Ouran High School

Club

D0462400

Ouran High School

Host Club

Vol.2

CONTENTS

CAST

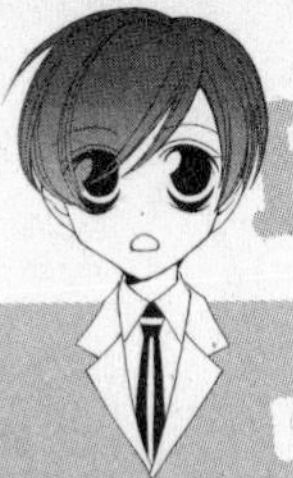

HARUHI FUJIOKA <1-A>
A SCHOLARSHIP STUDENT WITH A BLUNT PERSONALITY. THE CLUB'S CUSTOMERS ARE UNAWARE THAT SHE IS A GIRL. ♥

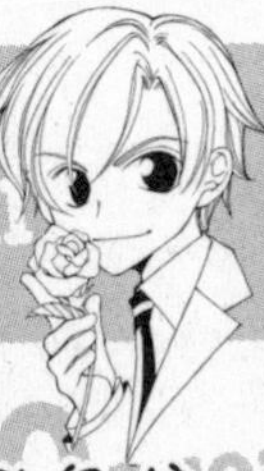

TAMAKI SUOH <2-A>
HOST CLUB PRESIDENT AND SUPPOSEDLY THE MOST REQUESTED HOST. SOMEWHAT NARCISSISTIC AND SLIGHTLY DENSE.

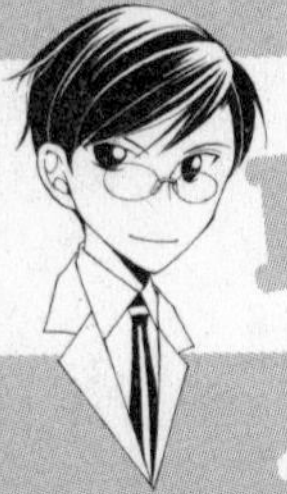

KYOYA OHTORI <2-A>
HOST CLUB VICE PRESIDENT. A COOL STRATEGIST. WHAT IS HE THINKING BEHIND THAT SMILE?

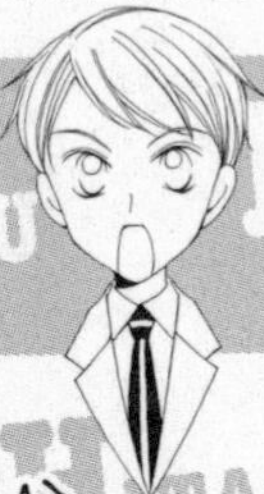

HIKARU HITACHIIN <1-A>
EASYGOING AND LIVES BY THE PHILOSOPHY OF "OTHERS = TOYS." THE OLDEST OF THE TWINS. VIRGO.

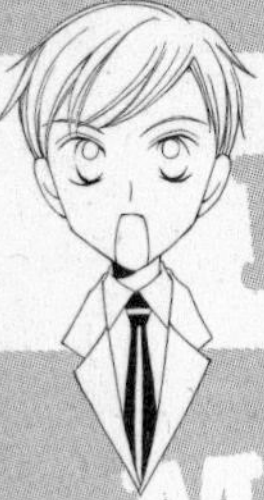

KAORU HITACHIIN <1-A>
HANDSOME HOMOSEXUAL + FORBIDDEN LOVE BETWEEN RELATIVES + SYMMETRY IS HIS NICHE. VIRGO.

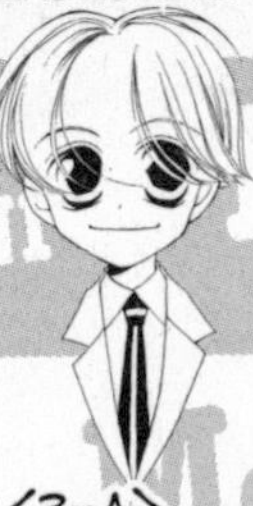

MITSUKUNI HANINOZUKA <3-A>
GOES BY THE NICKNAME "HUNNY." ALWAYS HAS HIS TOY BUNNY.

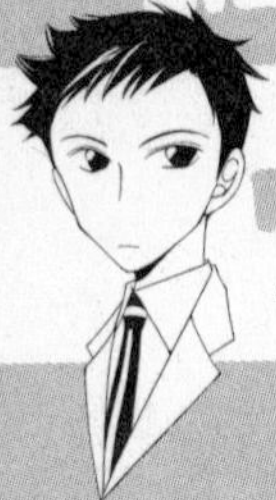

TAKASHI MORINOZUKA <3-A>
GOES BY THE NICKNAME "MORI." A MEMBER OF THE KENDO CLUB. HE QUIETLY WAITS UPON HUNNY.

STORY

THIS STORY TAKES PLACE AT OURAN INSTITUTE, AN ULTRAEXCLUSIVE PRIVATE HIGH SCHOOL. HARUHI, A SCHOLARSHIP STUDENT OF NO LINEAGE OR WEALTH, WANDERS INTO MUSIC ROOM 3 WHERE SHE ENCOUNTERS ALL SIX OF THE HANDSOME MEN OF THE HOST CLUB. UNIMPRESSED BY MERE APPEARANCES, SHE IS ABOUT TO TAKE HER LEAVE WHEN SHE ACCIDENTALLY BREAKS A VASE (MARKET PRICE: $80,000!) AND IS OBLIGED TO BECOME A MEMBER TO REPAY THE DEBT! HOW WILL THIS ALL WORK OUT?!

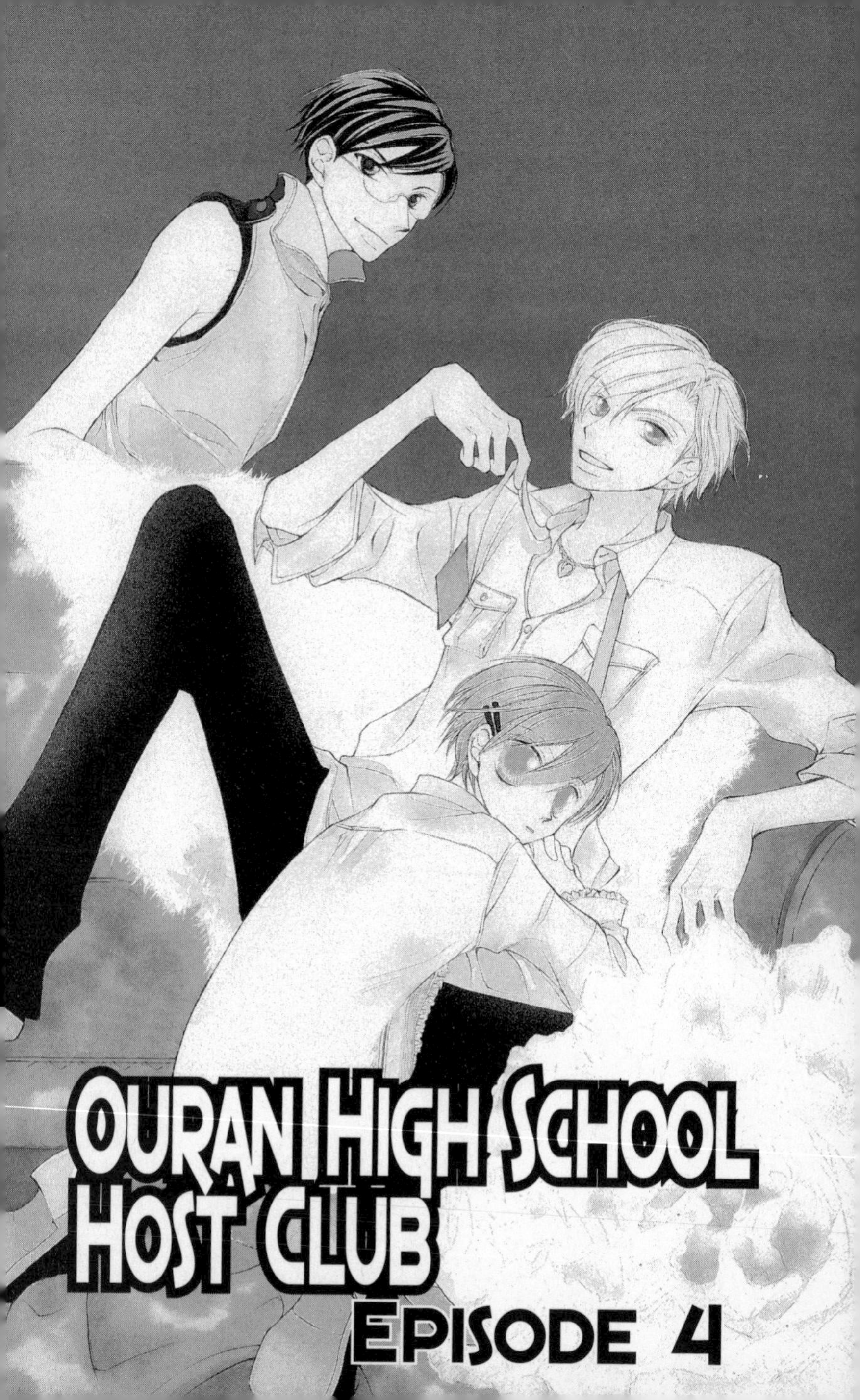
OURAN HIGH SCHOOL
HOST CLUB
EPISODE 4

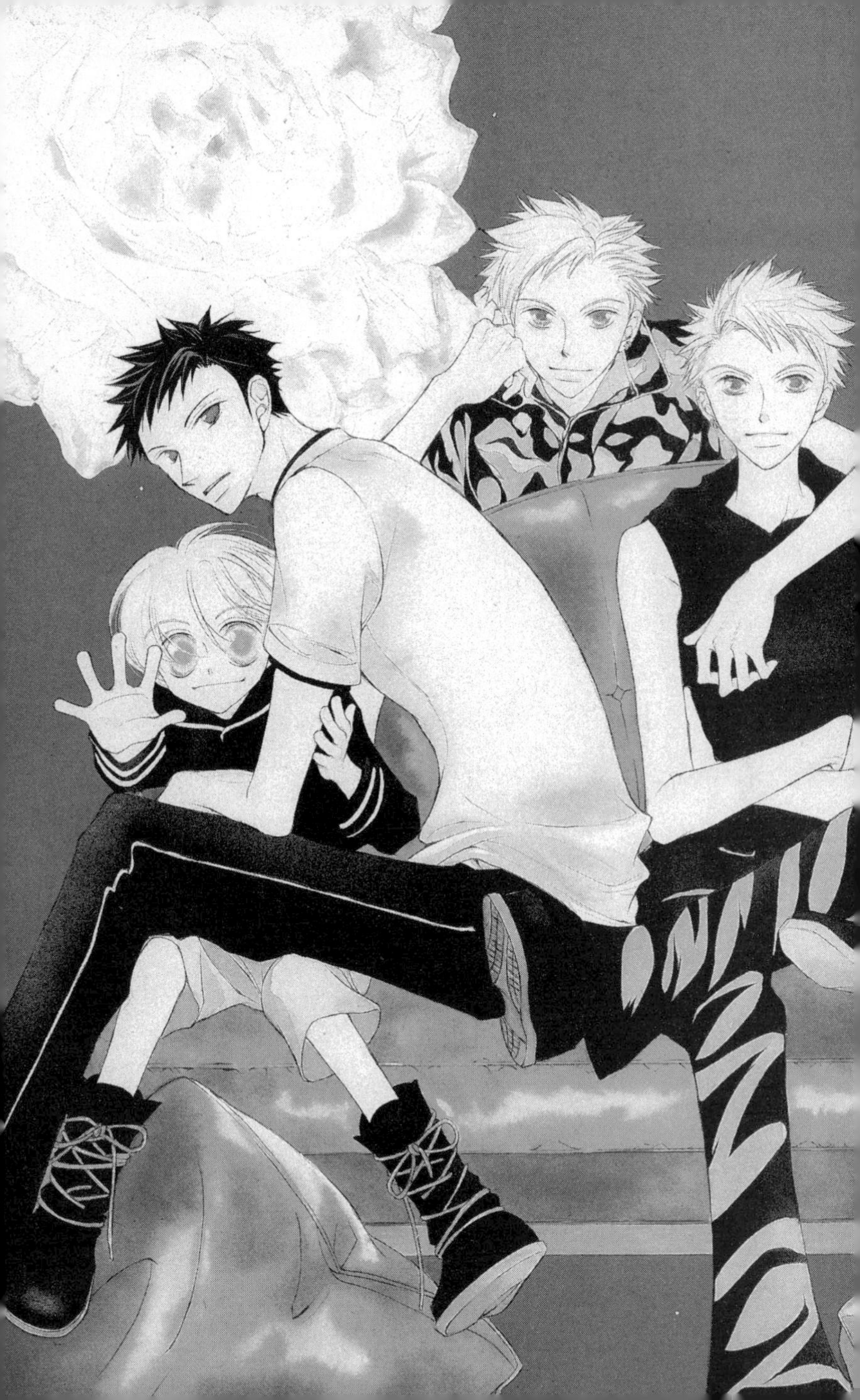

OURAN THEATER OF LOVE ~ SUOH FAMILY STORY ①

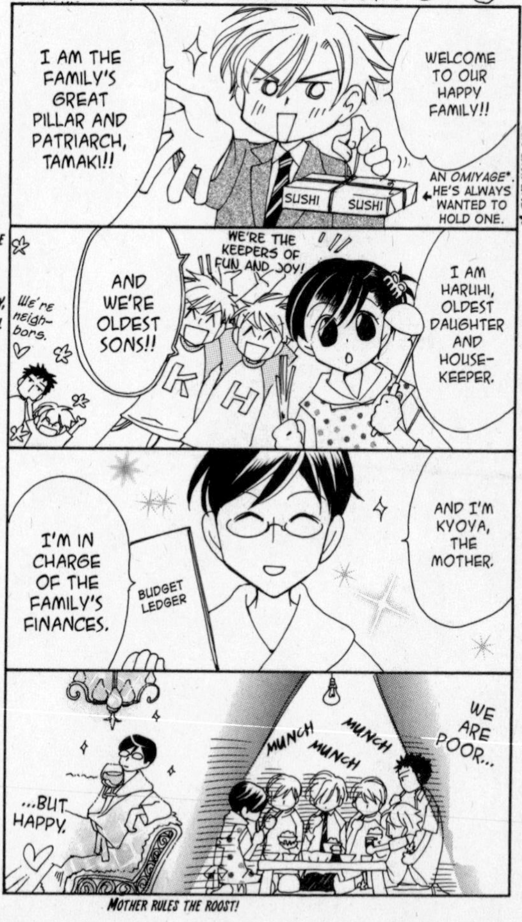
WELCOME TO OUR HAPPY FAMILY!!
I AM THE FAMILY'S GREAT PILLAR AND PATRIARCH, TAMAKI!!
SUSHI
SUSHI
I AM HARUHI, OLDEST DAUGHTER AND HOUSE-KEEPER.
WE'RE THE KEEPERS OF FUN AND JOY!
AND WE'RE OLDEST SONS!!
We're neighbors.
AND I'M KYOYA, THE MOTHER.
I'M IN CHARGE OF THE FAMILY'S FINANCES.
BUDGET LEDGER
WE ARE POOR...
MUNCH
MUNCH
MUNCH
...BUT HAPPY.

AN *OMIYAGE**. HE'S ALWAYS WANTED TO HOLD ONE.

THERE ARE OTHERS OUTSIDE THE FAMILY, BUT WE'LL IGNORE THEM.

MOTHER RULES THE ROOST!

*A TAKE-HOME GIFT

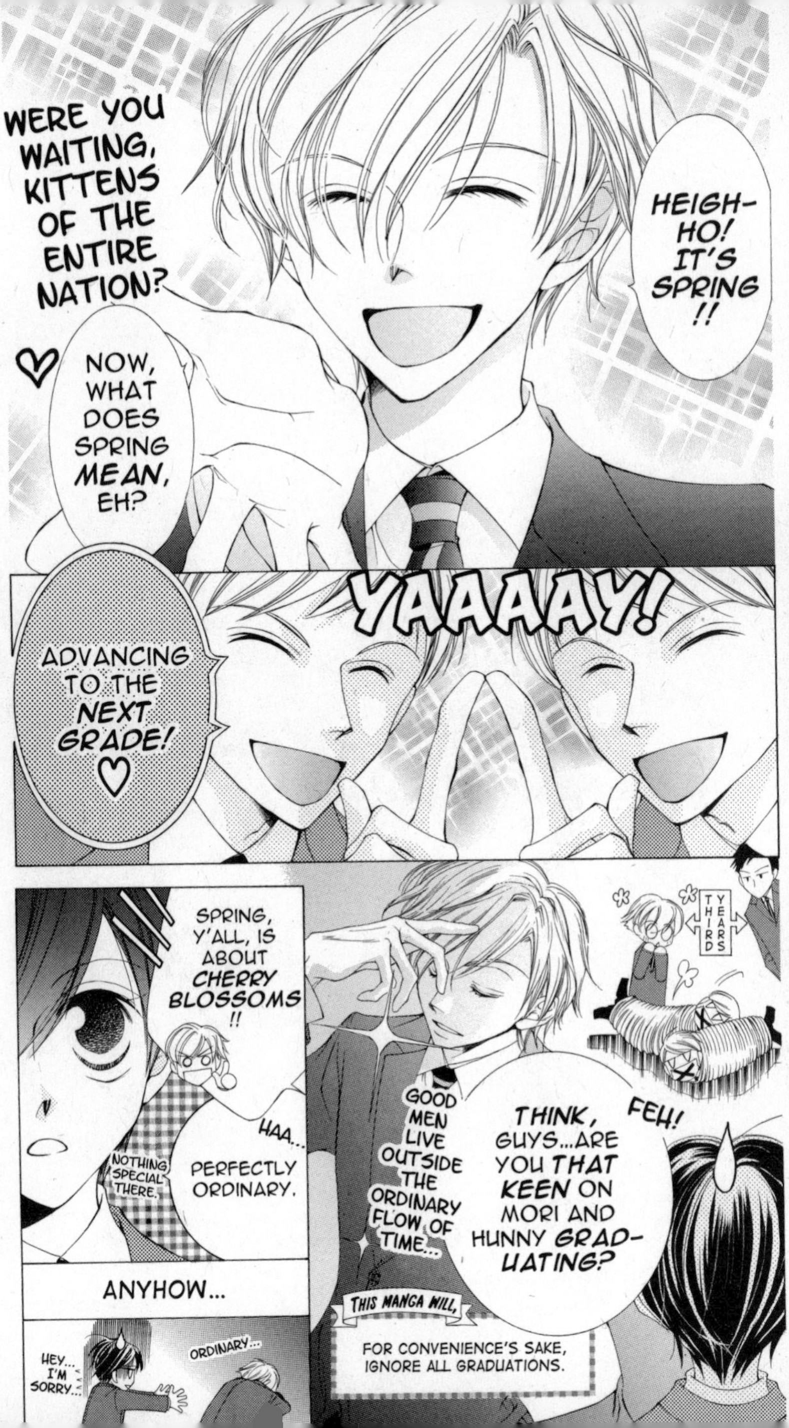
HEIGH-HO! IT'S SPRING!!
WERE YOU WAITING, KITTENS OF THE ENTIRE NATION?
NOW, WHAT DOES SPRING MEAN, EH?
YAAAAY!
ADVANCING TO THE NEXT GRADE!
THIRD YEARS
FEH!
THINK, GUYS...ARE YOU THAT KEEN ON MORI AND HUNNY GRADUATING?
GOOD MEN LIVE OUTSIDE THE ORDINARY FLOW OF TIME...
THIS MANGA WILL,
FOR CONVENIENCE'S SAKE, IGNORE ALL GRADUATIONS.
SPRING, Y'ALL, IS ABOUT CHERRY BLOSSOMS!!
HAA...
PERFECTLY ORDINARY.
NOTHING SPECIAL THERE.
ANYHOW...
ORDINARY...
HEY... I'M SORRY...

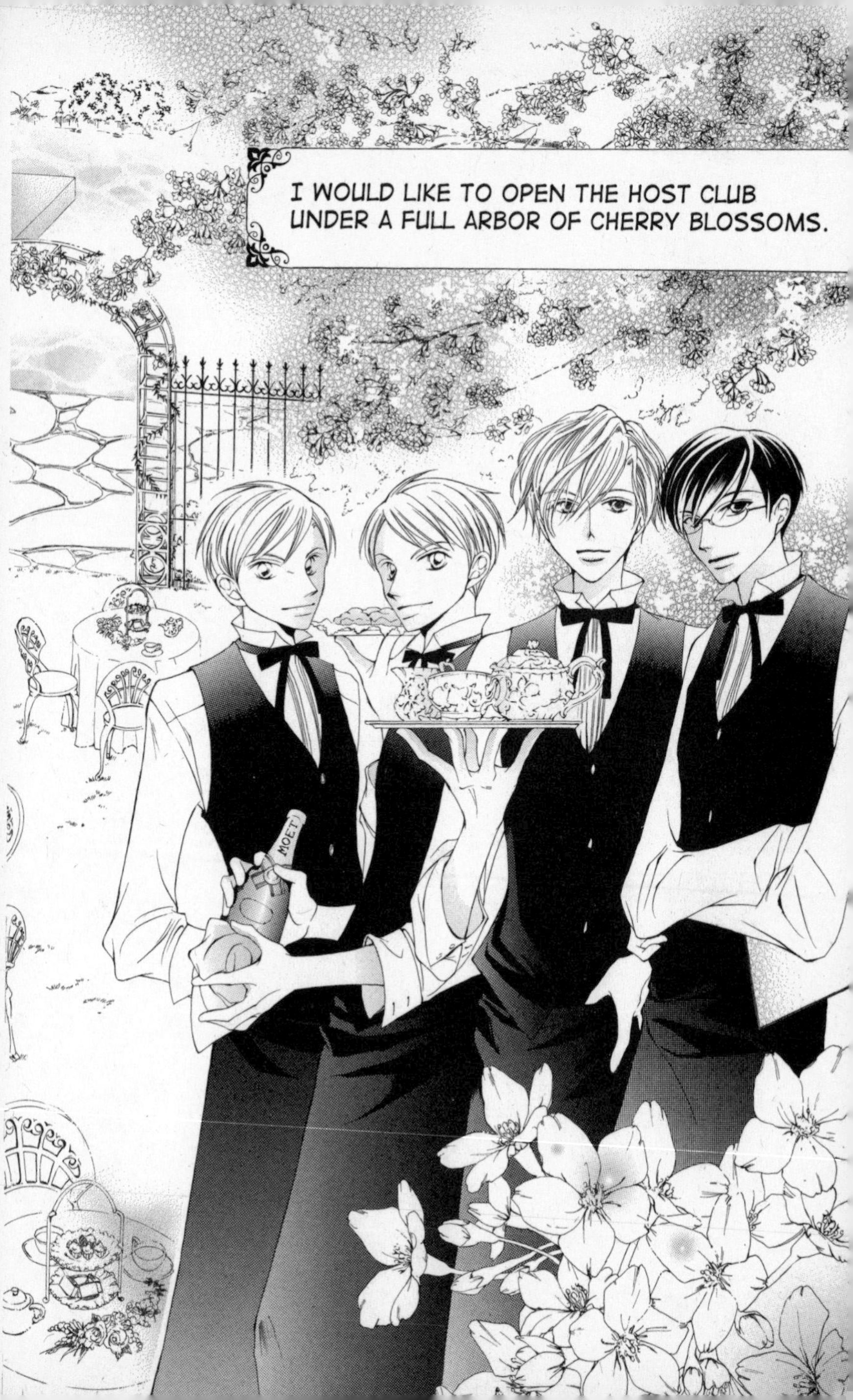
I WOULD LIKE TO OPEN THE HOST CLUB UNDER A FULL ARBOR OF CHERRY BLOSSOMS.
MOET

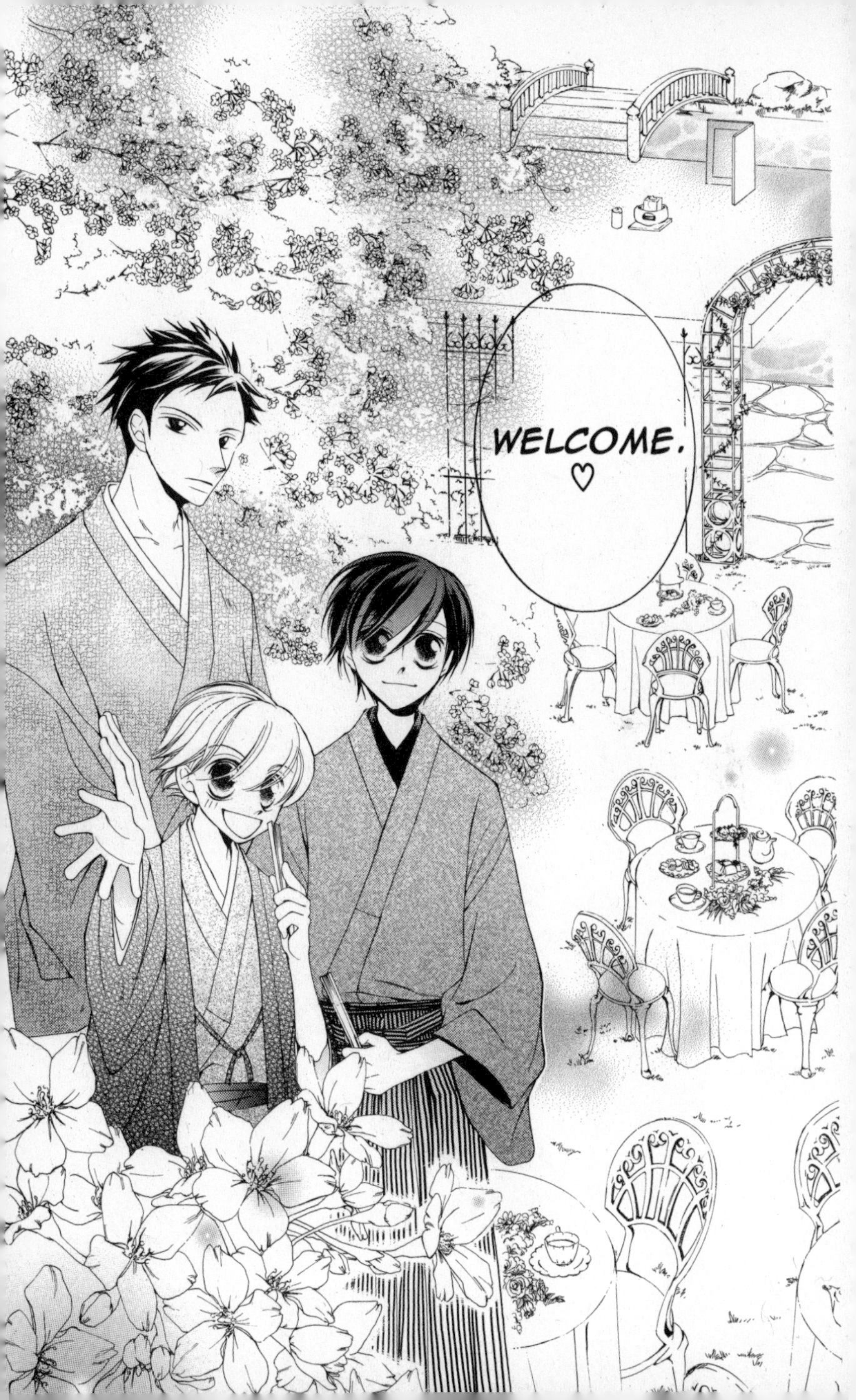
WELCOME. ♡

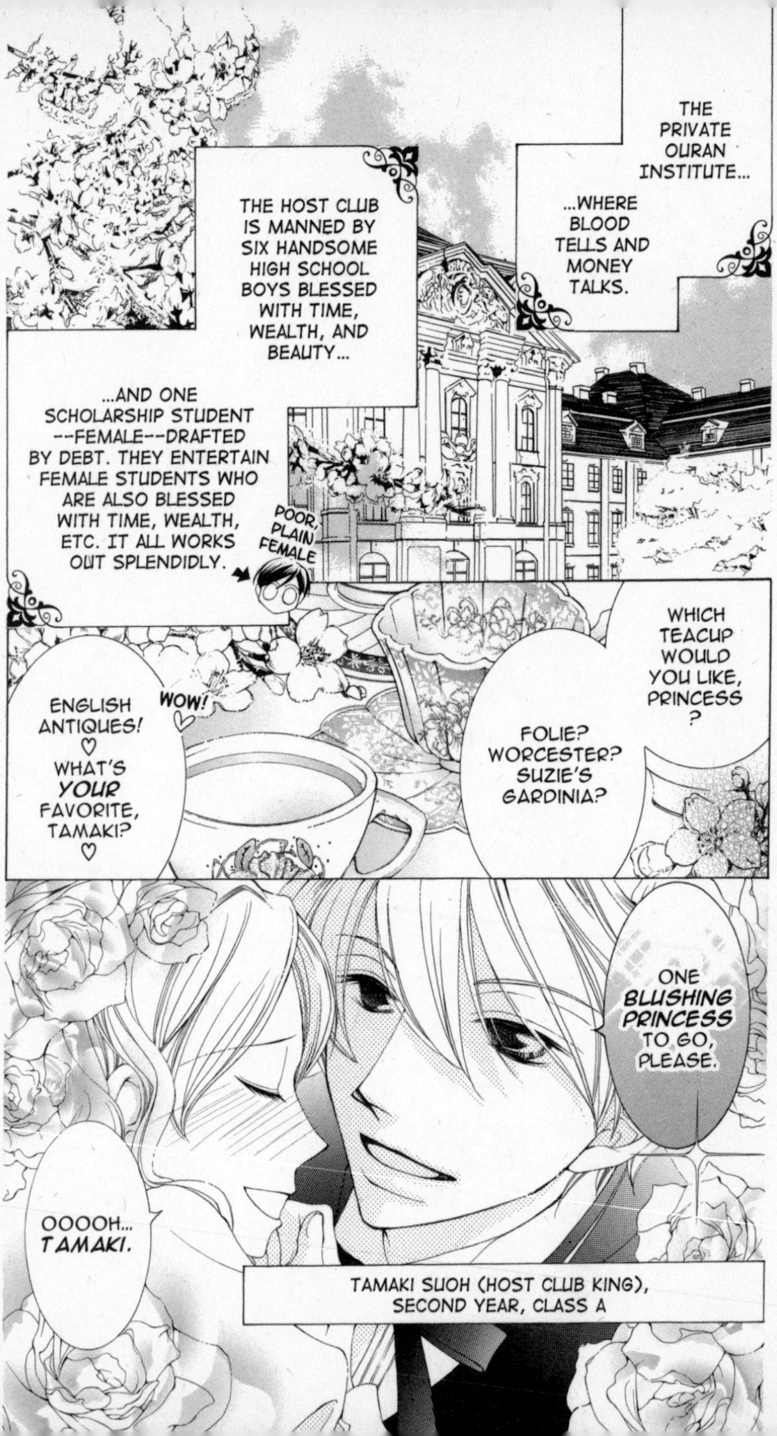
THE PRIVATE OURAN INSTITUTE...
...WHERE BLOOD TELLS AND MONEY TALKS.
THE HOST CLUB IS MANNED BY SIX HANDSOME HIGH SCHOOL BOYS BLESSED WITH TIME, WEALTH, AND BEAUTY...
...AND ONE SCHOLARSHIP STUDENT --FEMALE--DRAFTED BY DEBT. THEY ENTERTAIN FEMALE STUDENTS WHO ARE ALSO BLESSED WITH TIME, WEALTH, ETC. IT ALL WORKS OUT SPLENDIDLY.
POOR, PLAIN FEMALE
WHICH TEACUP WOULD YOU LIKE, PRINCESS?
FOLIE? WORCESTER? SUZIE'S GARDINIA?
WOW! ♡
ENGLISH ANTIQUES! ♡ WHAT'S ***YOUR*** FAVORITE, TAMAKI? ♡
ONE ***BLUSHING PRINCESS*** TO GO, PLEASE.
OOOOH... ***TAMAKI.***
TAMAKI SUOH (HOST CLUB KING), SECOND YEAR, CLASS A

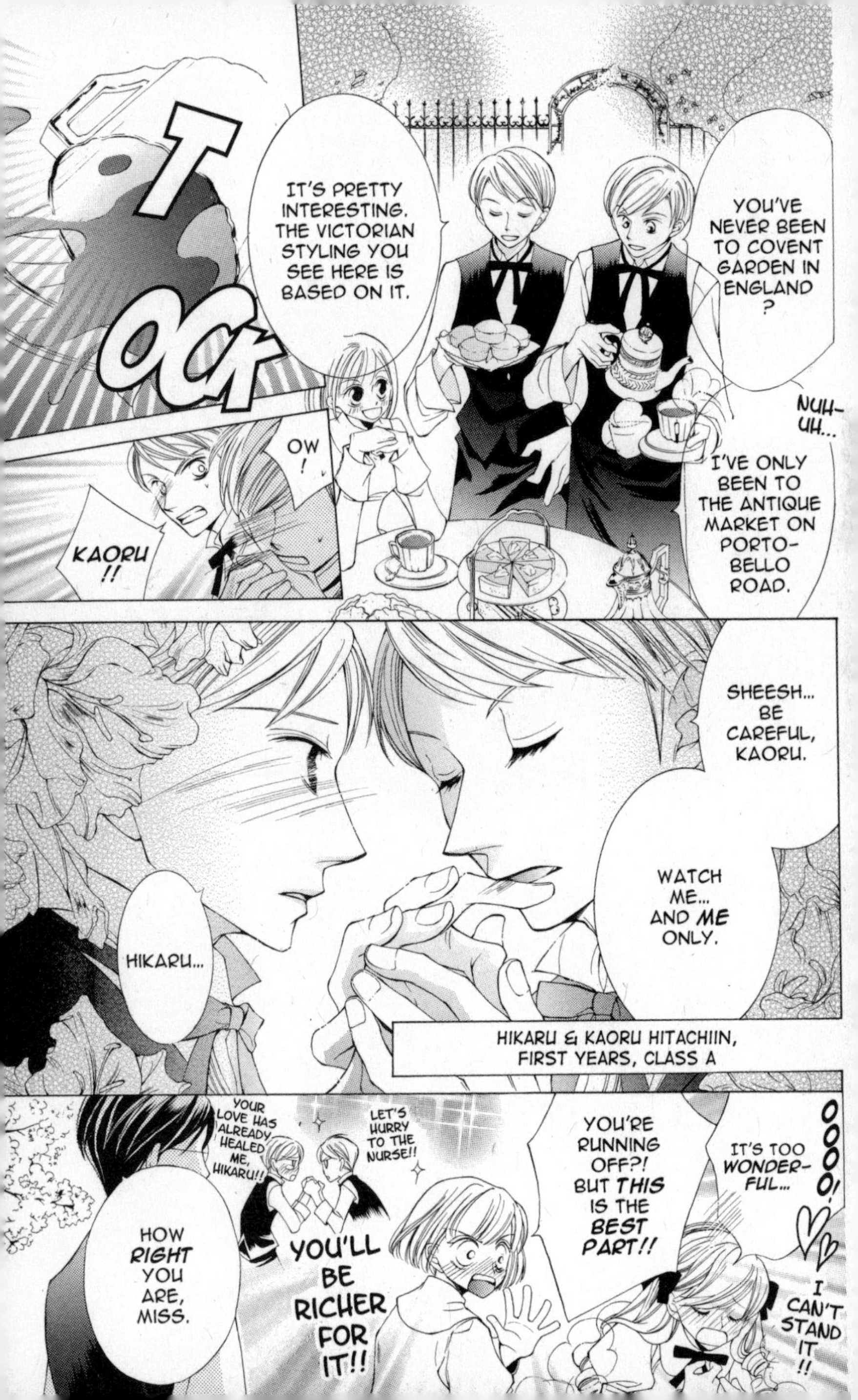
YOU'VE NEVER BEEN TO COVENT GARDEN IN ENGLAND?
IT'S PRETTY INTERESTING. THE VICTORIAN STYLING YOU SEE HERE IS BASED ON IT.
NUH-UH...
I'VE ONLY BEEN TO THE ANTIQUE MARKET ON PORTO-BELLO ROAD.
TOCK
OW!
KAORU!!
SHEESH... BE CAREFUL, KAORU.
WATCH ME... AND ME ONLY.
HIKARU...
HIKARU & KAORU HITACHIIN, FIRST YEARS, CLASS A
OOOOO!
IT'S TOO WONDERFUL...
I CAN'T STAND IT!!
YOU'RE RUNNING OFF?! BUT THIS IS THE BEST PART!!
LET'S HURRY TO THE NURSE!!
YOUR LOVE HAS ALREADY HEALED ME, HIKARU!!
YOU'LL BE RICHER FOR IT!!
HOW RIGHT YOU ARE, MISS.

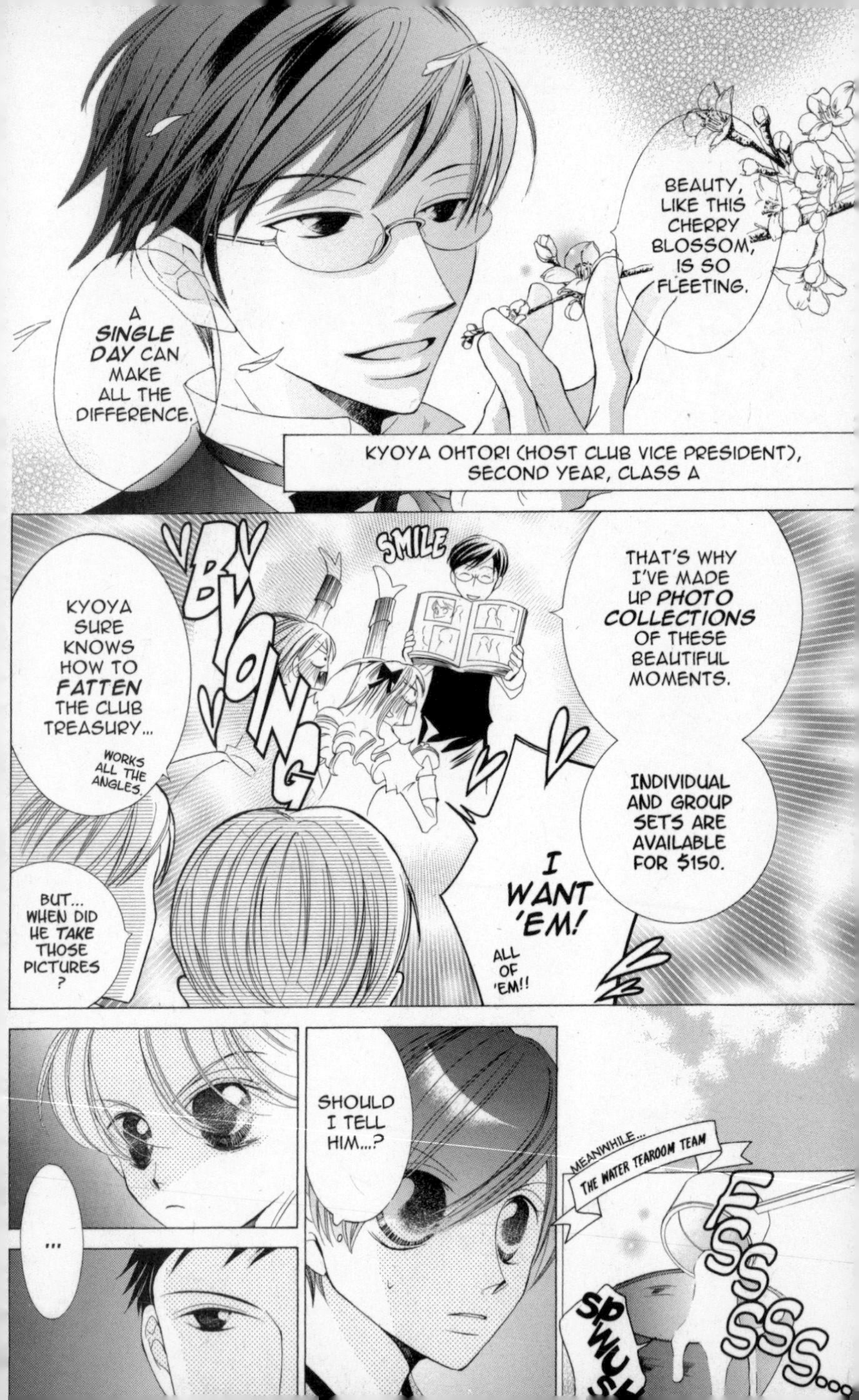
BEAUTY, LIKE THIS CHERRY BLOSSOM, IS SO FLEETING.
A SINGLE DAY CAN MAKE ALL THE DIFFERENCE.
KYOYA OHTORI (HOST CLUB VICE PRESIDENT), SECOND YEAR, CLASS A
THAT'S WHY I'VE MADE UP PHOTO COLLECTIONS OF THESE BEAUTIFUL MOMENTS.
SMILE
INDIVIDUAL AND GROUP SETS ARE AVAILABLE FOR $150.
I WANT 'EM!
ALL OF 'EM!!
BYOING
KYOYA SURE KNOWS HOW TO FATTEN THE CLUB TREASURY...
WORKS ALL THE ANGLES.
BUT... WHEN DID HE TAKE THOSE PICTURES?
MEANWHILE...
THE WATER TEAROOM TEAM
FSSSSSS...
SPWUSH
SHOULD I TELL HIM...?
...

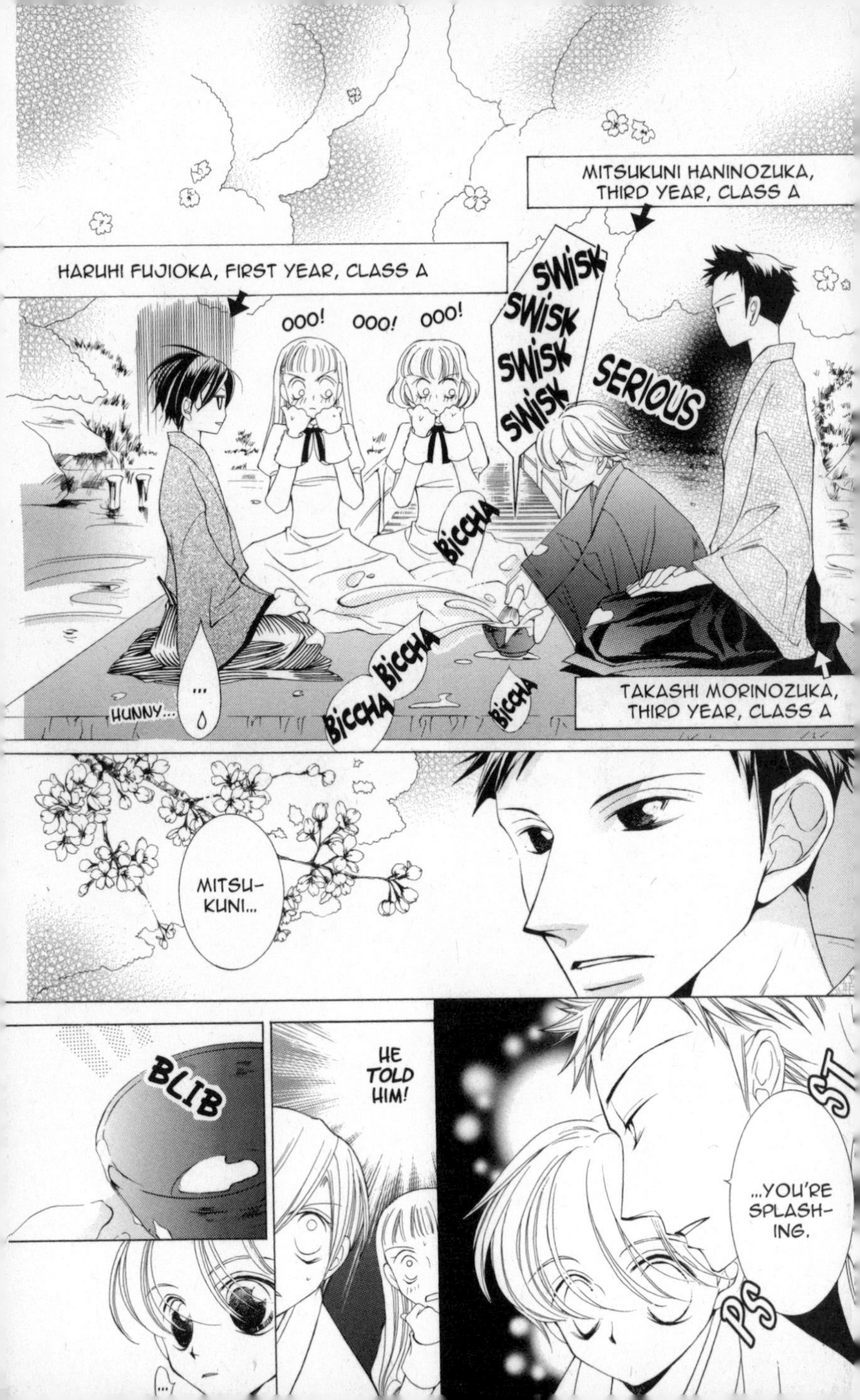
MITSUKUNI HANINOZUKA, THIRD YEAR, CLASS A
SWISK SWISK SWISK SWISK
SERIOUS
HARUHI FUJIOKA, FIRST YEAR, CLASS A
OOO! OOO! OOO!
BICCHA
TAKASHI MORINOZUKA, THIRD YEAR, CLASS A
BICCHA
BICCHA
BICCHA
...
HUNNY...
MITSU-KUNI...
ST
...YOU'RE SPLASH-ING.
PS
HE TOLD HIM!
BLIB
...

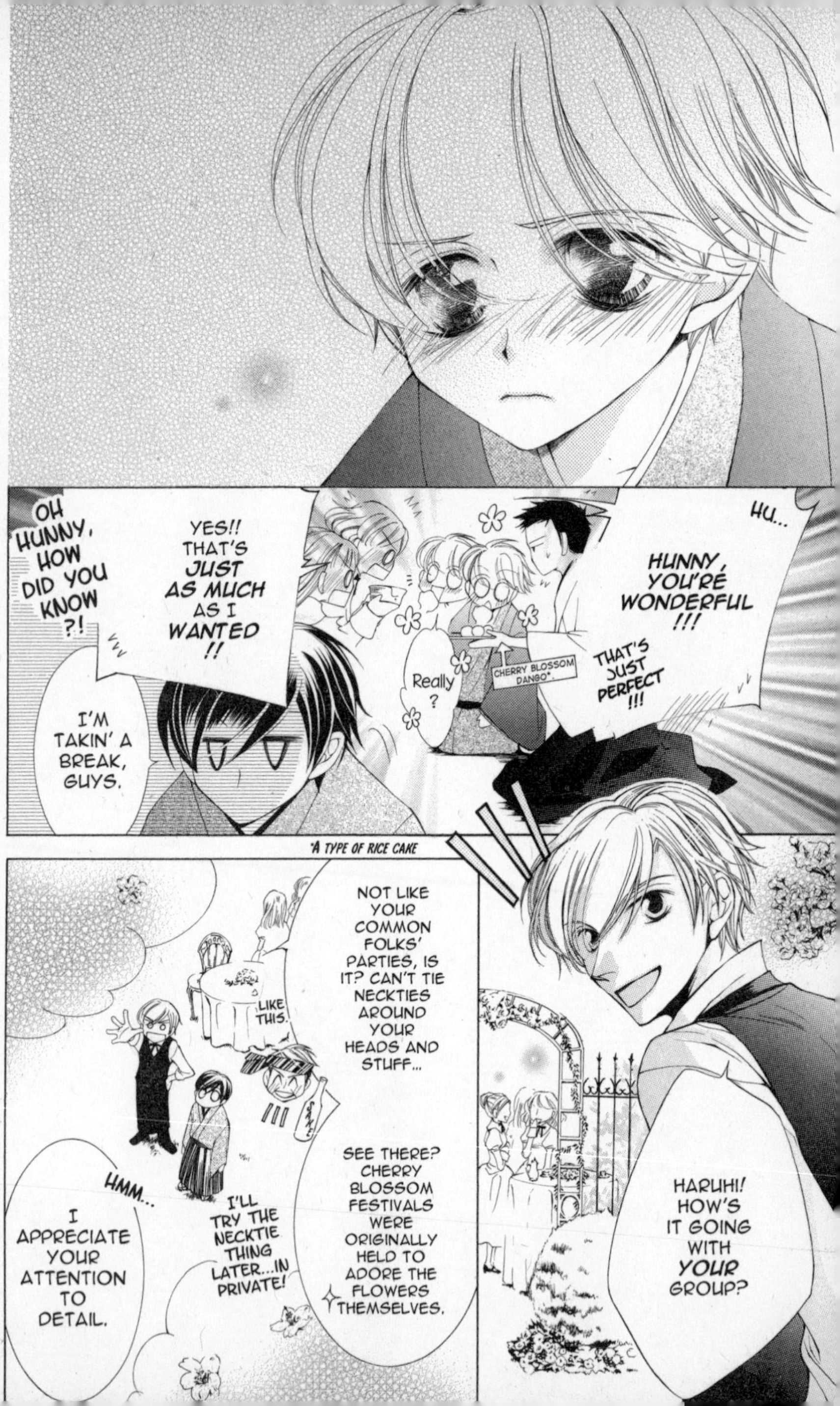
HU...
HUNNY, YOU'RE WONDERFUL!!!
THAT'S JUST PERFECT!!!
CHERRY BLOSSOM DANGO*.
Really?
YES!! THAT'S JUST AS MUCH AS I WANTED!!
OH HUNNY, HOW DID YOU KNOW?!
I'M TAKIN' A BREAK, GUYS.
HARUHI! HOW'S IT GOING WITH YOUR GROUP?
NOT LIKE YOUR COMMON FOLKS' PARTIES, IS IT? CAN'T TIE NECKTIES AROUND YOUR HEADS AND STUFF...
LIKE THIS.
SEE THERE? CHERRY BLOSSOM FESTIVALS WERE ORIGINALLY HELD TO ADORE THE FLOWERS THEMSELVES.
HMM...
I'LL TRY THE NECKTIE THING LATER...IN PRIVATE!
I APPRECIATE YOUR ATTENTION TO DETAIL.

*A TYPE OF RICE CAKE

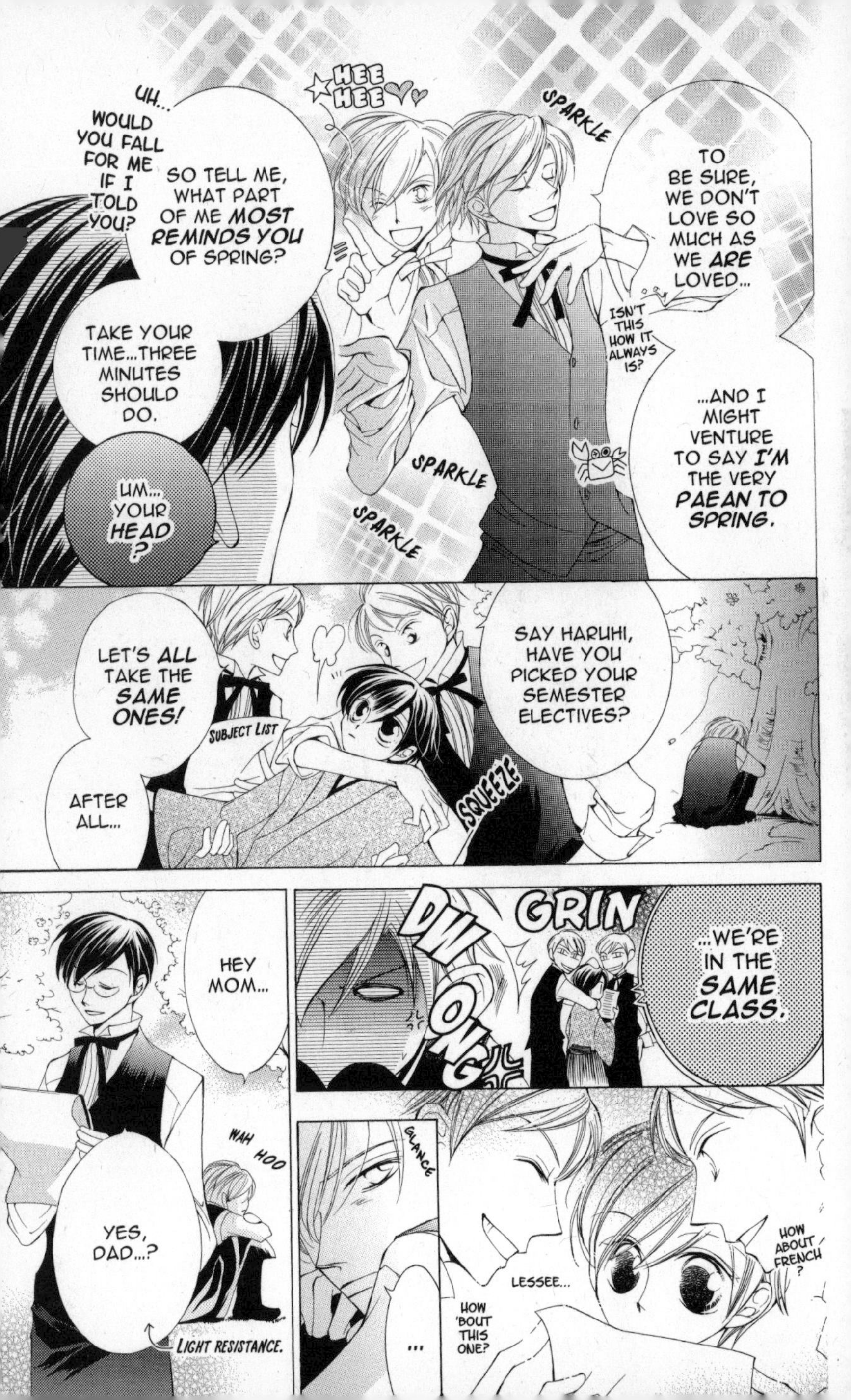
SPARKLE
TO BE SURE, WE DON'T LOVE SO MUCH AS WE ARE LOVED...
ISN'T THIS HOW IT ALWAYS IS?
...AND I MIGHT VENTURE TO SAY I'M THE VERY PAEAN TO SPRING.
HEE HEE
SO TELL ME, WHAT PART OF ME MOST REMINDS YOU OF SPRING?
UH... WOULD YOU FALL FOR ME IF I TOLD YOU?
TAKE YOUR TIME...THREE MINUTES SHOULD DO.
SPARKLE
SPARKLE
UM... YOUR HEAD?
SAY HARUHI, HAVE YOU PICKED YOUR SEMESTER ELECTIVES?
SQUEEZE
LET'S ALL TAKE THE SAME ONES!
SUBJECT LIST
AFTER ALL...
...WE'RE IN THE SAME CLASS.
GRIN
DWONG
HOW ABOUT FRENCH?
LESSEE...
GLANCE
HOW 'BOUT THIS ONE?
...
HEY MOM...
WAH HOO
YES, DAD...?
LIGHT RESISTANCE.

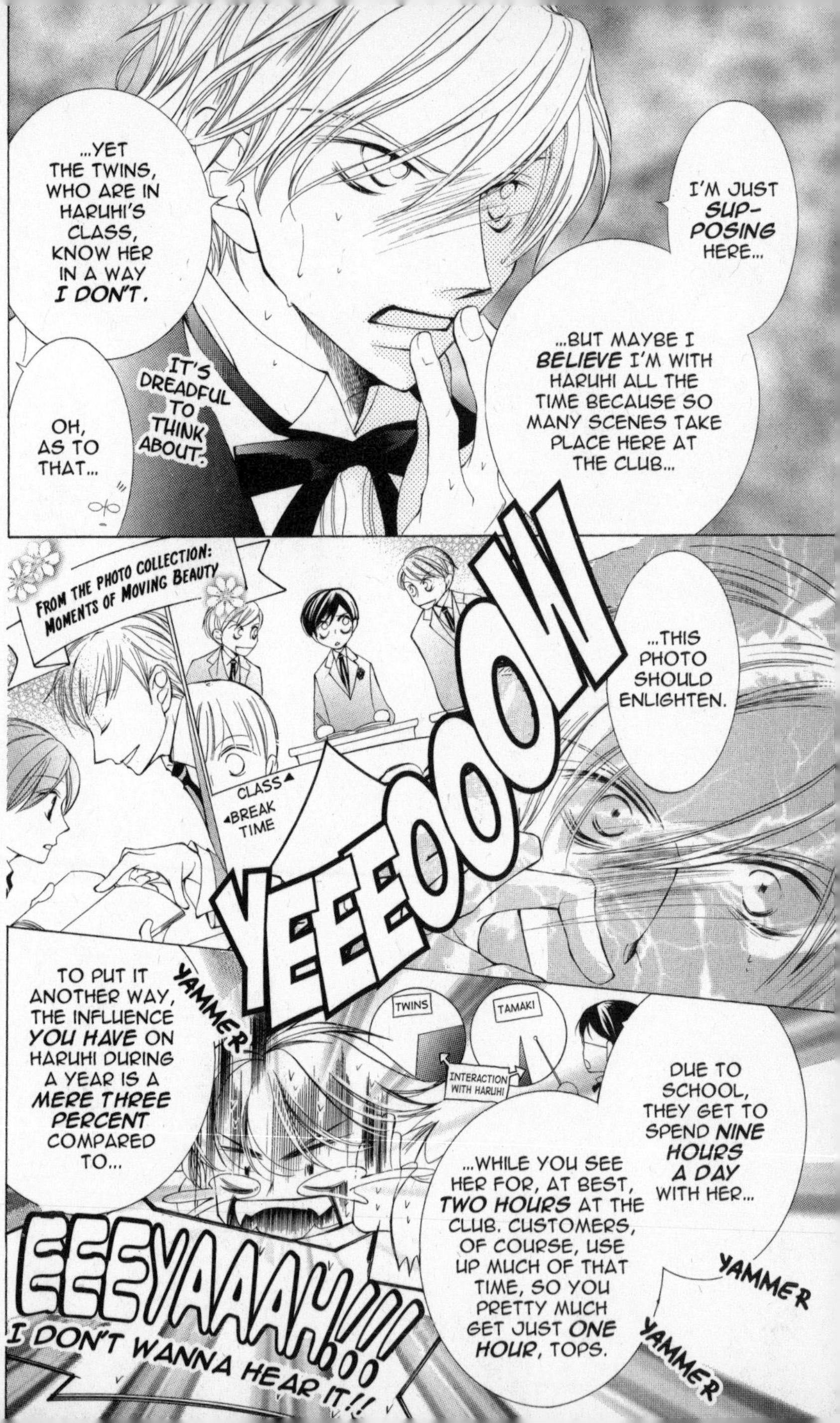
I'M JUST SUPPOSING HERE...
...BUT MAYBE I BELIEVE I'M WITH HARUHI ALL THE TIME BECAUSE SO MANY SCENES TAKE PLACE HERE AT THE CLUB...
...YET THE TWINS, WHO ARE IN HARUHI'S CLASS, KNOW HER IN A WAY I DON'T.
IT'S DREADFUL TO THINK ABOUT.
OH, AS TO THAT...
...THIS PHOTO SHOULD ENLIGHTEN.
YEEEOOOW
FROM THE PHOTO COLLECTION: MOMENTS OF MOVING BEAUTY
CLASS
BREAK TIME
DUE TO SCHOOL, THEY GET TO SPEND NINE HOURS A DAY WITH HER...
...WHILE YOU SEE HER FOR, AT BEST, TWO HOURS AT THE CLUB. CUSTOMERS, OF COURSE, USE UP MUCH OF THAT TIME, SO YOU PRETTY MUCH GET JUST ONE HOUR, TOPS.
YAMMER
YAMMER
TAMAKI
TWINS
INTERACTION WITH HARUHI
TO PUT IT ANOTHER WAY, THE INFLUENCE YOU HAVE ON HARUHI DURING A YEAR IS A MERE THREE PERCENT COMPARED TO...
YAMMER
EEEYAAAH!!!
I DON'T WANNA HEAR IT!!

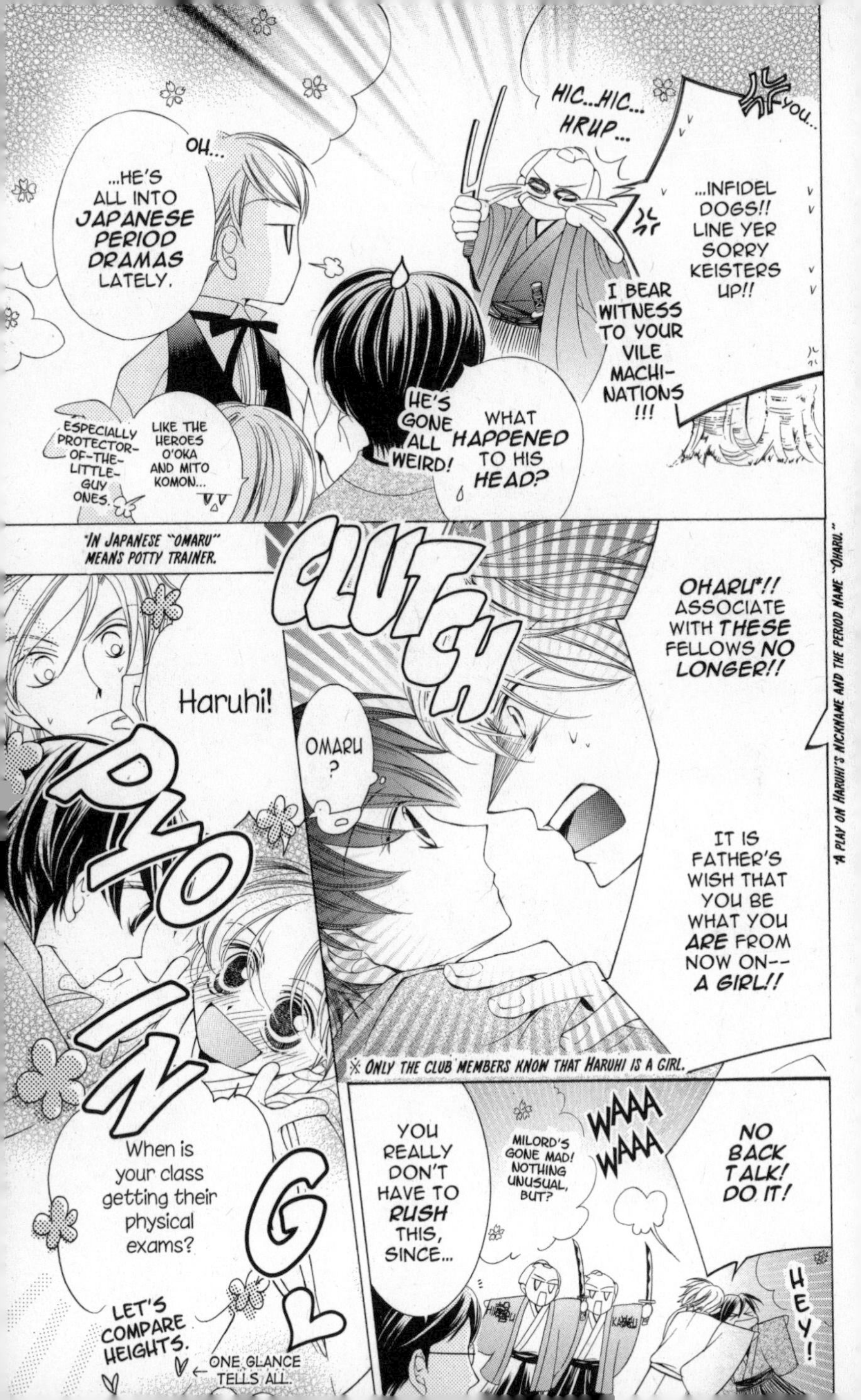
YOU...
HIC...HIC... HRUP...
...INFIDEL DOGS!! LINE YER SORRY KEISTERS UP!!
I BEAR WITNESS TO YOUR VILE MACHINATIONS!!!
WHAT HAPPENED TO HIS HEAD?
HE'S GONE ALL WEIRD!
OH...
...HE'S ALL INTO JAPANESE PERIOD DRAMAS LATELY.
LIKE THE HEROES O'OKA AND MITO KOMON...
ESPECIALLY PROTECTOR-OF-THE-LITTLE-GUY ONES.
*A PLAY ON HARUHI'S NICKNAME AND THE PERIOD NAME "OHARU."
*IN JAPANESE "OMARU" MEANS POTTY TRAINER.
OHARU*!! ASSOCIATE WITH THESE FELLOWS NO LONGER!!
CLUTCH
IT IS FATHER'S WISH THAT YOU BE WHAT YOU ARE FROM NOW ON-- A GIRL!!
OMARU ?
※ONLY THE CLUB MEMBERS KNOW THAT HARUHI IS A GIRL.
NO BACK TALK! DO IT!
HEY!
WAAA WAAA
MILORD'S GONE MAD! NOTHING UNUSUAL, BUT?
YOU REALLY DON'T HAVE TO RUSH THIS, SINCE...
Haruhi!
DYOING
When is your class getting their physical exams?
LET'S COMPARE HEIGHTS.
ONE GLANCE TELLS ALL.

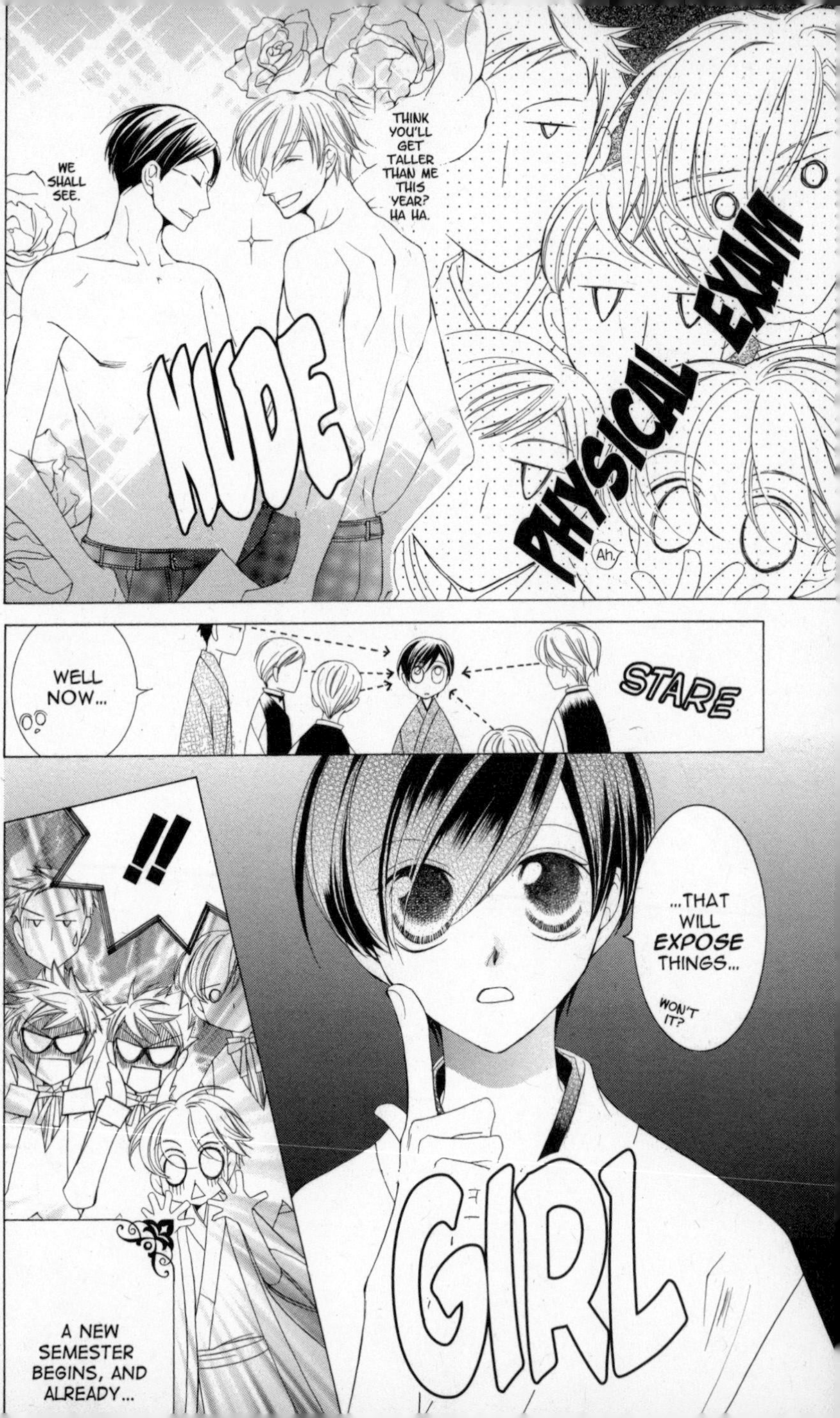
PHYSICAL EXAM
Ah.
THINK YOU'LL GET TALLER THAN ME THIS YEAR? HA HA.
WE SHALL SEE.
NUDE
STARE
WELL NOW...
...THAT WILL EXPOSE THINGS...
WON'T IT?
GIRL
!!
A NEW SEMESTER BEGINS, AND ALREADY...

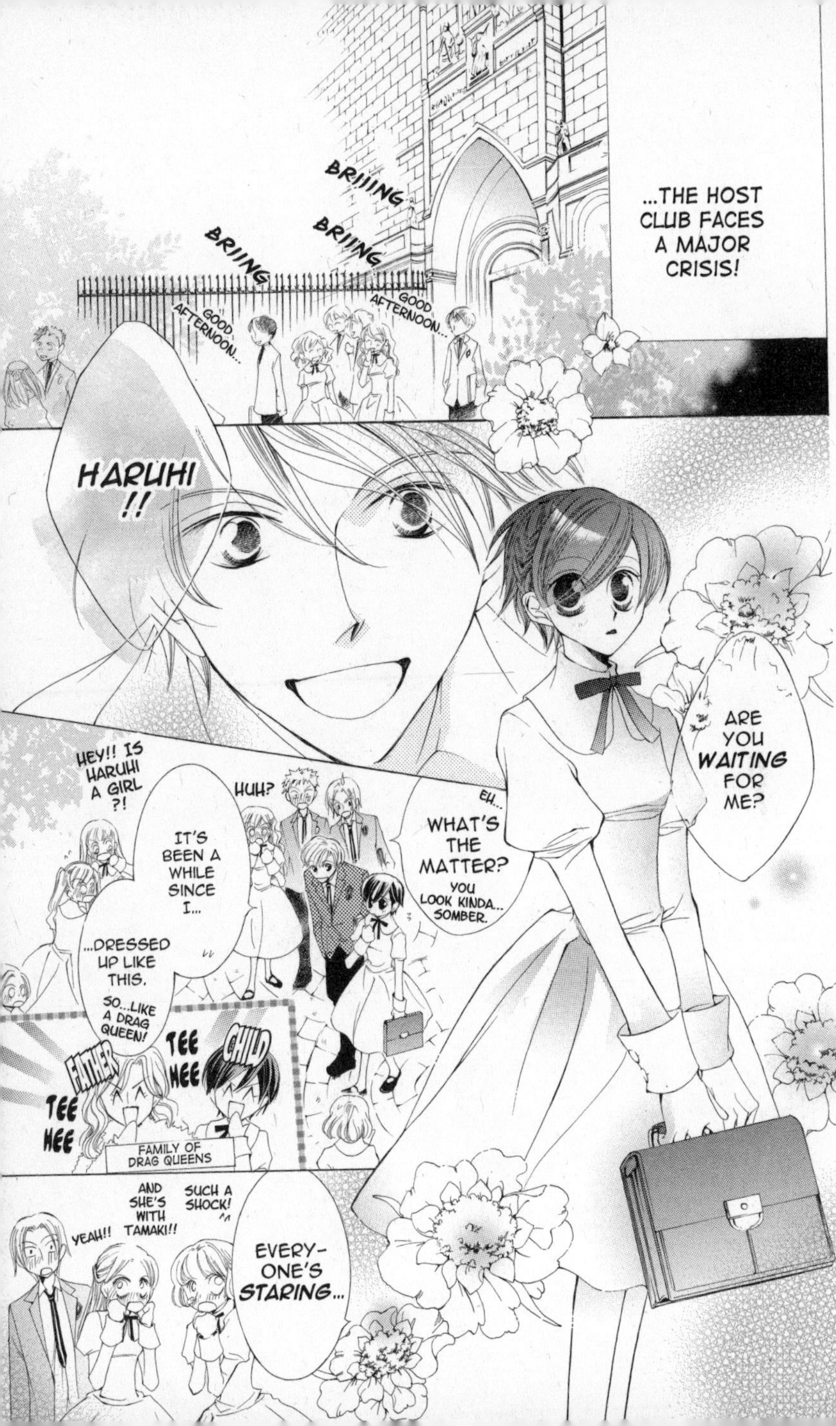
...THE HOST CLUB FACES A MAJOR CRISIS!
BRIIING
BRIIING
BRIIING
GOOD AFTERNOON...
GOOD AFTERNOON...
HARUHI !!
ARE YOU WAITING FOR ME?
EH... WHAT'S THE MATTER? YOU LOOK KINDA... SOMBER.
IT'S BEEN A WHILE SINCE I... ...DRESSED UP LIKE THIS.
HUH?
HEY!! IS HARUHI A GIRL ?!
SO...LIKE A DRAG QUEEN!
TEE HEE
CHILD
FATHER
TEE HEE
FAMILY OF DRAG QUEENS
EVERY-ONE'S STARING...
SUCH A SHOCK!
AND SHE'S WITH TAMAKI!!
YEAH!!

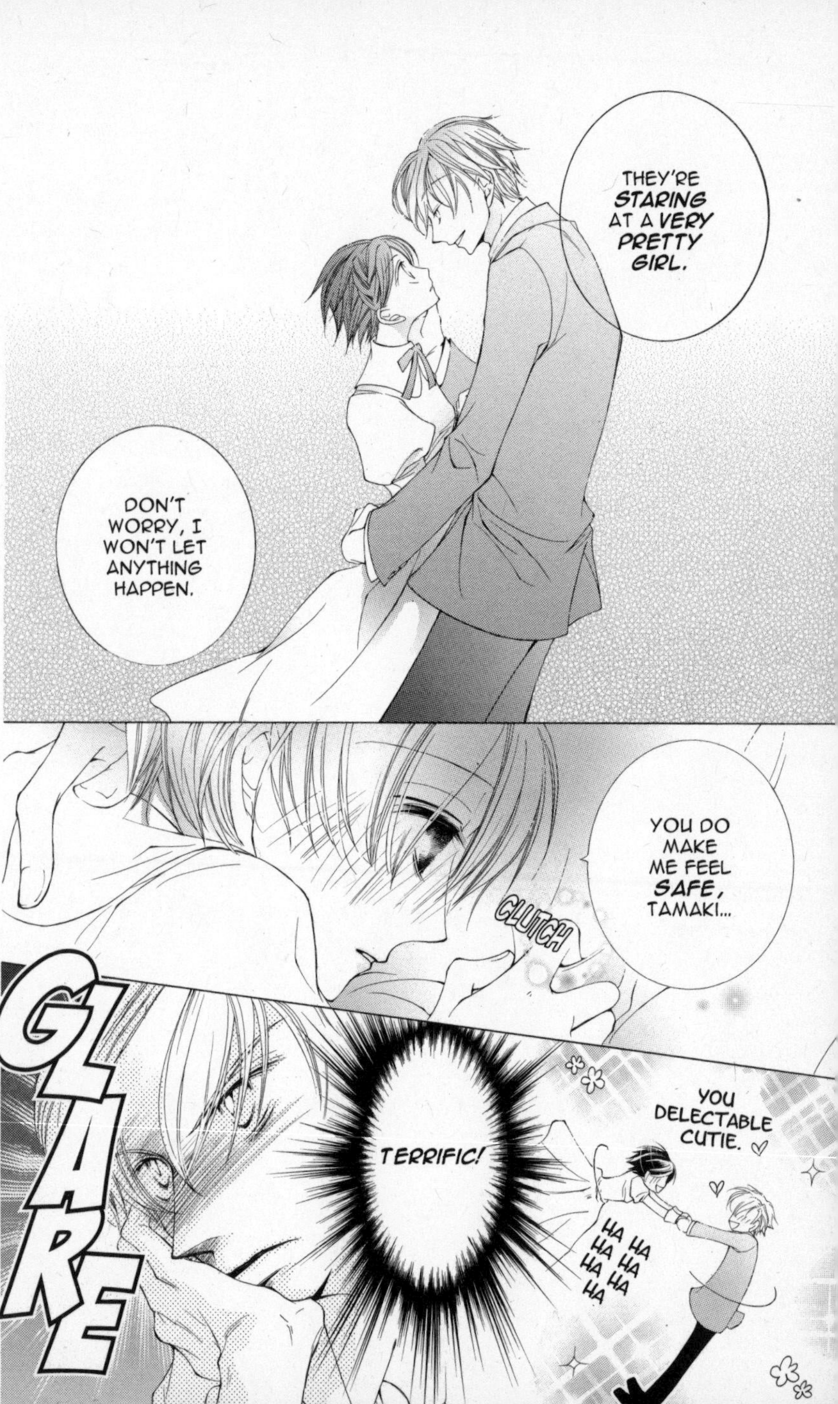
THEY'RE STARING AT A VERY PRETTY GIRL.
DON'T WORRY, I WON'T LET ANYTHING HAPPEN.
YOU DO MAKE ME FEEL SAFE, TAMAKI...
CLUTCH
YOU DELECTABLE CUTIE. ♡
HA HA HA HA HA HA HA
TERRIFIC!
GLARE

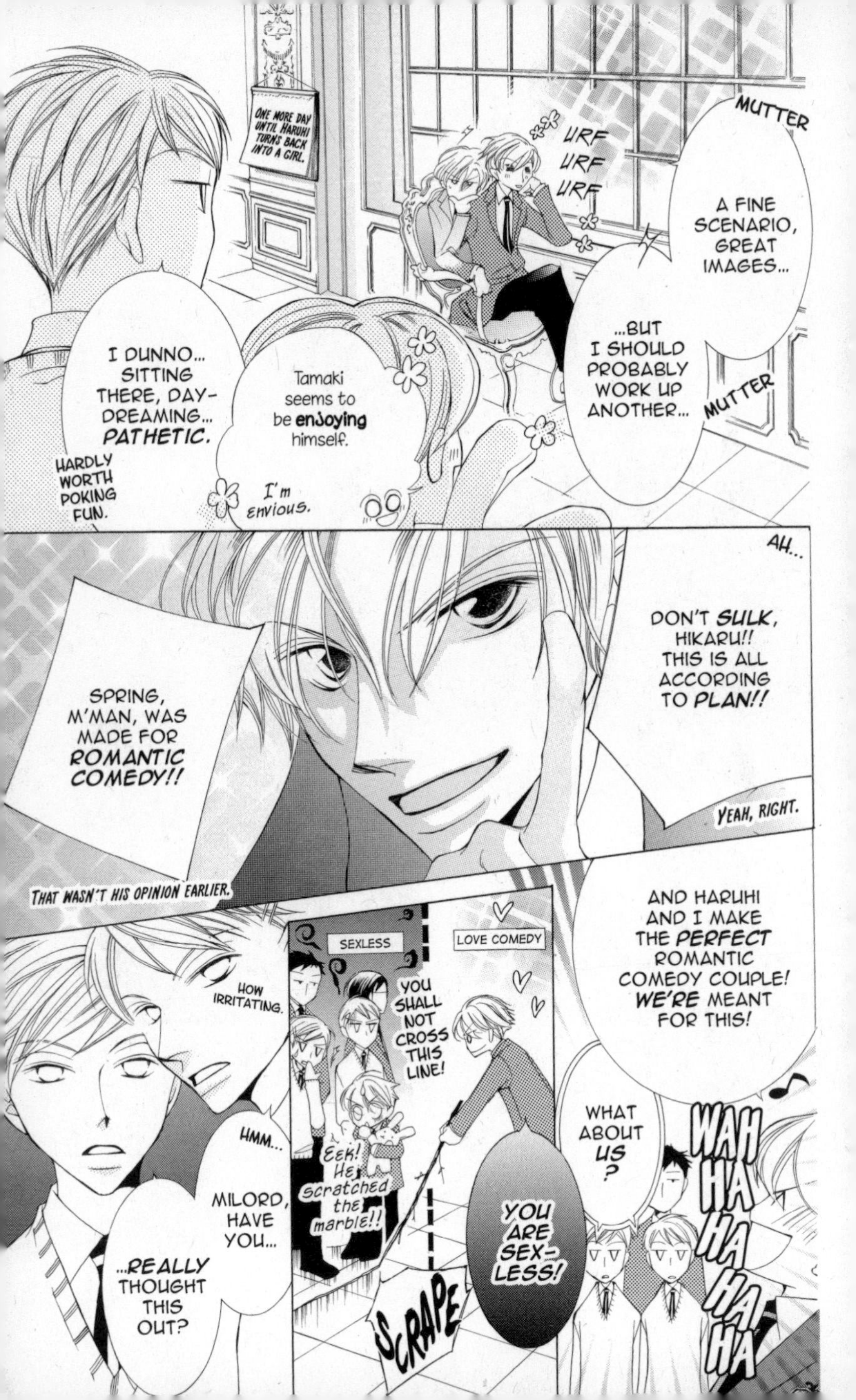
MUTTER
A FINE SCENARIO, GREAT IMAGES...
...BUT I SHOULD PROBABLY WORK UP ANOTHER...
MUTTER
URF URF URF
ONE MORE DAY UNTIL HARUHI TURNS BACK INTO A GIRL.
Tamaki seems to be enjoying himself.
I'm envious.
I DUNNO... SITTING THERE, DAY-DREAMING... PATHETIC.
HARDLY WORTH POKING FUN.
AH...
DON'T SULK, HIKARU!! THIS IS ALL ACCORDING TO PLAN!!
YEAH, RIGHT.
SPRING, M'MAN, WAS MADE FOR ROMANTIC COMEDY!!
THAT WASN'T HIS OPINION EARLIER.
AND HARUHI AND I MAKE THE PERFECT ROMANTIC COMEDY COUPLE! WE'RE MEANT FOR THIS!
WAH HA HA HA HA HA
WHAT ABOUT US?
YOU ARE SEXLESS!
LOVE COMEDY
SEXLESS
YOU SHALL NOT CROSS THIS LINE!
Eek! He scratched the marble!!
SCRAPE
HOW IRRITATING.
HMM...
MILORD, HAVE YOU...
...REALLY THOUGHT THIS OUT?

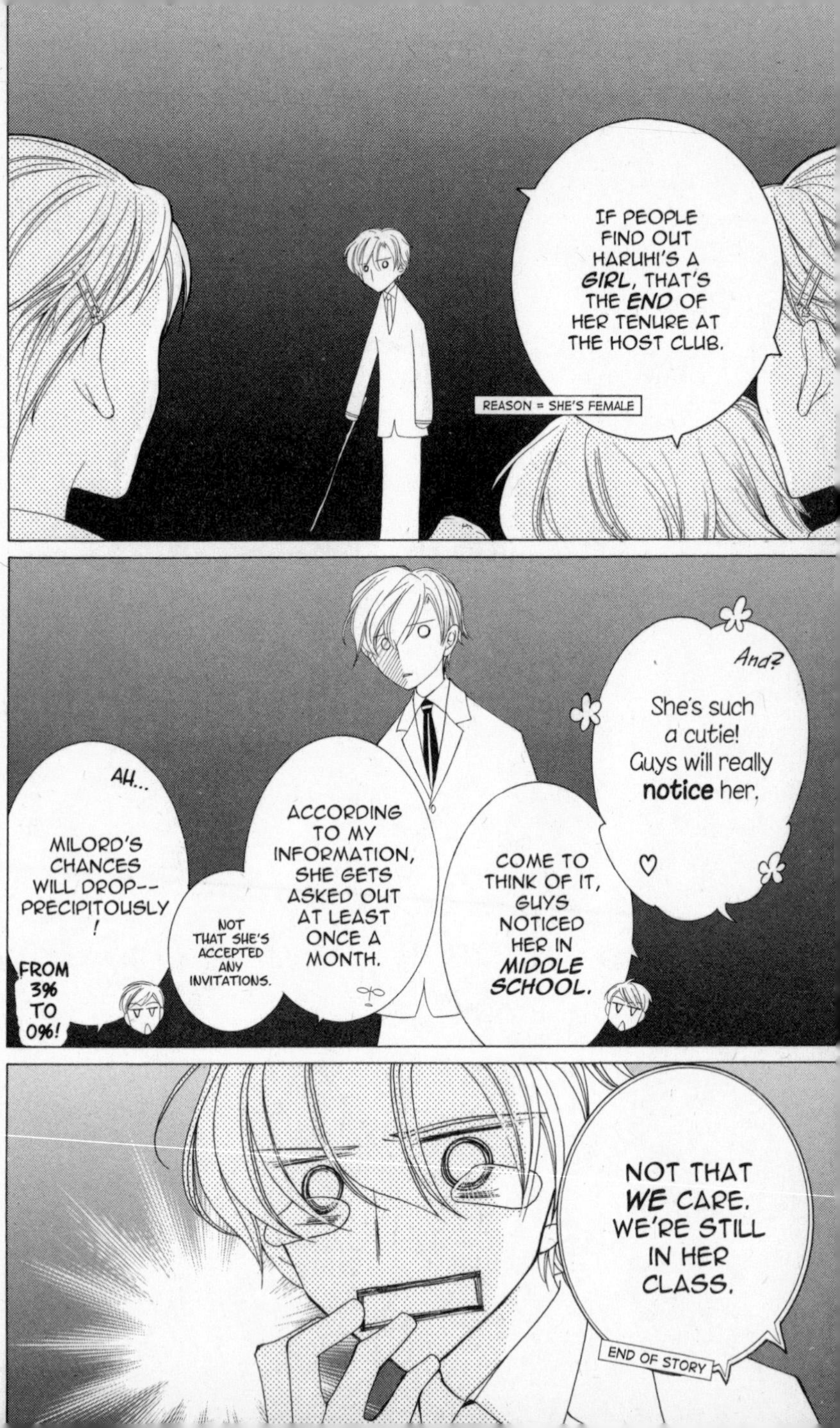
IF PEOPLE FIND OUT HARUHI'S A GIRL, THAT'S THE END OF HER TENURE AT THE HOST CLUB.
REASON = SHE'S FEMALE
And? She's such a cutie! Guys will really notice her. ♡
COME TO THINK OF IT, GUYS NOTICED HER IN MIDDLE SCHOOL.
ACCORDING TO MY INFORMATION, SHE GETS ASKED OUT AT LEAST ONCE A MONTH.
NOT THAT SHE'S ACCEPTED ANY INVITATIONS.
AH... MILORD'S CHANCES WILL DROP--PRECIPITOUSLY!
FROM 3% TO 0%!
NOT THAT WE CARE. WE'RE STILL IN HER CLASS.
END OF STORY

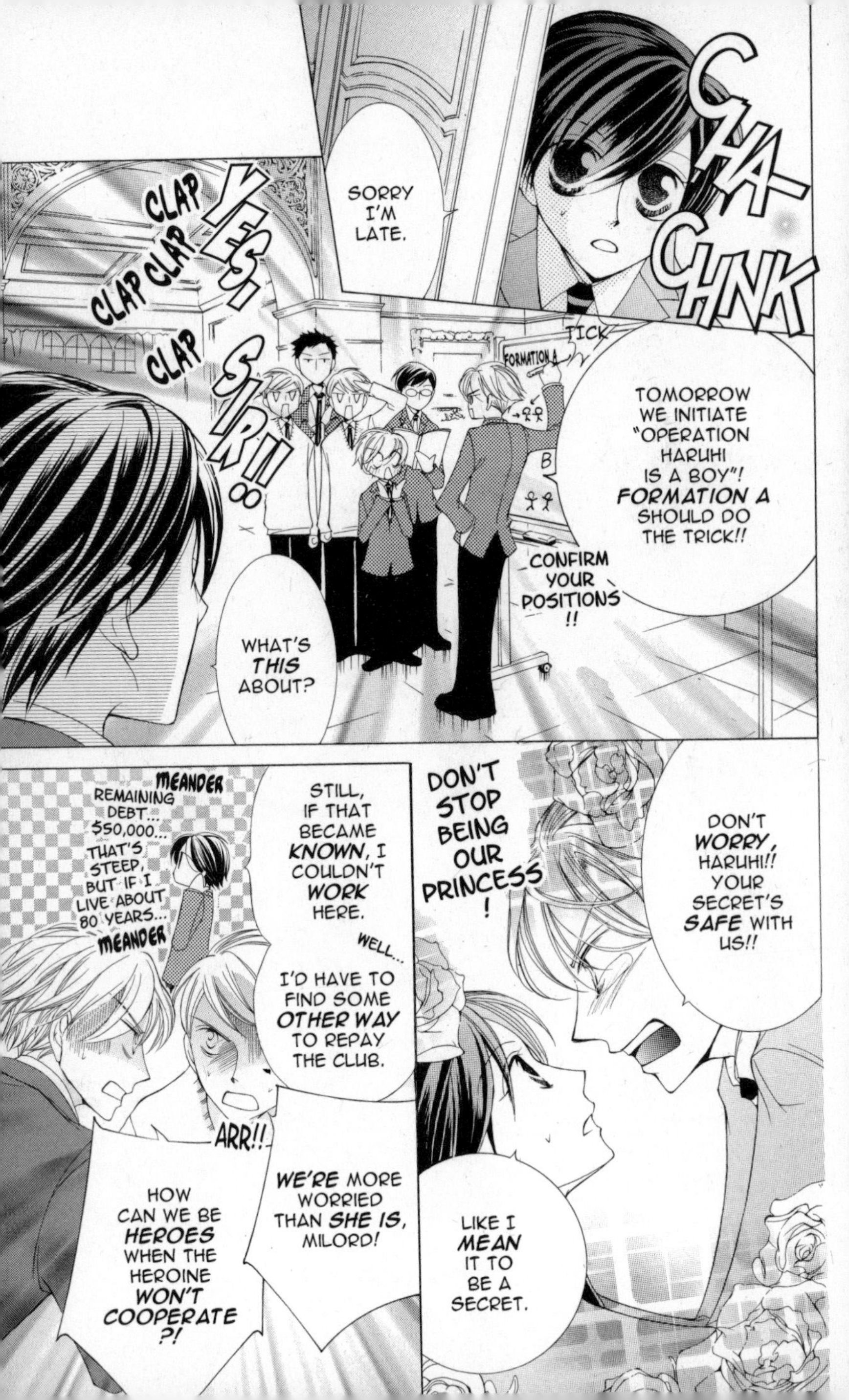
CHA-CHUNK
SORRY I'M LATE.
TOMORROW WE INITIATE "OPERATION HARUHI IS A BOY"! FORMATION A SHOULD DO THE TRICK!!
TICK
FORMATION A
B
CONFIRM YOUR POSITIONS!!
YES, SIR!!
CLAP CLAP CLAP CLAP CLAP
WHAT'S THIS ABOUT?
DON'T WORRY, HARUHI!! YOUR SECRET'S SAFE WITH US!!
DON'T STOP BEING OUR PRINCESS!
LIKE I MEAN IT TO BE A SECRET.
STILL, IF THAT BECAME KNOWN, I COULDN'T WORK HERE.
WELL...
I'D HAVE TO FIND SOME OTHER WAY TO REPAY THE CLUB.
MEANDER
REMAINING DEBT... $50,000... THAT'S STEEP, BUT IF I LIVE ABOUT 80 YEARS...
MEANDER
ARR!!
WE'RE MORE WORRIED THAN SHE IS, MILORD!
HOW CAN WE BE HEROES WHEN THE HEROINE WON'T COOPERATE?!

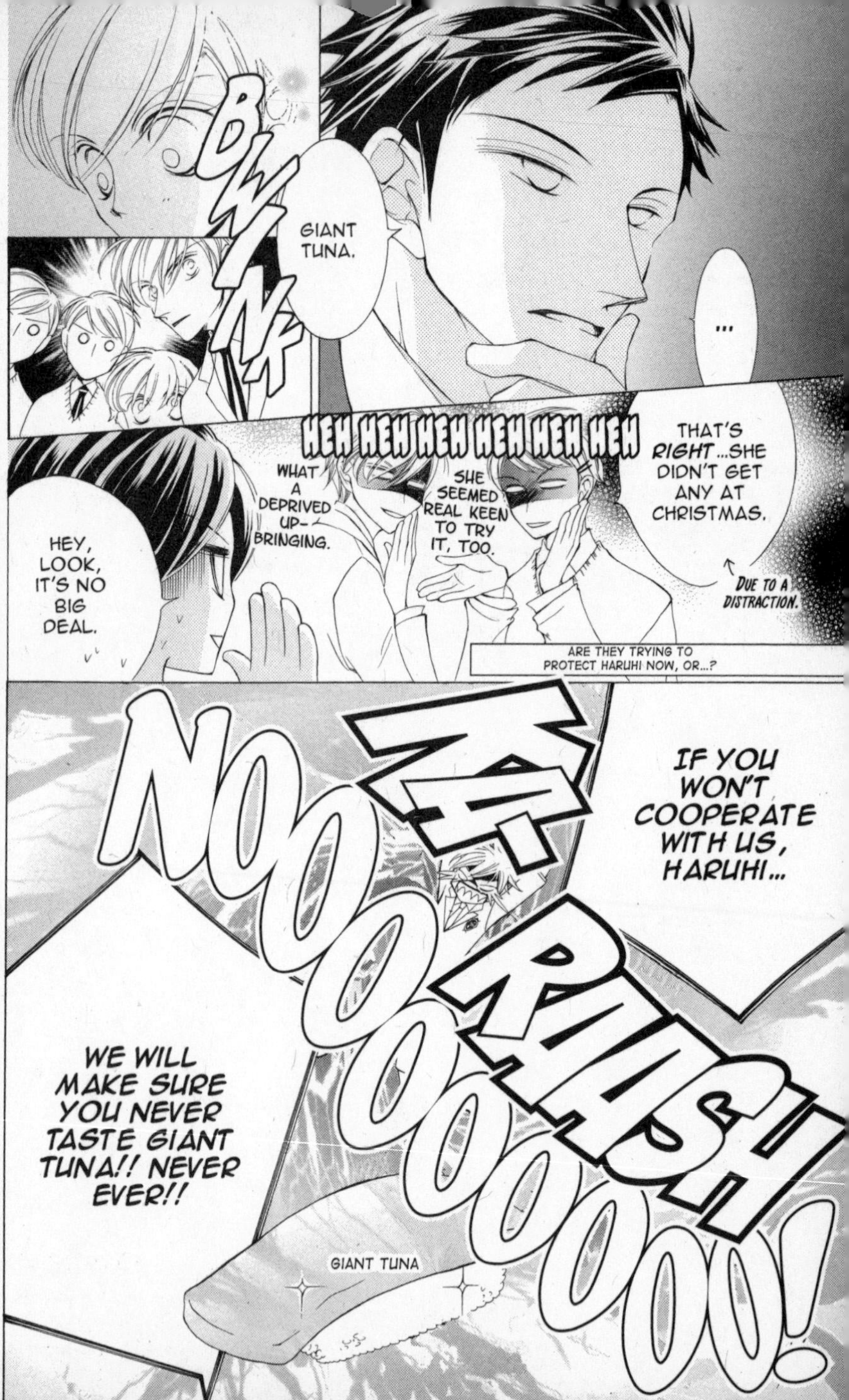
...
BOWINK
GIANT TUNA.
THAT'S *RIGHT*...SHE DIDN'T GET ANY AT CHRISTMAS.
DUE TO A DISTRACTION.
HEH HEH HEH HEH HEH HEH
SHE SEEMED REAL KEEN TO TRY IT, TOO.
WHAT A DEPRIVED UP-BRINGING.
HEY, LOOK, IT'S NO BIG DEAL.
ARE THEY TRYING TO PROTECT HARUHI NOW, OR...?
IF YOU WON'T COOPERATE WITH US, HARUHI...
KA-RATSH
NOOOOOOOOOOOO!
WE WILL MAKE SURE YOU NEVER TASTE GIANT TUNA!! NEVER EVER!!
GIANT TUNA

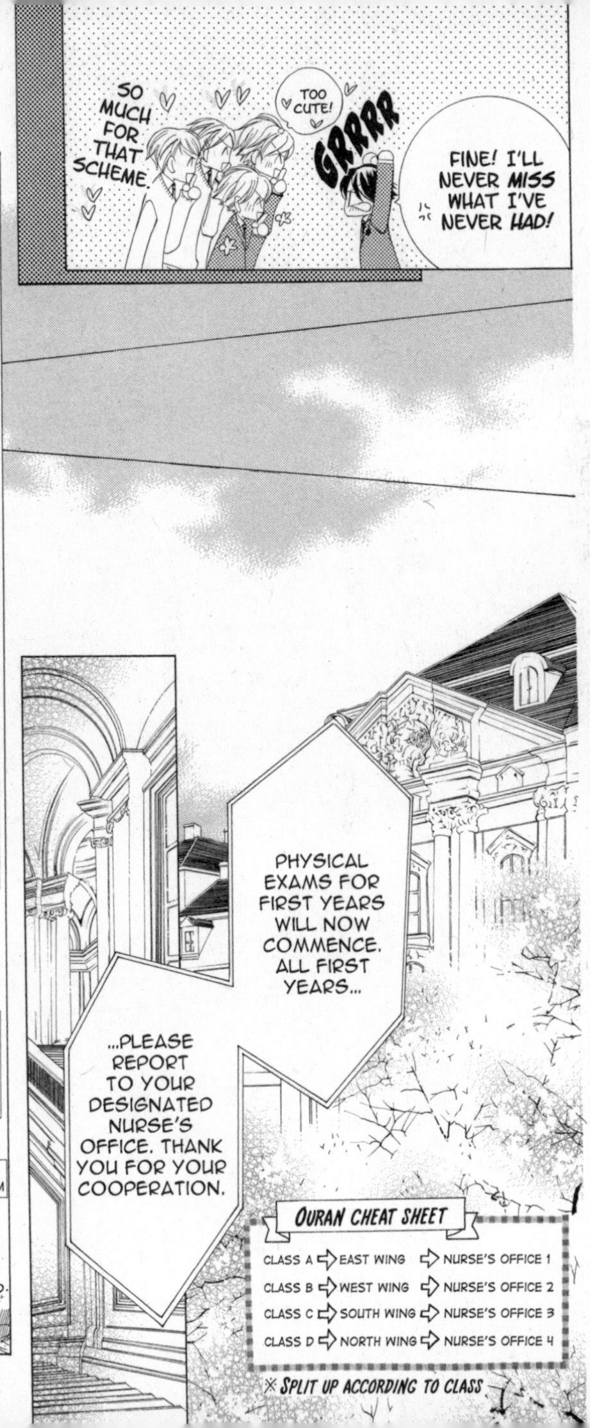
FINE! I'LL NEVER MISS WHAT I'VE NEVER HAD!
GRRRR
TOO CUTE!
SO MUCH FOR THAT SCHEME.
PHYSICAL EXAMS FOR FIRST YEARS WILL NOW COMMENCE. ALL FIRST YEARS...
...PLEASE REPORT TO YOUR DESIGNATED NURSE'S OFFICE. THANK YOU FOR YOUR COOPERATION.
OURAN CHEAT SHEET
CLASS A ⇨ EAST WING ⇨ NURSE'S OFFICE 1
CLASS B ⇨ WEST WING ⇨ NURSE'S OFFICE 2
CLASS C ⇨ SOUTH WING ⇨ NURSE'S OFFICE 3
CLASS D ⇨ NORTH WING ⇨ NURSE'S OFFICE 4
※ SPLIT UP ACCORDING TO CLASS

1

✿ HELLO. THIS IS HATORI FOR *HOST CLUB*, VOLUME 2. VOLUME 1 WAS BASED ON SINGLE SEGMENTS. VOLUME 2 AND ON IS A PUBLISHED SERIES. HOWEVER, THIS FIRST ROUND OF THE PUBLISHED SERIES (APRIL ISSUE) WAS A DISASTER...

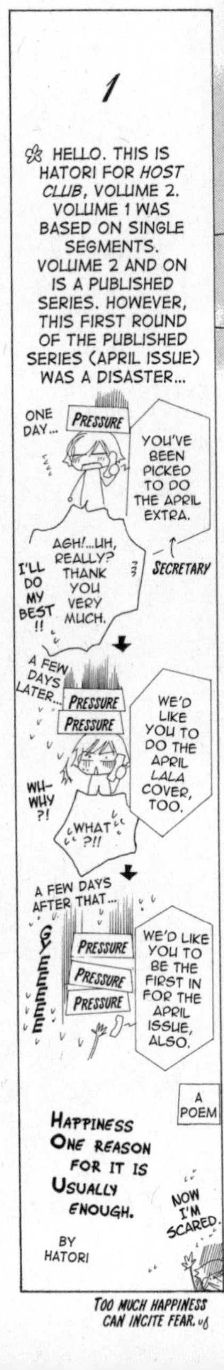
ONE DAY...
PRESSURE
YOU'VE BEEN PICKED TO DO THE APRIL EXTRA.
SECRETARY
AGH!...UH, REALLY? THANK YOU VERY MUCH.
I'LL DO MY BEST!!
A FEW DAYS LATER...
PRESSURE
PRESSURE
WE'D LIKE YOU TO DO THE APRIL LALA COVER, TOO.
WH-WHY?!
WHAT?!!
A FEW DAYS AFTER THAT...
PRESSURE
PRESSURE
PRESSURE
WE'D LIKE YOU TO BE THE FIRST IN FOR THE APRIL ISSUE, ALSO.

A POEM

HAPPINESS
ONE REASON
FOR IT IS
USUALLY
ENOUGH.

BY
HATORI

NOW I'M SCARED.

TOO MUCH HAPPINESS CAN INCITE FEAR.

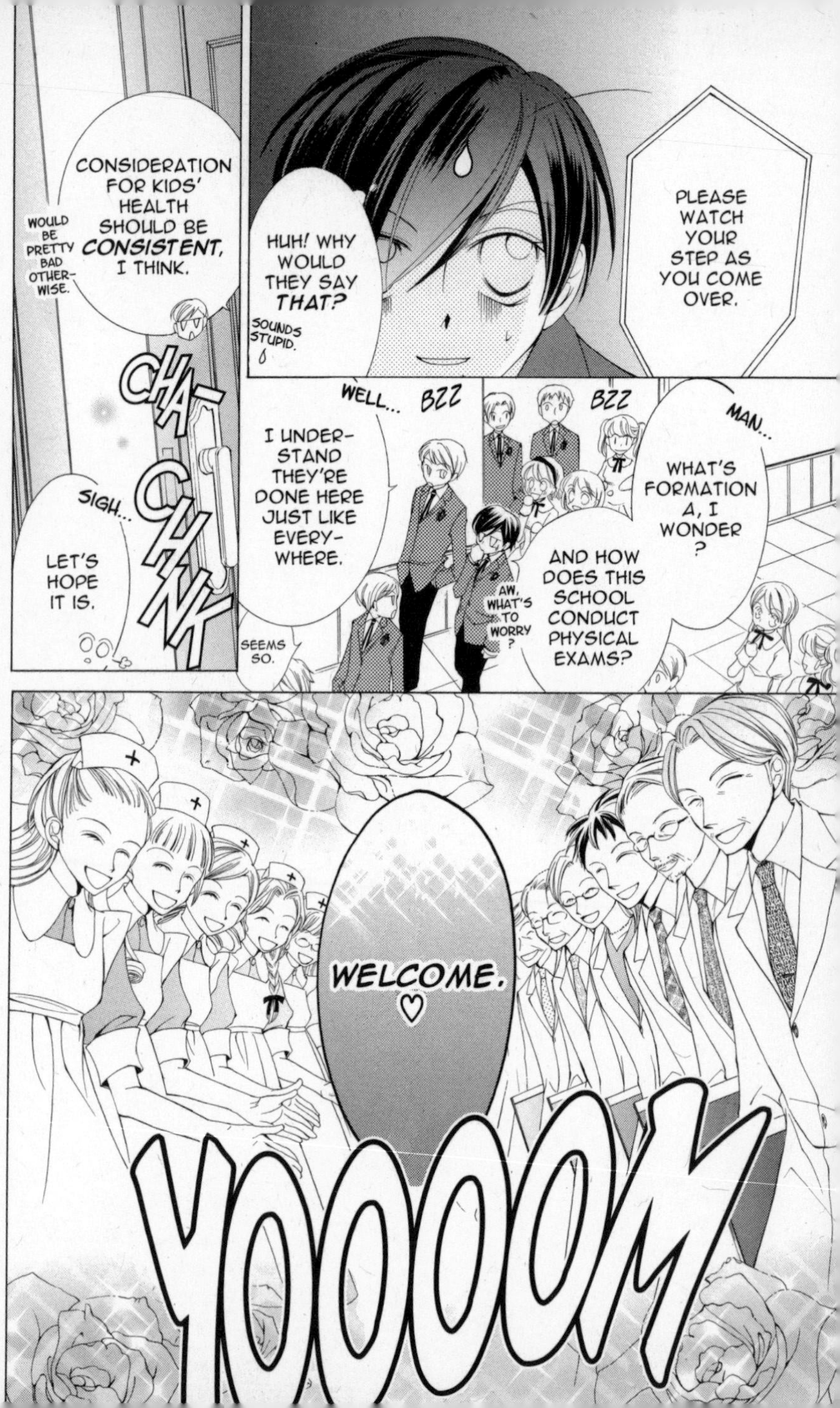
PLEASE WATCH YOUR STEP AS YOU COME OVER.
HUH! WHY WOULD THEY SAY THAT?
SOUNDS STUPID.
BZZ
MAN...
WHAT'S FORMATION A, I WONDER?
AND HOW DOES THIS SCHOOL CONDUCT PHYSICAL EXAMS?
AW, WHAT'S TO WORRY?
WELL... BZZ
I UNDERSTAND THEY'RE DONE HERE JUST LIKE EVERYWHERE.
SEEMS SO.
CONSIDERATION FOR KIDS' HEALTH SHOULD BE CONSISTENT, I THINK.
WOULD BE PRETTY BAD OTHERWISE.
CHA-CHUNK
SIGH...
LET'S HOPE IT IS.
WELCOME. ♡
YOOOOM

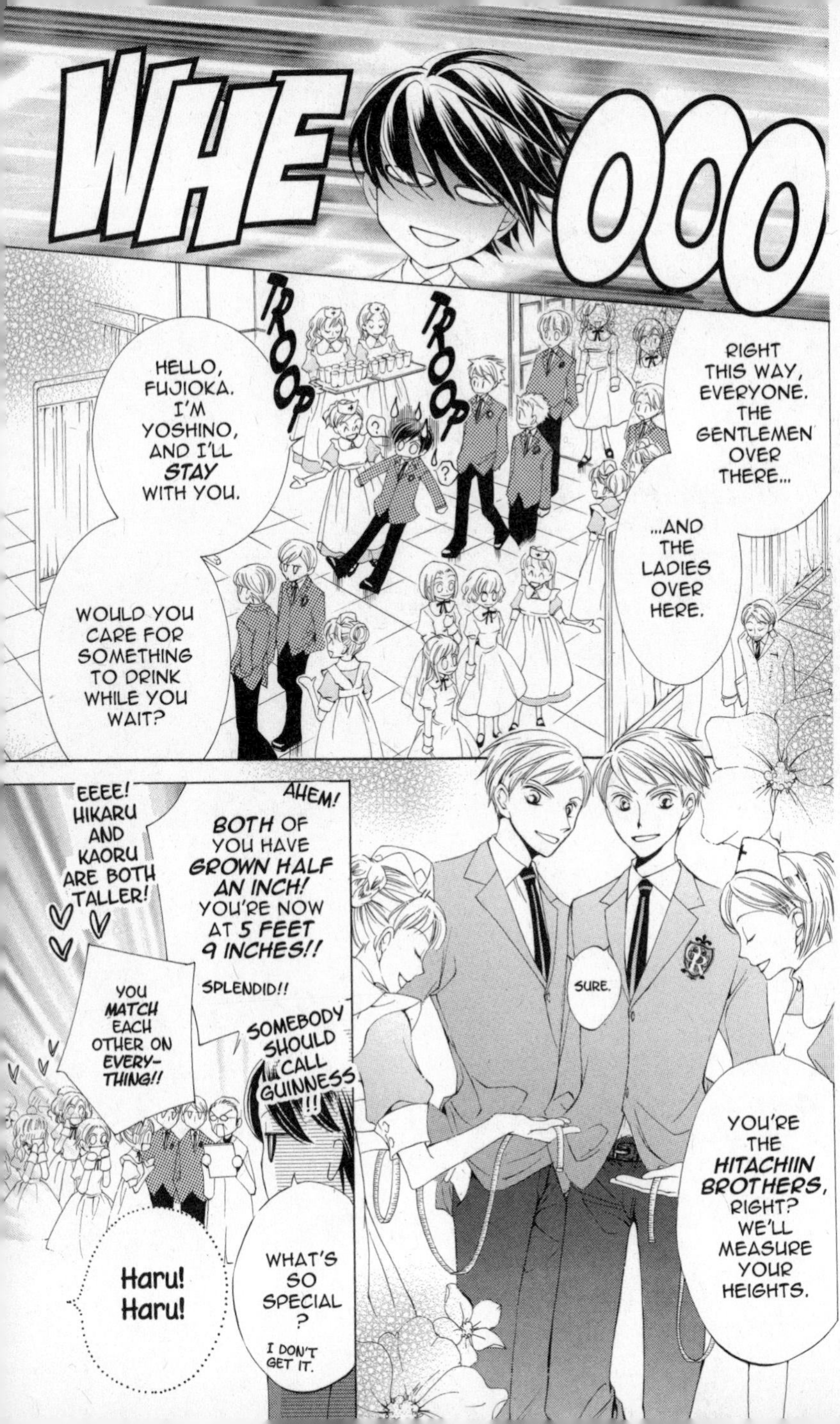
WHEOOO
RIGHT THIS WAY, EVERYONE. THE GENTLEMEN OVER THERE...
...AND THE LADIES OVER HERE.
TROOP TROOP
HELLO, FUJIOKA. I'M YOSHINO, AND I'LL STAY WITH YOU.
WOULD YOU CARE FOR SOMETHING TO DRINK WHILE YOU WAIT?
YOU'RE THE HITACHIIN BROTHERS, RIGHT? WE'LL MEASURE YOUR HEIGHTS.
SURE.
AHEM!
BOTH OF YOU HAVE GROWN HALF AN INCH! YOU'RE NOW AT 5 FEET 9 INCHES!!
SPLENDID!!
EEEE! HIKARU AND KAORU ARE BOTH TALLER!
YOU MATCH EACH OTHER ON EVERY-THING!!
SOMEBODY SHOULD CALL GUINNESS!!!
WHAT'S SO SPECIAL?
I DON'T GET IT.
Haru! Haru!

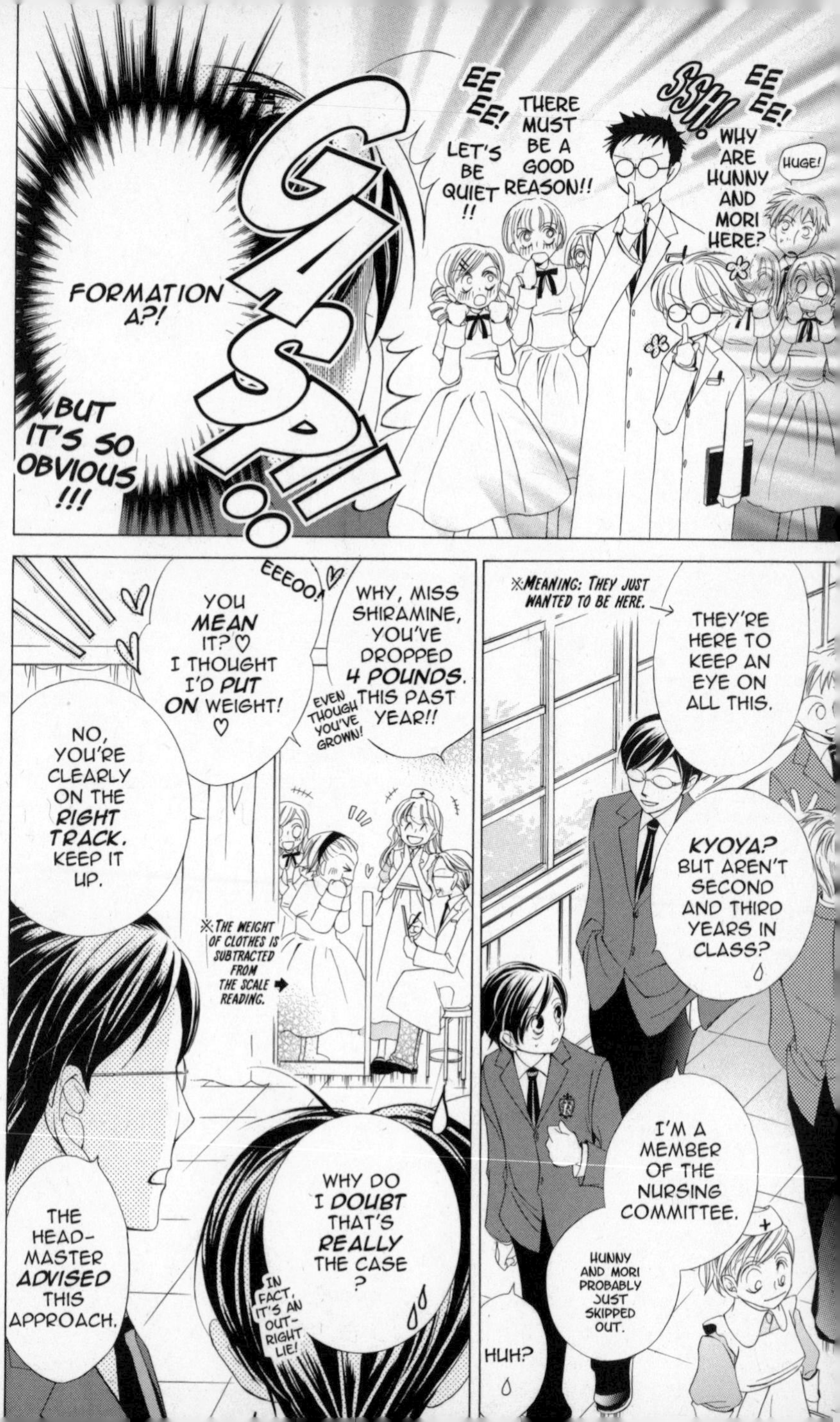
EE EE!
SSH!!
WHY ARE HUNNY AND MORI HERE?
HUGE!
THERE MUST BE A GOOD REASON!!
EE EE!
LET'S BE QUIET!!
GASP!!
FORMATION A?!
BUT IT'S SO OBVIOUS!!!
※MEANING: THEY JUST WANTED TO BE HERE.
THEY'RE HERE TO KEEP AN EYE ON ALL THIS.
KYOYA? BUT AREN'T SECOND AND THIRD YEARS IN CLASS?
I'M A MEMBER OF THE NURSING COMMITTEE.
HUNNY AND MORI PROBABLY JUST SKIPPED OUT.
HUH?
WHY, MISS SHIRAMINE, YOU'VE DROPPED 4 POUNDS THIS PAST YEAR!!
EVEN THOUGH YOU'VE GROWN!
EEEOO!
YOU MEAN IT? I THOUGHT I'D PUT ON WEIGHT!
NO, YOU'RE CLEARLY ON THE RIGHT TRACK. KEEP IT UP.
※THE WEIGHT OF CLOTHES IS SUBTRACTED FROM THE SCALE READING.
THE HEAD-MASTER ADVISED THIS APPROACH.
WHY DO I DOUBT THAT'S REALLY THE CASE?
IN FACT, IT'S AN OUT-RIGHT LIE!

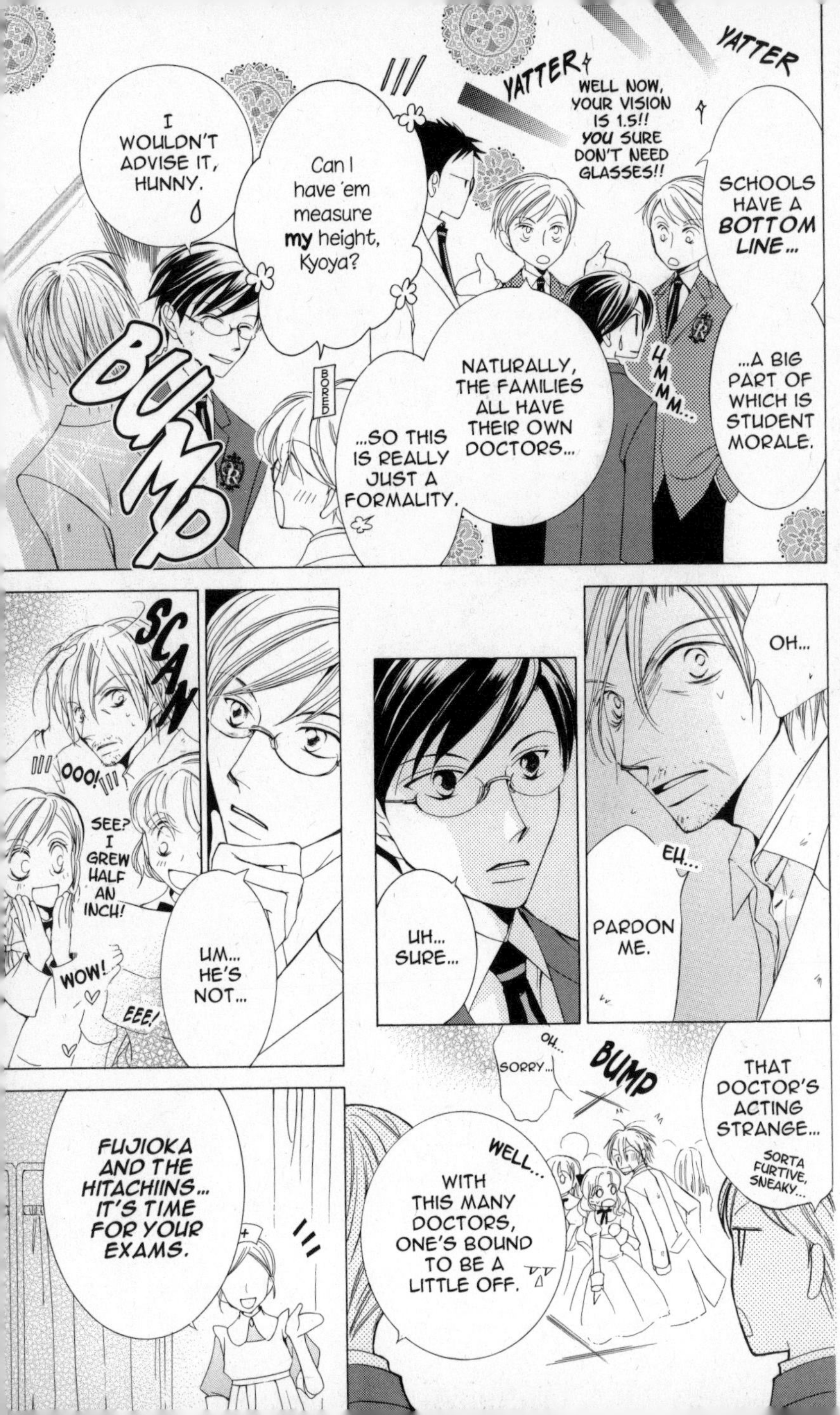
YATTER
SCHOOLS HAVE A BOTTOM LINE...
...A BIG PART OF WHICH IS STUDENT MORALE.
YATTER
WELL NOW, YOUR VISION IS 1.5!! YOU SURE DON'T NEED GLASSES!!
HMMM...
NATURALLY, THE FAMILIES ALL HAVE THEIR OWN DOCTORS...
...SO THIS IS REALLY JUST A FORMALITY.
Can I have 'em measure my height, Kyoya?
BORED
I WOULDN'T ADVISE IT, HUNNY.
BUMP
OH...
EH...
PARDON ME.
UH... SURE...
SCAN
UM... HE'S NOT...
OOO!
SEE? I GREW HALF AN INCH!
WOW!
EEE!
OH...
SORRY...
BUMP
THAT DOCTOR'S ACTING STRANGE...
SORTA FURTIVE, SNEAKY...
WELL...
WITH THIS MANY DOCTORS, ONE'S BOUND TO BE A LITTLE OFF.
FUJIOKA AND THE HITACHIINS... IT'S TIME FOR YOUR EXAMS.

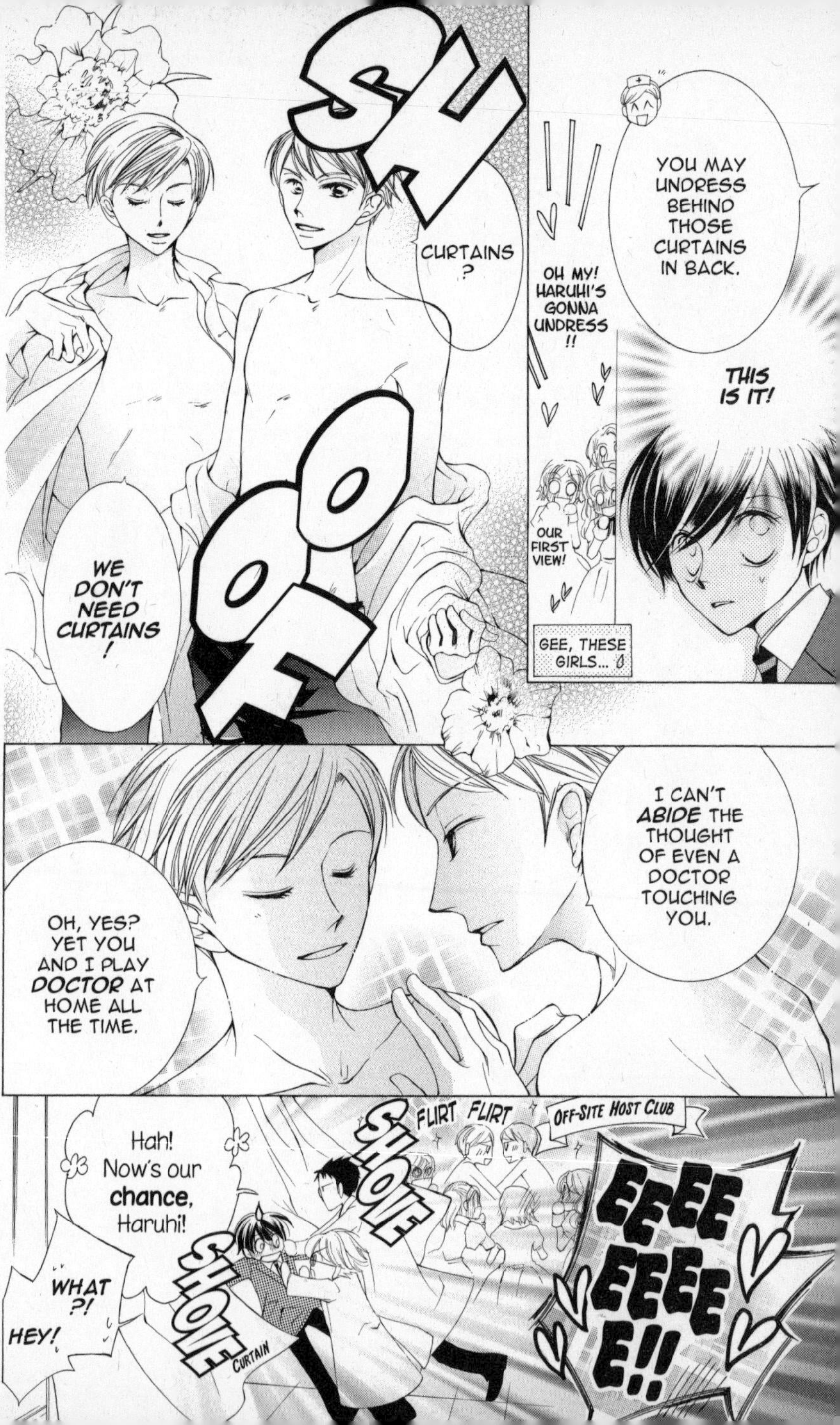

YOU MAY UNDRESS BEHIND THOSE CURTAINS IN BACK.
OH MY! HARUHI'S GONNA UNDRESS!!
THIS IS IT!
OUR FIRST VIEW!
GEE, THESE GIRLS...
SH
CURTAINS?
WE DON'T NEED CURTAINS!
I CAN'T *ABIDE* THE THOUGHT OF EVEN A DOCTOR TOUCHING YOU.
OH, YES? YET YOU AND I PLAY *DOCTOR* AT HOME ALL THE TIME.
EEEEEEEEE!!
OFF-SITE HOST CLUB
FLIRT FLIRT
SHOVE
SHOVE
SHOVE
CURTAIN
Hah! Now's our **chance**, Haruhi!
WHAT?!
HEY!

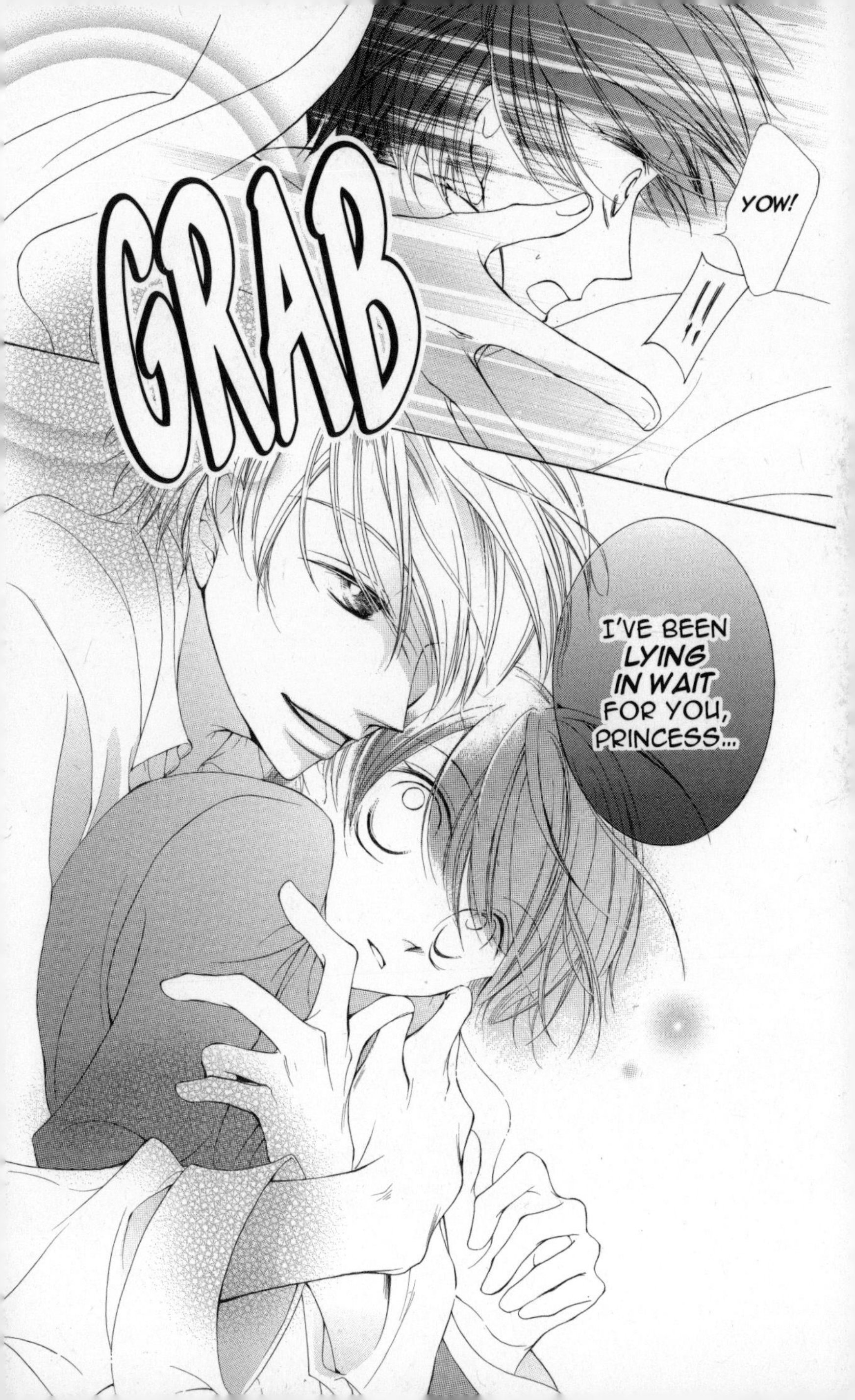
YOW!
!!
GRAB
I'VE BEEN LYING IN WAIT FOR YOU, PRINCESS...

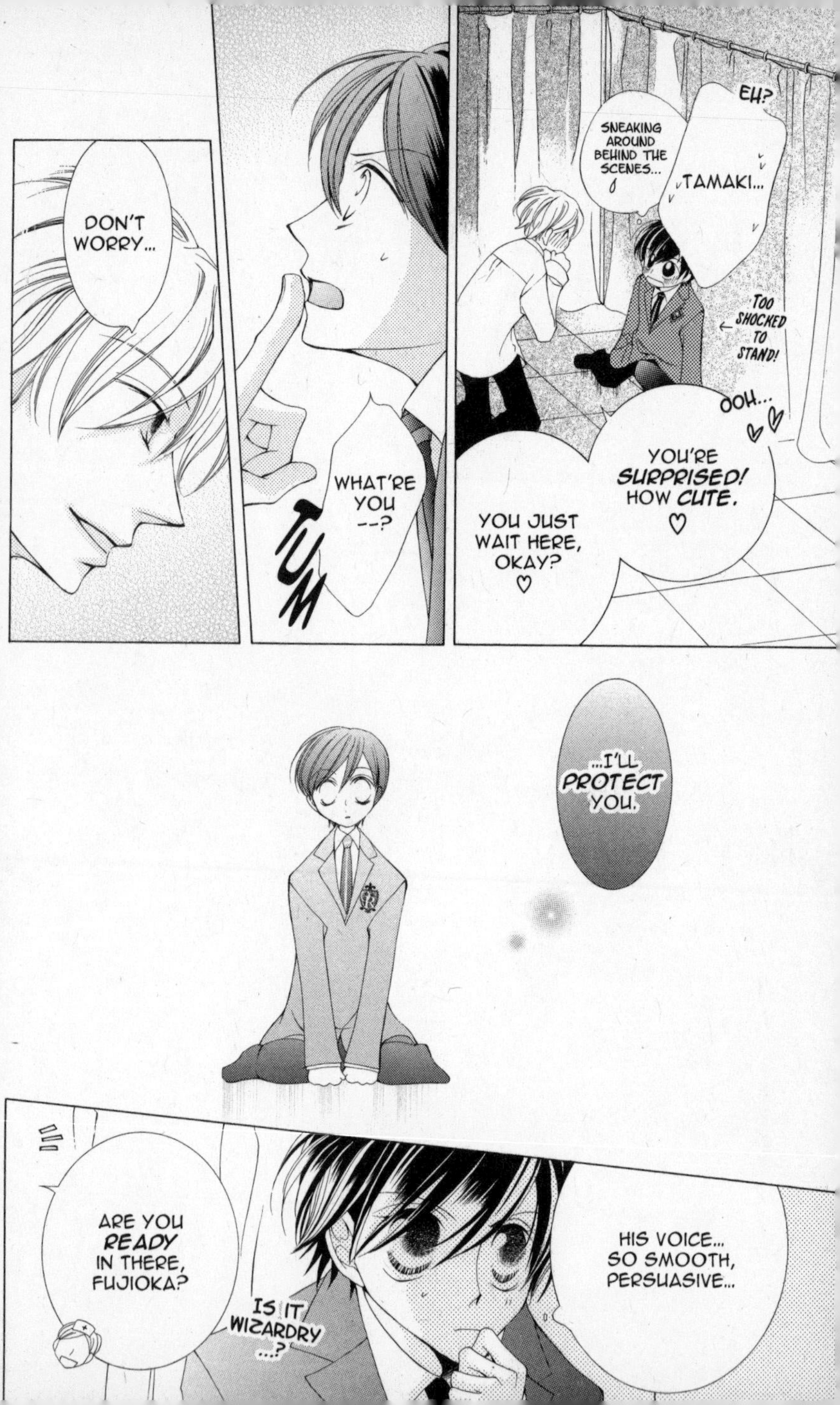
EH?
TAMAKI...
SNEAKING AROUND BEHIND THE SCENES...
TOO SHOCKED TO STAND!
OOH...
YOU'RE SURPRISED! HOW CUTE.
YOU JUST WAIT HERE, OKAY?
WHAT'RE YOU --?
TUM
DON'T WORRY...
...I'LL PROTECT YOU.
HIS VOICE... SO SMOOTH, PERSUASIVE...
IS IT WIZARDRY ...?
ARE YOU READY IN THERE, FUJIOKA?

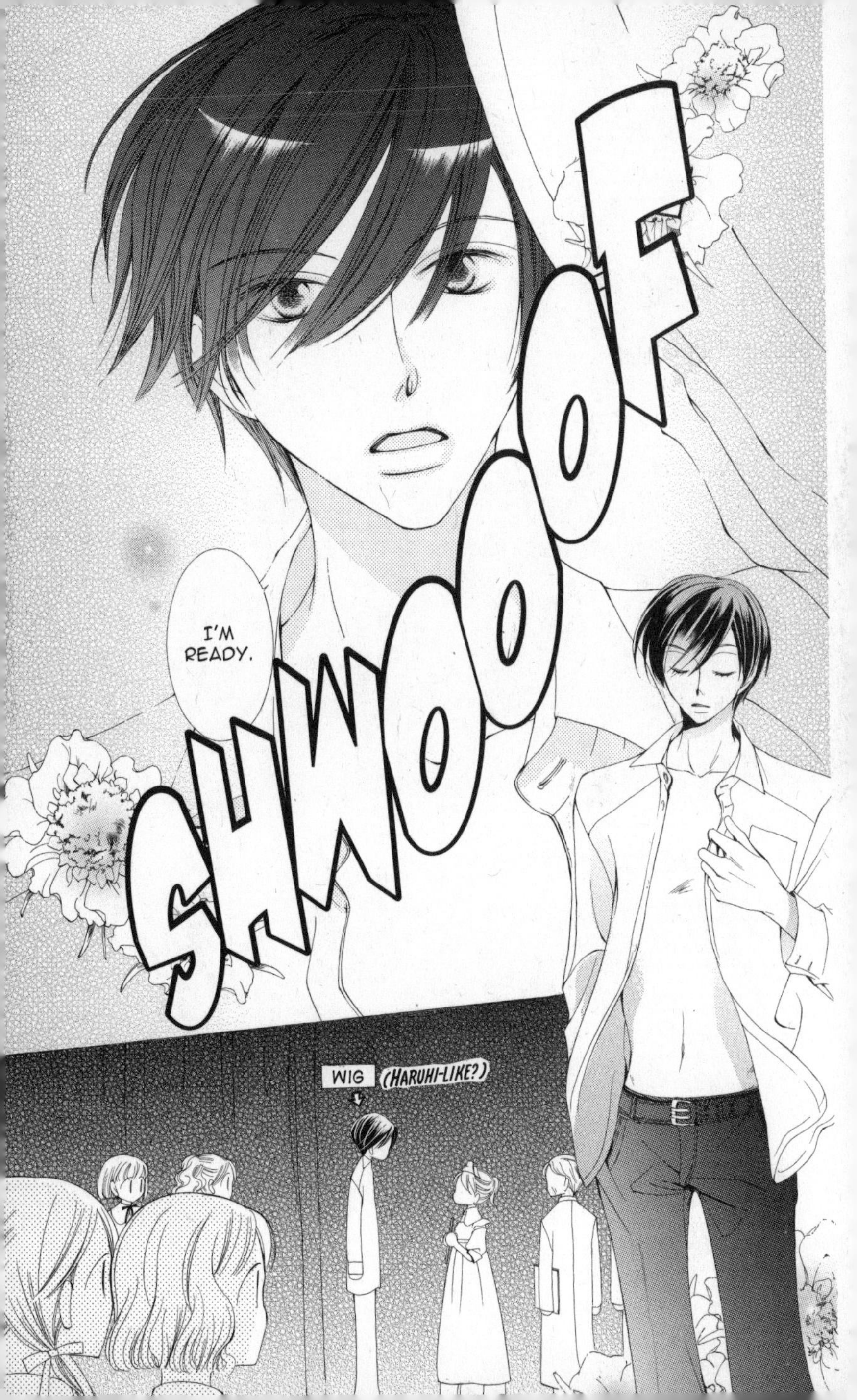
SHWOOOOF
I'M READY.
WIG
(HARUHI-LIKE?)

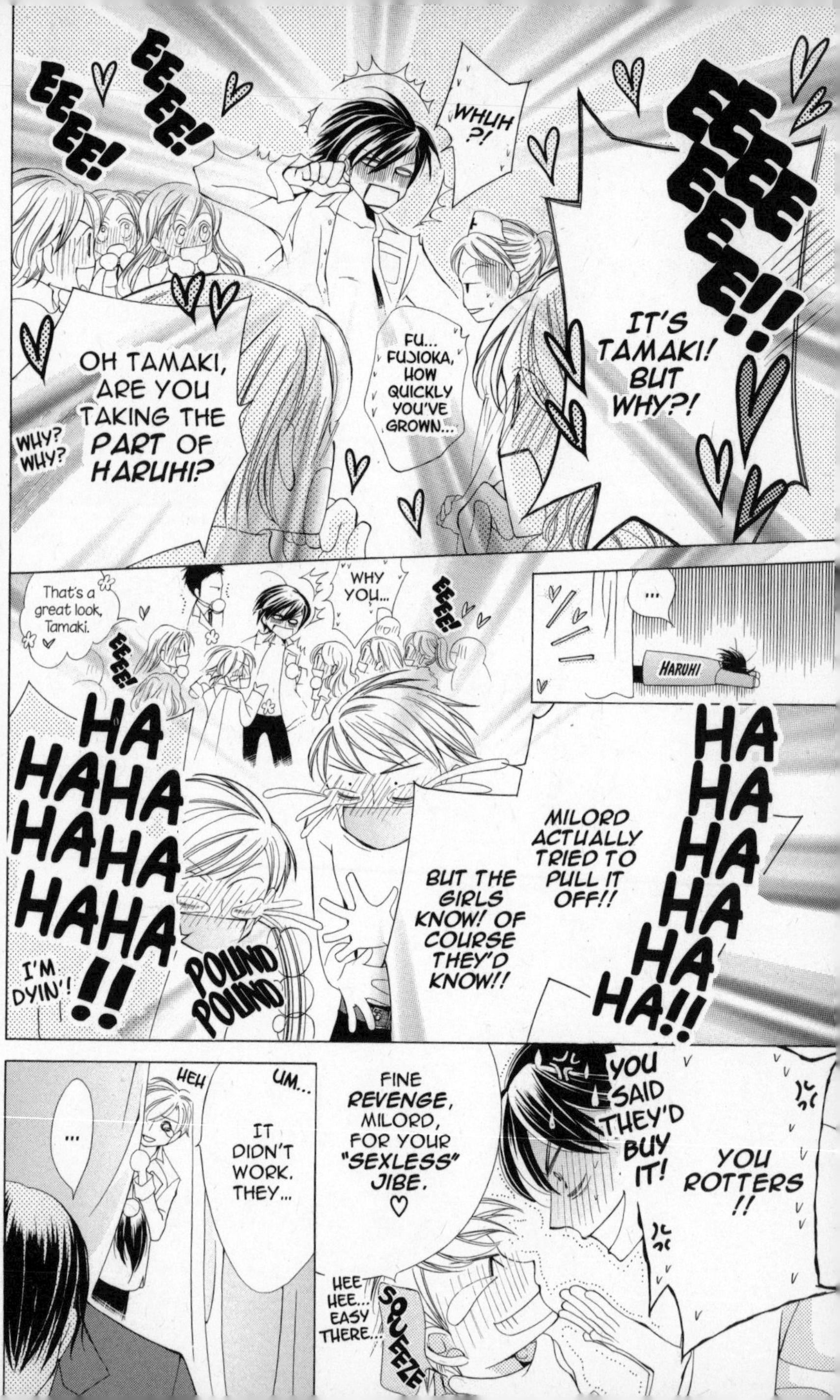
EEEEEEE!!
IT'S TAMAKI! BUT WHY?!
WHUH?!
EEEEE!
EEEEE!
FU... FUJIOKA, HOW QUICKLY YOU'VE GROWN...
OH TAMAKI, ARE YOU TAKING THE PART OF HARUHI?
WHY? WHY?
...
HARUHI
WHY YOU...
EEEE!
That's a great look, Tamaki.
EEEE!
HA HA HA HA HA HA HA!!
MILORD ACTUALLY TRIED TO PULL IT OFF!!
BUT THE GIRLS KNOW! OF COURSE THEY'D KNOW!!
POUND POUND
HA HAHA HAHA HAHA HAHA!!
I'M DYIN'!
YOU ROTTERS!!
YOU SAID THEY'D BUY IT!
FINE REVENGE, MILORD, FOR YOUR "SEXLESS" JIBE.
SQUEEZE
HEE HEE... EASY THERE...
UM...
HEH
IT DIDN'T WORK. THEY...
...

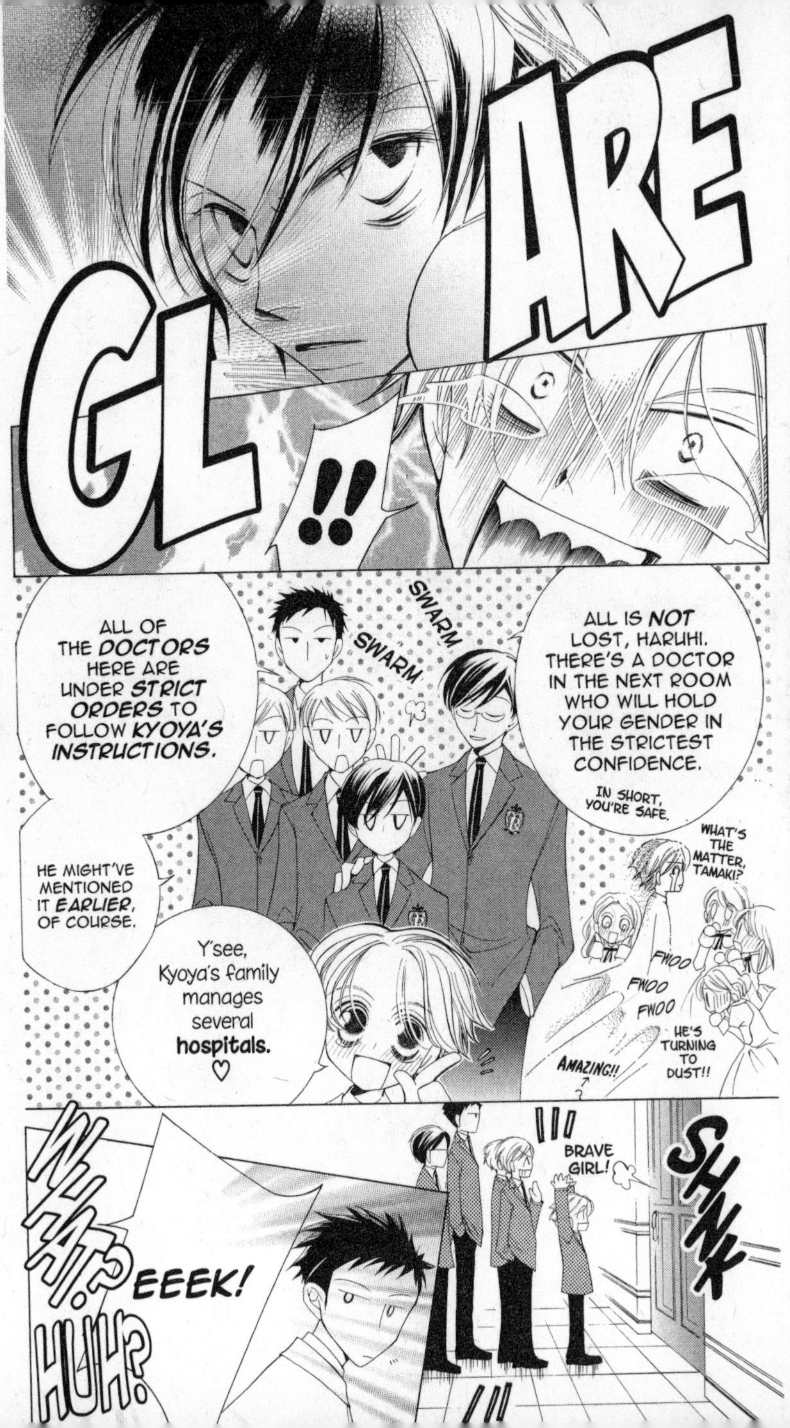
GLARE
!!
ALL IS NOT LOST, HARUHI. THERE'S A DOCTOR IN THE NEXT ROOM WHO WILL HOLD YOUR GENDER IN THE STRICTEST CONFIDENCE.
IN SHORT, YOU'RE SAFE.
SWARM
SWARM
ALL OF THE DOCTORS HERE ARE UNDER STRICT ORDERS TO FOLLOW KYOYA'S INSTRUCTIONS.
WHAT'S THE MATTER, TAMAKI!?
FWOO
FWOO
FWOO
HE'S TURNING TO DUST!!
AMAZING!!
?
HE MIGHT'VE MENTIONED IT EARLIER, OF COURSE.
Y'see, Kyoya's family manages several hospitals. ♡
SHHNK
BRAVE GIRL!
EEEK!
WHAT?!
HUH?

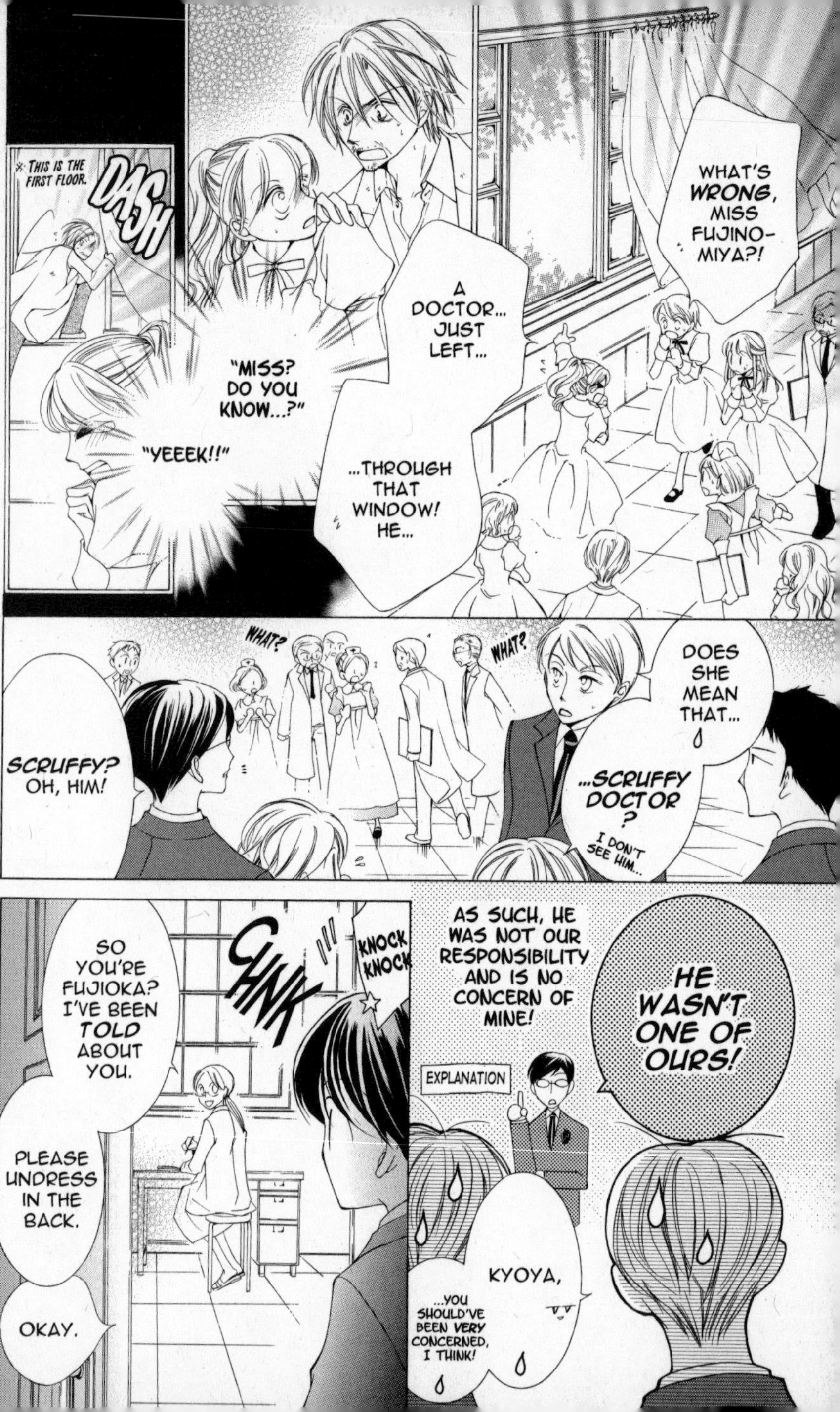
WHAT'S WRONG, MISS FUJINO-MIYA?!
A DOCTOR... JUST LEFT...
...THROUGH THAT WINDOW! HE...
"MISS? DO YOU KNOW...?"
"YEEEK!!"
DASH
※ THIS IS THE FIRST FLOOR.
DOES SHE MEAN THAT...
...SCRUFFY DOCTOR?
I DON'T SEE HIM...
WHAT?
WHAT?
SCRUFFY? OH, HIM!
HE WASN'T ONE OF OURS!
AS SUCH, HE WAS NOT OUR RESPONSIBILITY AND IS NO CONCERN OF MINE!
EXPLANATION
KYOYA,
...YOU SHOULD'VE BEEN VERY CONCERNED, I THINK!
KNOCK KNOCK
CHNK
SO YOU'RE FUJIOKA? I'VE BEEN TOLD ABOUT YOU.
PLEASE UNDRESS IN THE BACK.
OKAY.

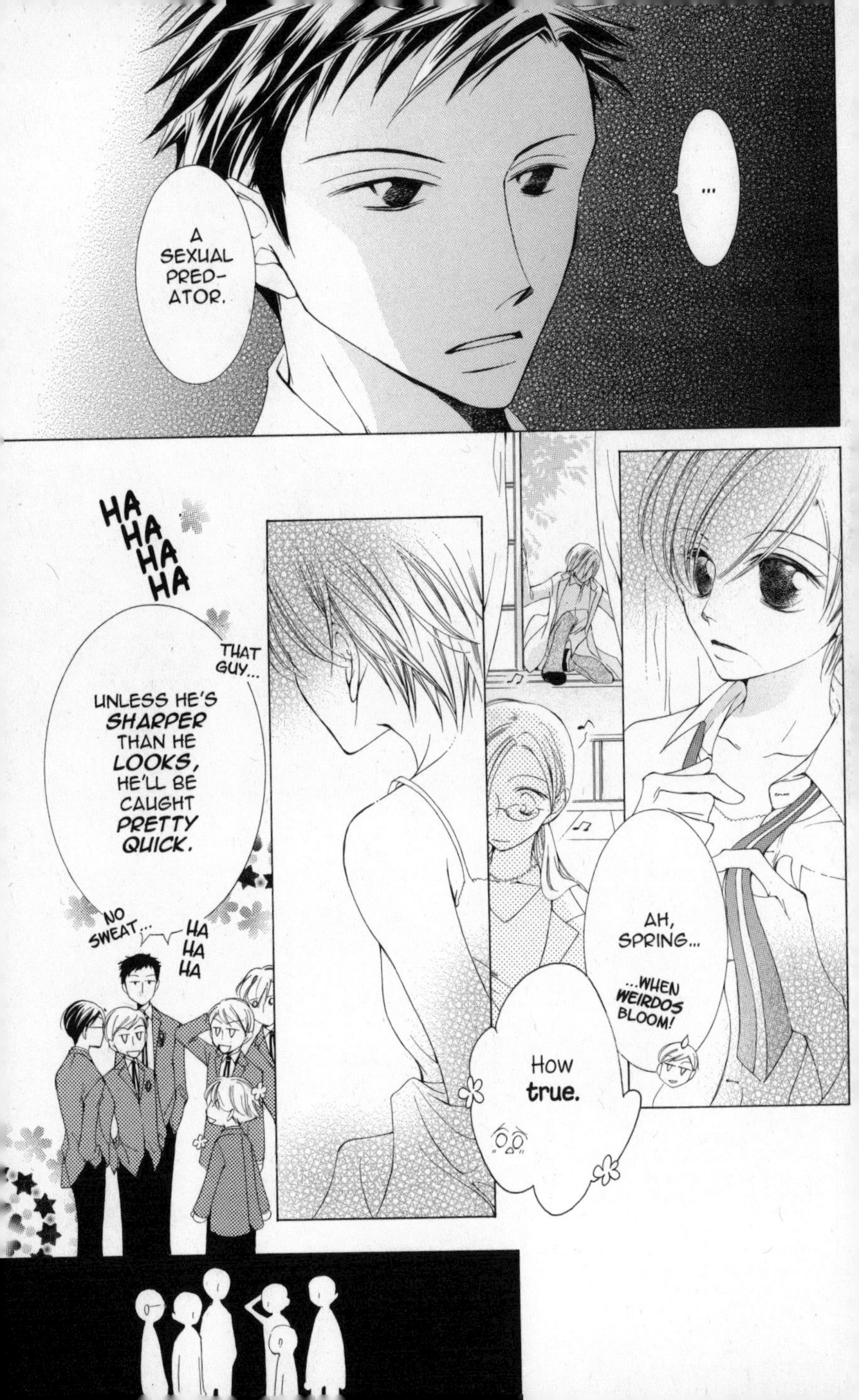
...
A SEXUAL PRED-ATOR.
AH, SPRING...
...WHEN WEIRDOS BLOOM!
How true.
HA HA HA HA
THAT GUY...
UNLESS HE'S SHARPER THAN HE LOOKS, HE'LL BE CAUGHT PRETTY QUICK.
NO SWEAT...
HA HA HA

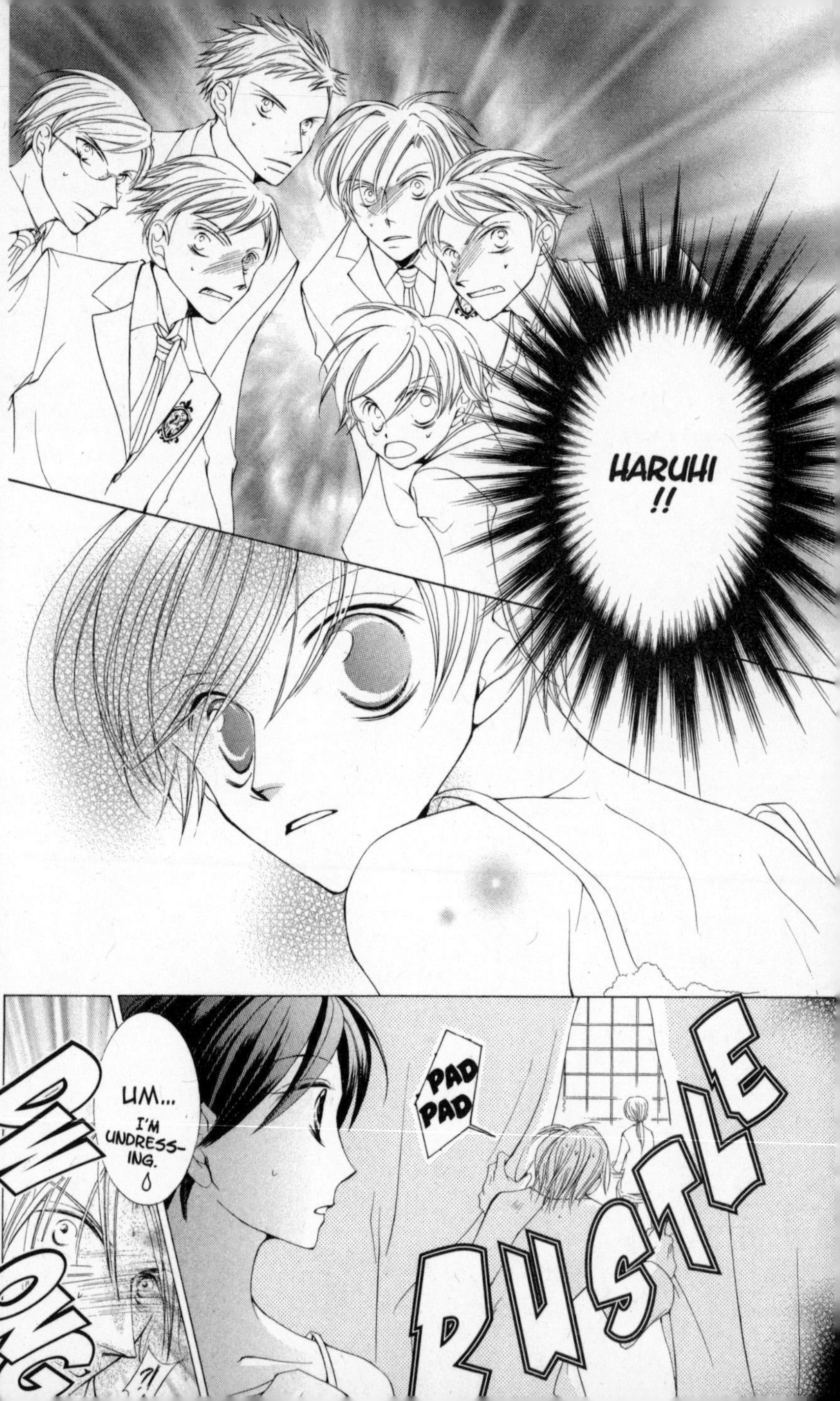
HARUHI !!
RUSTLE
PAD PAD
UM... I'M UNDRESSING.

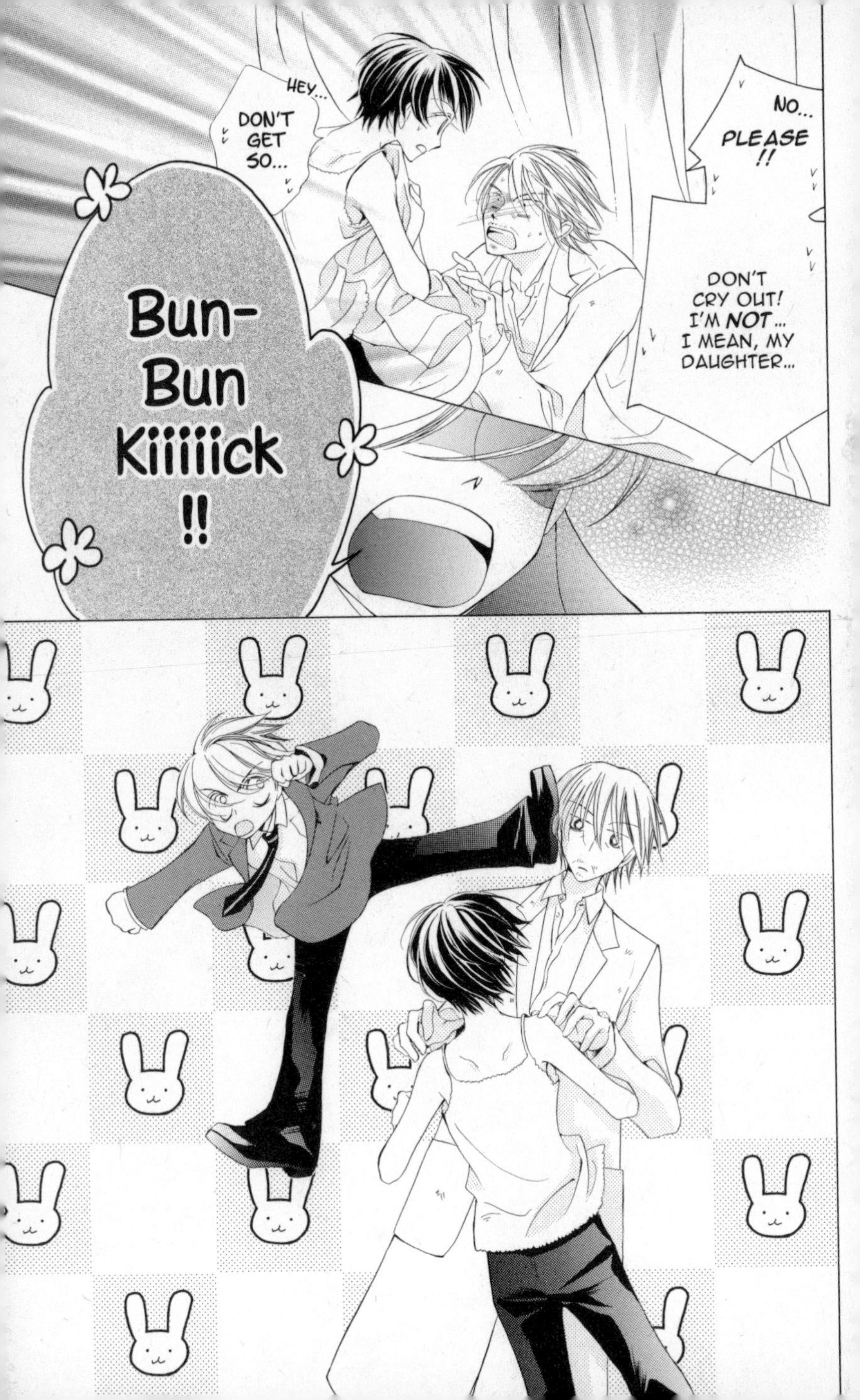
NO... PLEASE !!
DON'T CRY OUT! I'M *NOT*... I MEAN, MY DAUGHTER...
HEY... DON'T GET SO...
Bun-Bun Kiiiiick !!

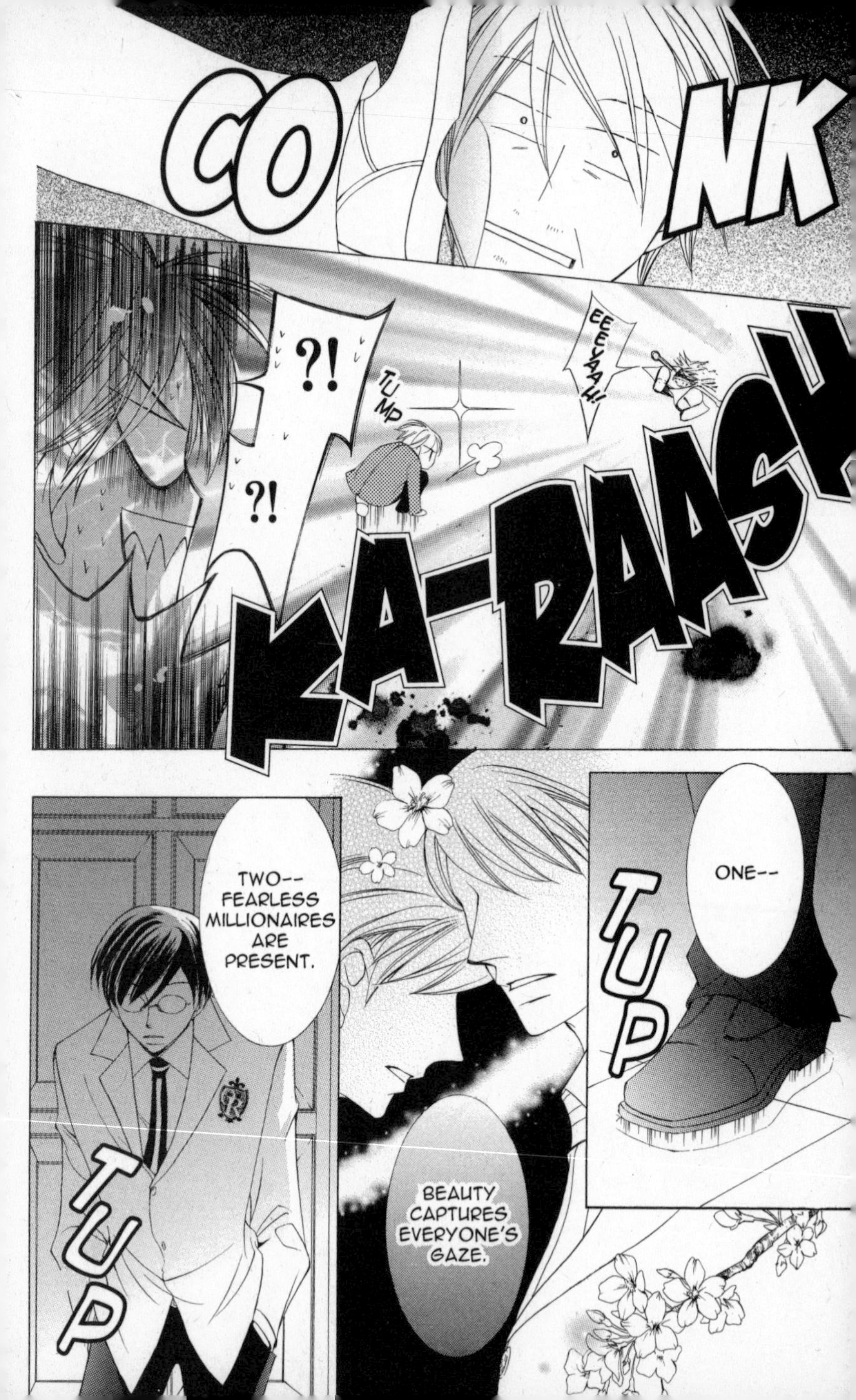
CO
NK
EEEYAAAH!!
KA-RAASH!
TUMP
?!
?!
ONE--
TUP
BEAUTY CAPTURES EVERYONE'S GAZE.
TWO--FEARLESS MILLIONAIRES ARE PRESENT.
TUP

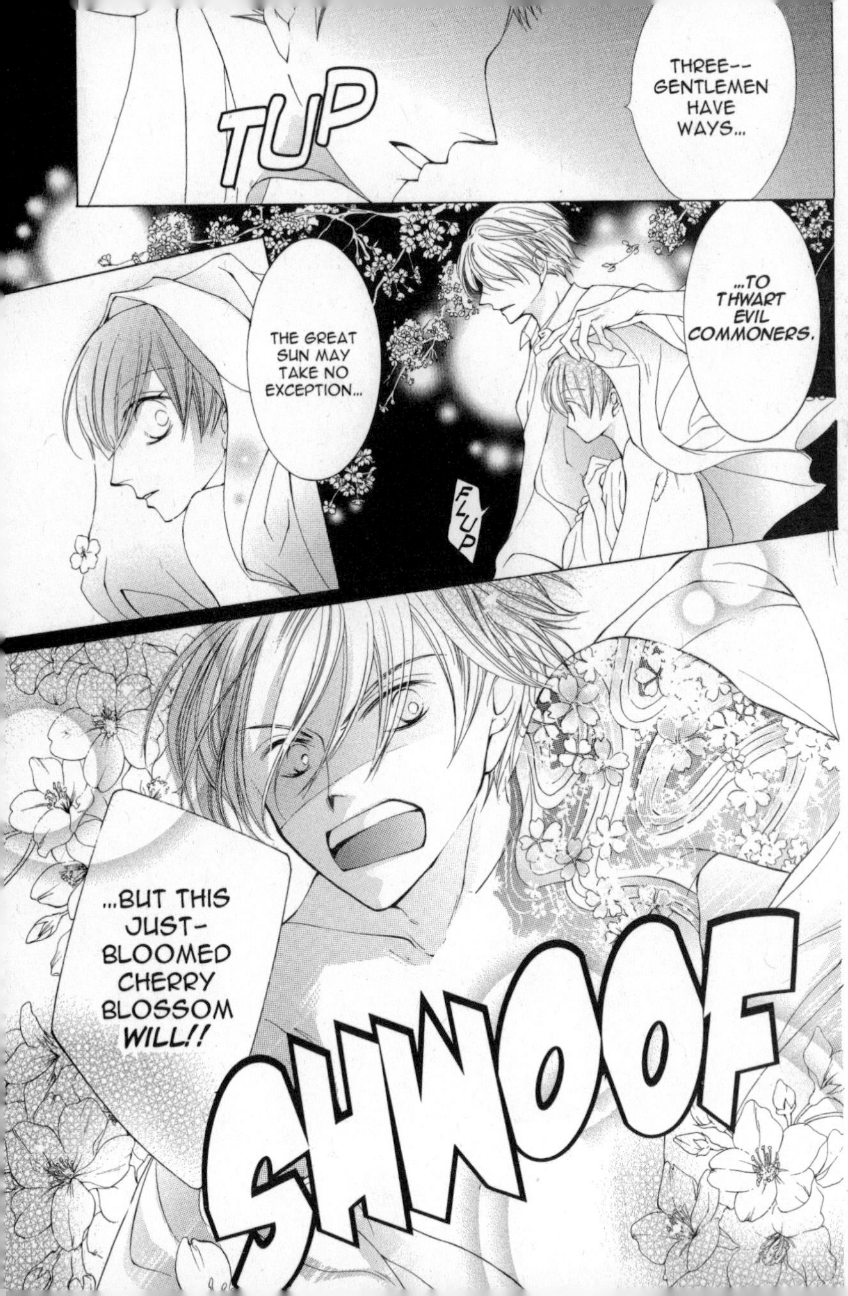
THREE--GENTLEMEN HAVE WAYS...
TUP
...TO THWART EVIL COMMONERS.
FLUP
THE GREAT SUN MAY TAKE NO EXCEPTION...
...BUT THIS JUST-BLOOMED CHERRY BLOSSOM WILL!!
SHWOOF

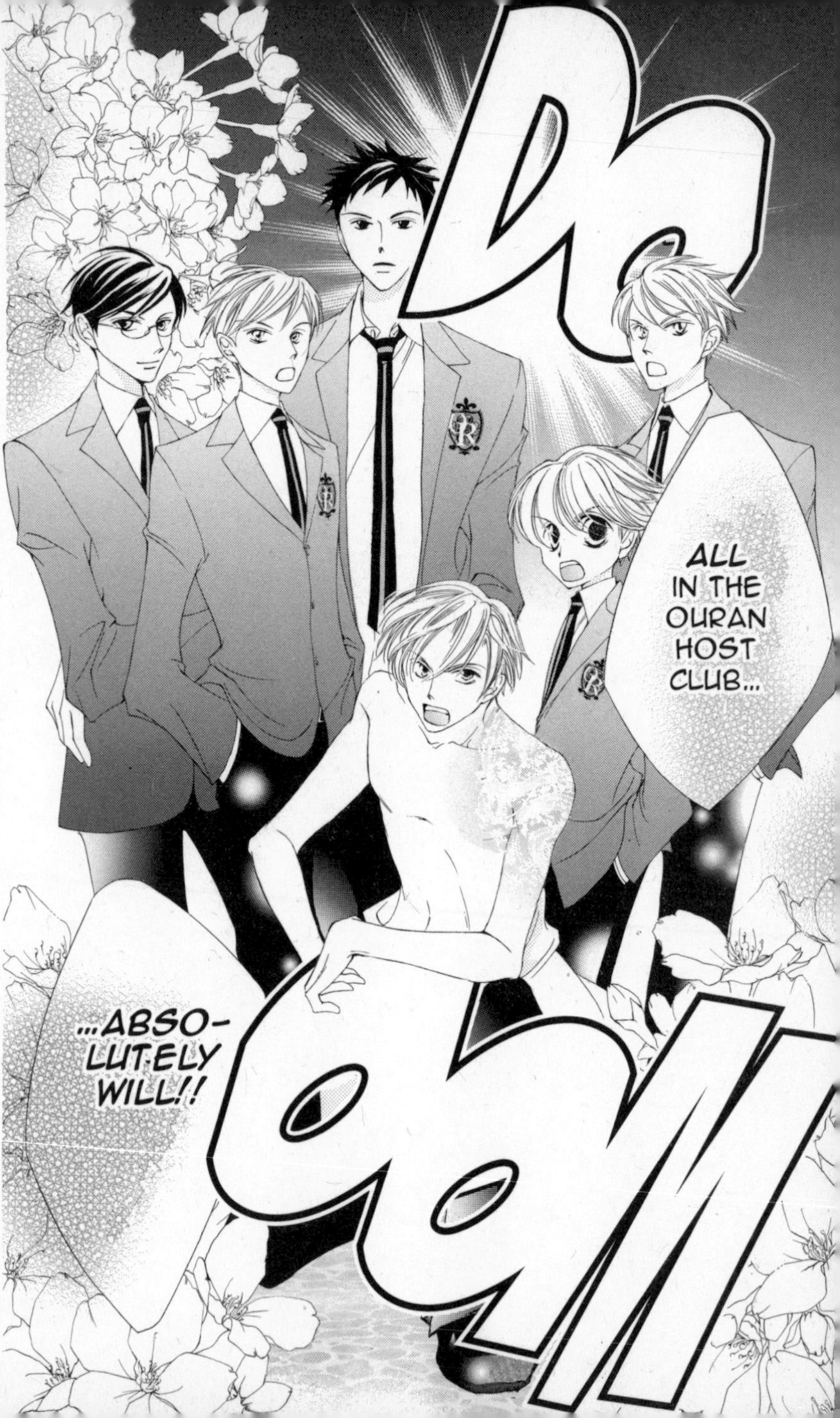
ALL IN THE OURAN HOST CLUB...
...ABSO-LUTELY WILL!!

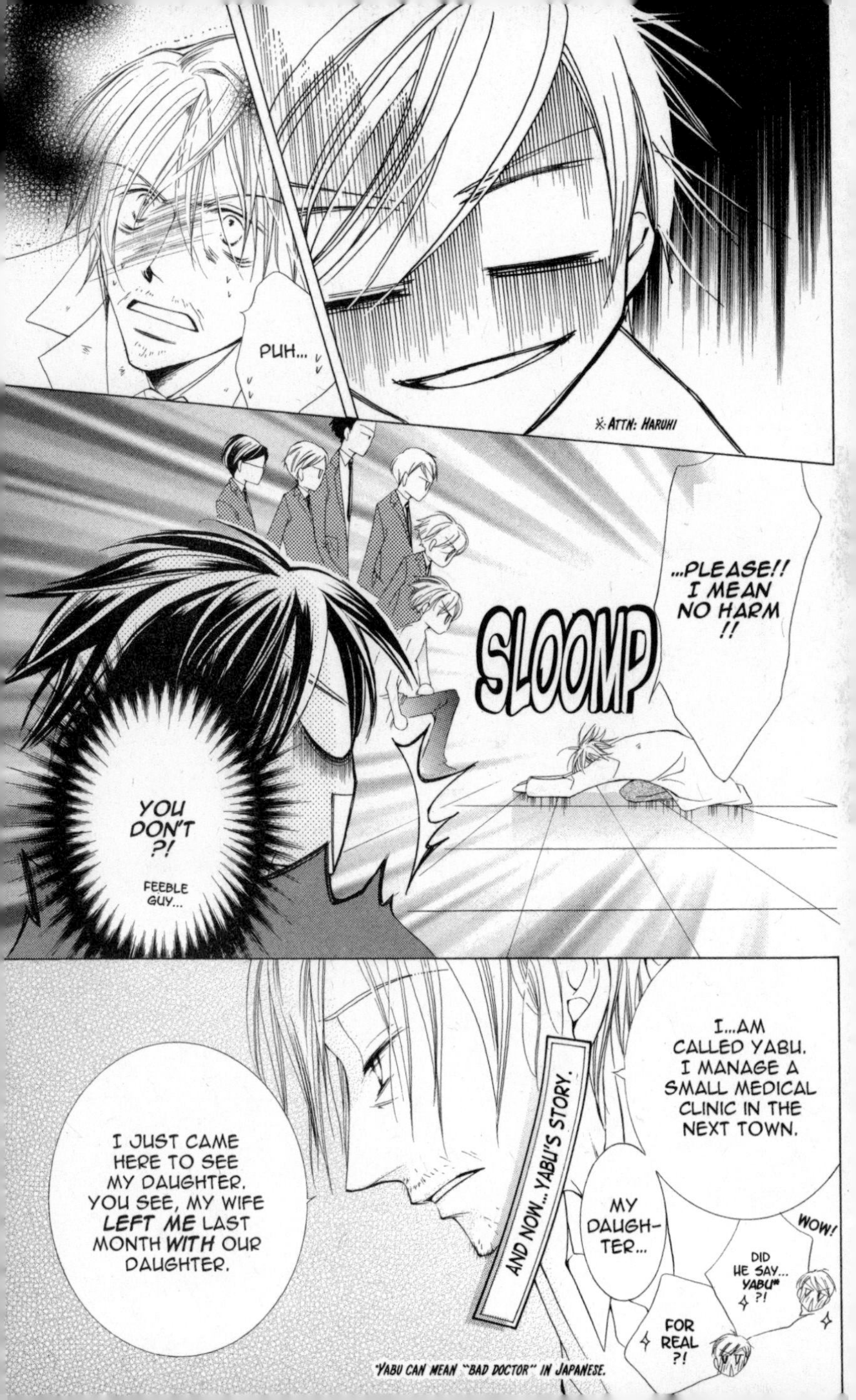

PUH...
※ATTN: HARUHI
...PLEASE!! I MEAN NO HARM !!
SLOOMP
YOU DON'T ?!
FEEBLE GUY...
I...AM CALLED YABU. I MANAGE A SMALL MEDICAL CLINIC IN THE NEXT TOWN.
WOW!
DID HE SAY... YABU* ?!
FOR REAL ?!
MY DAUGHTER...
AND NOW... YABU'S STORY.
I JUST CAME HERE TO SEE MY DAUGHTER. YOU SEE, MY WIFE LEFT ME LAST MONTH WITH OUR DAUGHTER.

*YABU CAN MEAN "BAD DOCTOR" IN JAPANESE.

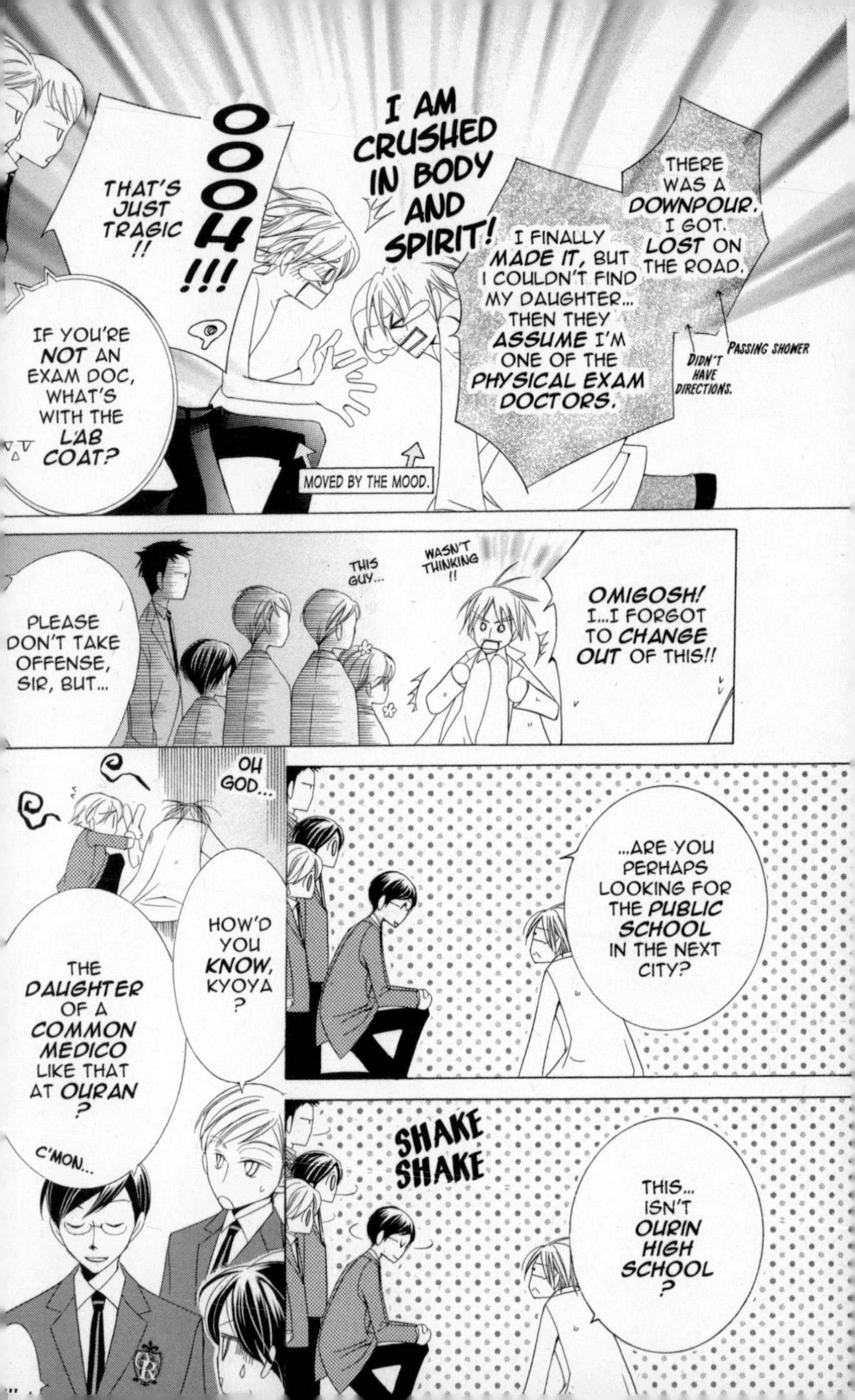

THERE WAS A DOWNPOUR. I GOT. LOST ON THE ROAD.
PASSING SHOWER
DIDN'T HAVE DIRECTIONS.
I FINALLY MADE IT, BUT I COULDN'T FIND MY DAUGHTER... THEN THEY ASSUME I'M ONE OF THE PHYSICAL EXAM DOCTORS.
I AM CRUSHED IN BODY AND SPIRIT!
MOVED BY THE MOOD.
OOOOH!!!
THAT'S JUST TRAGIC!!
IF YOU'RE NOT AN EXAM DOC, WHAT'S WITH THE LAB COAT?
OMIGOSH! I...I FORGOT TO CHANGE OUT OF THIS!!
WASN'T THINKING!!
THIS GUY...
PLEASE DON'T TAKE OFFENSE, SIR, BUT...
...ARE YOU PERHAPS LOOKING FOR THE PUBLIC SCHOOL IN THE NEXT CITY?
SHAKE SHAKE
THIS... ISN'T OURIN HIGH SCHOOL?
OH GOD...
HOW'D YOU KNOW, KYOYA?
THE DAUGHTER OF A COMMON MEDICO LIKE THAT AT OURAN?
C'MON...

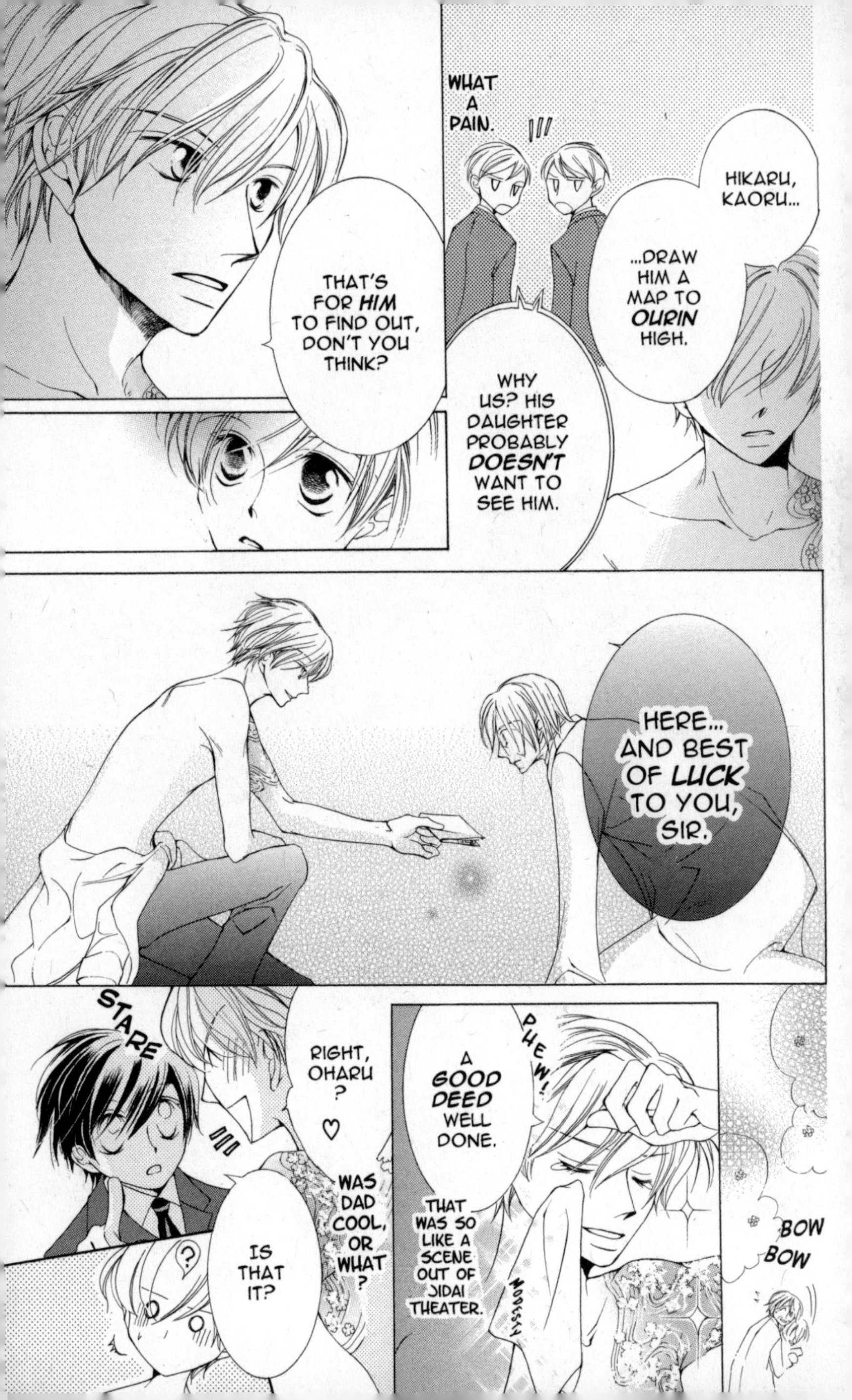
HIKARU, KAORU...
...DRAW HIM A MAP TO OURIN HIGH.
WHAT A PAIN.
///
WHY US? HIS DAUGHTER PROBABLY DOESN'T WANT TO SEE HIM.
THAT'S FOR HIM TO FIND OUT, DON'T YOU THINK?
HERE... AND BEST OF LUCK TO YOU, SIR.
BOW BOW
PHEW!
A GOOD DEED WELL DONE.
THAT WAS SO LIKE A SCENE OUT OF JIDAI THEATER.
STARE
RIGHT, OHARU? ♡
WAS DAD COOL, OR WHAT?
IS THAT IT?

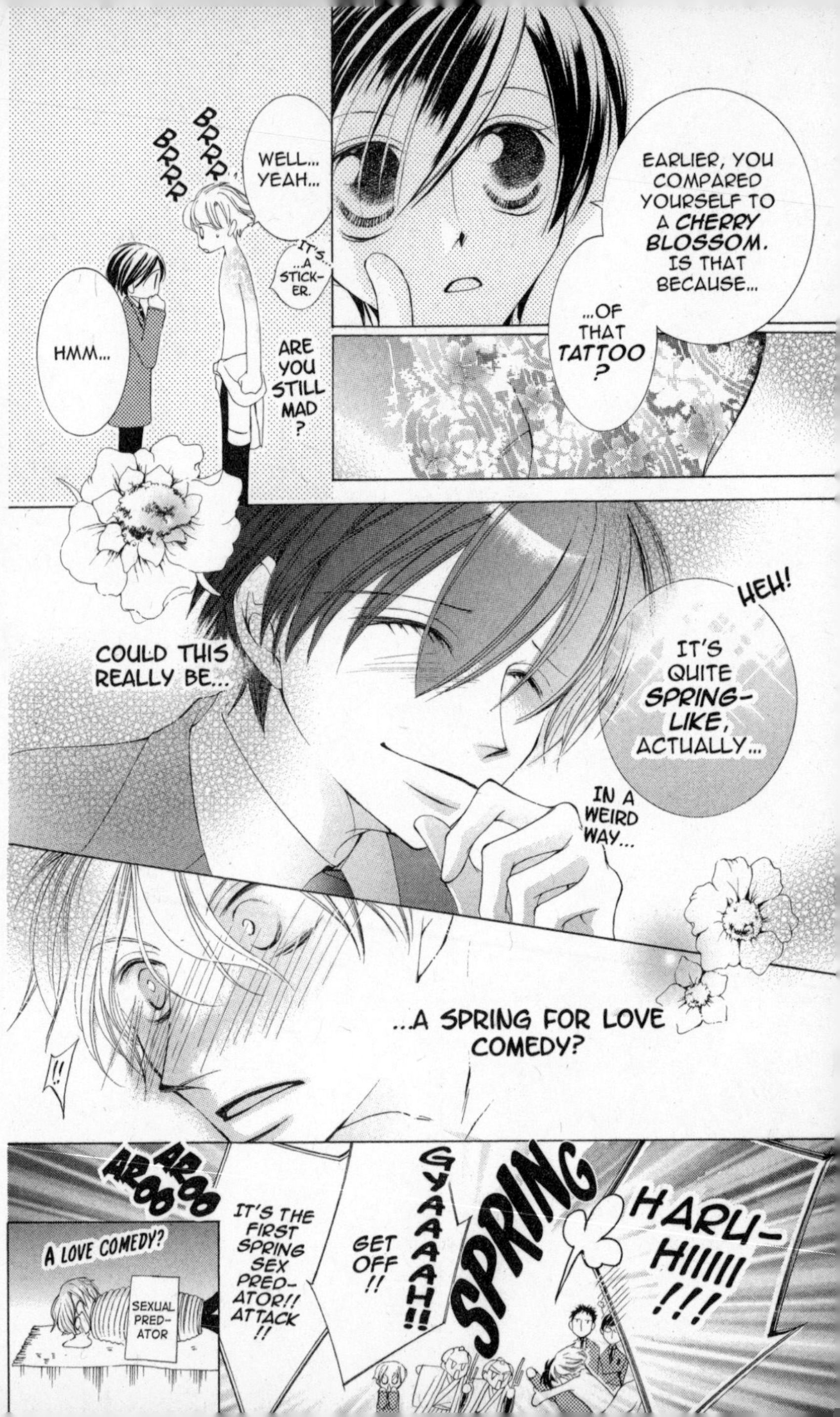
EARLIER, YOU COMPARED YOURSELF TO A CHERRY BLOSSOM. IS THAT BECAUSE...
...OF THAT TATTOO?
WELL... YEAH...
IT'S... ...A STICKER.
BRRR BRRR
ARE YOU STILL MAD?
HMM...
HEH!
IT'S QUITE SPRING-LIKE, ACTUALLY...
IN A WEIRD WAY...
COULD THIS REALLY BE...
...A SPRING FOR LOVE COMEDY?
!!
HARU-HI!!!!! !!!
SPRING
GYAAAAAH!!
GET OFF!!
IT'S THE FIRST SPRING SEX PREDATOR!! ATTACK!!
AROOO AROOO
A LOVE COMEDY?
SEXUAL PREDATOR

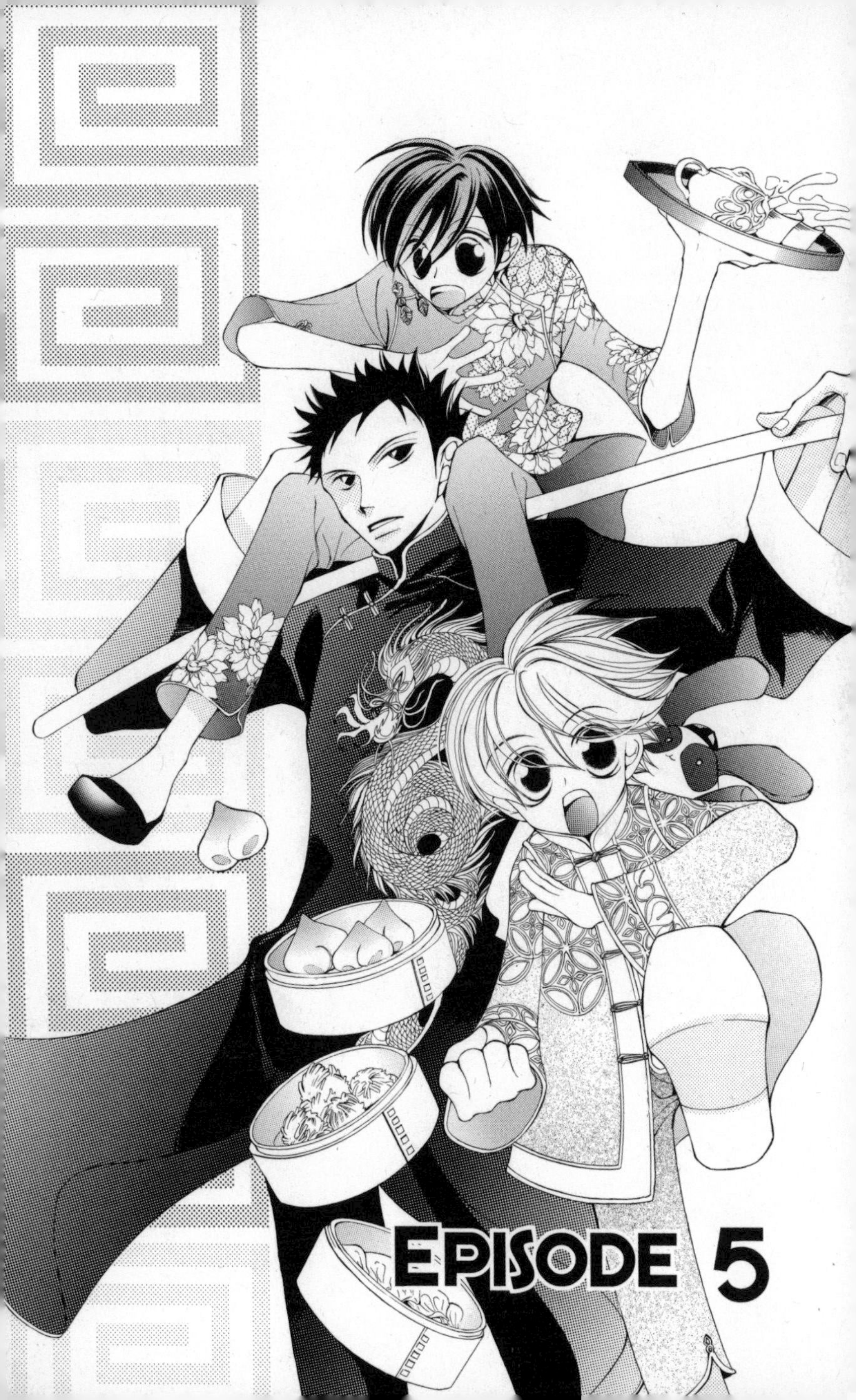
EPISODE 5

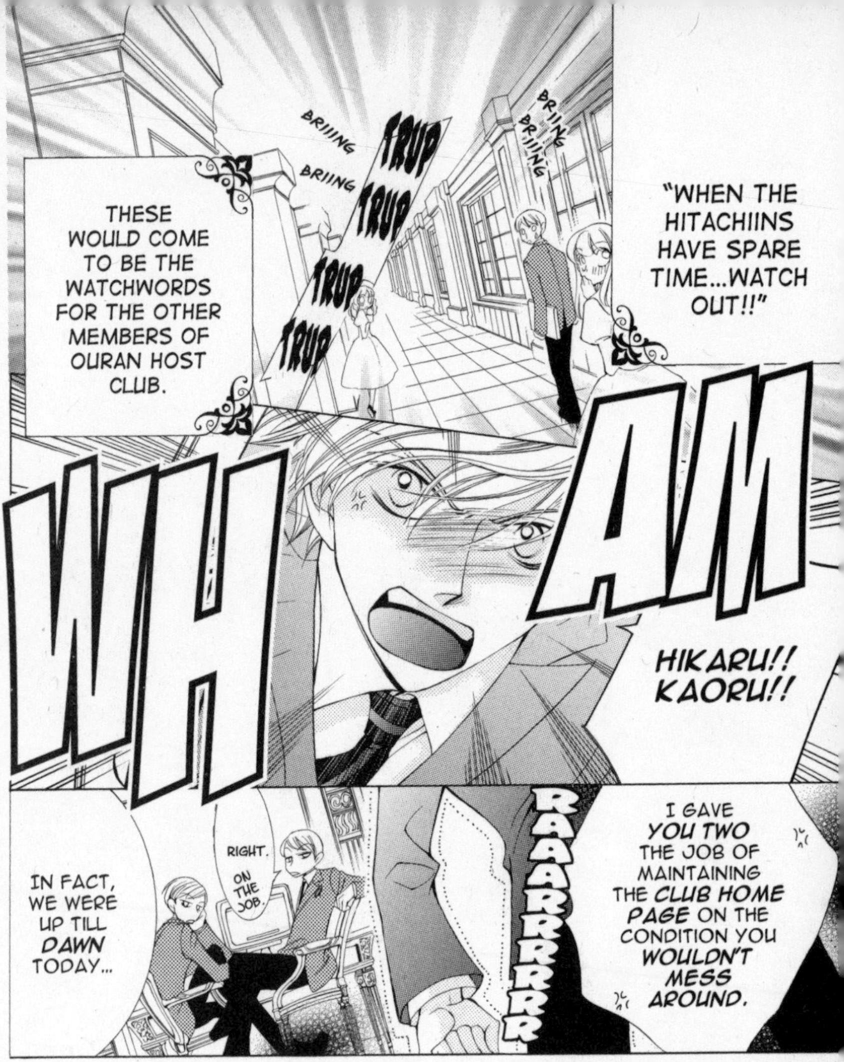
"WHEN THE HITACHIINS HAVE SPARE TIME...WATCH OUT!!"
BRIIING
BRIIIING
TRUP TRUP TRUP TRUP
BRIIING
BRIIING
THESE WOULD COME TO BE THE WATCHWORDS FOR THE OTHER MEMBERS OF OURAN HOST CLUB.
WHAM
HIKARU!! KAORU!!
RAAAARRRRR
I GAVE YOU TWO THE JOB OF MAINTAINING THE CLUB HOME PAGE ON THE CONDITION YOU WOULDN'T MESS AROUND.
RIGHT.
ON THE JOB.
IN FACT, WE WERE UP TILL DAWN TODAY...

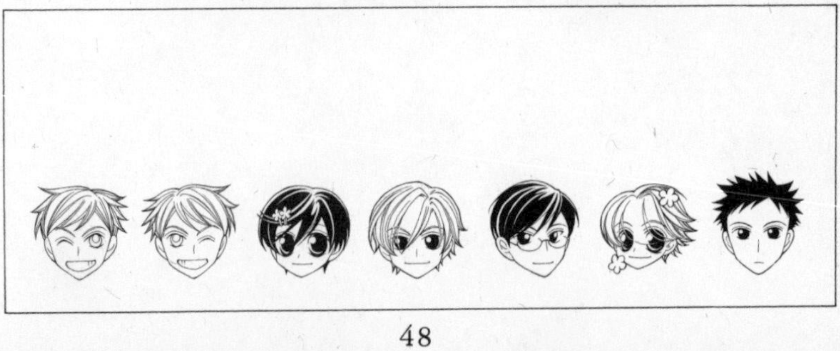

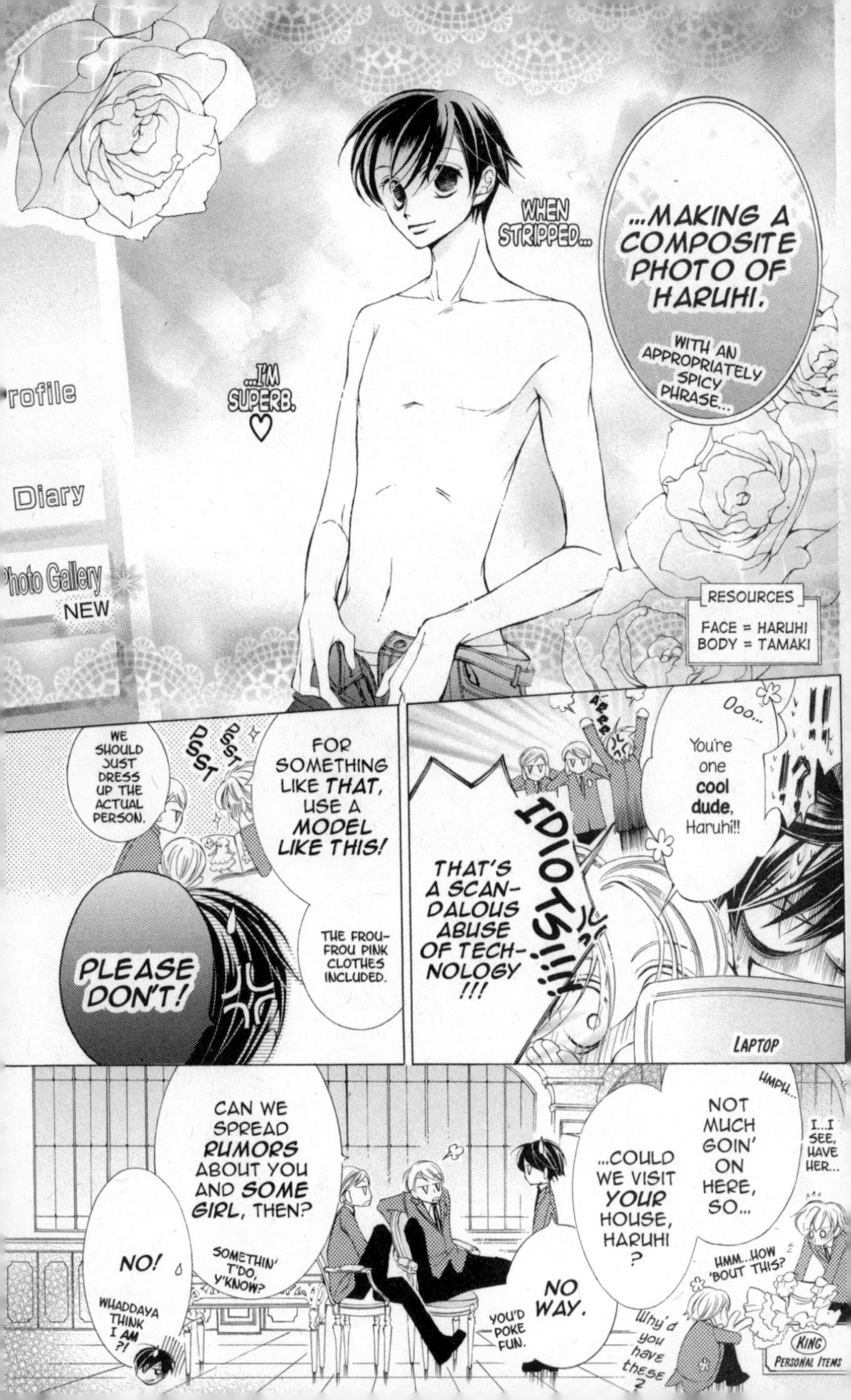
...MAKING A COMPOSITE PHOTO OF HARUHI.
WITH AN APPROPRIATELY SPICY PHRASE...
WHEN STRIPPED...
...I'M SUPERB. ♡
RESOURCES
FACE = HARUHI
BODY = TAMAKI
rofile
Diary
Photo Gallery
NEW
Ooo...
You're one cool dude, Haruhi!!
!!
!?
ARRR
IDIOTS!!!!
THAT'S A SCAN-DALOUS ABUSE OF TECH-NOLOGY!!!
LAPTOP
FOR SOMETHING LIKE THAT, USE A MODEL LIKE THIS!
PSST
PSST
WE SHOULD JUST DRESS UP THE ACTUAL PERSON.
THE FROU-FROU PINK CLOTHES INCLUDED.
PLEASE DON'T!
HMPH...
NOT MUCH GOIN' ON HERE, SO...
I...I SEE, HAVE HER...
...COULD WE VISIT YOUR HOUSE, HARUHI?
NO WAY.
YOU'D POKE FUN.
HMM...HOW 'BOUT THIS?
Why'd you have these?
KING
PERSONAL ITEMS
CAN WE SPREAD RUMORS ABOUT YOU AND SOME GIRL, THEN?
SOMETHIN' T'DO, Y'KNOW?
NO!
WHADDAYA THINK I AM?!

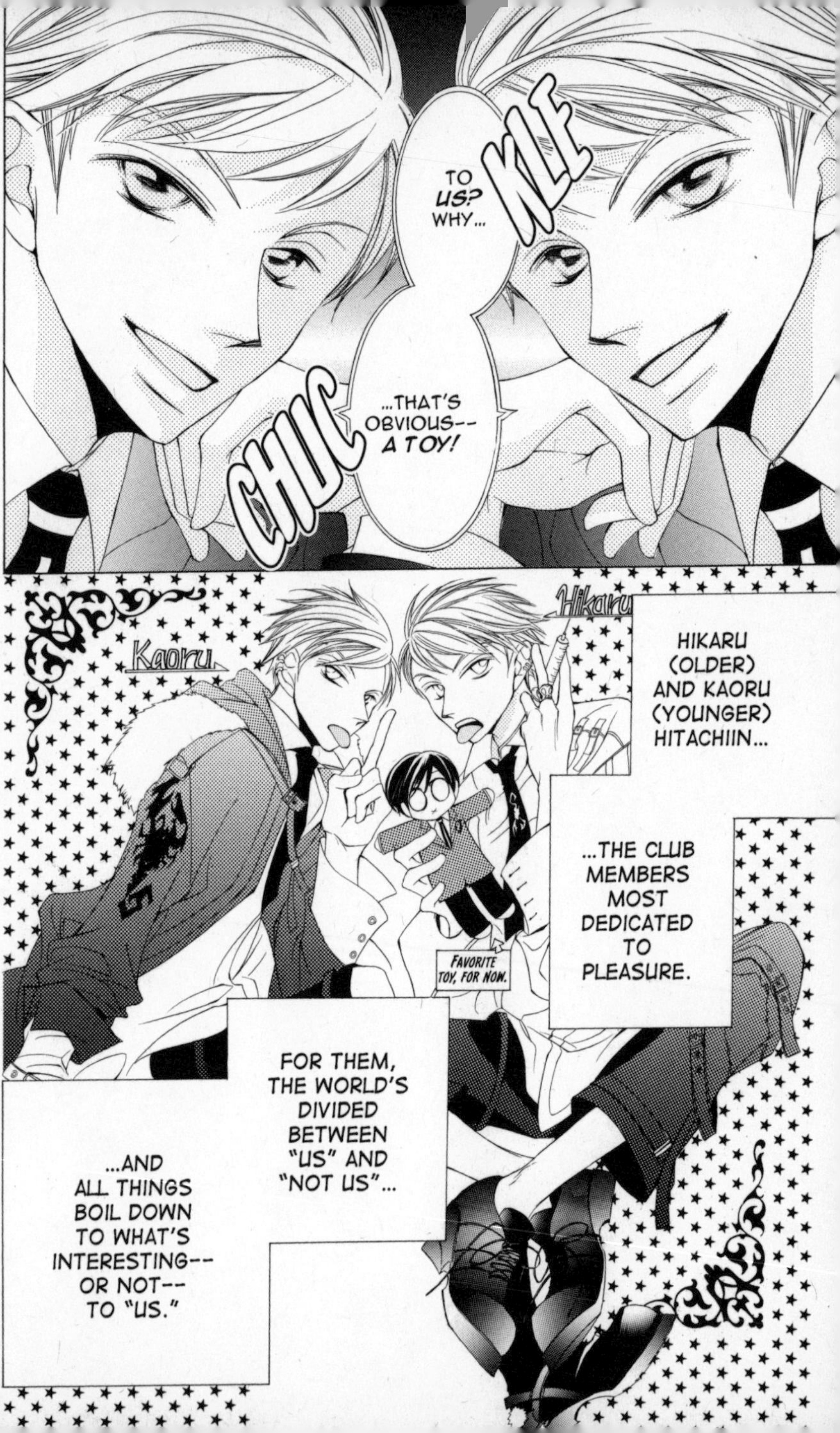
KLIF
TO US? WHY...
...THAT'S OBVIOUS-- A TOY!
CHUC
Hikaru
Kaoru
HIKARU (OLDER) AND KAORU (YOUNGER) HITACHIIN...
...THE CLUB MEMBERS MOST DEDICATED TO PLEASURE.
FAVORITE TOY, FOR NOW.
FOR THEM, THE WORLD'S DIVIDED BETWEEN "US" AND "NOT US"...
...AND ALL THINGS BOIL DOWN TO WHAT'S INTERESTING-- OR NOT-- TO "US."

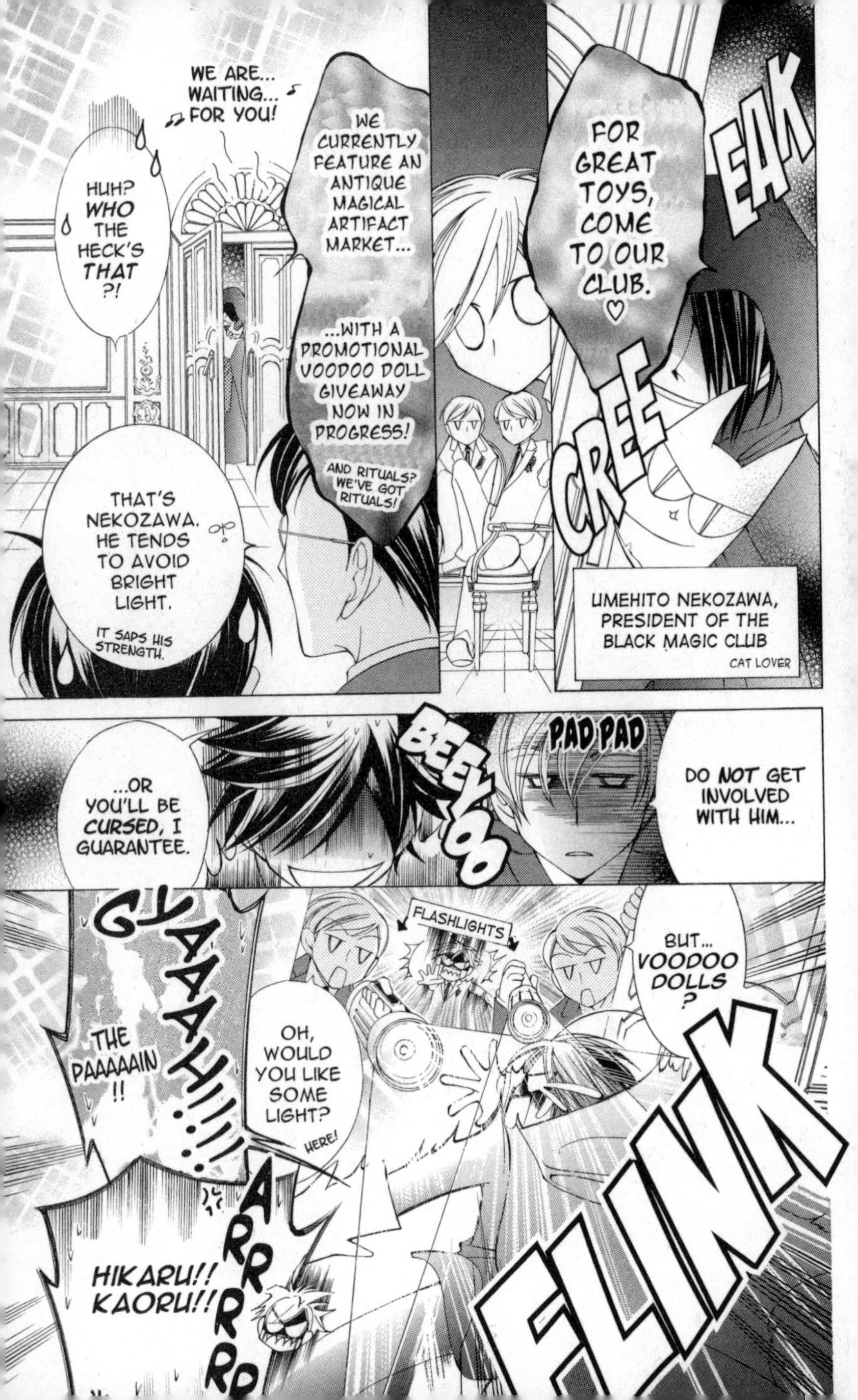
FOR GREAT TOYS, COME TO OUR CLUB. ♡
CREEEAK
UMEHITO NEKOZAWA, PRESIDENT OF THE BLACK MAGIC CLUB
CAT LOVER
WE CURRENTLY FEATURE AN ANTIQUE MAGICAL ARTIFACT MARKET...
...WITH A PROMOTIONAL VOODOO DOLL GIVEAWAY NOW IN PROGRESS!
AND RITUALS? WE'VE GOT RITUALS!
WE ARE... WAITING... FOR YOU!
HUH? WHO THE HECK'S THAT?!
THAT'S NEKOZAWA. HE TENDS TO AVOID BRIGHT LIGHT.
IT SAPS HIS STRENGTH.
DO NOT GET INVOLVED WITH HIM...
PAD PAD
BEEYOO
...OR YOU'LL BE CURSED, I GUARANTEE.
BUT... VOODOO DOLLS?
FLASHLIGHTS
FLINK
OH, WOULD YOU LIKE SOME LIGHT?
HERE!
GYAAAH!!!!!
THE PAAAAAIN!!
ARRRRR
HIKARU!! KAORU!!

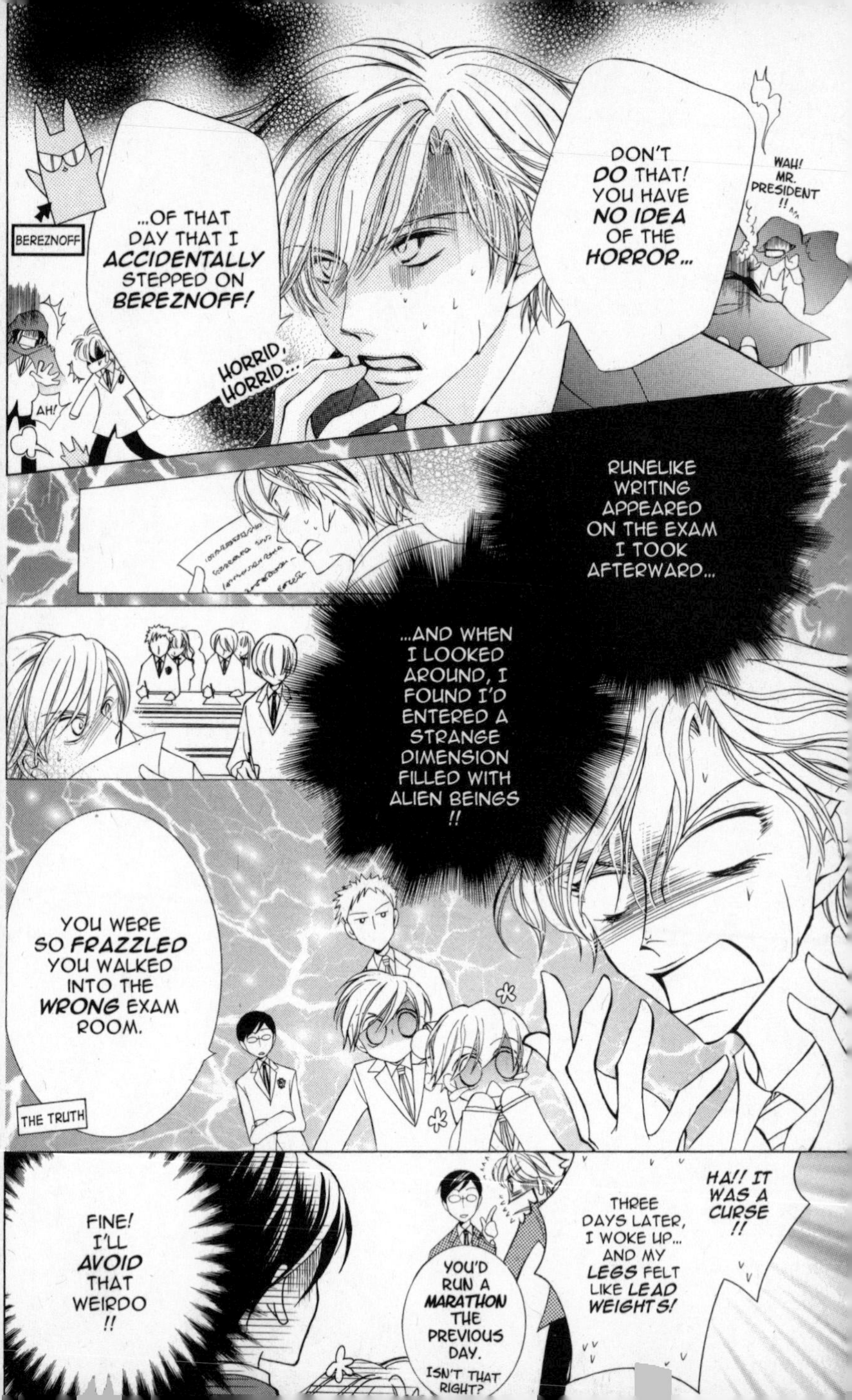
WAH! MR. PRESIDENT !!
DON'T DO THAT! YOU HAVE NO IDEA OF THE HORROR...
...OF THAT DAY THAT I ACCIDENTALLY STEPPED ON BEREZNOFF!
BEREZNOFF
HORRID, HORRID...
AH!
RUNELIKE WRITING APPEARED ON THE EXAM I TOOK AFTERWARD...
...AND WHEN I LOOKED AROUND, I FOUND I'D ENTERED A STRANGE DIMENSION FILLED WITH ALIEN BEINGS !!
YOU WERE SO FRAZZLED YOU WALKED INTO THE WRONG EXAM ROOM.
THE TRUTH
HA!! IT WAS A CURSE !!
THREE DAYS LATER, I WOKE UP... AND MY LEGS FELT LIKE LEAD WEIGHTS!
YOU'D RUN A MARATHON THE PREVIOUS DAY. ISN'T THAT RIGHT?
FINE! I'LL AVOID THAT WEIRDO !!

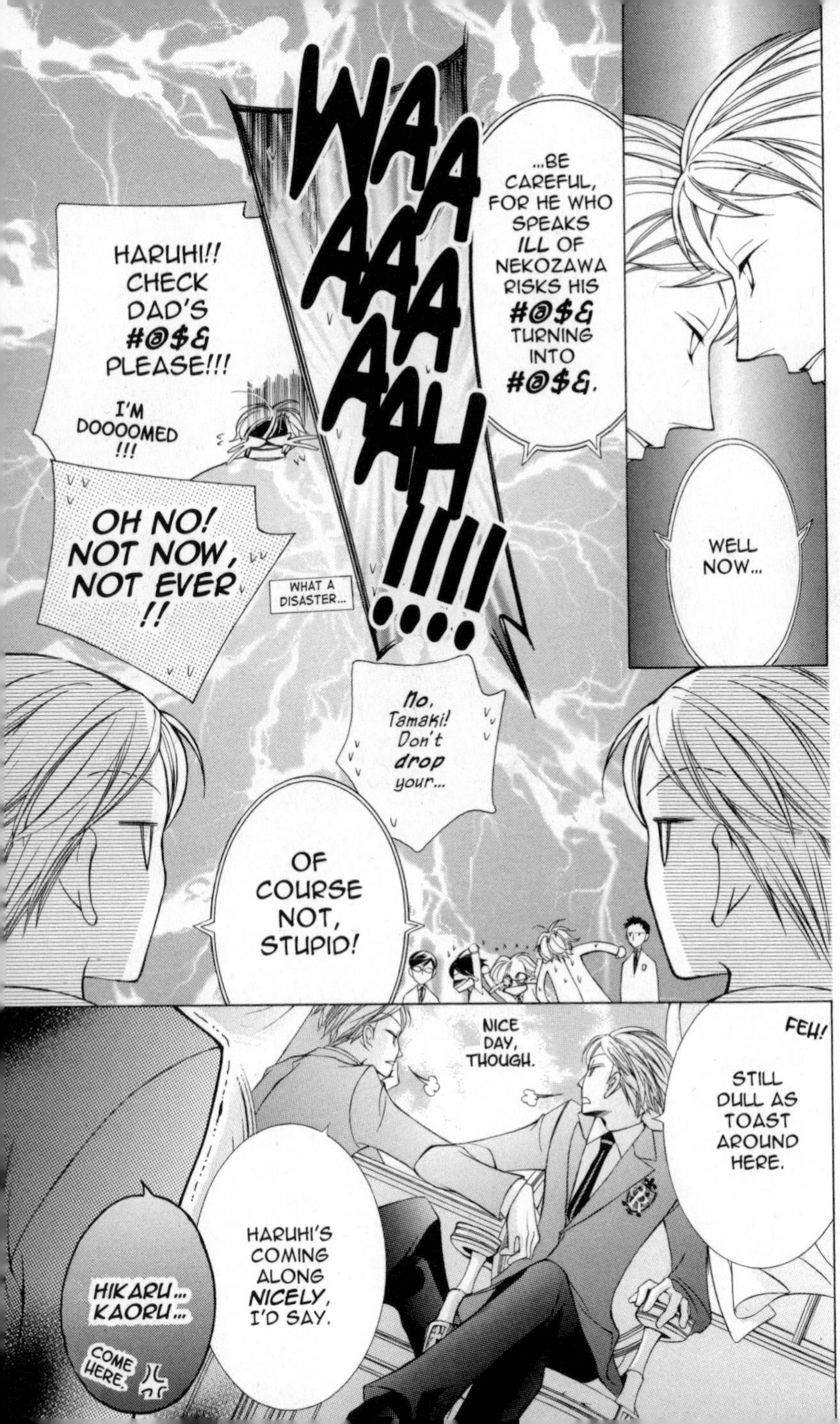

WELL NOW...
...BE CAREFUL, FOR HE WHO SPEAKS ILL OF NEKOZAWA RISKS HIS #@$& TURNING INTO #@$&.
WAAAAAAAAAAH!!!!....
HARUHI!! CHECK DAD'S #@$& PLEASE!!!
I'M DOOOOMED!!!
OH NO! NOT NOW, NOT EVER!!
WHAT A DISASTER...
No, Tamaki! Don't drop your...
OF COURSE NOT, STUPID!
FEH!
STILL DULL AS TOAST AROUND HERE.
NICE DAY, THOUGH.
HARUHI'S COMING ALONG NICELY, I'D SAY.
HIKARU... KAORU...
COME HERE.

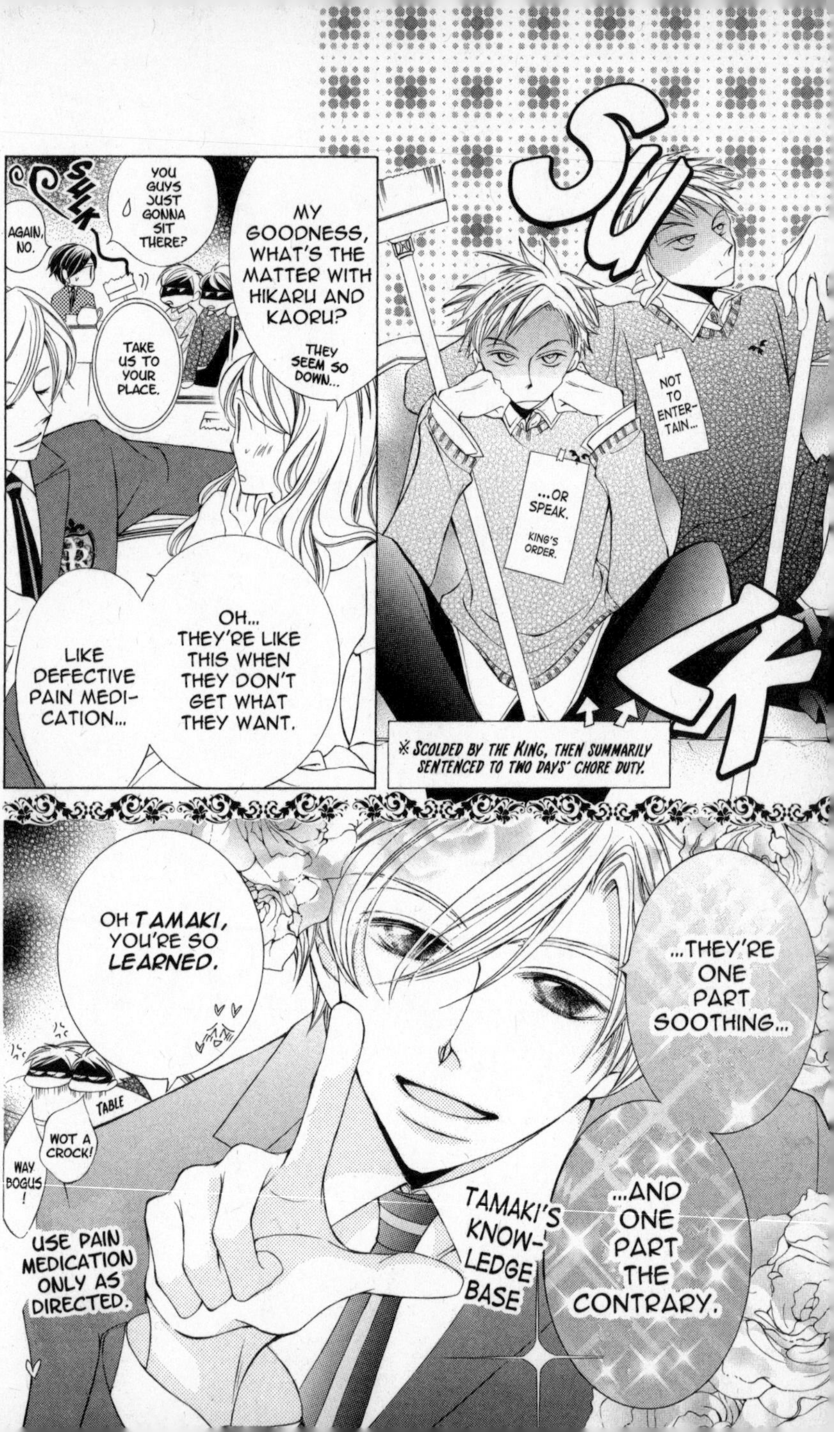
SULK
NOT TO ENTERTAIN...
...OR SPEAK.
KING'S ORDER.
※ SCOLDED BY THE KING, THEN SUMMARILY SENTENCED TO TWO DAYS' CHORE DUTY.
MY GOODNESS, WHAT'S THE MATTER WITH HIKARU AND KAORU?
THEY SEEM SO DOWN...
YOU GUYS JUST GONNA SIT THERE?
SULK
AGAIN, NO.
TAKE US TO YOUR PLACE.
OH... THEY'RE LIKE THIS WHEN THEY DON'T GET WHAT THEY WANT.
LIKE DEFECTIVE PAIN MEDICATION...
...THEY'RE ONE PART SOOTHING...
...AND ONE PART THE CONTRARY.
TAMAKI'S KNOWLEDGE BASE
OH TAMAKI, YOU'RE SO LEARNED.
TABLE
WOT A CROCK!
WAY BOGUS!
USE PAIN MEDICATION ONLY AS DIRECTED.

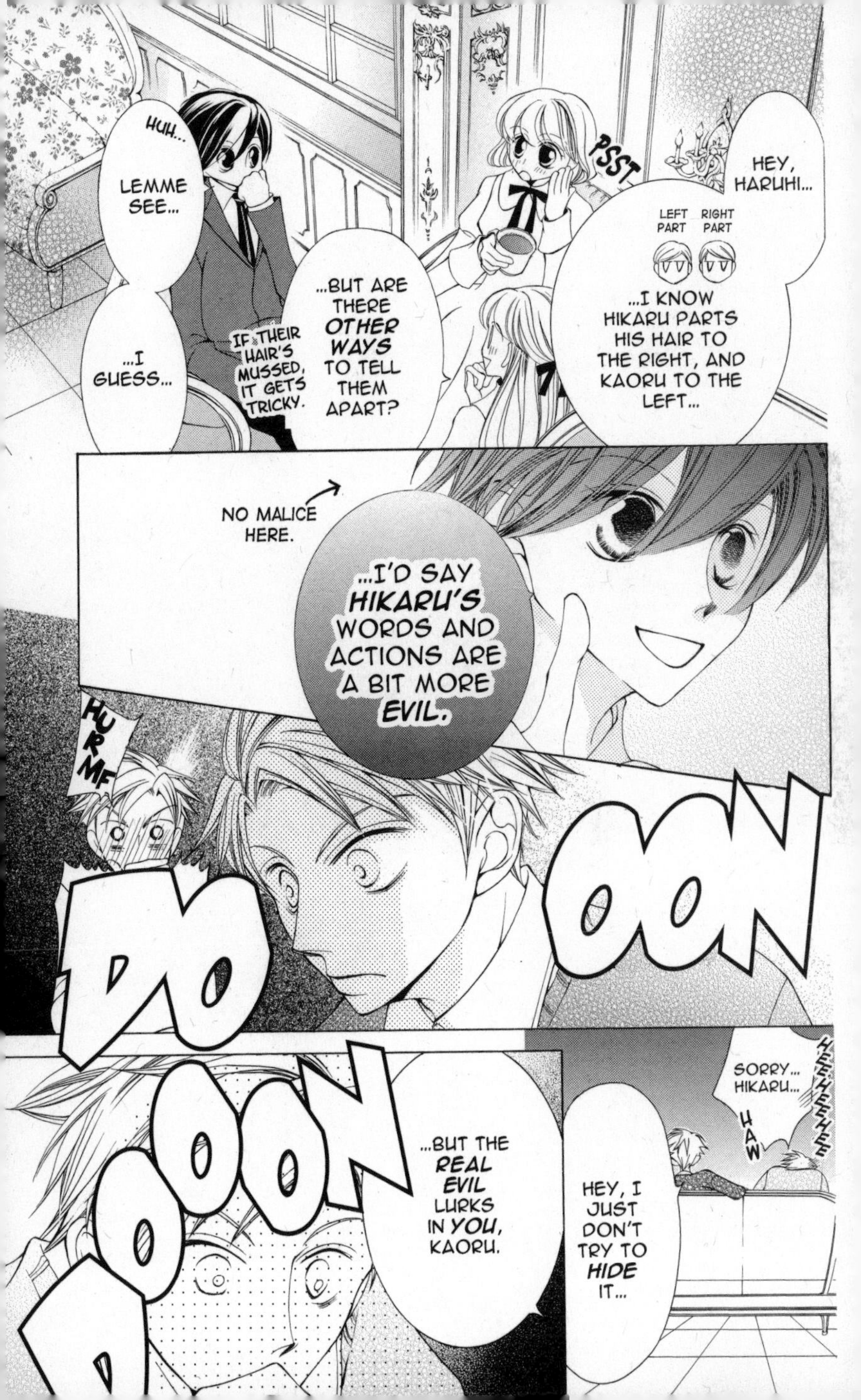
HEY, HARUHI...
LEFT PART RIGHT PART
...I KNOW HIKARU PARTS HIS HAIR TO THE RIGHT, AND KAORU TO THE LEFT...
PSST
...BUT ARE THERE OTHER WAYS TO TELL THEM APART?
IF THEIR HAIR'S MUSSED, IT GETS TRICKY.
HUH... LEMME SEE...
...I GUESS...
...I'D SAY HIKARU'S WORDS AND ACTIONS ARE A BIT MORE EVIL.
NO MALICE HERE.
DOOON
HURMF
SORRY... HIKARU...
HEHEHEHE
HAW
HEY, I JUST DON'T TRY TO HIDE IT...
...BUT THE REAL EVIL LURKS IN YOU, KAORU.
DOOON

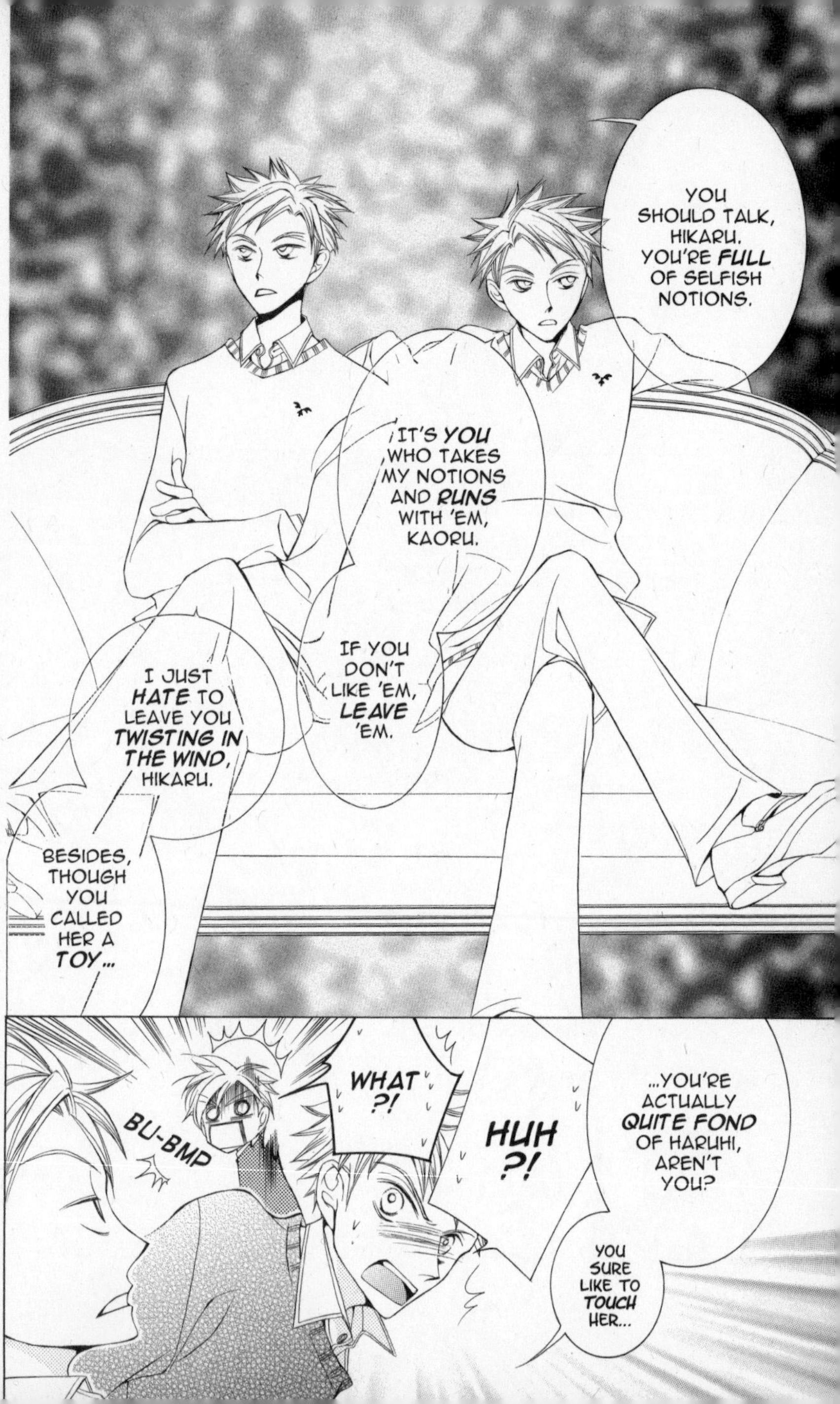
YOU SHOULD TALK, HIKARU. YOU'RE FULL OF SELFISH NOTIONS.
IT'S YOU WHO TAKES MY NOTIONS AND RUNS WITH 'EM, KAORU.
IF YOU DON'T LIKE 'EM, LEAVE 'EM.
I JUST HATE TO LEAVE YOU TWISTING IN THE WIND, HIKARU.
BESIDES, THOUGH YOU CALLED HER A TOY...
...YOU'RE ACTUALLY QUITE FOND OF HARUHI, AREN'T YOU?
YOU SURE LIKE TO TOUCH HER...
HUH ?!
WHAT ?!
BU-BMP

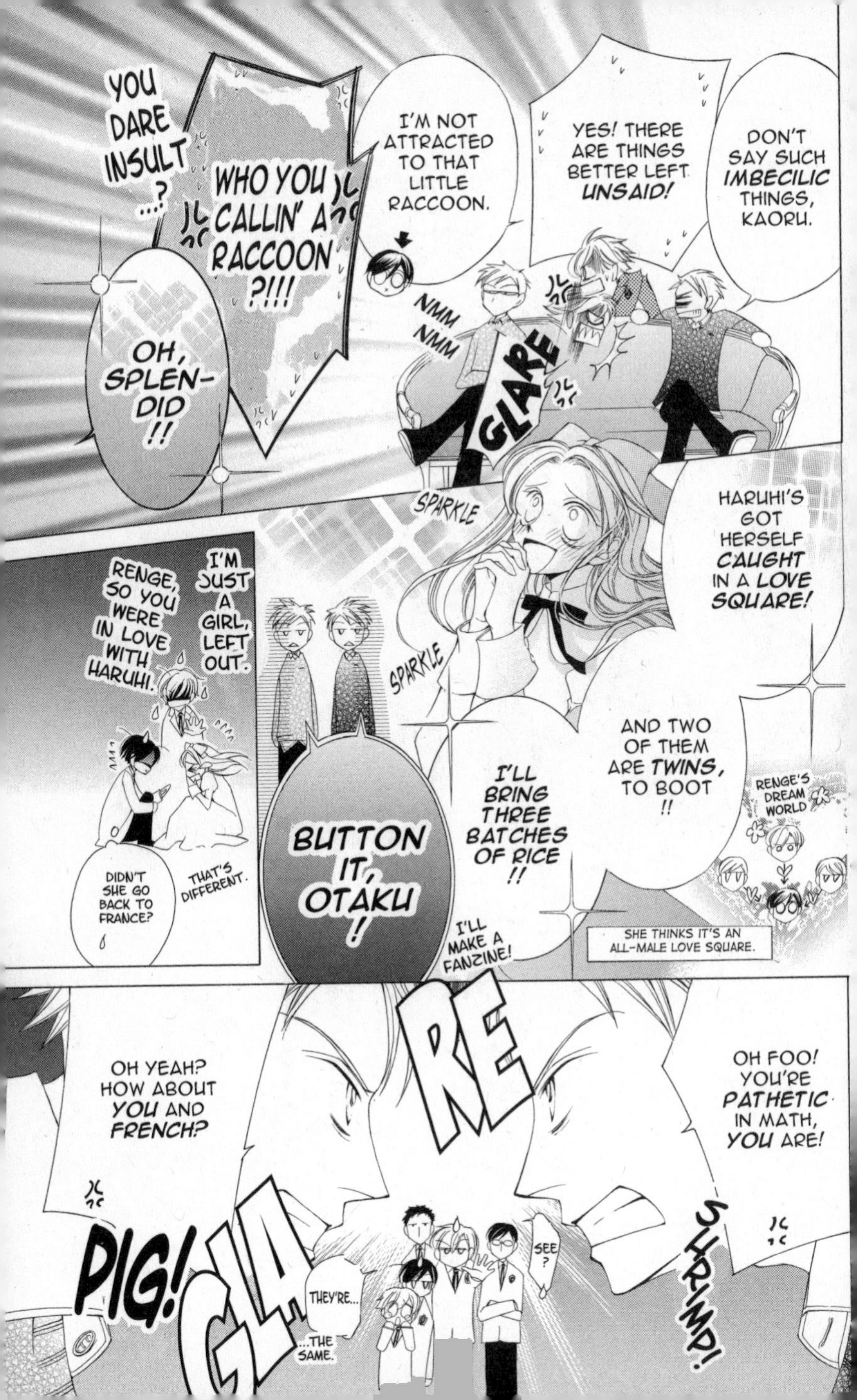
DON'T SAY SUCH IMBECILIC THINGS, KAORU.
YES! THERE ARE THINGS BETTER LEFT UNSAID!
I'M NOT ATTRACTED TO THAT LITTLE RACCOON.
NMM NMM
GLARE
WHO YOU CALLIN' A RACCOON?!!!
YOU DARE INSULT...?
OH, SPLENDID!!
HARUHI'S GOT HERSELF CAUGHT IN A LOVE SQUARE!
SPARKLE
SPARKLE
AND TWO OF THEM ARE TWINS, TO BOOT!!
RENGE'S DREAM WORLD
I'LL BRING THREE BATCHES OF RICE!!
SHE THINKS IT'S AN ALL-MALE LOVE SQUARE.
I'LL MAKE A FANZINE!
BUTTON IT, OTAKU!
I'M JUST A GIRL, LEFT OUT.
RENGE, SO YOU WERE IN LOVE WITH HARUHI.
THAT'S DIFFERENT.
DIDN'T SHE GO BACK TO FRANCE?
OH FOO! YOU'RE PATHETIC IN MATH, YOU ARE!
RE
OH YEAH? HOW ABOUT YOU AND FRENCH?
SHRIMP!
SEE?
THEY'RE...
...THE SAME.
PIG!

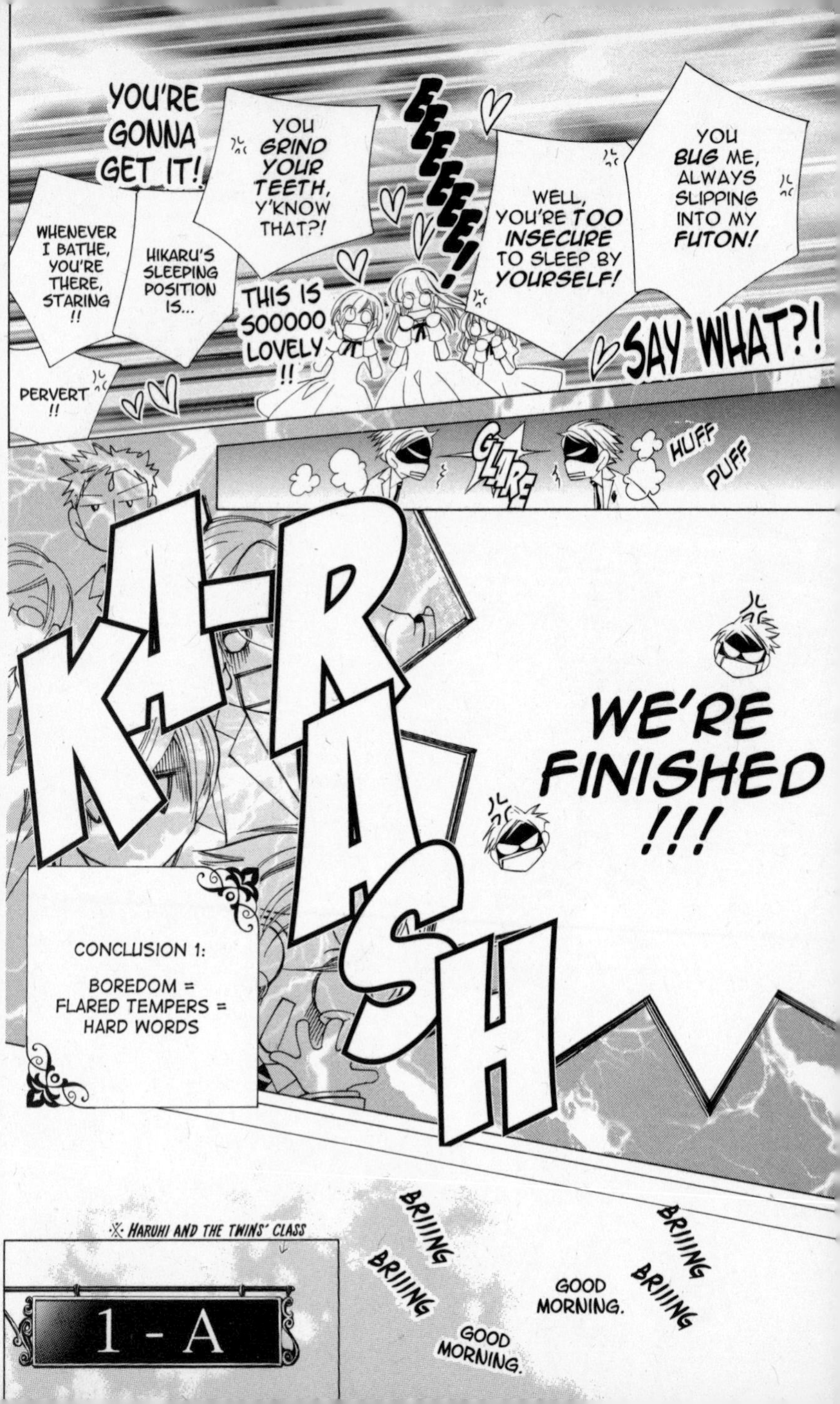
YOU BUG ME, ALWAYS SLIPPING INTO MY FUTON!
SAY WHAT?!
WELL, YOU'RE TOO INSECURE TO SLEEP BY YOURSELF!
EEEEEE!
THIS IS SOOOOO LOVELY!!
YOU GRIND YOUR TEETH, Y'KNOW THAT?!
YOU'RE GONNA GET IT!
HIKARU'S SLEEPING POSITION IS...
WHENEVER I BATHE, YOU'RE THERE, STARING!!
PERVERT!!
HUFF
PUFF
GLARE
WE'RE FINISHED!!!
KA-RASH
CONCLUSION 1:
BOREDOM = FLARED TEMPERS = HARD WORDS
BRIIING
BRIIING
GOOD MORNING.
BRIIING
BRIIING
GOOD MORNING.
※ HARUHI AND THE TWINS' CLASS
1 - A

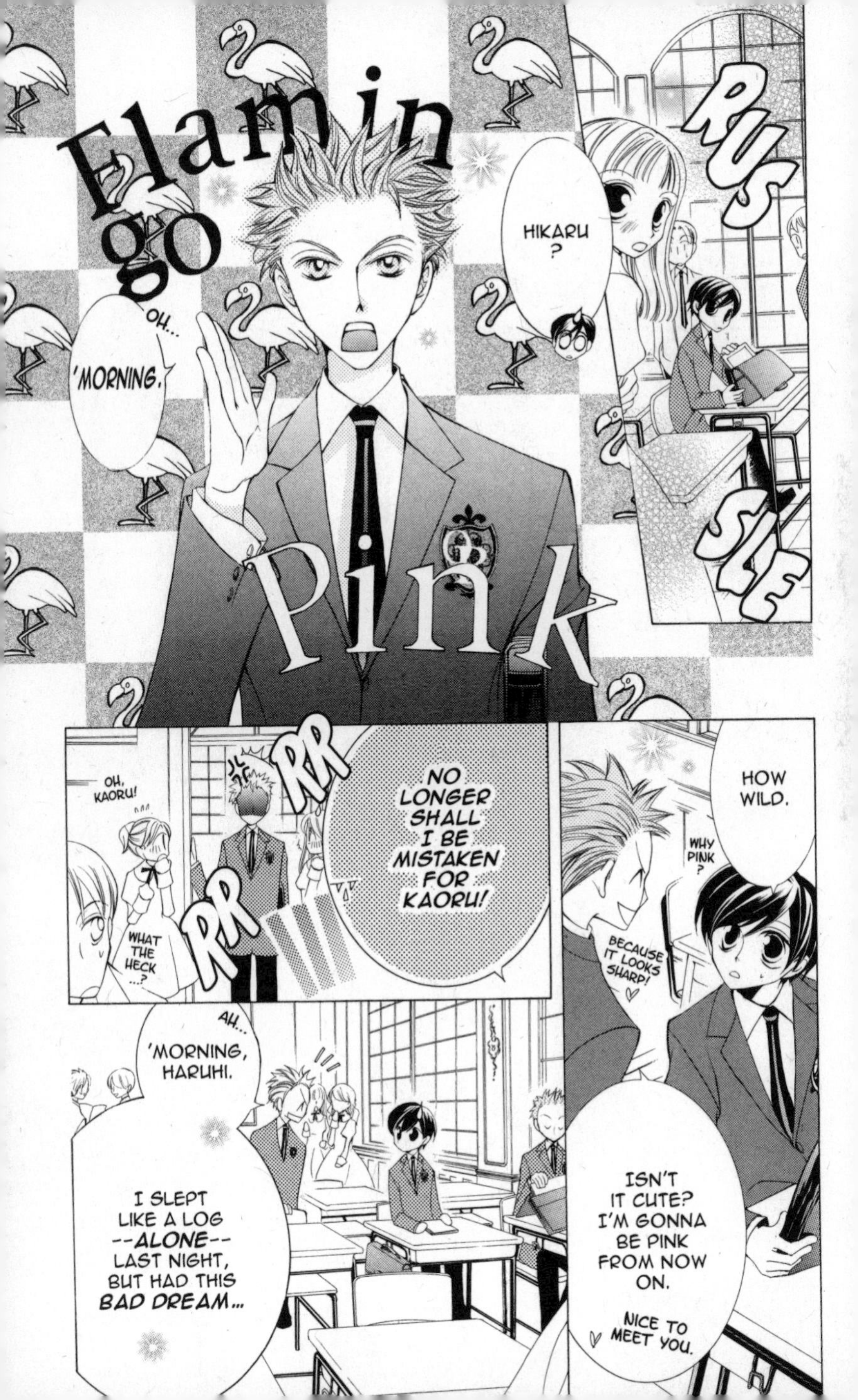
RUS
HIKARU ?
SLE
Flamin go
OH... 'MORNING.
Pink
HOW WILD.
WHY PINK ?
BECAUSE IT LOOKS SHARP!
ISN'T IT CUTE? I'M GONNA BE PINK FROM NOW ON.
NICE TO MEET YOU.
NO LONGER SHALL I BE MISTAKEN FOR KAORU!
RR
OH, KAORU!
RR
WHAT THE HECK ...?
AH... 'MORNING, HARUHI.
I SLEPT LIKE A LOG --ALONE-- LAST NIGHT, BUT HAD THIS BAD DREAM...

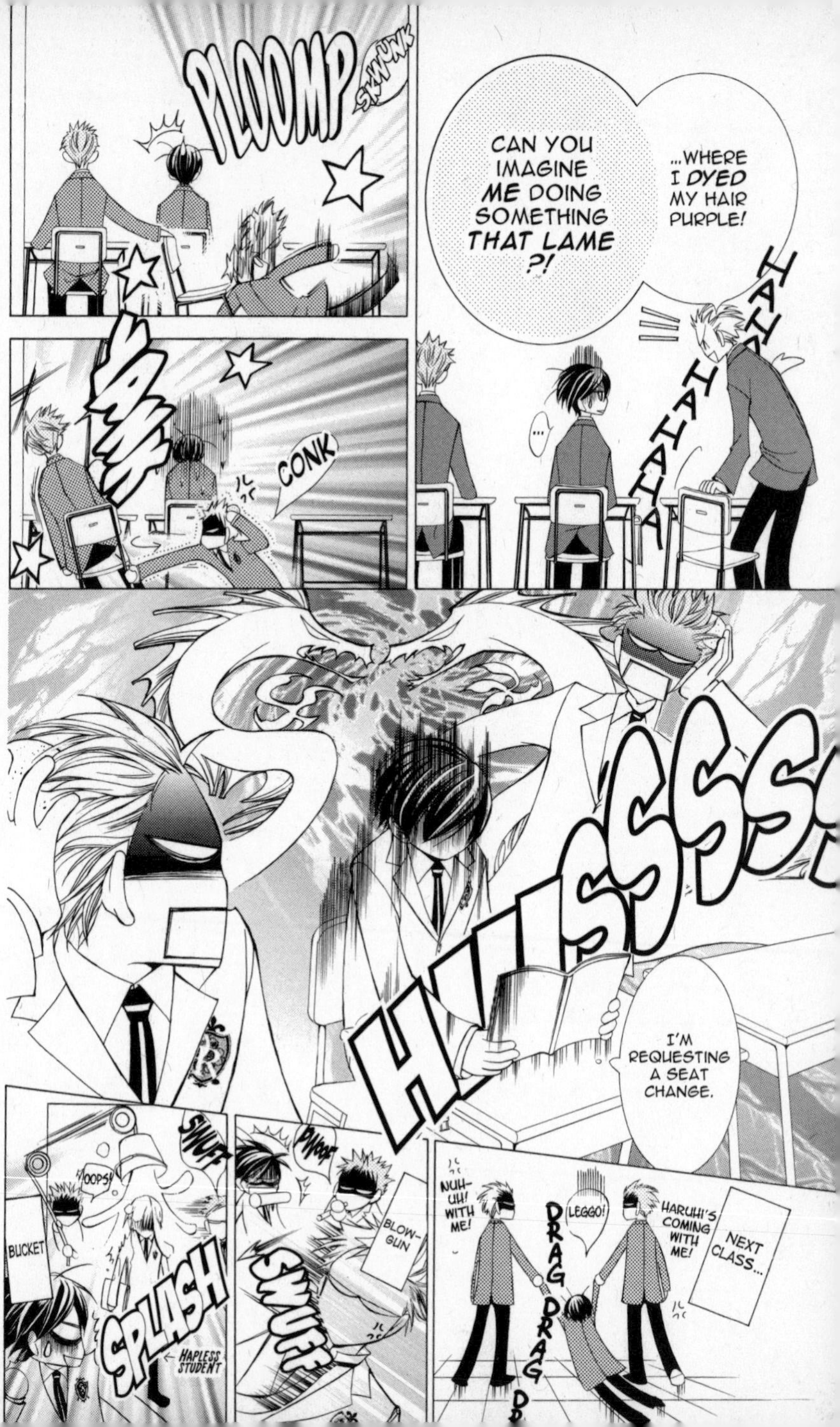
...WHERE I DYED MY HAIR PURPLE!
CAN YOU IMAGINE ME DOING SOMETHING THAT LAME?!
HAHAHAHAHAHA
...
PLOOMP
SKWUNK
YANK
CONK
HISSSSS
I'M REQUESTING A SEAT CHANGE.
NEXT CLASS...
HARUHI'S COMING WITH ME!
LEGGO!
NUH-UH! WITH ME!
DRAG DRAG DRAG
PWOOF
BLOW-GUN
SWUFF
SWUF
OOPS!
BUCKET
SPLASH
HAPLESS STUDENT

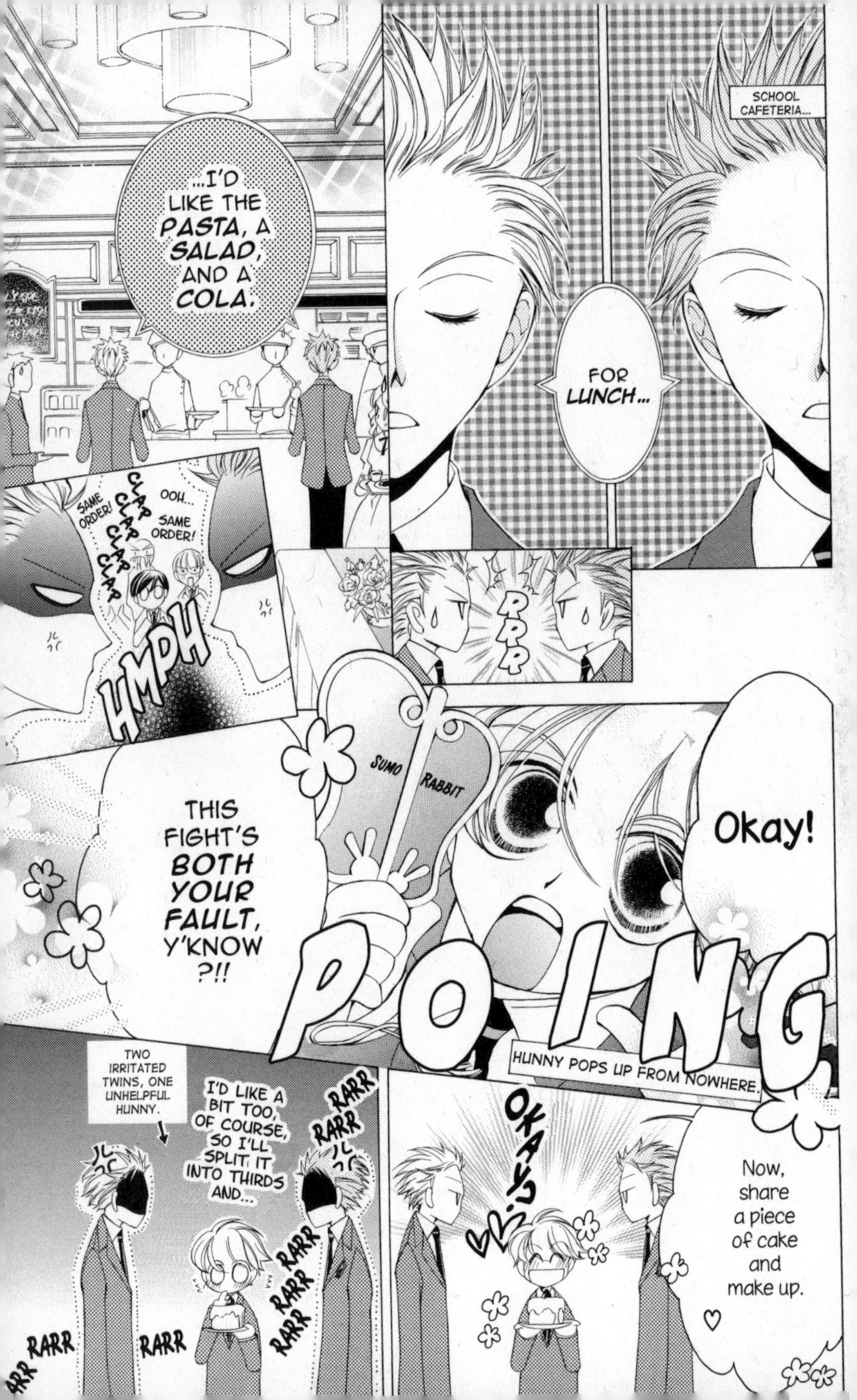
SCHOOL CAFETERIA...
FOR LUNCH...
...I'D LIKE THE PASTA, A SALAD, AND A COLA.
RRR
OOH... SAME ORDER!
SAME ORDER!
CLAP CLAP CLAP CLAP CLAP
HMPH
Okay!
SUMO RABBIT
POING
HUNNY POPS UP FROM NOWHERE.
THIS FIGHT'S BOTH YOUR FAULT, Y'KNOW?!!
Now, share a piece of cake and make up.
OKAY?
TWO IRRITATED TWINS, ONE UNHELPFUL HUNNY.
I'D LIKE A BIT TOO, OF COURSE, SO I'LL SPLIT IT INTO THIRDS AND...
RARR RARR
RARR RARR RARR RARR
RARR RARR ARR

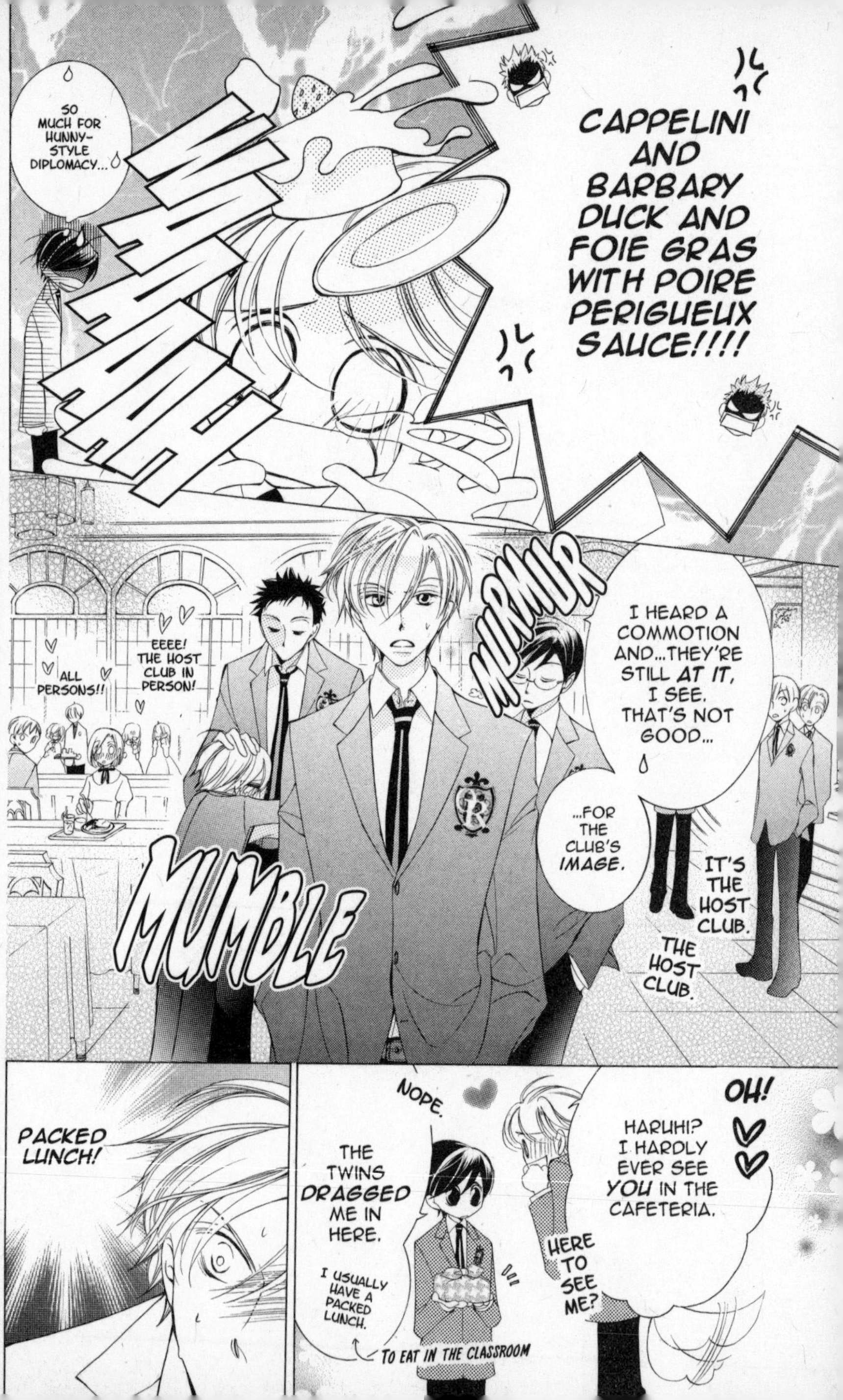
CAPPELINI AND BARBARY DUCK AND FOIE GRAS WITH POIRE PERIGUEUX SAUCE!!!!
SO MUCH FOR HUNNY-STYLE DIPLOMACY...
MURMUR
I HEARD A COMMOTION AND...THEY'RE STILL AT IT, I SEE. THAT'S NOT GOOD...
...FOR THE CLUB'S IMAGE.
IT'S THE HOST CLUB.
THE HOST CLUB.
EEEE! THE HOST CLUB IN PERSON!
ALL PERSONS!!
MUMBLE
OH!
HARUHI? I HARDLY EVER SEE YOU IN THE CAFETERIA.
HERE TO SEE ME?
NOPE.
THE TWINS DRAGGED ME IN HERE.
I USUALLY HAVE A PACKED LUNCH.
TO EAT IN THE CLASSROOM
PACKED LUNCH!

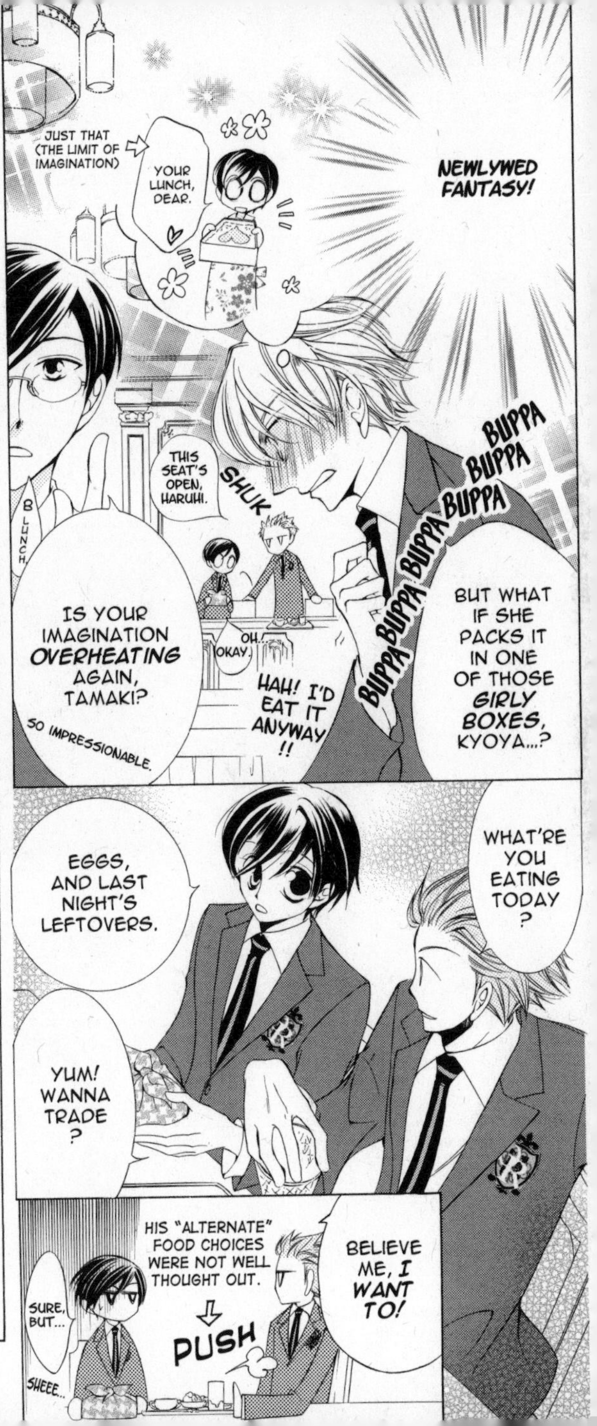
NEWLYWED FANTASY!
YOUR LUNCH, DEAR.
JUST THAT (THE LIMIT OF IMAGINATION)
BUT WHAT IF SHE PACKS IT IN ONE OF THOSE GIRLY BOXES, KYOYA...?
BUPPA BUPPA BUPPA BUPPA BUPPA BUPPA BUPPA
THIS SEAT'S OPEN, HARUHI.
SHUK
OH... OKAY.
HAH! I'D EAT IT ANYWAY!!
IS YOUR IMAGINATION OVERHEATING AGAIN, TAMAKI?
SO IMPRESSIONABLE.
B LUNCH
WHAT'RE YOU EATING TODAY?
EGGS, AND LAST NIGHT'S LEFTOVERS.
YUM! WANNA TRADE?
BELIEVE ME, I WANT TO!
HIS "ALTERNATE" FOOD CHOICES WERE NOT WELL THOUGHT OUT.
PUSH
SURE, BUT...
SHEEE...

2

✿ IN THIS EPISODE, THE TWINS FIGHT! THE COVER FOR THIS WAS A NICE CHANGE. FOR THE FIRST TIME I DIDN'T HAVE TO DRAW ALL SEVEN CLUB MEMBERS AT ONCE (LAUGH), SO I DECIDED TO MAKE IT MORE DYNAMIC. AFTER THIS, I DID THE COLOR PREVIEW WITH TAMAKI, KYOYA, AND MORI IN CHINESE OUTFITS--I'D LIKE TO DO THAT WITH THE TWINS, TOO.

✿ MY OWN GOAL IN THIS EPISODE WAS TO DEVELOP THE CHARACTERS OF THE TWINS. THE SLIGHTLY MORE NEFARIOUS PERSONALITY (HARSH WORDS) AND ACTIONS OF HIKARU, COUPLED WITH HIS TOUCHING OF HARUHI, WAS SOMETHING I HAD KEPT IN MIND DURING VOLUME 1. (WHAT KIND OF MIND...?) I AM HOPING TO GRADUALLY REVEAL THE DIFFERENCES IN THEIR PERSONALITIES.

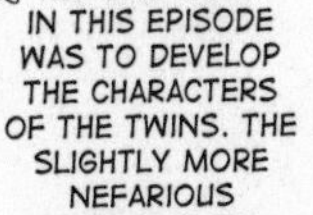
YAAAAY!
KAORUN
PIKARI

※ VISUALLY, THE ONLY DIFFERENCE IS THE WAY THEY PART THEIR HAIR (LAUGH).

IF YOU THINK TO YOURSELF, "THEY LOOK DIFFERENT!!," THAT'S A PROBLEM WITH HATORI'S ARTISTIC ABILITIES... (LAUGH).

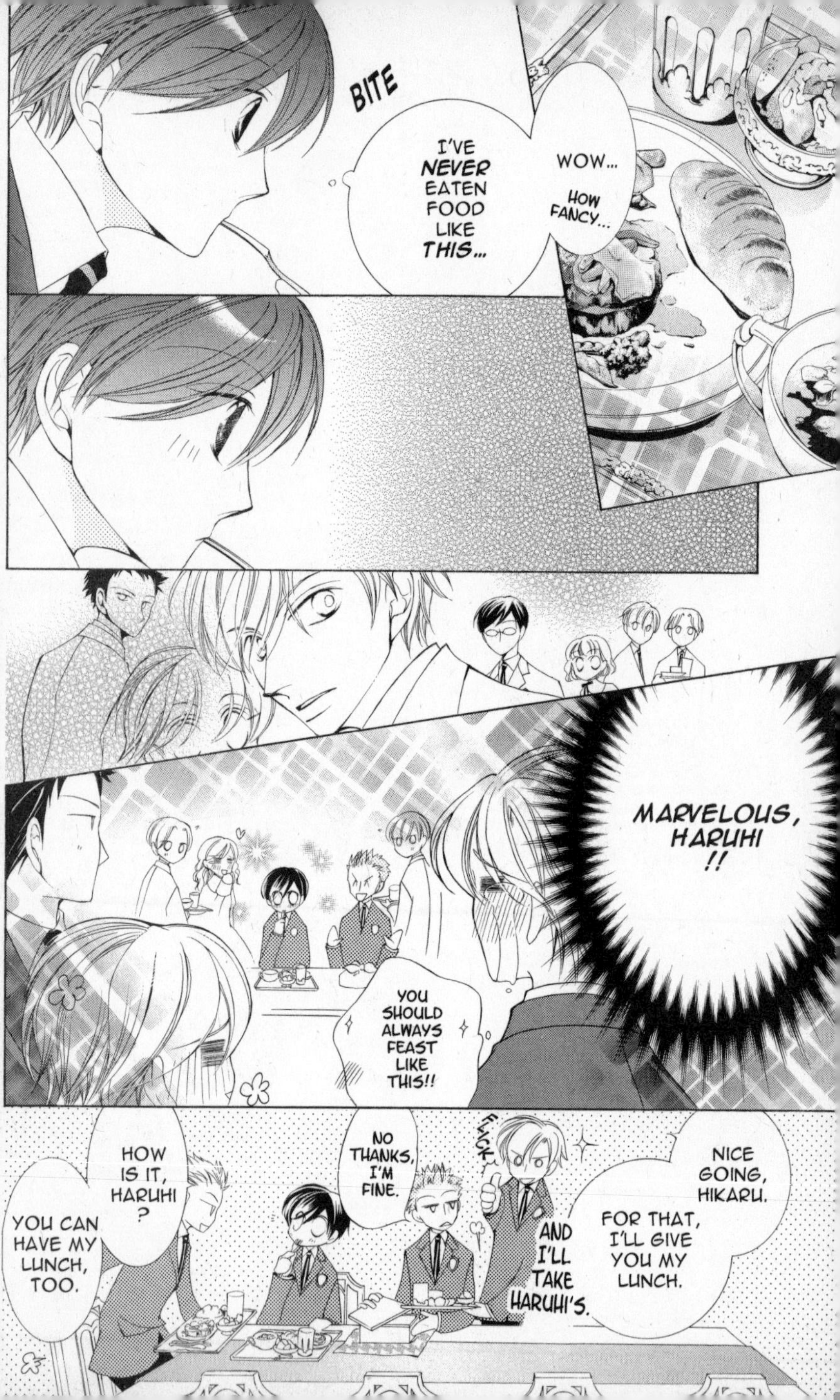
BITE
WOW...
HOW FANCY...
I'VE NEVER EATEN FOOD LIKE THIS...
MARVELOUS, HARUHI!!
YOU SHOULD ALWAYS FEAST LIKE THIS!!
NICE GOING, HIKARU.
FOR THAT, I'LL GIVE YOU MY LUNCH.
FLICK
AND I'LL TAKE HARUHI'S.
NO THANKS, I'M FINE.
HOW IS IT, HARUHI?
YOU CAN HAVE MY LUNCH, TOO.

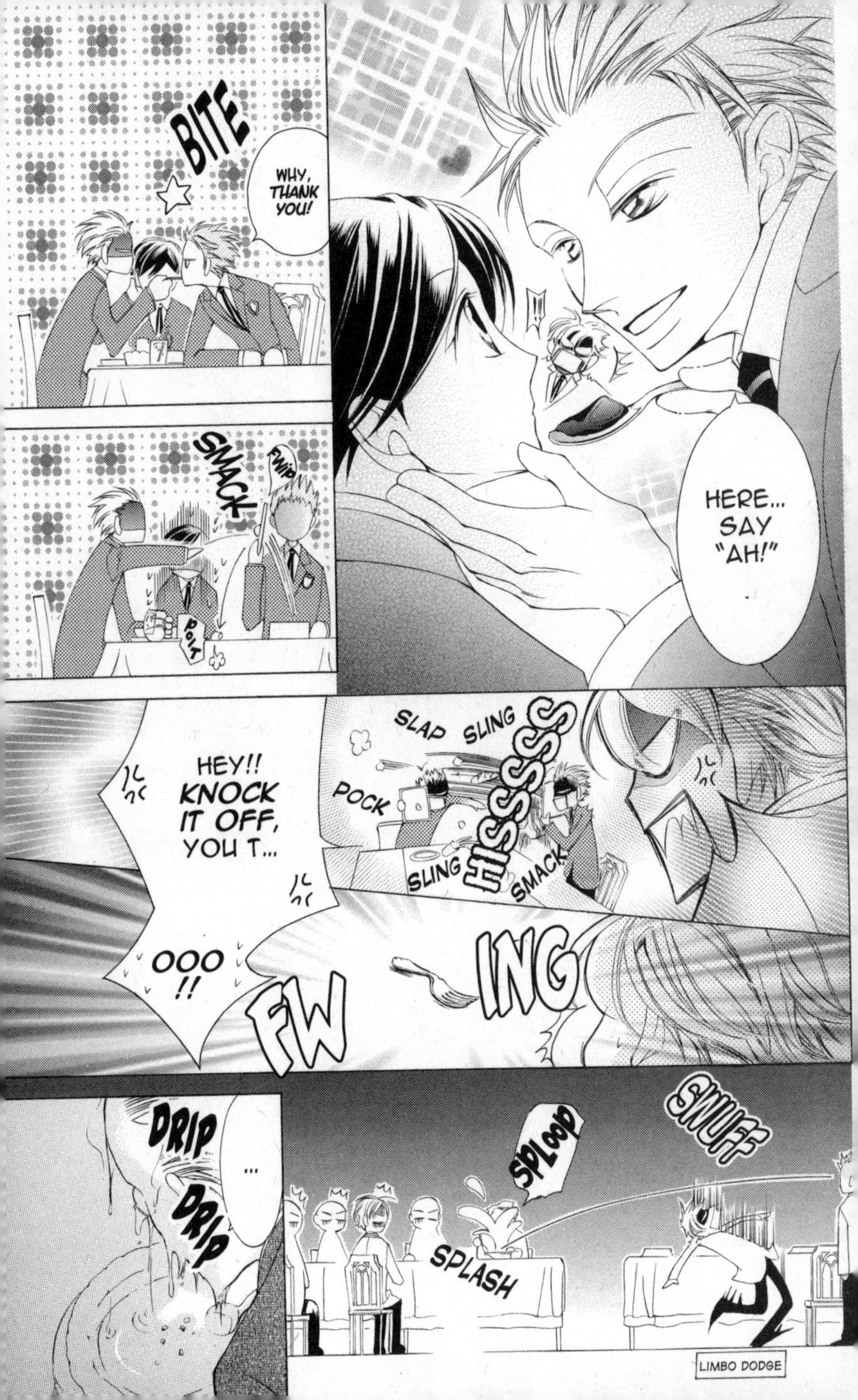
HERE... SAY "AH!"
!!
BITE
WHY, THANK YOU!
SMACK
FWIP
POIT
SLAP
SLING
HISSSSSS
POCK
SLING
SMACK
HEY!! KNOCK IT OFF, YOU T...
OOO !!
FW ING
SNUFF
SPLOOP
SPLASH
LIMBO DODGE
DRIP
DRIP
...

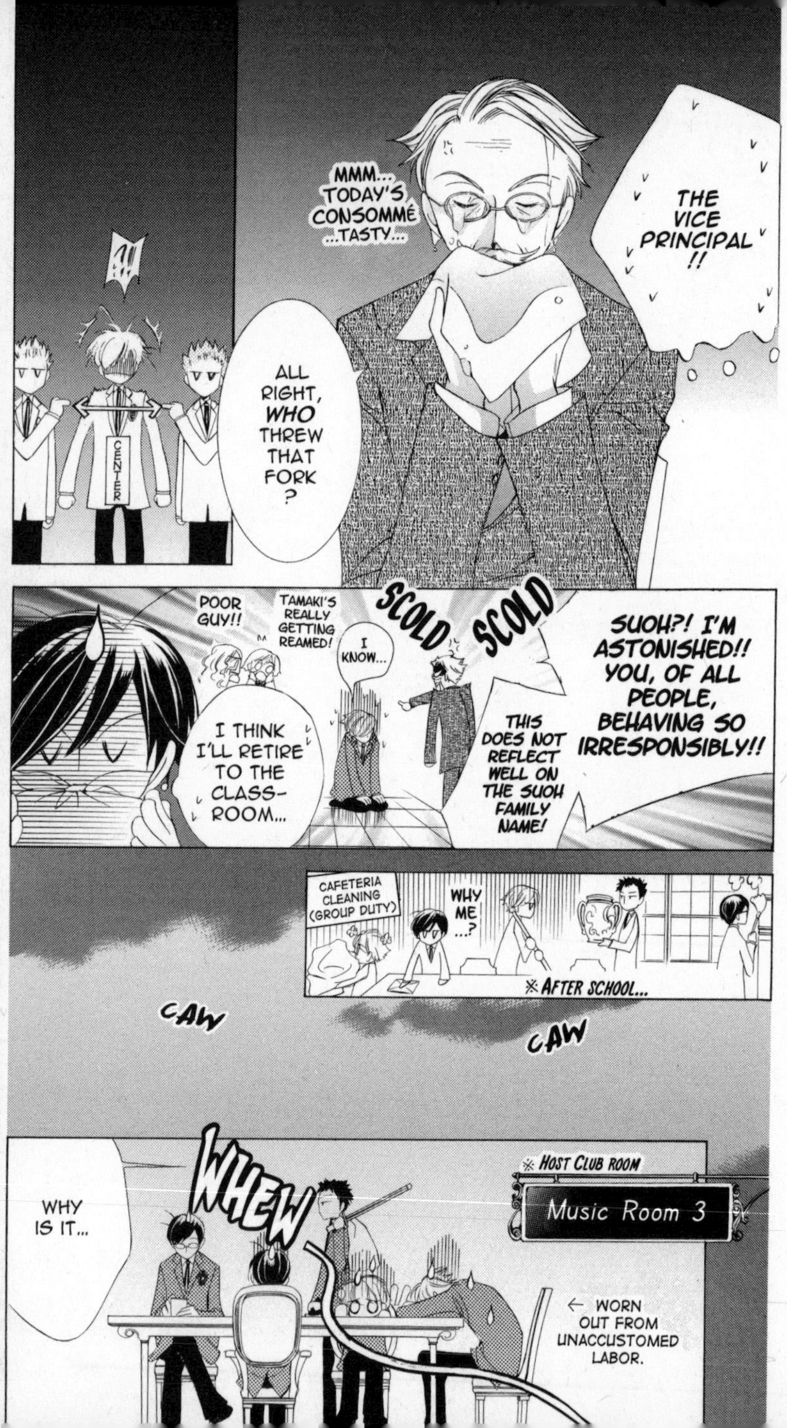
THE VICE PRINCIPAL!!
MMM... TODAY'S CONSOMMÉ ...TASTY...
ALL RIGHT, WHO THREW THAT FORK?
?!!
CENTER
SUOH?! I'M ASTONISHED!! YOU, OF ALL PEOPLE, BEHAVING SO IRRESPONSIBLY!!
THIS DOES NOT REFLECT WELL ON THE SUOH FAMILY NAME!
SCOLD
SCOLD
TAMAKI'S REALLY GETTING REAMED!
POOR GUY!!
I KNOW...
I THINK I'LL RETIRE TO THE CLASS-ROOM...
CAFETERIA CLEANING (GROUP DUTY)
WHY ME ...?
※AFTER SCHOOL...
CAW
CAW
※HOST CLUB ROOM
Music Room 3
WHEW
WHY IS IT...
← WORN OUT FROM UNACCUSTOMED LABOR.

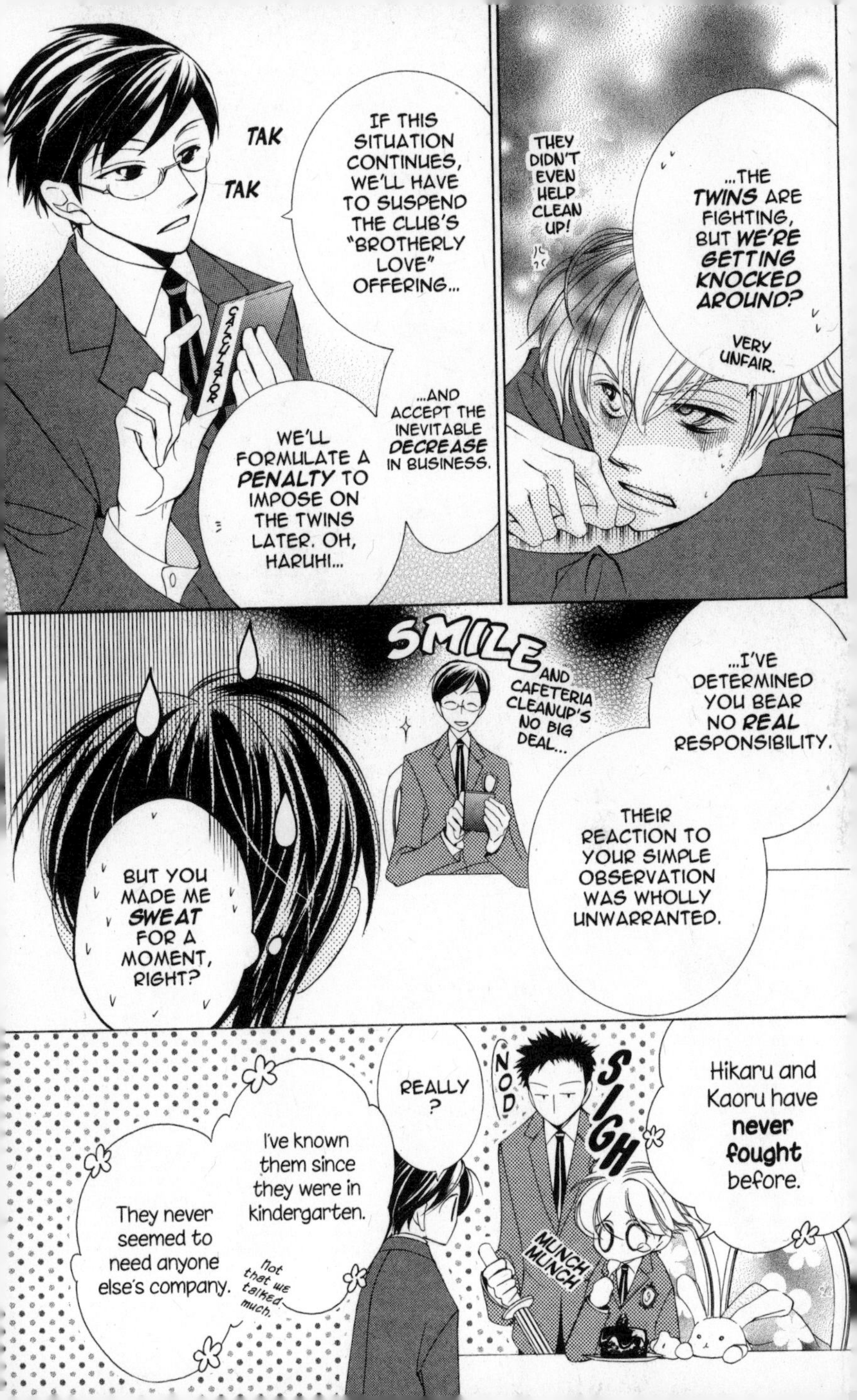

...THE TWINS ARE FIGHTING, BUT WE'RE GETTING KNOCKED AROUND?
VERY UNFAIR.
THEY DIDN'T EVEN HELP CLEAN UP!
TAK
TAK
IF THIS SITUATION CONTINUES, WE'LL HAVE TO SUSPEND THE CLUB'S "BROTHERLY LOVE" OFFERING...
...AND ACCEPT THE INEVITABLE DECREASE IN BUSINESS.
CALCULATOR
WE'LL FORMULATE A PENALTY TO IMPOSE ON THE TWINS LATER. OH, HARUHI...
...I'VE DETERMINED YOU BEAR NO REAL RESPONSIBILITY.
THEIR REACTION TO YOUR SIMPLE OBSERVATION WAS WHOLLY UNWARRANTED.
SMILE
AND CAFETERIA CLEANUP'S NO BIG DEAL...
BUT YOU MADE ME SWEAT FOR A MOMENT, RIGHT?
Hikaru and Kaoru have never fought before.
SIGH
NOD
MUNCH MUNCH
REALLY?
I've known them since they were in kindergarten.
They never seemed to need anyone else's company.
Not that we talked much.

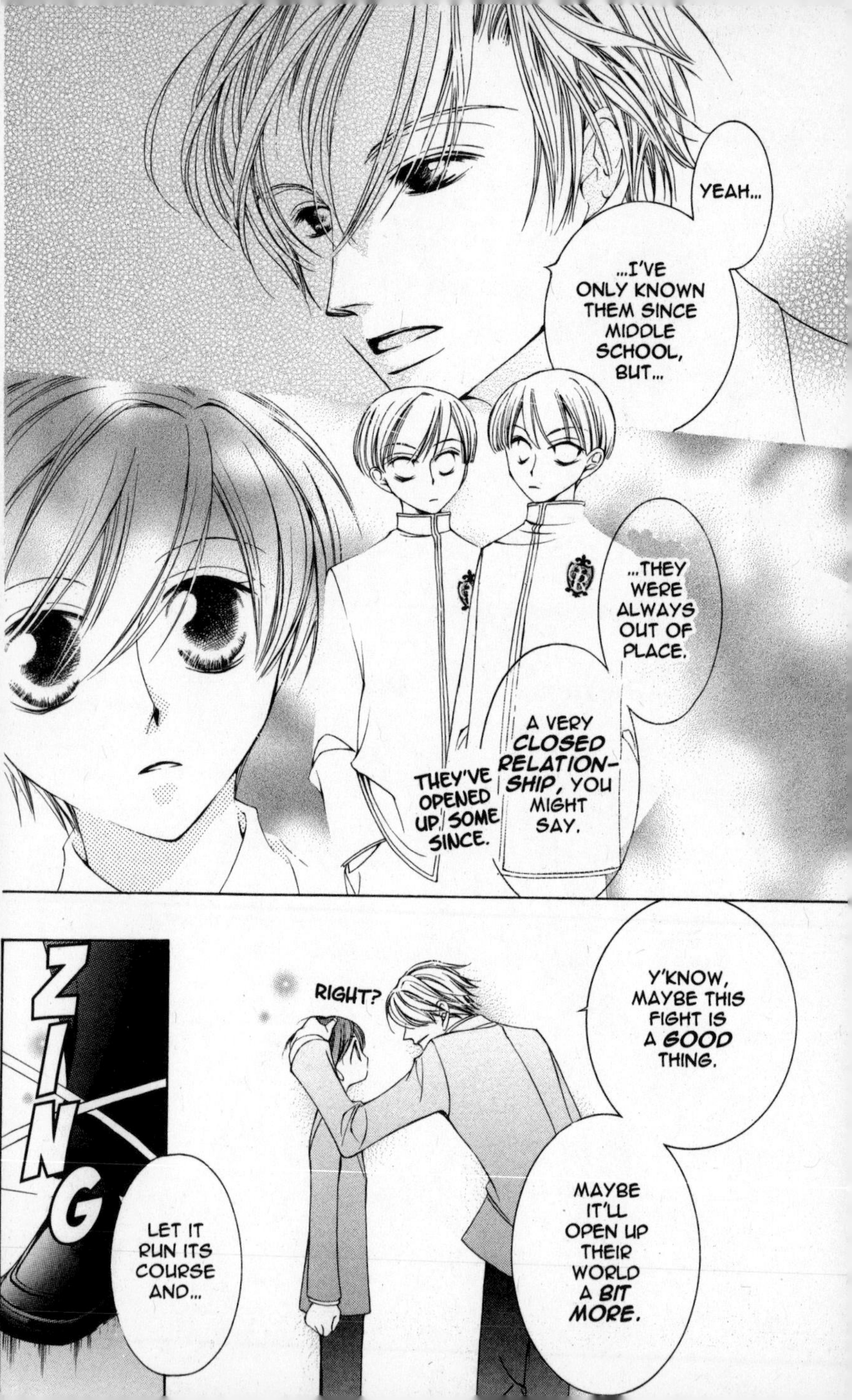
YEAH...
...I'VE ONLY KNOWN THEM SINCE MIDDLE SCHOOL, BUT...
...THEY WERE ALWAYS OUT OF PLACE.
A VERY CLOSED RELATIONSHIP, YOU MIGHT SAY.
THEY'VE OPENED UP SOME SINCE.
Y'KNOW, MAYBE THIS FIGHT IS A GOOD THING.
MAYBE IT'LL OPEN UP THEIR WORLD A BIT MORE.
RIGHT?
LET IT RUN ITS COURSE AND...
ZING

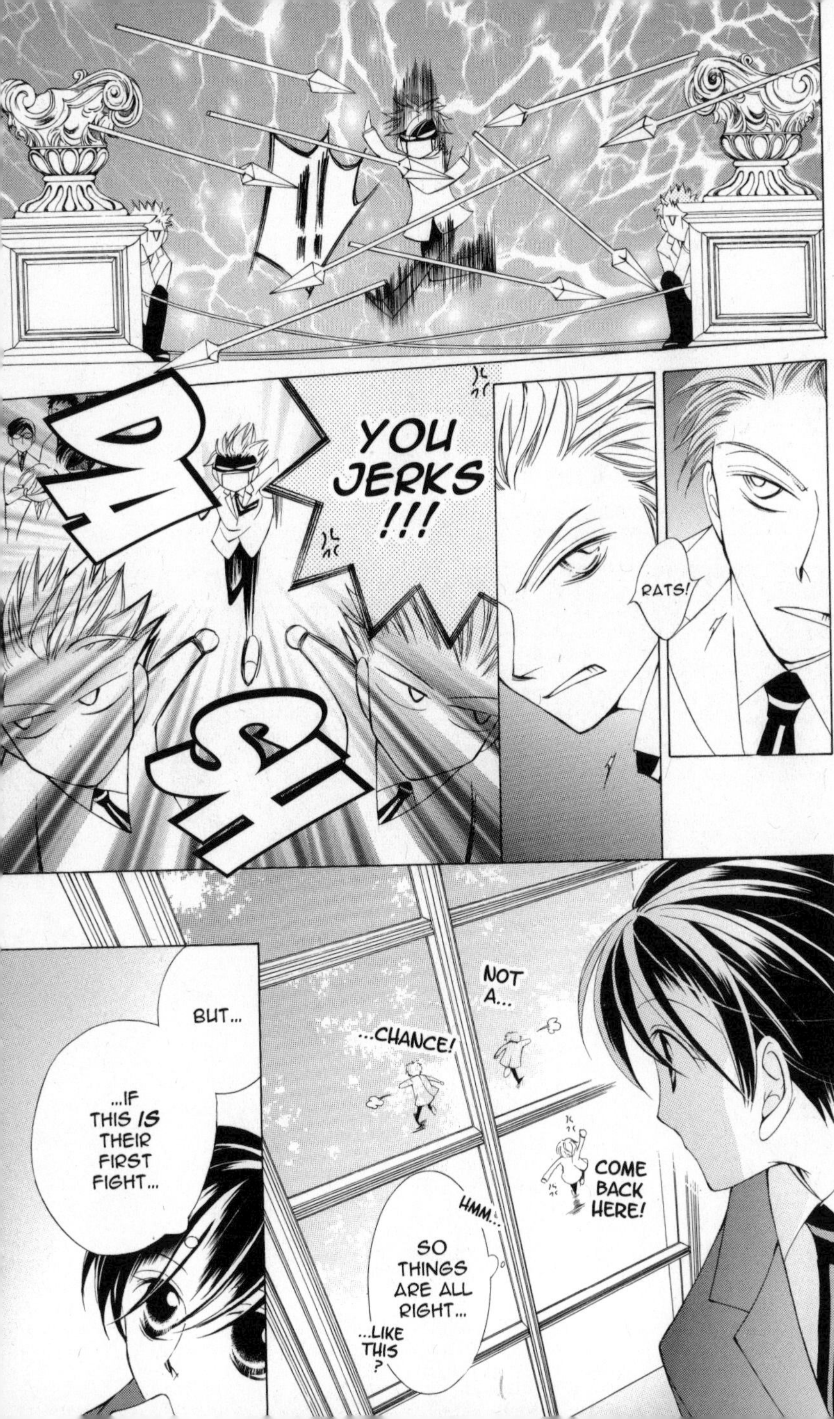

!!
RATS!
YOU JERKS!!!
DASH
NOT A...
...CHANCE!
COME BACK HERE!
HMM...
SO THINGS ARE ALL RIGHT...
...LIKE THIS?
BUT...
...IF THIS IS THEIR FIRST FIGHT...

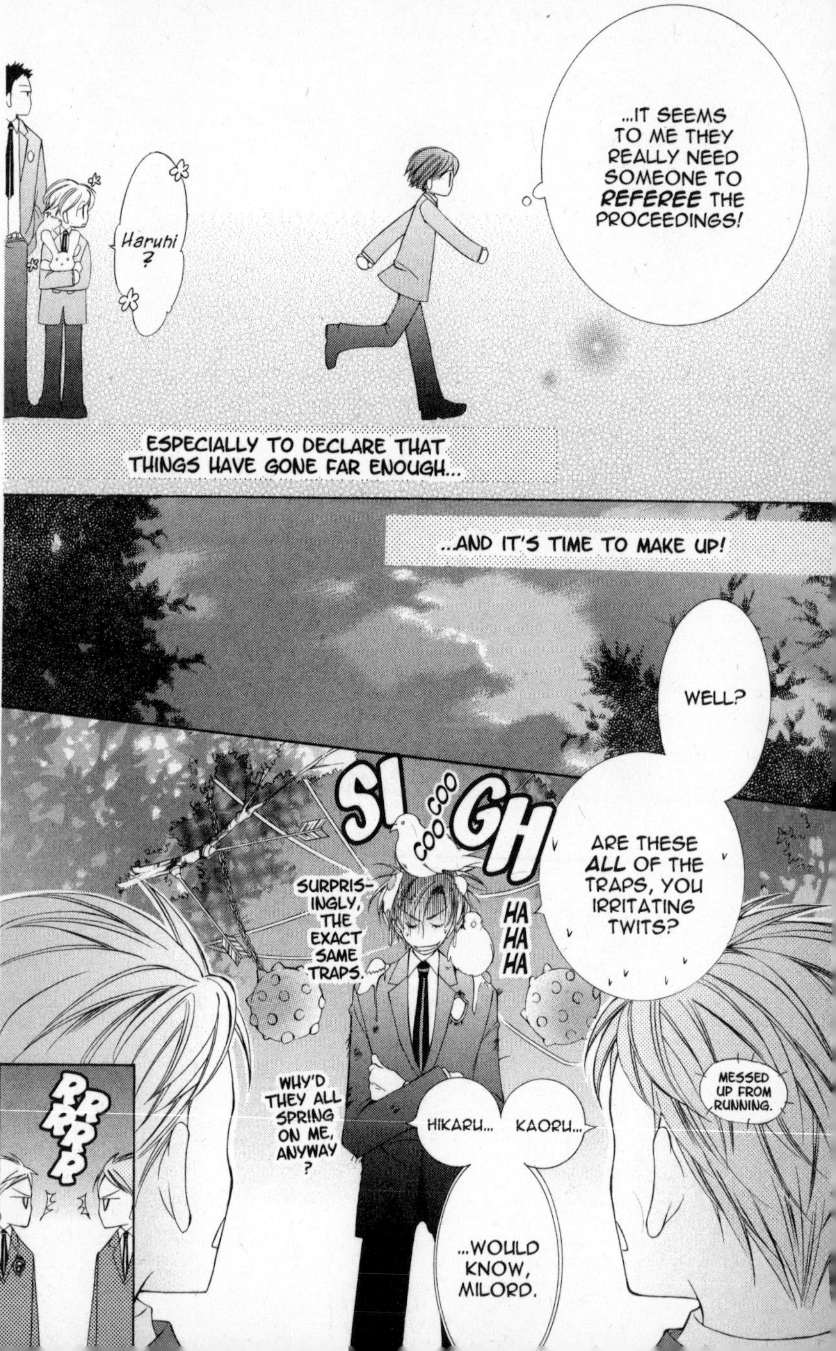
...IT SEEMS TO ME THEY REALLY NEED SOMEONE TO REFEREE THE PROCEEDINGS!
Haruhi?
ESPECIALLY TO DECLARE THAT THINGS HAVE GONE FAR ENOUGH...
...AND IT'S TIME TO MAKE UP!
WELL?
ARE THESE ALL OF THE TRAPS, YOU IRRITATING TWITS?
SIGH
COO COO
HA HA HA
SURPRIS-INGLY, THE EXACT SAME TRAPS.
MESSED UP FROM RUNNING.
HIKARU...
KAORU...
...WOULD KNOW, MILORD.
WHY'D THEY ALL SPRING ON ME, ANYWAY?
RRRRR

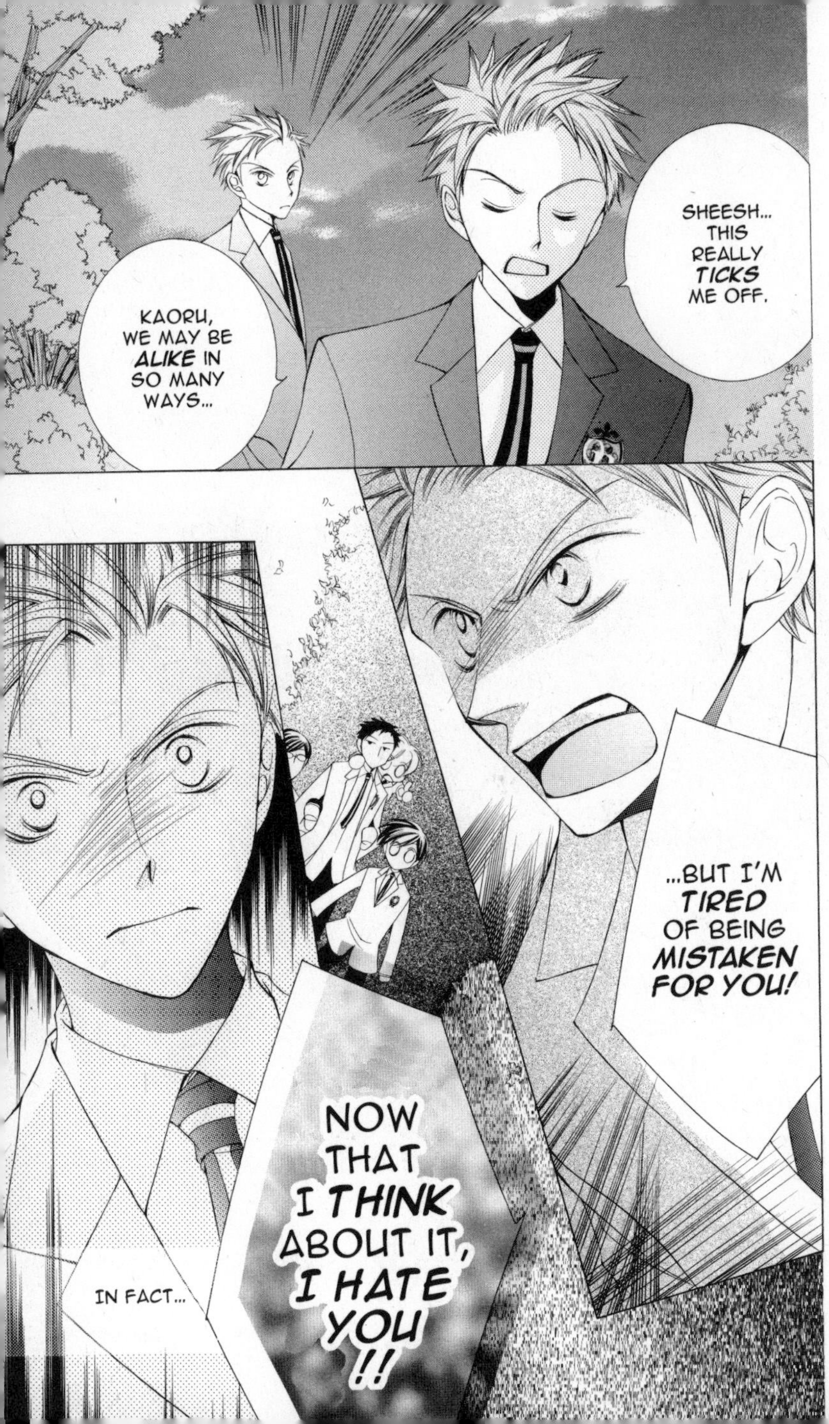
SHEESH... THIS REALLY TICKS ME OFF.
KAORU, WE MAY BE ALIKE IN SO MANY WAYS...
...BUT I'M TIRED OF BEING MISTAKEN FOR YOU!
IN FACT...
NOW THAT I THINK ABOUT IT, I HATE YOU!!

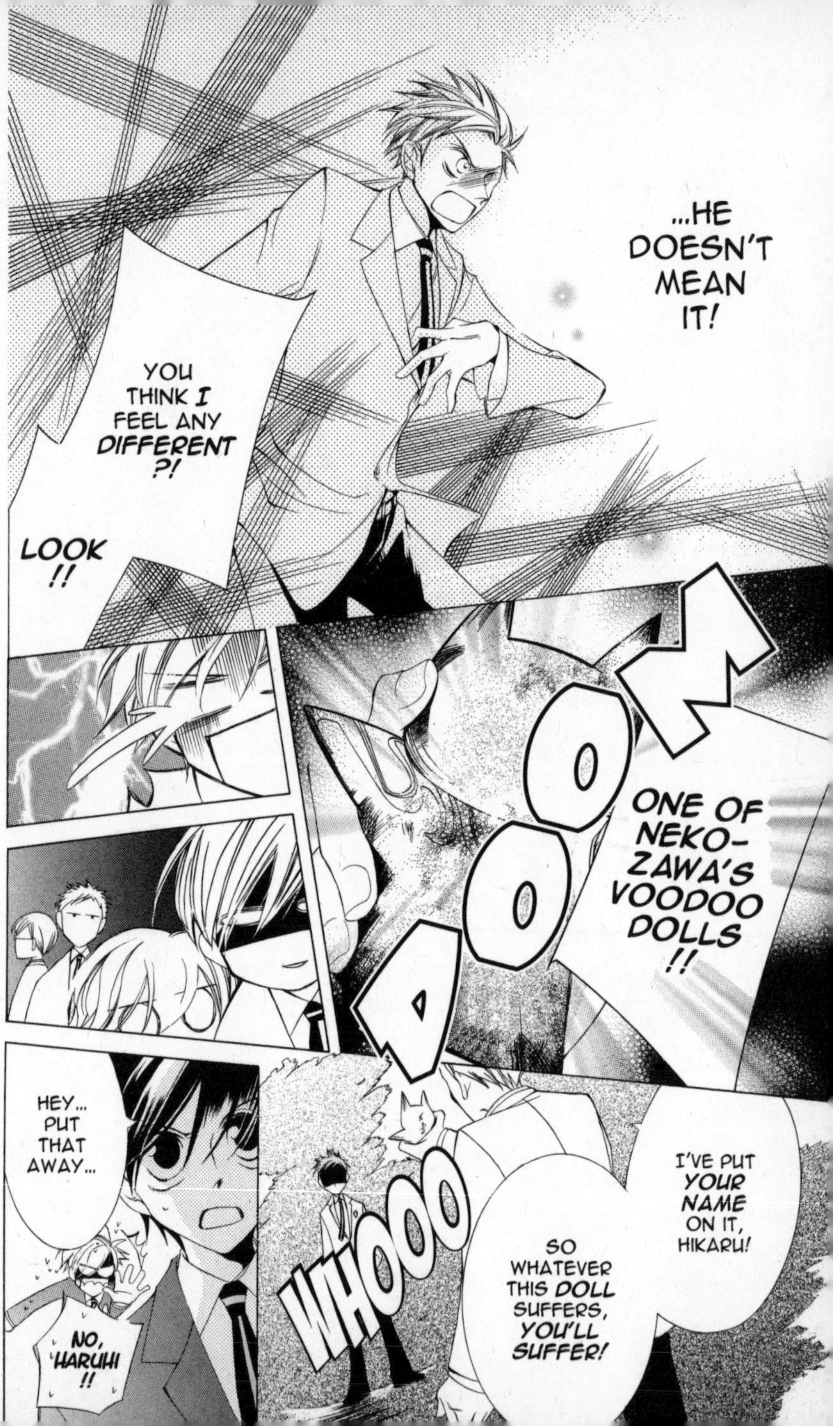
...HE DOESN'T MEAN IT!
YOU THINK I FEEL ANY DIFFERENT ?!
LOOK !!
DOOOM
ONE OF NEKO-ZAWA'S VOODOO DOLLS !!
I'VE PUT YOUR NAME ON IT, HIKARU!
SO WHATEVER THIS DOLL SUFFERS, YOU'LL SUFFER!
WHOOO
HEY... PUT THAT AWAY...
NO, HARUHI !!

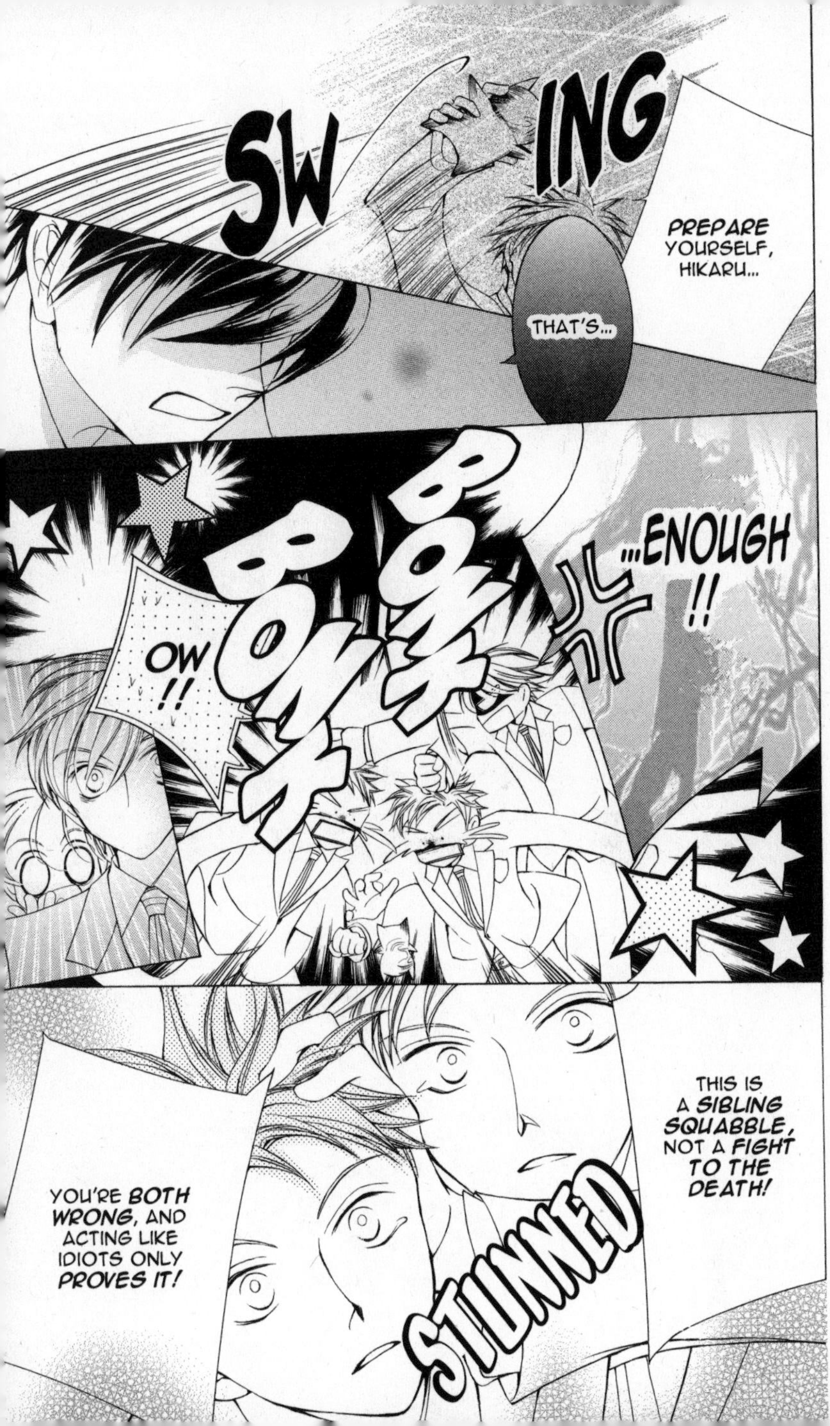
PREPARE YOURSELF, HIKARU...
THAT'S...
SW ING
...ENOUGH !!
BONK
BONK
OW !!
THIS IS A SIBLING SQUABBLE, NOT A FIGHT TO THE DEATH!
YOU'RE BOTH WRONG, AND ACTING LIKE IDIOTS ONLY PROVES IT!
STUNNED

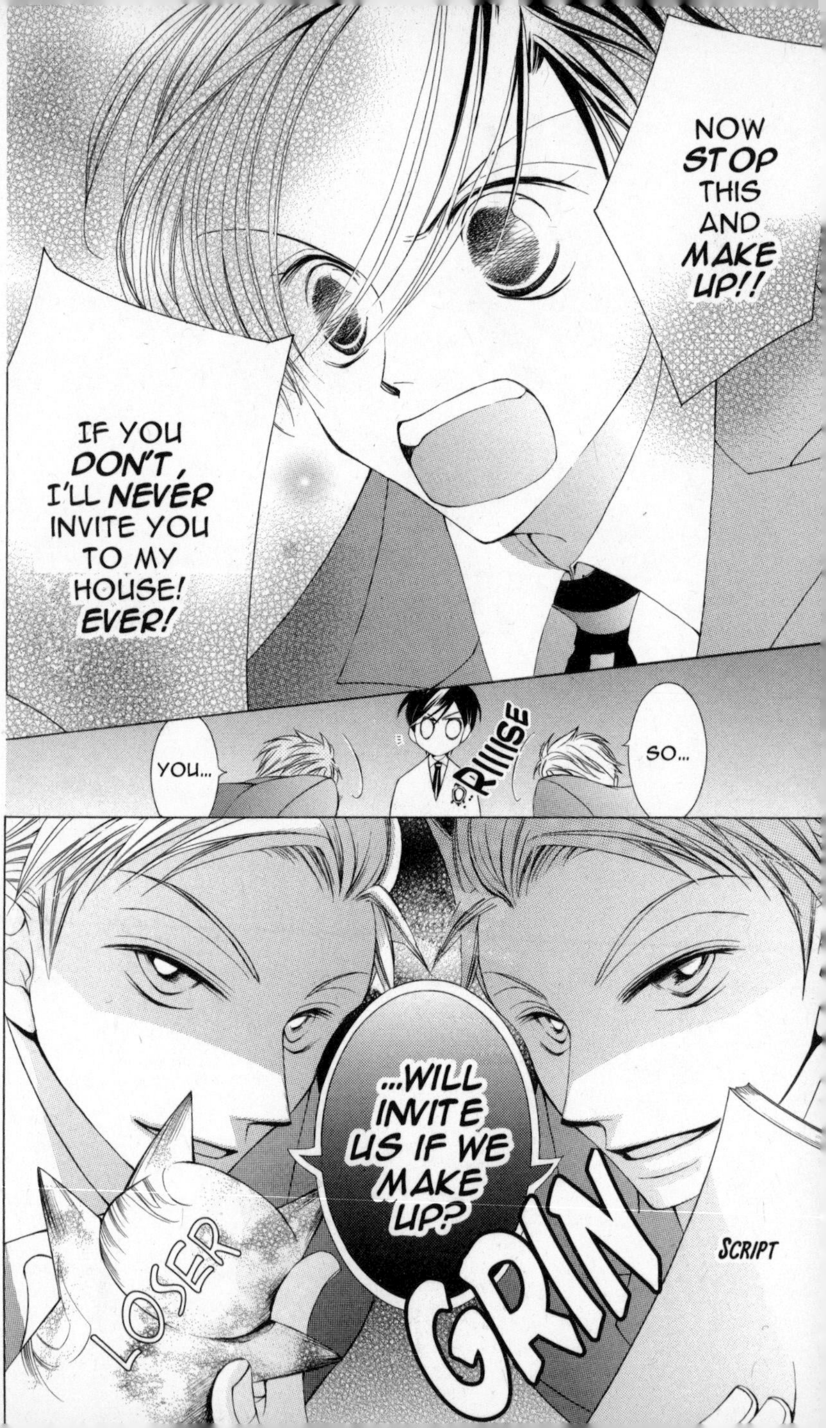
NOW STOP THIS AND MAKE UP!!
IF YOU DON'T, I'LL NEVER INVITE YOU TO MY HOUSE! EVER!
SO...
RIIIISE
YOU...
...WILL INVITE US IF WE MAKE UP?
SCRIPT
GRIN
LOSER

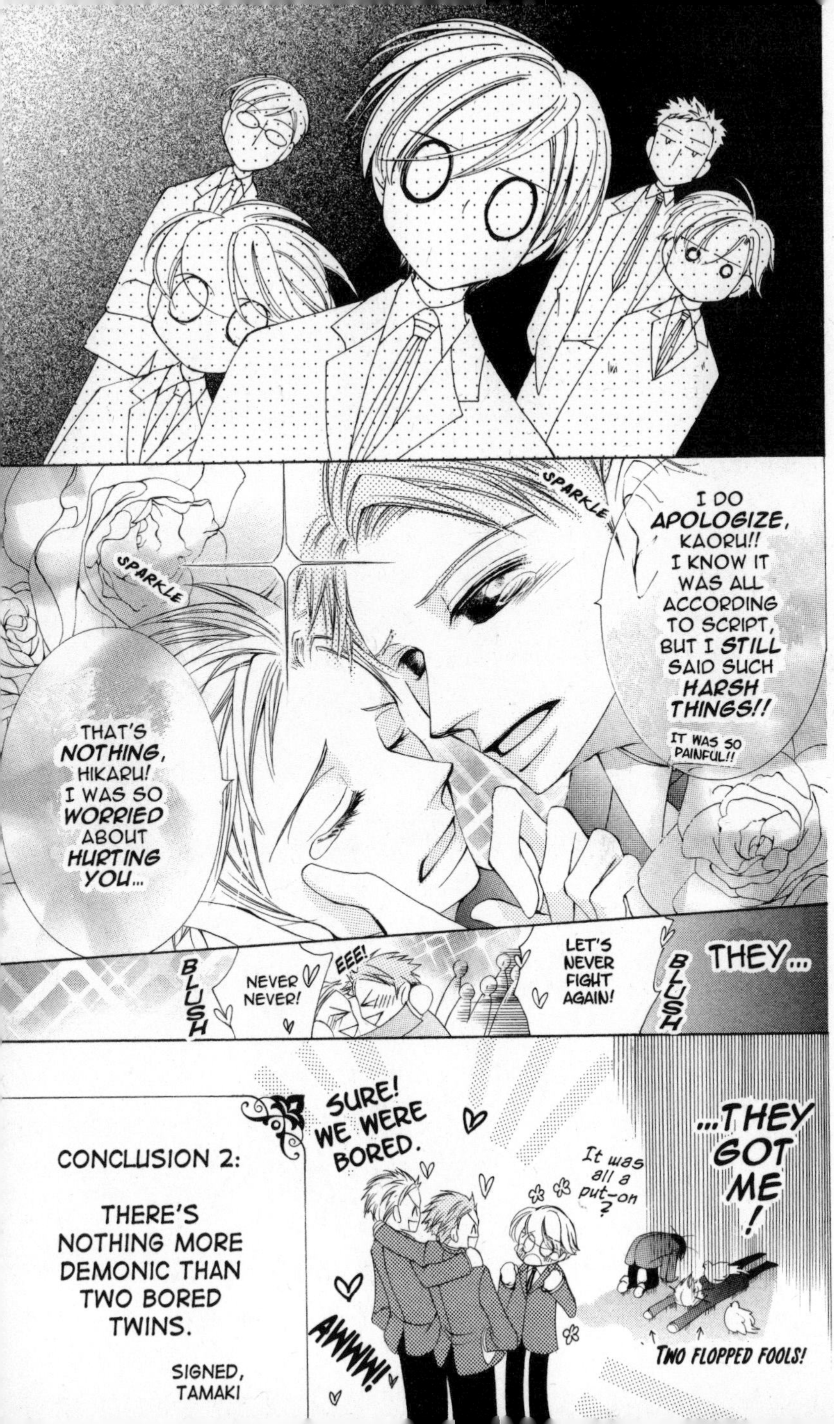

SPARKLE
I DO APOLOGIZE, KAORU!! I KNOW IT WAS ALL ACCORDING TO SCRIPT, BUT I STILL SAID SUCH HARSH THINGS!!
IT WAS SO PAINFUL!!
SPARKLE
THAT'S NOTHING, HIKARU! I WAS SO WORRIED ABOUT HURTING YOU...
THEY...
BLUSH
LET'S NEVER FIGHT AGAIN!
EEE!
NEVER NEVER!
BLUSH
...THEY GOT ME!
It was all a put-on?
TWO FLOPPED FOOLS!
SURE! WE WERE BORED.
AWWW!
CONCLUSION 2:
THERE'S NOTHING MORE DEMONIC THAN TWO BORED TWINS.
SIGNED, TAMAKI

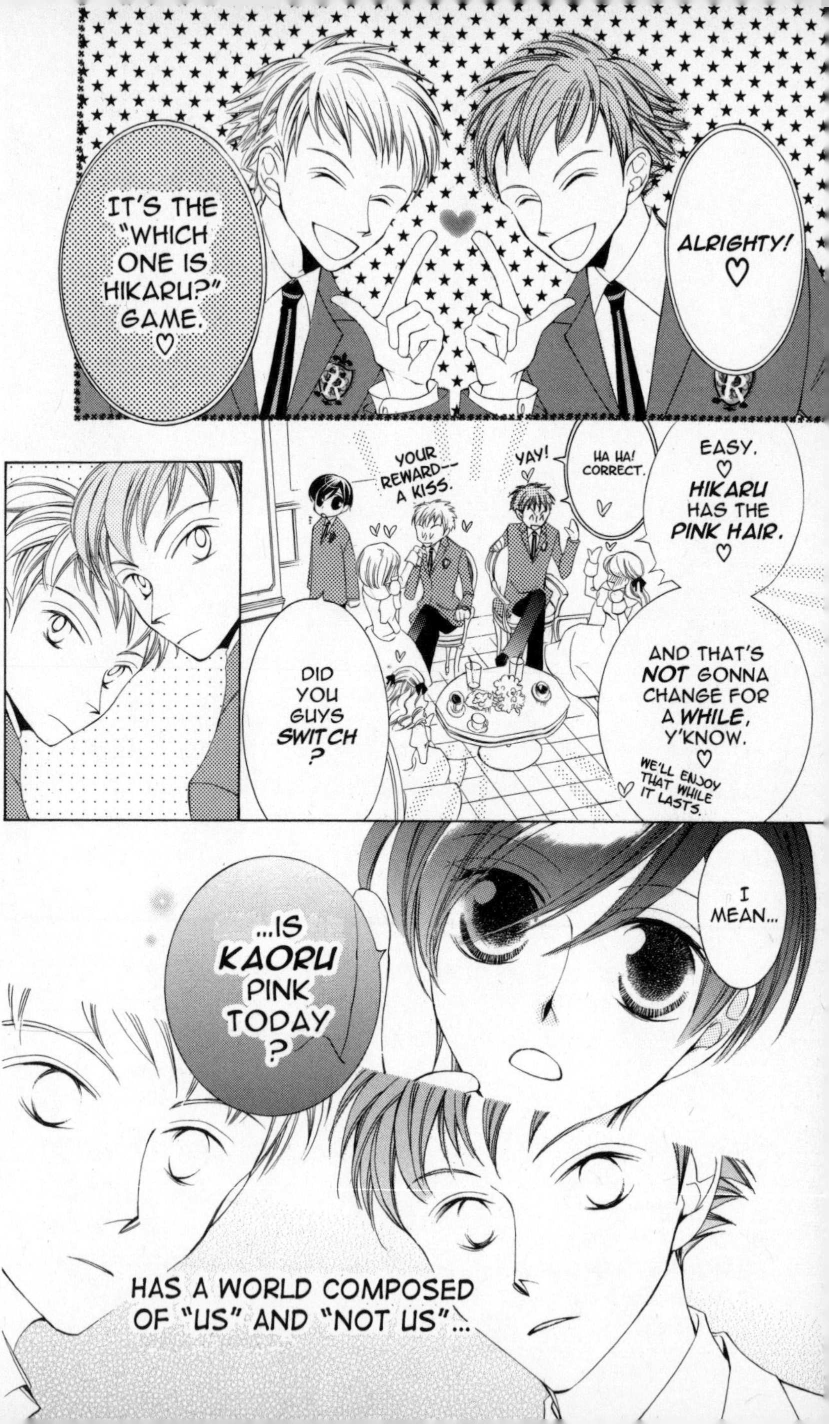
ALRIGHTY! ♡
IT'S THE "WHICH ONE IS HIKARU?" GAME. ♡
EASY. ♡ HIKARU HAS THE PINK HAIR. ♡
HA HA! CORRECT. ♡
YAY!
YOUR REWARD-- A KISS.
AND THAT'S NOT GONNA CHANGE FOR A WHILE, Y'KNOW. ♡
WE'LL ENJOY THAT WHILE IT LASTS.
DID YOU GUYS SWITCH?
I MEAN...
...IS KAORU PINK TODAY?
HAS A WORLD COMPOSED OF "US" AND "NOT US"...

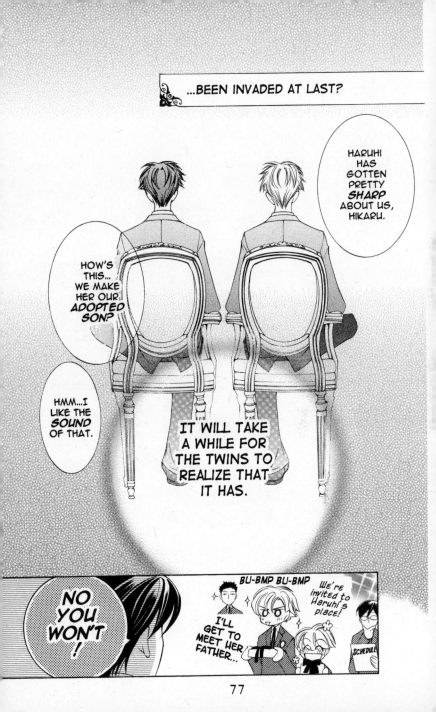

HARUHI HAS GOTTEN PRETTY *SHARP* ABOUT US, HIKARU.

HOW'S THIS... WE MAKE HER OUR *ADOPTED SON?*

HMM...I LIKE THE *SOUND* OF THAT.

IT WILL TAKE A WHILE FOR THE TWINS TO REALIZE THAT IT HAS.

NO YOU WON'T!

BU-BMP BU-BMP

We're invited to Haruhi's place!

I'LL GET TO MEET HER FATHER...

SCHEDULE

OURAN THEATER OF LOVE ~ SUOH FAMILY STORY ②

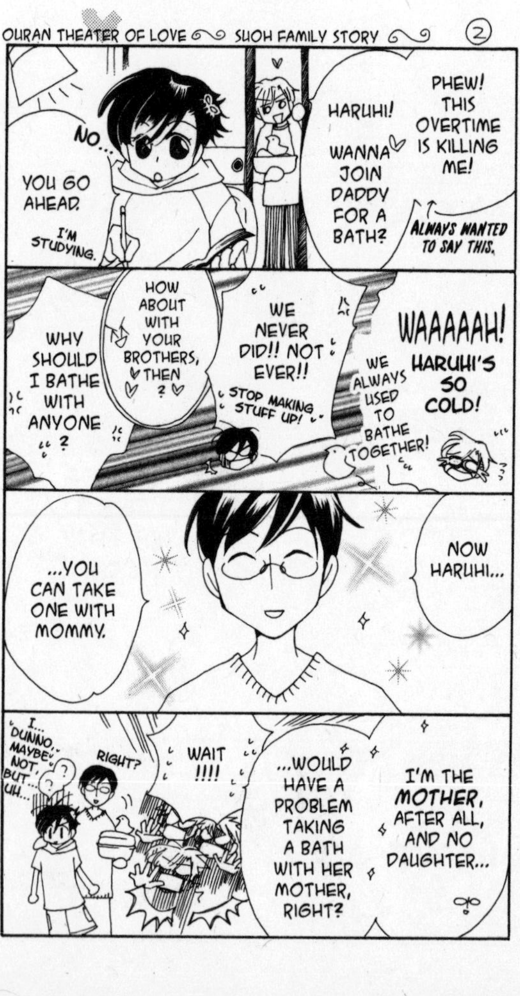
PHEW! THIS OVERTIME IS KILLING ME!
ALWAYS WANTED TO SAY THIS.
HARUHI! WANNA JOIN DADDY FOR A BATH?
NO...
YOU GO AHEAD.
I'M STUDYING.
WAAAAAH! HARUHI'S SO COLD!
WE ALWAYS USED TO BATHE TOGETHER!
WE NEVER DID!! NOT EVER!!
STOP MAKING STUFF UP!
HOW ABOUT WITH YOUR BROTHERS, THEN?
WHY SHOULD I BATHE WITH ANYONE?
NOW HARUHI...
...YOU CAN TAKE ONE WITH MOMMY.
I'M THE MOTHER, AFTER ALL, AND NO DAUGHTER...
...WOULD HAVE A PROBLEM TAKING A BATH WITH HER MOTHER, RIGHT?
WAIT!!!!
RIGHT?
I... DUNNO. MAYBE NOT, BUT... UH...

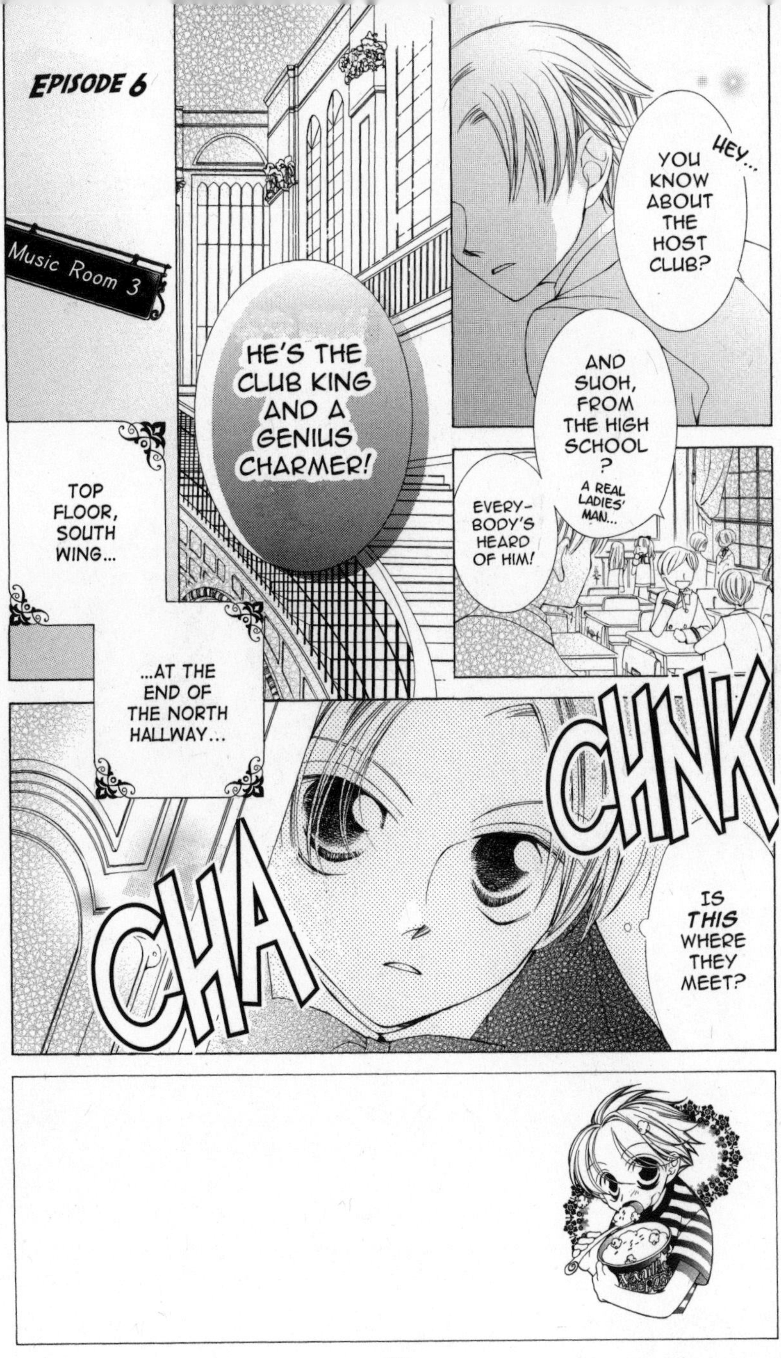
EPISODE 6
HEY...
YOU KNOW ABOUT THE HOST CLUB?
AND SUOH, FROM THE HIGH SCHOOL?
A REAL LADIES' MAN...
EVERY-BODY'S HEARD OF HIM!
HE'S THE CLUB KING AND A GENIUS CHARMER!
Music Room 3
TOP FLOOR, SOUTH WING...
...AT THE END OF THE NORTH HALLWAY...
CHA
CHNK
IS THIS WHERE THEY MEET?

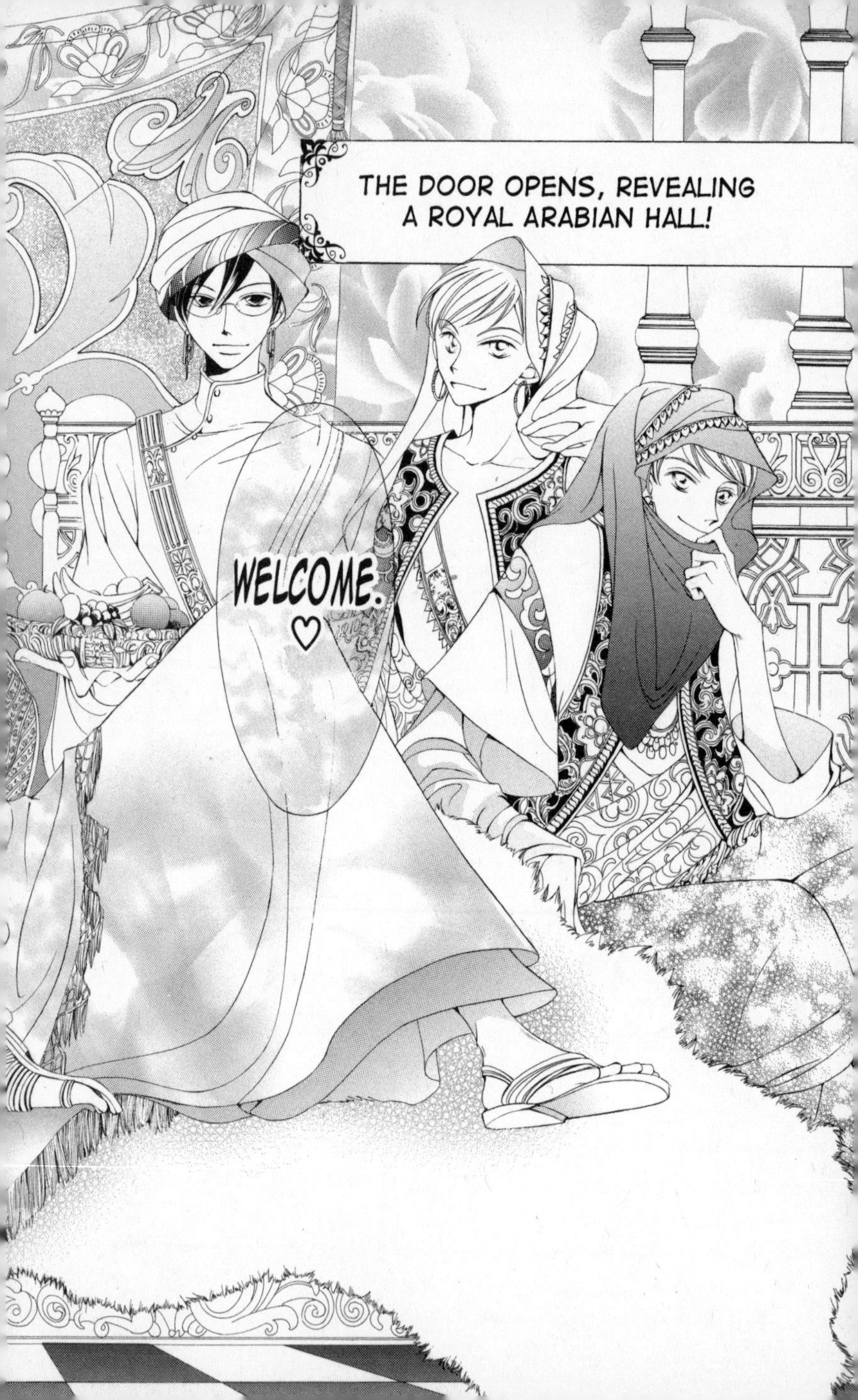
THE DOOR OPENS, REVEALING A ROYAL ARABIAN HALL!
WELCOME. ♡

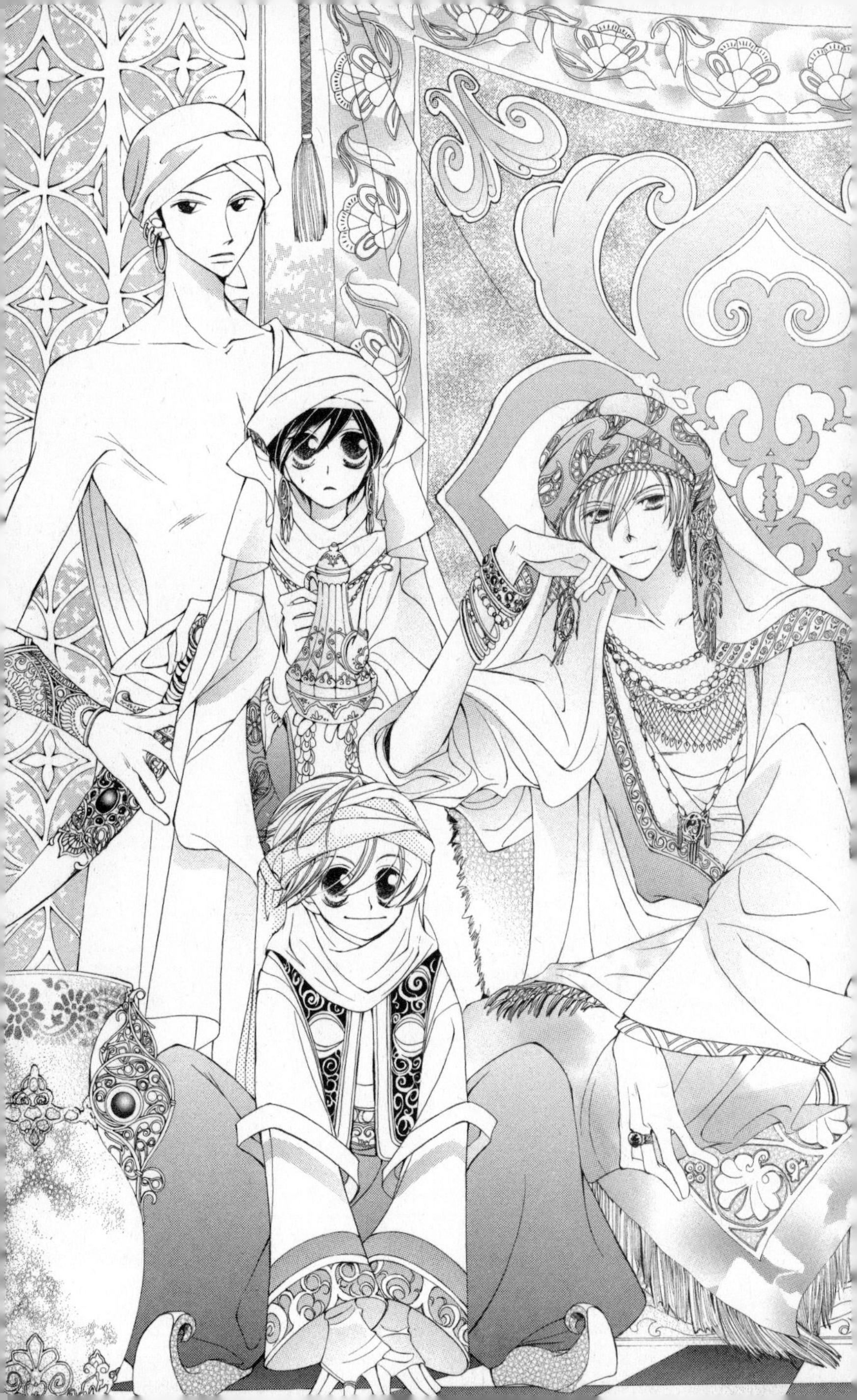

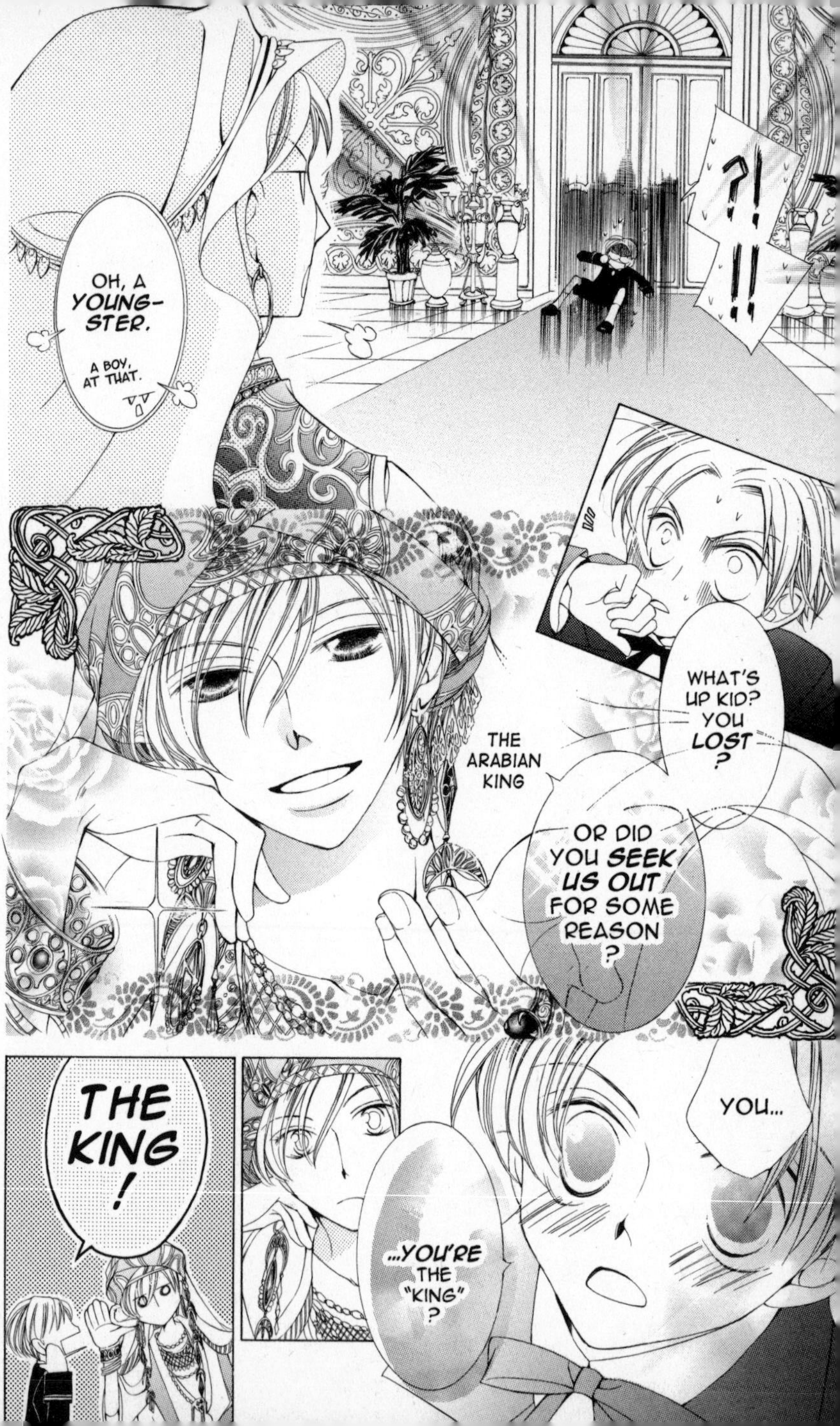
?!!!
OH, A YOUNGSTER.
A BOY, AT THAT.
WHAT'S UP KID? YOU LOST?
THE ARABIAN KING
OR DID YOU SEEK US OUT FOR SOME REASON?
YOU...
...YOU'RE THE "KING"?
THE KING!

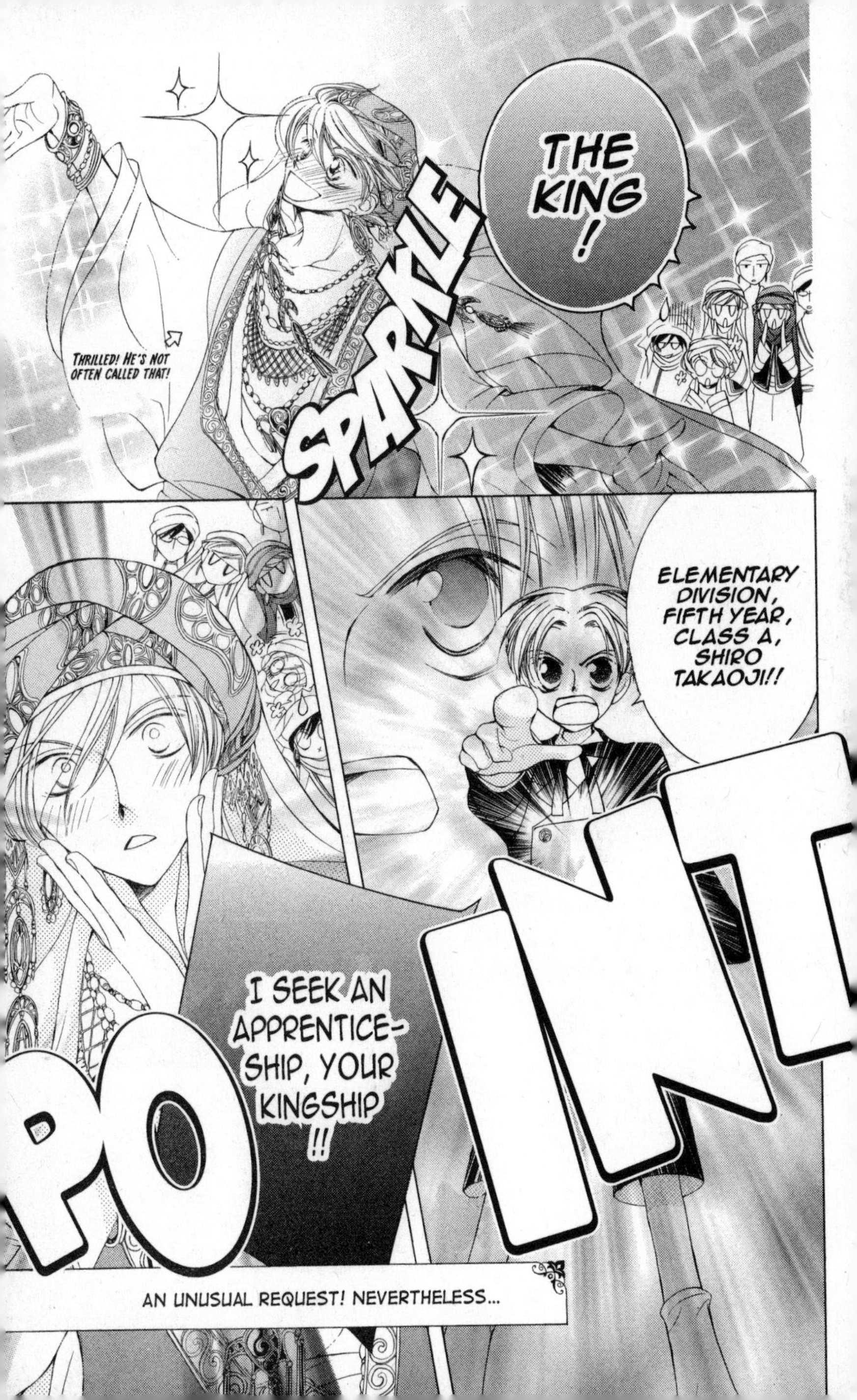
THE KING!
SPARKLE
THRILLED! HE'S NOT OFTEN CALLED THAT!
ELEMENTARY DIVISION, FIFTH YEAR, CLASS A, SHIRO TAKAOJI!!
POINT
I SEEK AN APPRENTICE-SHIP, YOUR KINGSHIP!!
AN UNUSUAL REQUEST! NEVERTHELESS...

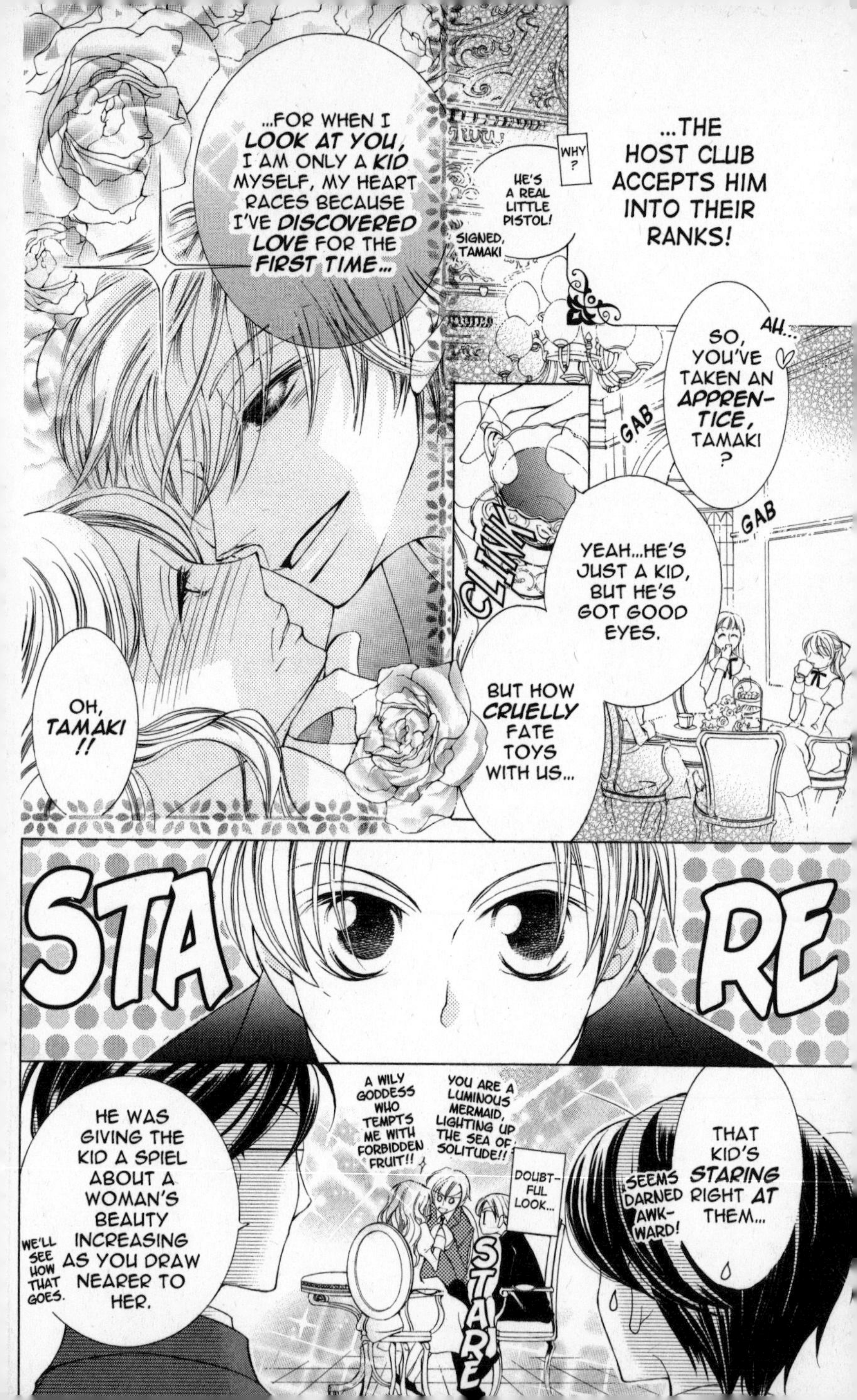
...THE HOST CLUB ACCEPTS HIM INTO THEIR RANKS!
WHY?
HE'S A REAL LITTLE PISTOL!
SIGNED, TAMAKI
AH...
SO, YOU'VE TAKEN AN APPREN-TICE, TAMAKI?
GAB
GAB
CLINK
YEAH...HE'S JUST A KID, BUT HE'S GOT GOOD EYES.
BUT HOW CRUELLY FATE TOYS WITH US...
...FOR WHEN I LOOK AT YOU, I AM ONLY A KID MYSELF, MY HEART RACES BECAUSE I'VE DISCOVERED LOVE FOR THE FIRST TIME...
OH, TAMAKI!!
STARE
THAT KID'S STARING RIGHT AT THEM...
SEEMS DARNED AWK-WARD!
DOUBT-FUL LOOK...
YOU ARE A LUMINOUS MERMAID, LIGHTING UP THE SEA OF SOLITUDE!!
A WILY GODDESS WHO TEMPTS ME WITH FORBIDDEN FRUIT!!
STARE
HE WAS GIVING THE KID A SPIEL ABOUT A WOMAN'S BEAUTY INCREASING AS YOU DRAW NEARER TO HER.
WE'LL SEE HOW THAT GOES.

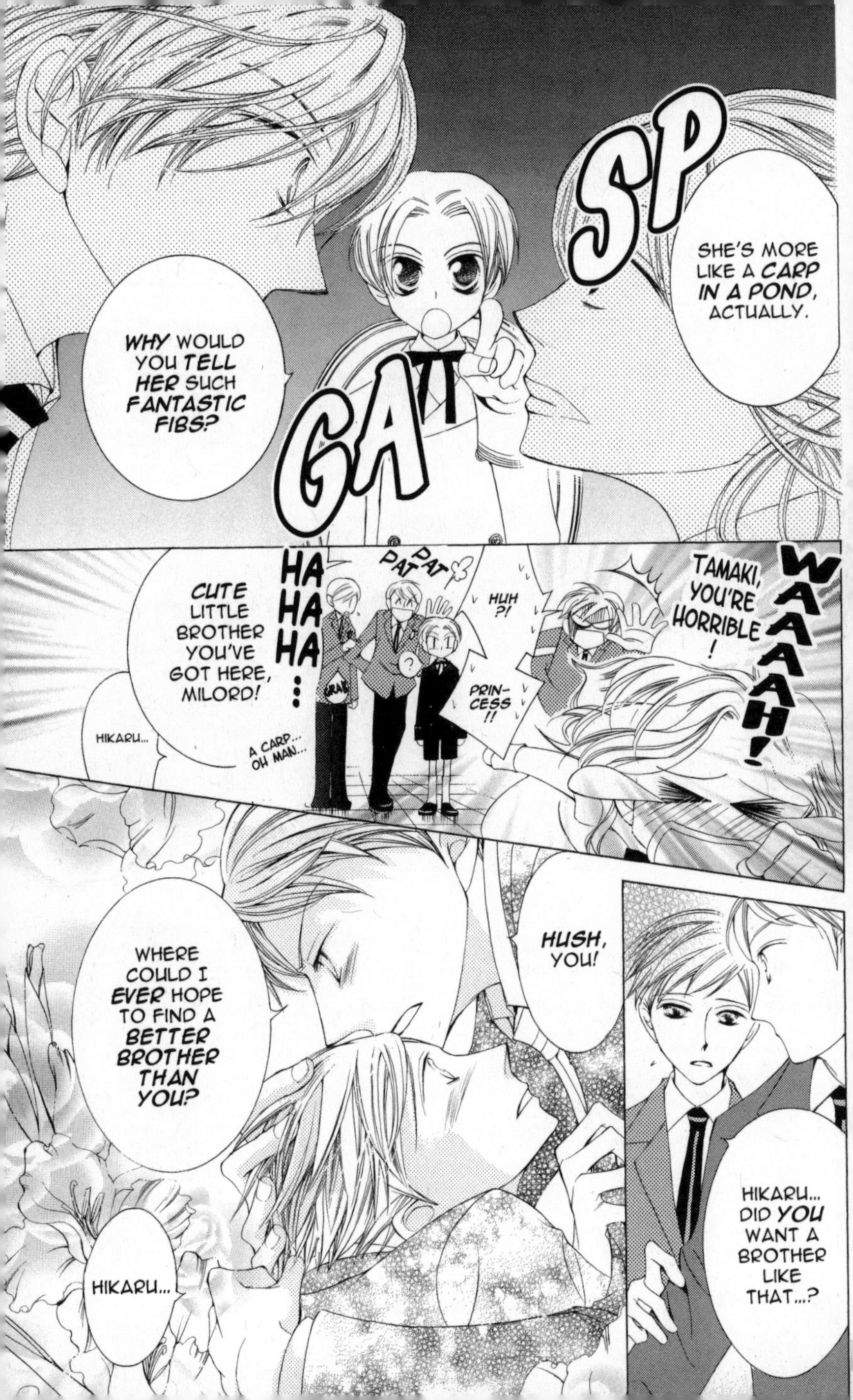
SHE'S MORE LIKE A CARP IN A POND, ACTUALLY.
SP
GA
WHY WOULD YOU TELL HER SUCH FANTASTIC FIBS?
WAAAAAH!
TAMAKI, YOU'RE HORRIBLE!
HUH ?!
PRIN-CESS !!
PAT PAT
HA HA HA...
CUTE LITTLE BROTHER YOU'VE GOT HERE, MILORD!
GRAB
A CARP... OH MAN...
HIKARU...
HIKARU... DID YOU WANT A BROTHER LIKE THAT...?
HUSH, YOU!
WHERE COULD I EVER HOPE TO FIND A BETTER BROTHER THAN YOU?
HIKARU...

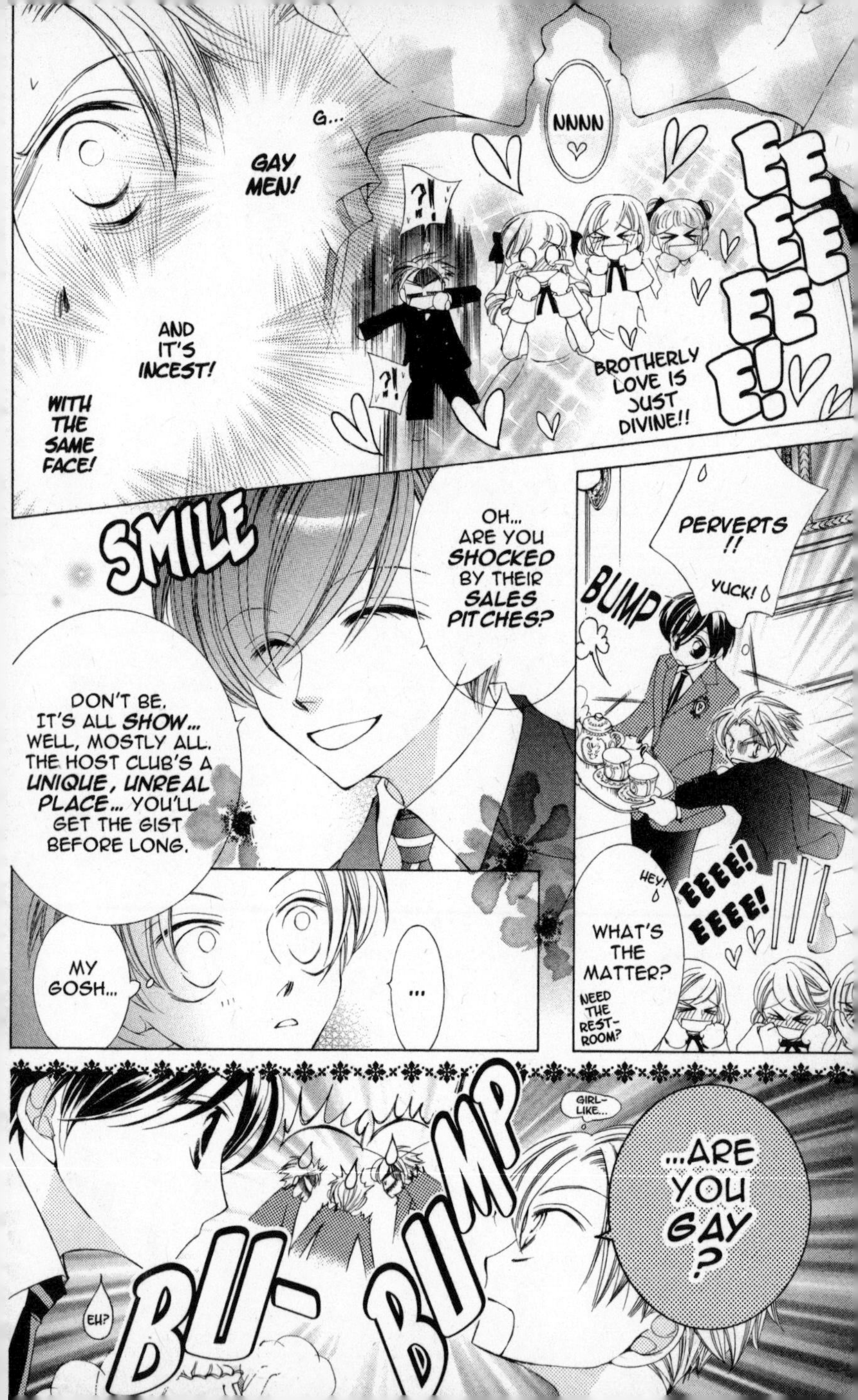
EE EE EE E!
NNNN
BROTHERLY LOVE IS JUST DIVINE!!
?!
?!
G...
GAY MEN!
AND IT'S INCEST!
WITH THE SAME FACE!
PERVERTS!!
YUCK!
BUMP
HEY!
EEEE! EEEE!
WHAT'S THE MATTER?
NEED THE REST-ROOM?
SMILE
OH... ARE YOU SHOCKED BY THEIR SALES PITCHES?
DON'T BE. IT'S ALL SHOW... WELL, MOSTLY ALL. THE HOST CLUB'S A UNIQUE, UNREAL PLACE... YOU'LL GET THE GIST BEFORE LONG.
...
MY GOSH...
GIRL-LIKE...
...ARE YOU GAY?
BU-BUMP
EH?

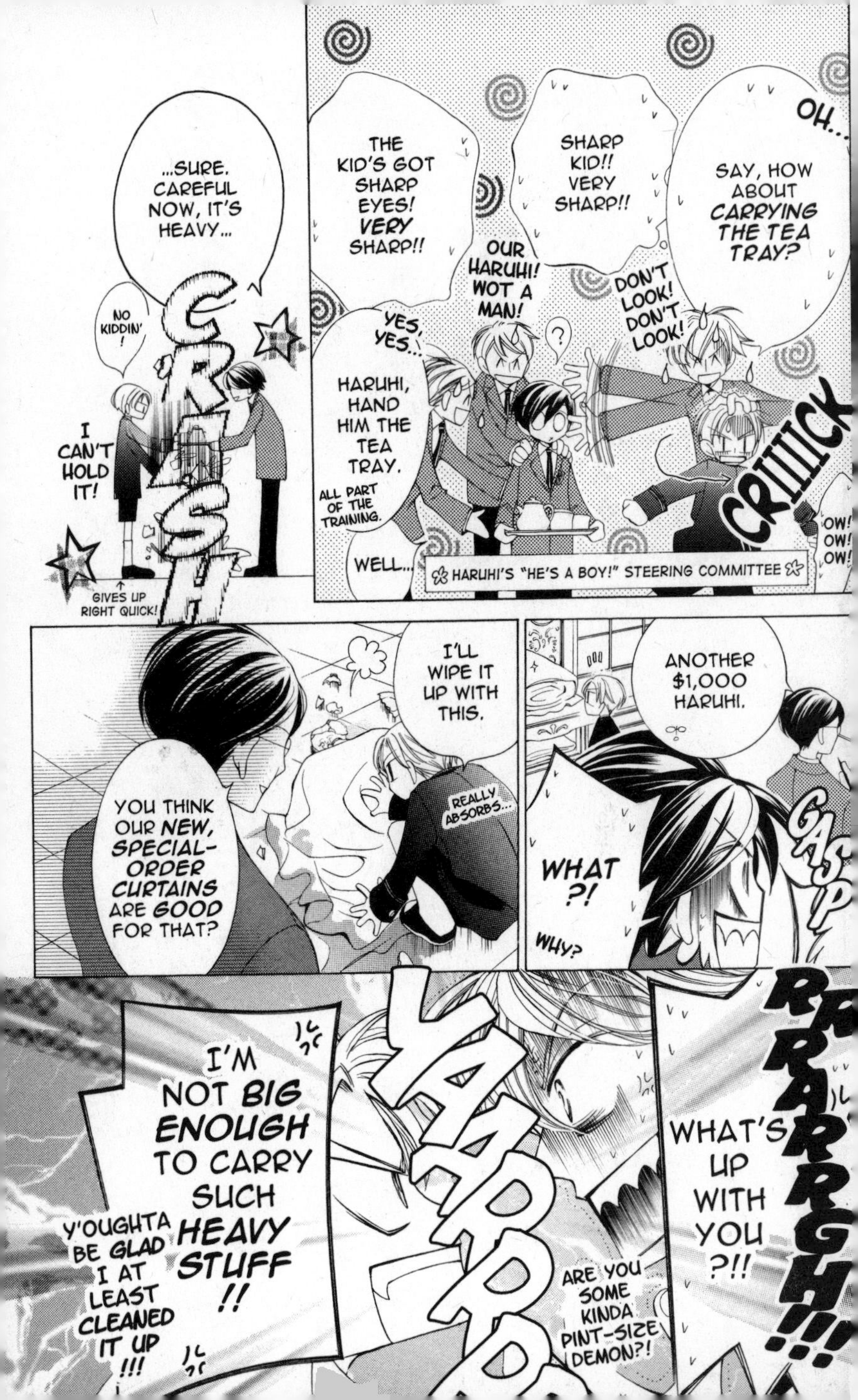
OH...
SAY, HOW ABOUT CARRYING THE TEA TRAY?
SHARP KID!! VERY SHARP!!
THE KID'S GOT SHARP EYES! VERY SHARP!!
DON'T LOOK! DON'T LOOK!
OUR HARUHI! WOT A MAN!
?
CRIIICK
OW! OW! OW!
YES, YES...
HARUHI, HAND HIM THE TEA TRAY.
ALL PART OF THE TRAINING.
WELL...
HARUHI'S "HE'S A BOY!" STEERING COMMITTEE
...SURE. CAREFUL NOW, IT'S HEAVY...
NO KIDDIN'!
CRASH
I CAN'T HOLD IT!
GIVES UP RIGHT QUICK!
ANOTHER $1,000 HARUHI.
GASP
WHAT?!
WHY?
I'LL WIPE IT UP WITH THIS.
REALLY ABSORBS...
YOU THINK OUR NEW, SPECIAL-ORDER CURTAINS ARE GOOD FOR THAT?
RRRARRGH!!!
WHAT'S UP WITH YOU?!!
ARE YOU SOME KINDA PINT-SIZE DEMON?!
I'M NOT BIG ENOUGH TO CARRY SUCH HEAVY STUFF!!
Y'OUGHTA BE GLAD I AT LEAST CLEANED IT UP!!!

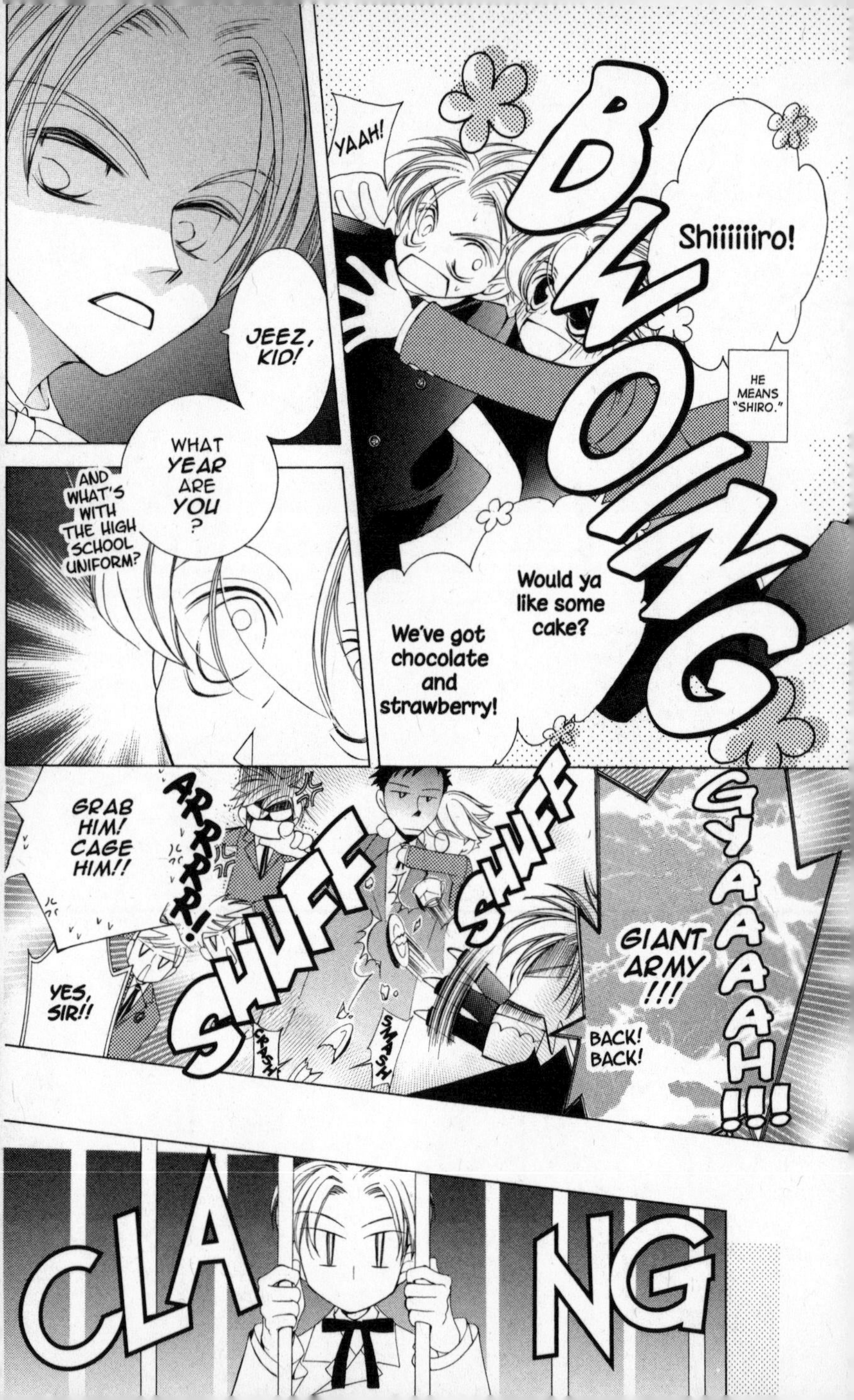
Shiiiiiiro!
BWOING
HE MEANS "SHIRO."
YAAH!
Would ya like some cake?
We've got chocolate and strawberry!
JEEZ, KID!
WHAT YEAR ARE YOU?
AND WHAT'S WITH THE HIGH SCHOOL UNIFORM?
GYAAAAAH!!!
GIANT ARMY!!!
BACK! BACK!
SHUFF
SHUFF
SMASH
CRASH
ARRRR!
GRAB HIM! CAGE HIM!!
YES, SIR!!
CLANG

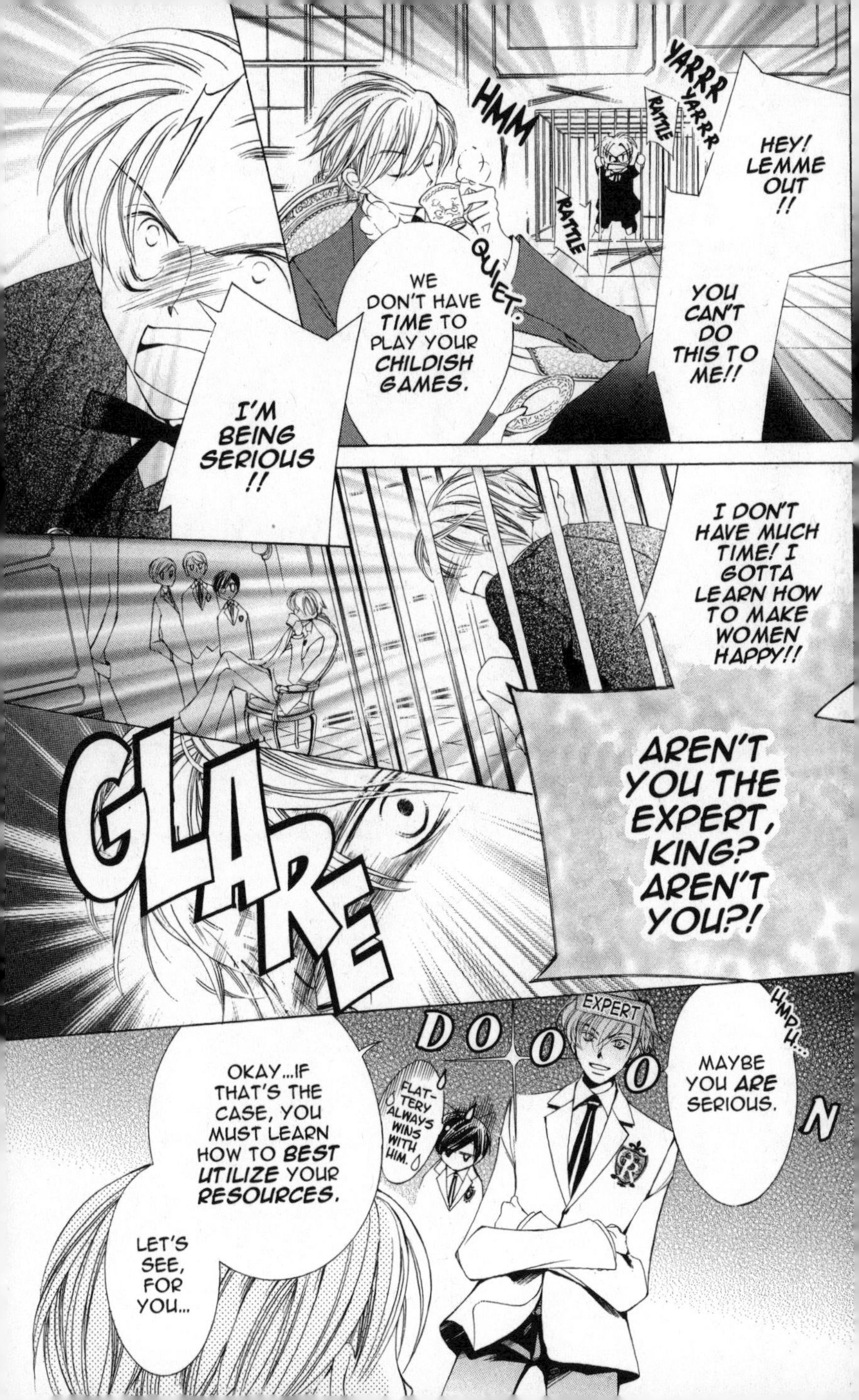
YARRR
YARRR
RATTLE
RATTLE
HEY! LEMME OUT!!
YOU CAN'T DO THIS TO ME!!
HMM
QUIET.
WE DON'T HAVE TIME TO PLAY YOUR CHILDISH GAMES.
I'M BEING SERIOUS!!
I DON'T HAVE MUCH TIME! I GOTTA LEARN HOW TO MAKE WOMEN HAPPY!!
AREN'T YOU THE EXPERT, KING? AREN'T YOU?!
GLARE
HMPH...
MAYBE YOU ARE SERIOUS.
EXPERT
DOOOON
FLATTERY ALWAYS WINS WITH HIM.
OKAY...IF THAT'S THE CASE, YOU MUST LEARN HOW TO BEST UTILIZE YOUR RESOURCES.
LET'S SEE, FOR YOU...

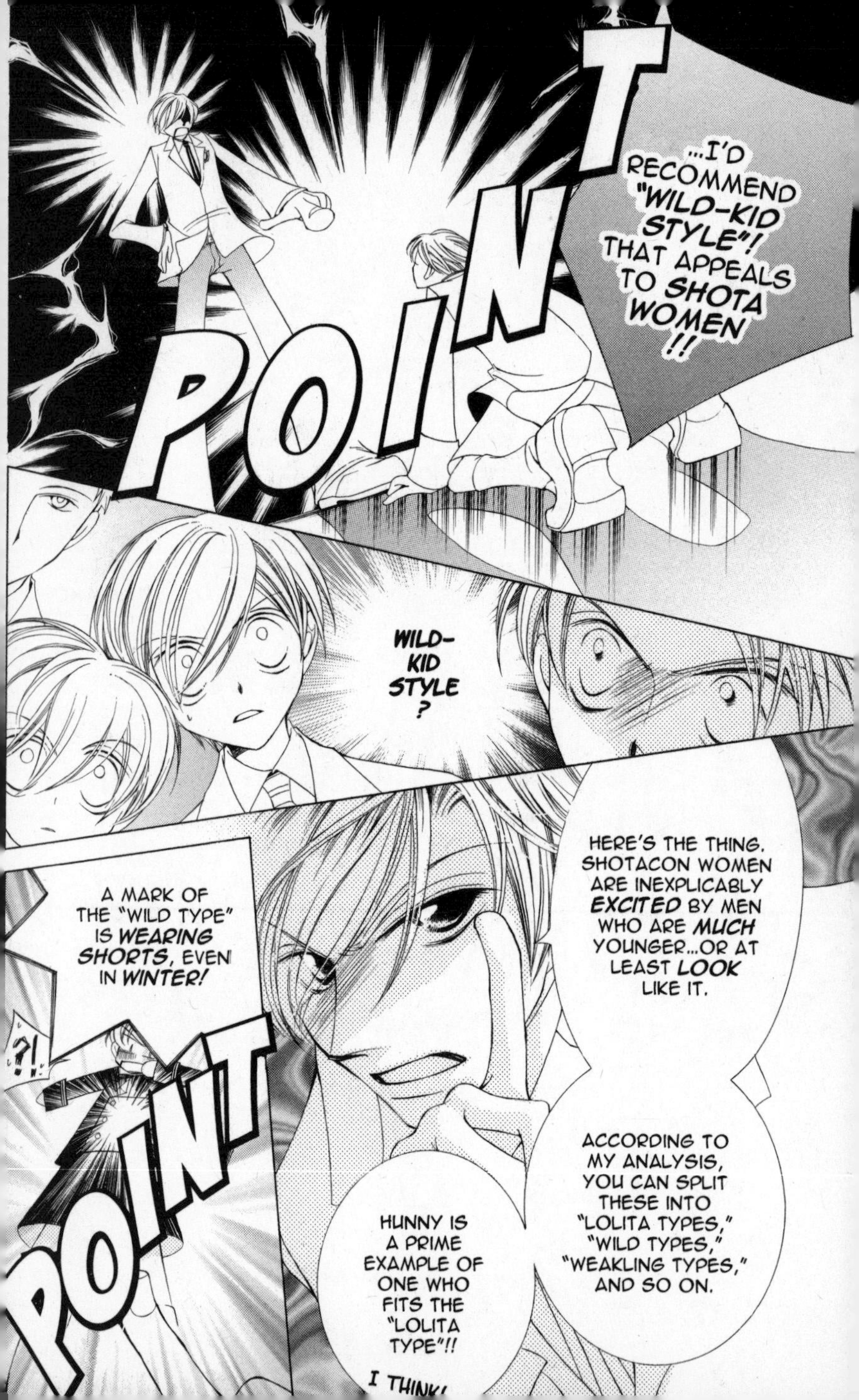

...I'D RECOMMEND "WILD-KID STYLE"! THAT APPEALS TO SHOTA WOMEN!!
POINT
WILD-KID STYLE?
HERE'S THE THING. SHOTACON WOMEN ARE INEXPLICABLY EXCITED BY MEN WHO ARE MUCH YOUNGER...OR AT LEAST LOOK LIKE IT.
ACCORDING TO MY ANALYSIS, YOU CAN SPLIT THESE INTO "LOLITA TYPES," "WILD TYPES," "WEAKLING TYPES," AND SO ON.
HUNNY IS A PRIME EXAMPLE OF ONE WHO FITS THE "LOLITA TYPE"!!
I THINK!
A MARK OF THE "WILD TYPE" IS WEARING SHORTS, EVEN IN WINTER!
?!
POINT

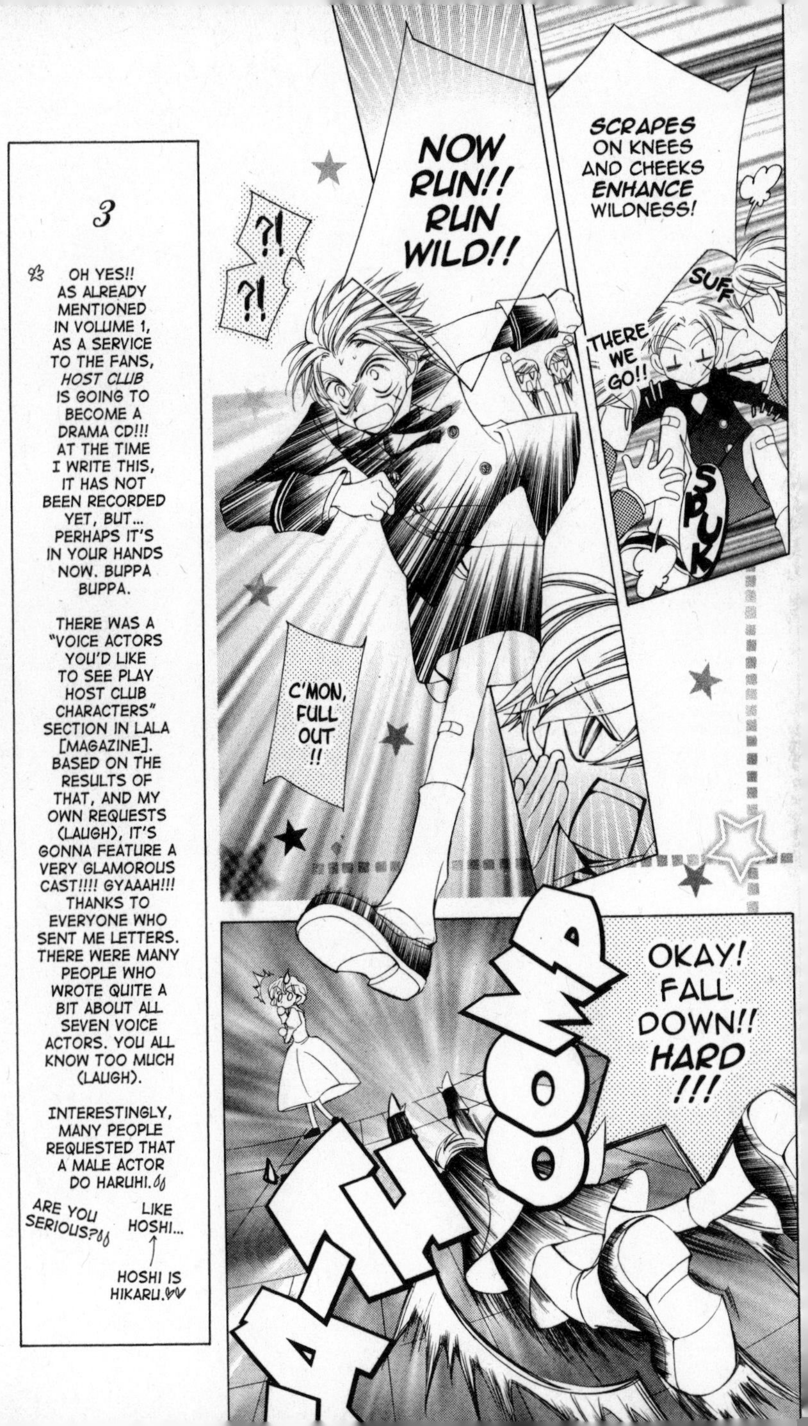
SCRAPES ON KNEES AND CHEEKS ENHANCE WILDNESS!
SUFF
THERE WE GO!!
SPUK
NOW RUN!! RUN WILD!!
?!
?!
C'MON, FULL OUT !!
OKAY! FALL DOWN!! HARD !!!
THOOMP

3

OH YES!! AS ALREADY MENTIONED IN VOLUME 1, AS A SERVICE TO THE FANS, *HOST CLUB* IS GOING TO BECOME A DRAMA CD!!! AT THE TIME I WRITE THIS, IT HAS NOT BEEN RECORDED YET, BUT... PERHAPS IT'S IN YOUR HANDS NOW. BUPPA BUPPA.

THERE WAS A "VOICE ACTORS YOU'D LIKE TO SEE PLAY HOST CLUB CHARACTERS" SECTION IN LALA [MAGAZINE]. BASED ON THE RESULTS OF THAT, AND MY OWN REQUESTS (LAUGH), IT'S GONNA FEATURE A VERY GLAMOROUS CAST!!!! GYAAAH!!! THANKS TO EVERYONE WHO SENT ME LETTERS. THERE WERE MANY PEOPLE WHO WROTE QUITE A BIT ABOUT ALL SEVEN VOICE ACTORS. YOU ALL KNOW TOO MUCH (LAUGH).

INTERESTINGLY, MANY PEOPLE REQUESTED THAT A MALE ACTOR DO HARUHI.

ARE YOU SERIOUS?!

LIKE HOSHI...

HOSHI IS HIKARU.

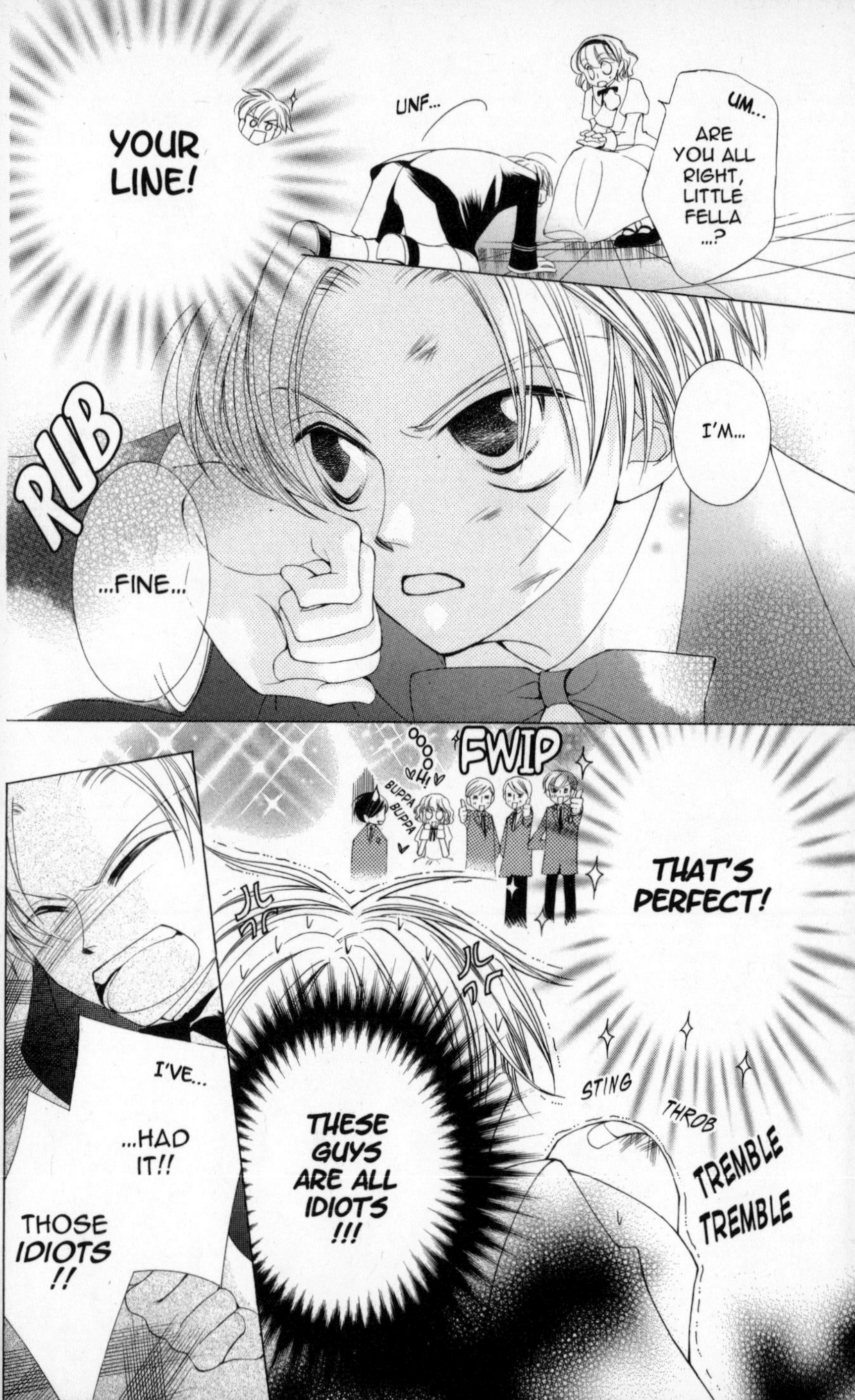
UM...
ARE YOU ALL RIGHT, LITTLE FELLA ...?
UNF...
YOUR LINE!
I'M...
RUB
...FINE...
THAT'S PERFECT!
FWIP
OOOOH!
BUPPA BUPPA
TREMBLE TREMBLE
THROB
STING
THESE GUYS ARE ALL IDIOTS !!!
I'VE...
...HAD IT!!
THOSE IDIOTS !!

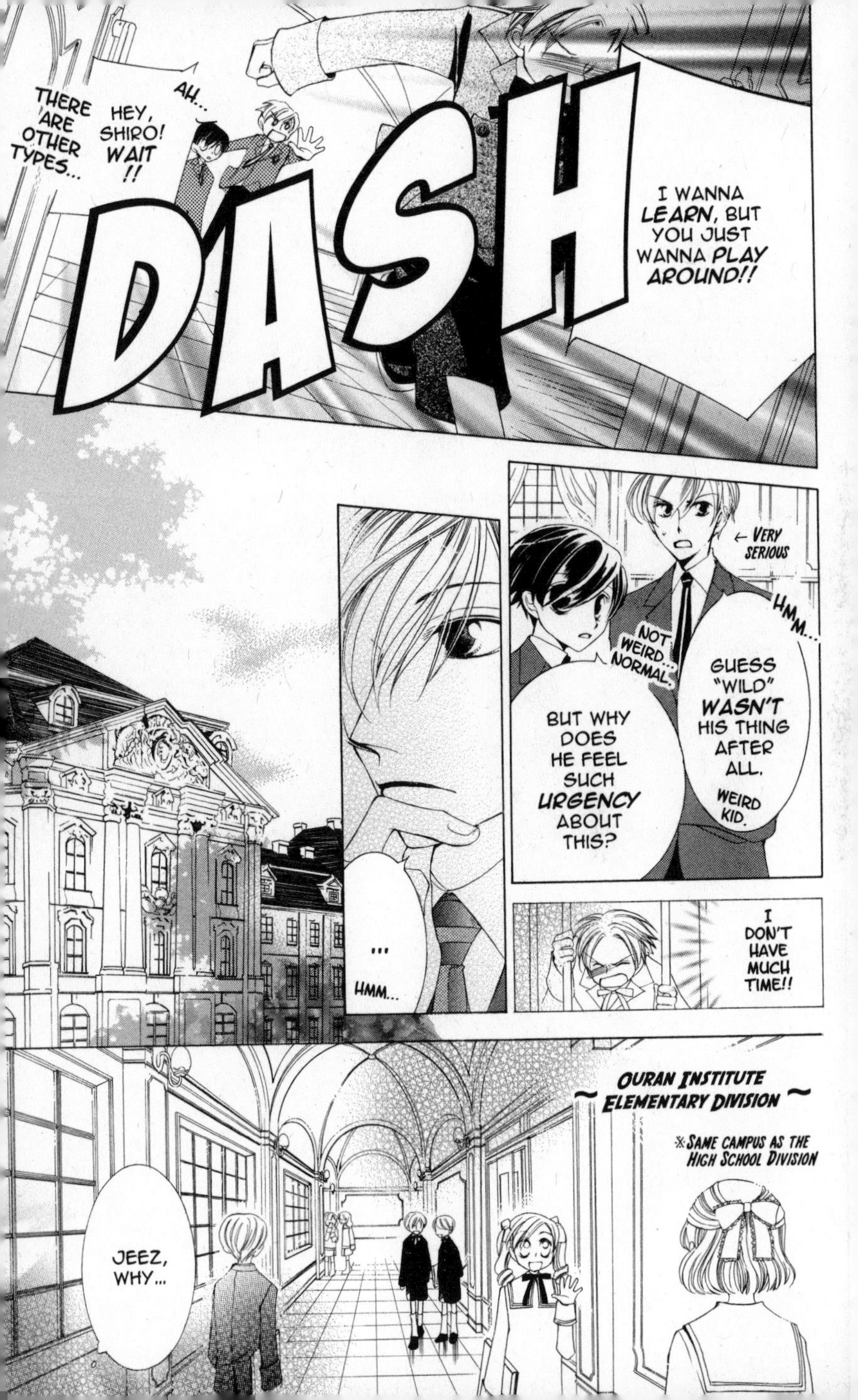
I WANNA LEARN, BUT YOU JUST WANNA PLAY AROUND!!
DASH
AH...
HEY, SHIRO! WAIT!!
THERE ARE OTHER TYPES...
← VERY SERIOUS
HMM...
GUESS "WILD" WASN'T HIS THING AFTER ALL.
WEIRD KID.
NOT WEIRD... NORMAL.
BUT WHY DOES HE FEEL SUCH URGENCY ABOUT THIS?
I DON'T HAVE MUCH TIME!!
...
HMM...
OURAN INSTITUTE ~ELEMENTARY DIVISION~
※SAME CAMPUS AS THE HIGH SCHOOL DIVISION
JEEZ, WHY...

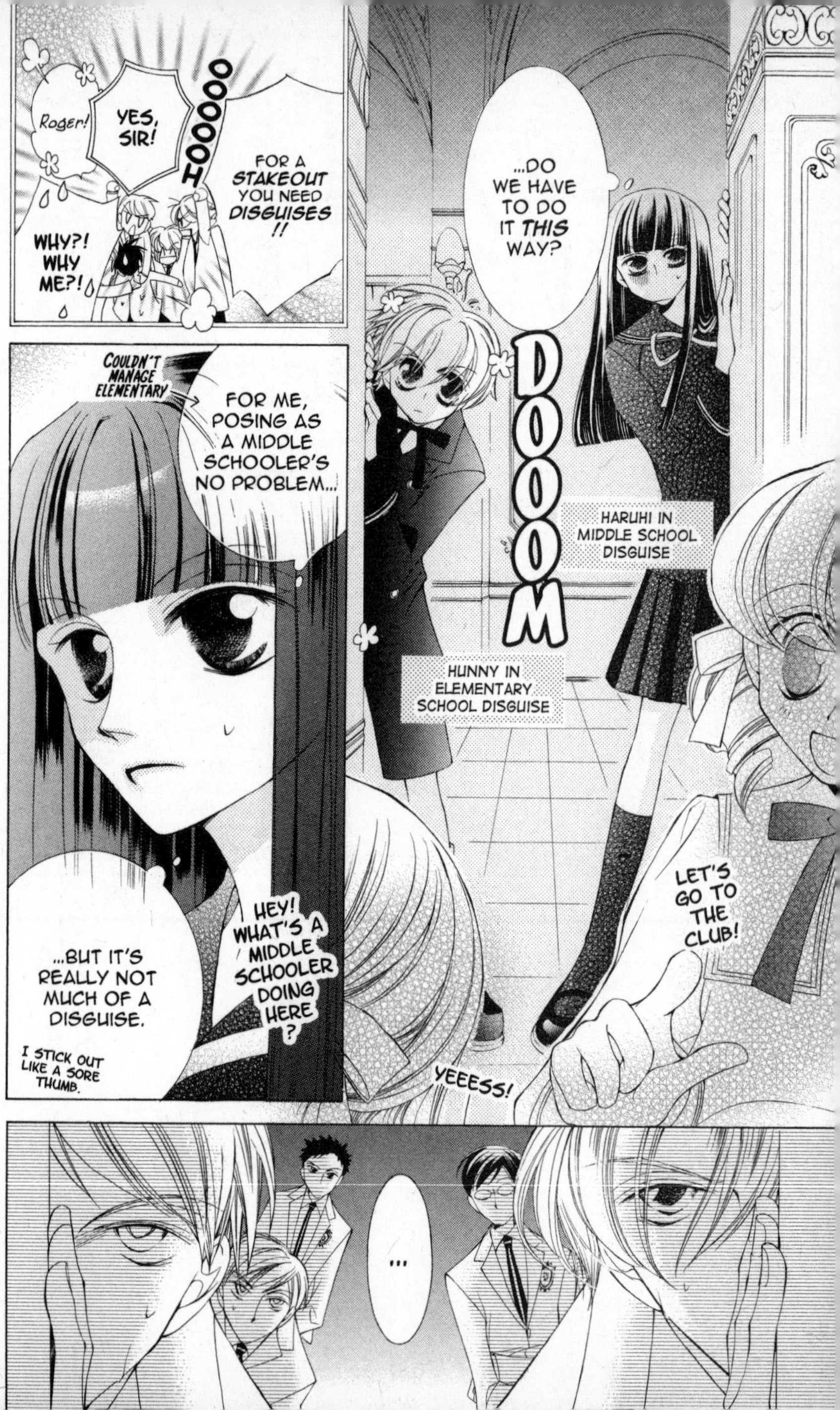
...DO WE HAVE TO DO IT THIS WAY?
DOOOOM
HARUHI IN MIDDLE SCHOOL DISGUISE
HUNNY IN ELEMENTARY SCHOOL DISGUISE
LET'S GO TO THE CLUB!
YEEESS!
Roger!
YES, SIR!
HOOOOOO
FOR A STAKEOUT YOU NEED DISGUISES!!
WHY?! WHY ME?!
COULDN'T MANAGE ELEMENTARY
FOR ME, POSING AS A MIDDLE SCHOOLER'S NO PROBLEM...
HEY! WHAT'S A MIDDLE SCHOOLER DOING HERE?
...BUT IT'S REALLY NOT MUCH OF A DISGUISE.
I STICK OUT LIKE A SORE THUMB.
...

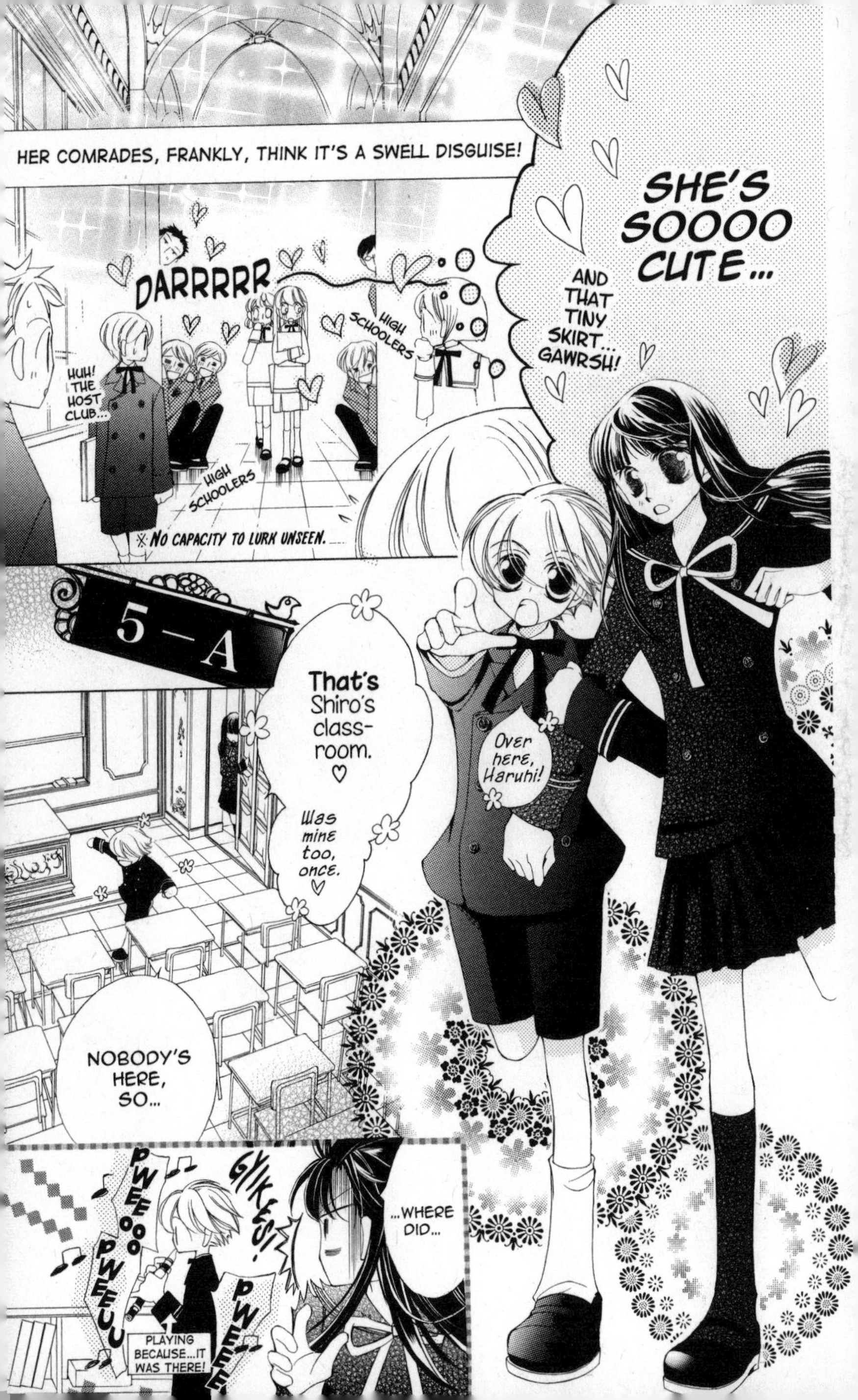
HER COMRADES, FRANKLY, THINK IT'S A SWELL DISGUISE!
SHE'S SOOOO CUTE...
AND THAT TINY SKIRT... GAWRSH!
HIGH SCHOOLERS
DARRRRR
HUH! THE HOST CLUB...
HIGH SCHOOLERS
※No capacity to lurk unseen.
Over here, Haruhi!
5-A
That's Shiro's class-room. ♡
Was mine too, once. ♡
NOBODY'S HERE, SO...
...WHERE DID...
GYIKES!
PWEEE
PWEEOOO
PWEEUU
PLAYING BECAUSE...IT WAS THERE!

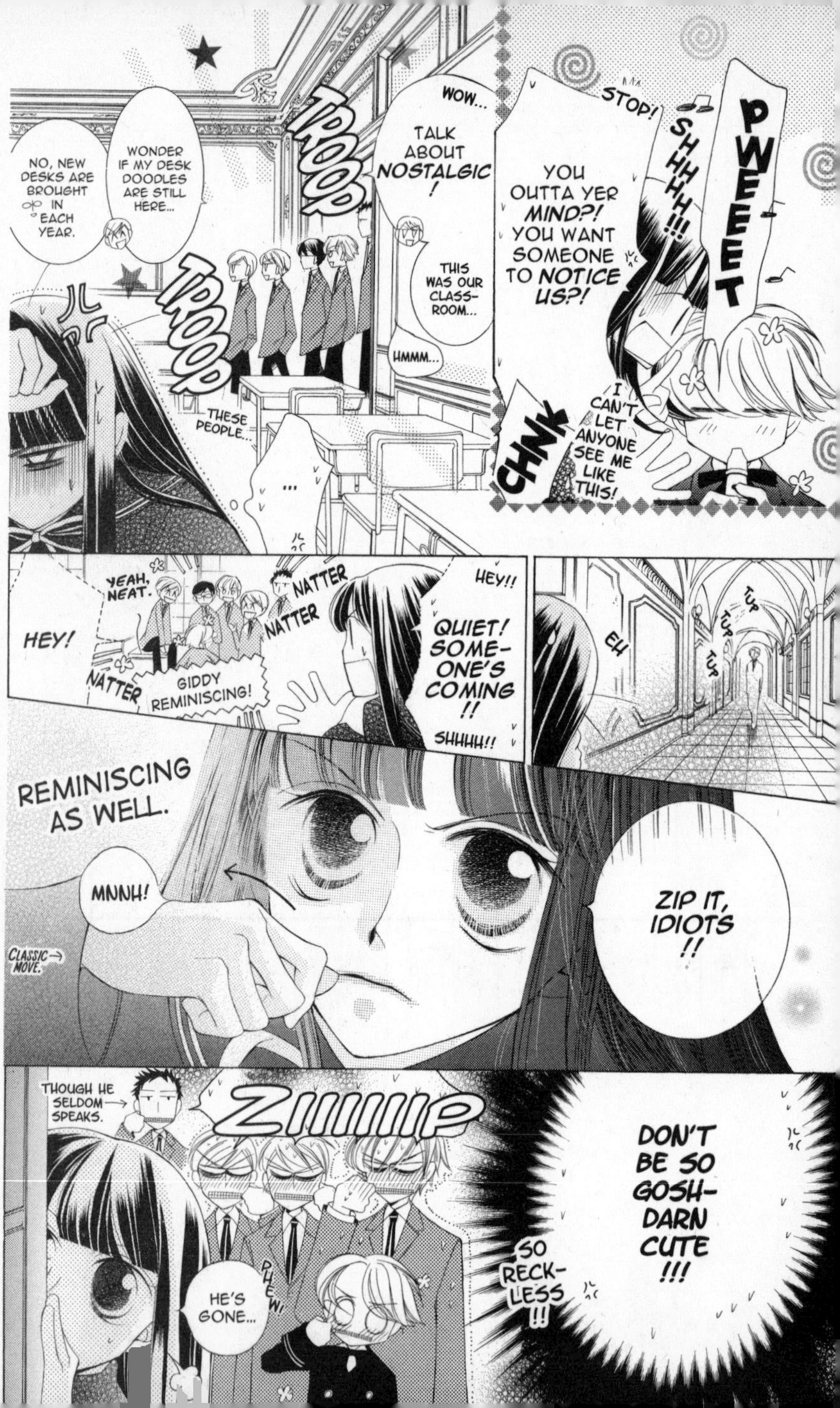
STOP!
PWEEET
SHHHH!!!
YOU OUTTA YER MIND?! YOU WANT SOMEONE TO NOTICE US?!
CHNK
I CAN'T LET ANYONE SEE ME LIKE THIS!
WOW...
TALK ABOUT NOSTALGIC!
TROOP
THIS WAS OUR CLASSROOM...
HMMM...
WONDER IF MY DESK DOODLES ARE STILL HERE...
NO, NEW DESKS ARE BROUGHT IN EACH YEAR.
TROOP
THESE PEOPLE...
...
TUP TUP TUP
EH
HEY!!
QUIET! SOMEONE'S COMING!!
SHHHH!!
NATTER
NATTER
YEAH, NEAT.
HEY!
NATTER
GIDDY REMINISCING!
ZIP IT, IDIOTS!!
REMINISCING AS WELL.
MNNH!
CLASSIC MOVE.
DON'T BE SO GOSH-DARN CUTE!!!
SO RECKLESS!!
ZIIIIIIP
THOUGH HE SELDOM SPEAKS.
PHEW!
HE'S GONE...

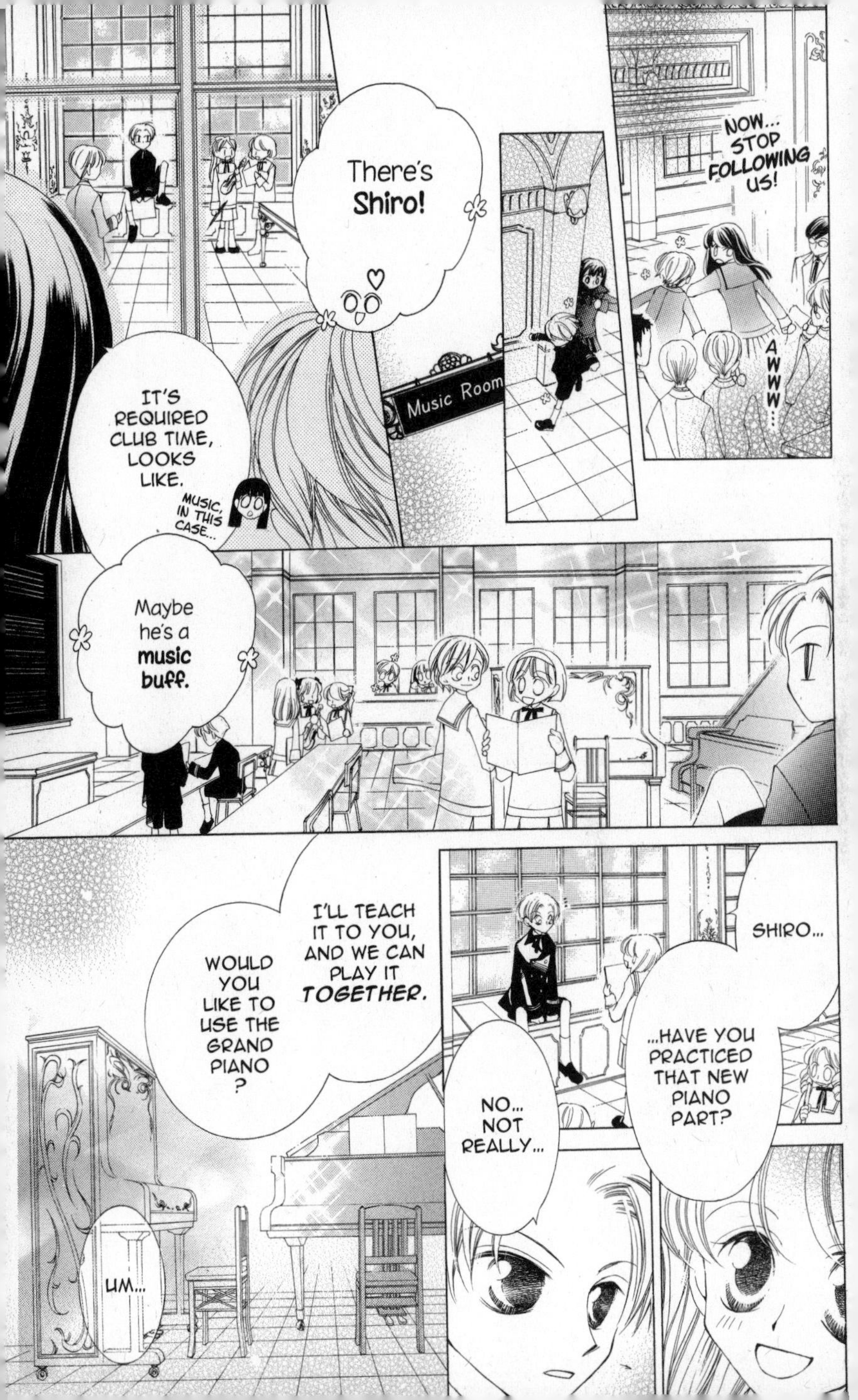
NOW... STOP FOLLOWING US!
AWWW...
Music Room
There's Shiro!
IT'S REQUIRED CLUB TIME, LOOKS LIKE.
MUSIC, IN THIS CASE...
Maybe he's a music buff.
SHIRO...
...HAVE YOU PRACTICED THAT NEW PIANO PART?
NO... NOT REALLY...
I'LL TEACH IT TO YOU, AND WE CAN PLAY IT TOGETHER.
WOULD YOU LIKE TO USE THE GRAND PIANO?
UM...

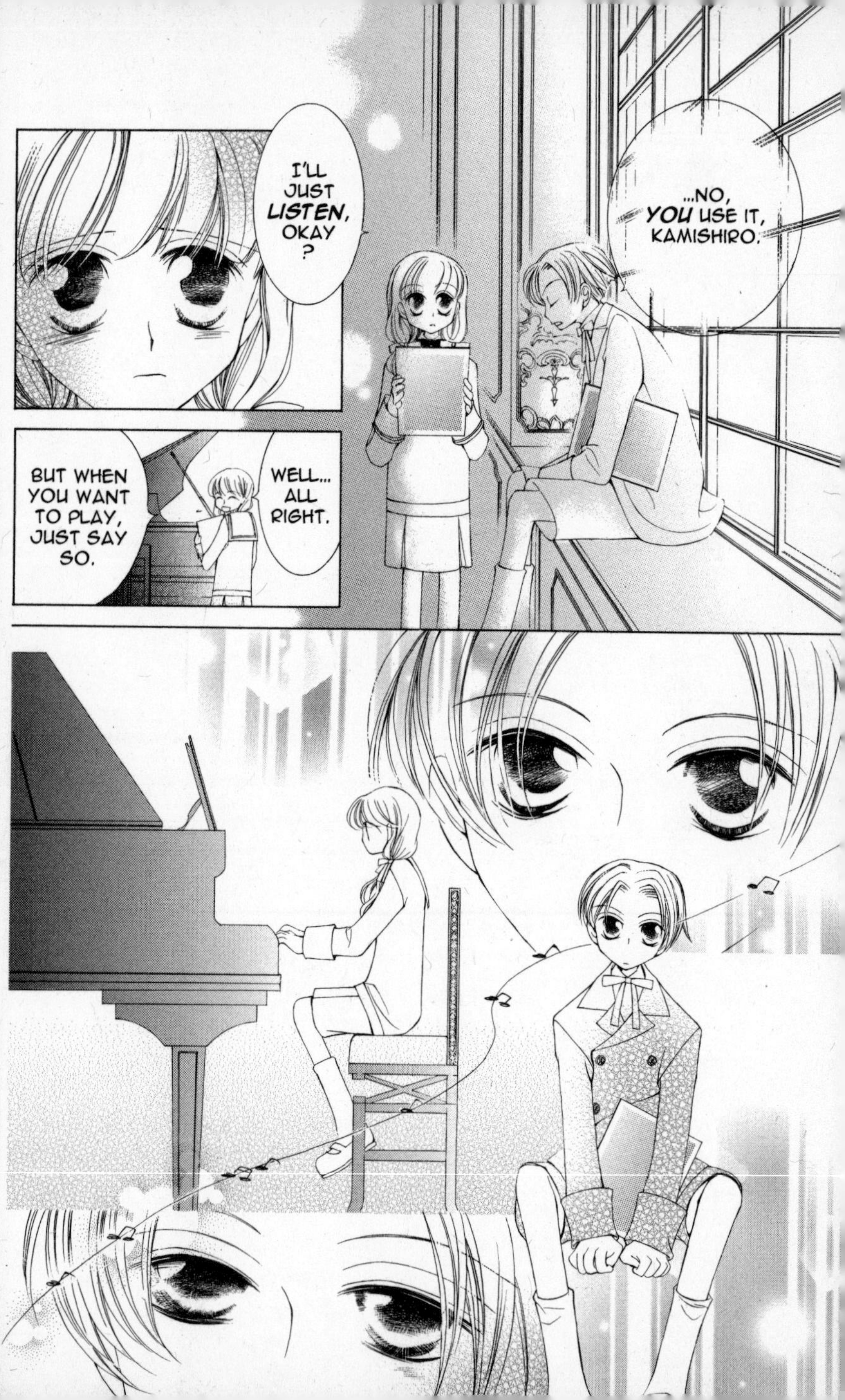
...NO, YOU USE IT, KAMISHIRO.
I'LL JUST LISTEN, OKAY?
WELL... ALL RIGHT.
BUT WHEN YOU WANT TO PLAY, JUST SAY SO.

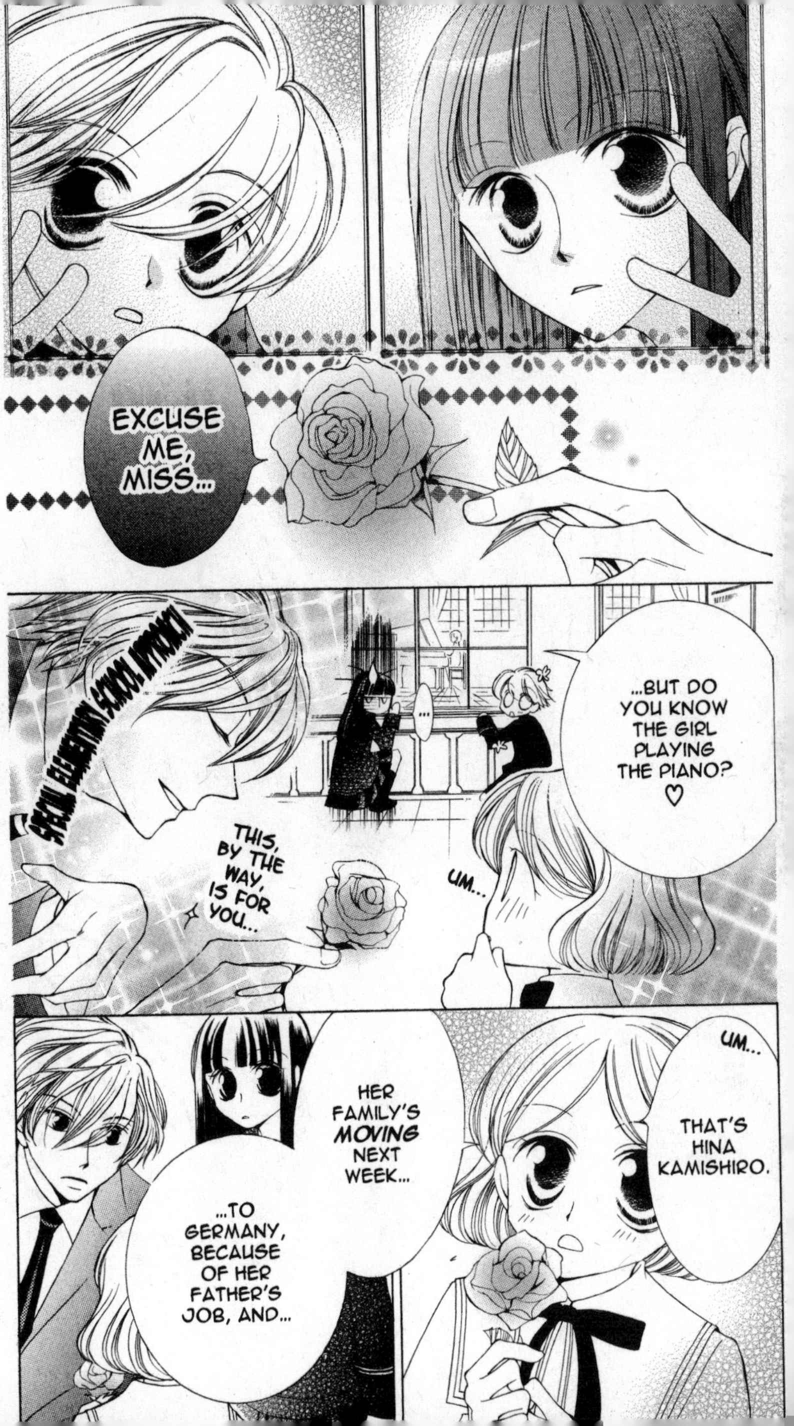
EXCUSE ME, MISS...
...BUT DO YOU KNOW THE GIRL PLAYING THE PIANO? ♡
...
SPECIAL ELEMENTARY SCHOOL APPROACH
UM...
THIS, BY THE WAY, IS FOR YOU...
UM...
THAT'S HINA KAMISHIRO.
HER FAMILY'S *MOVING* NEXT WEEK...
...TO GERMANY, BECAUSE OF HER FATHER'S JOB, AND...

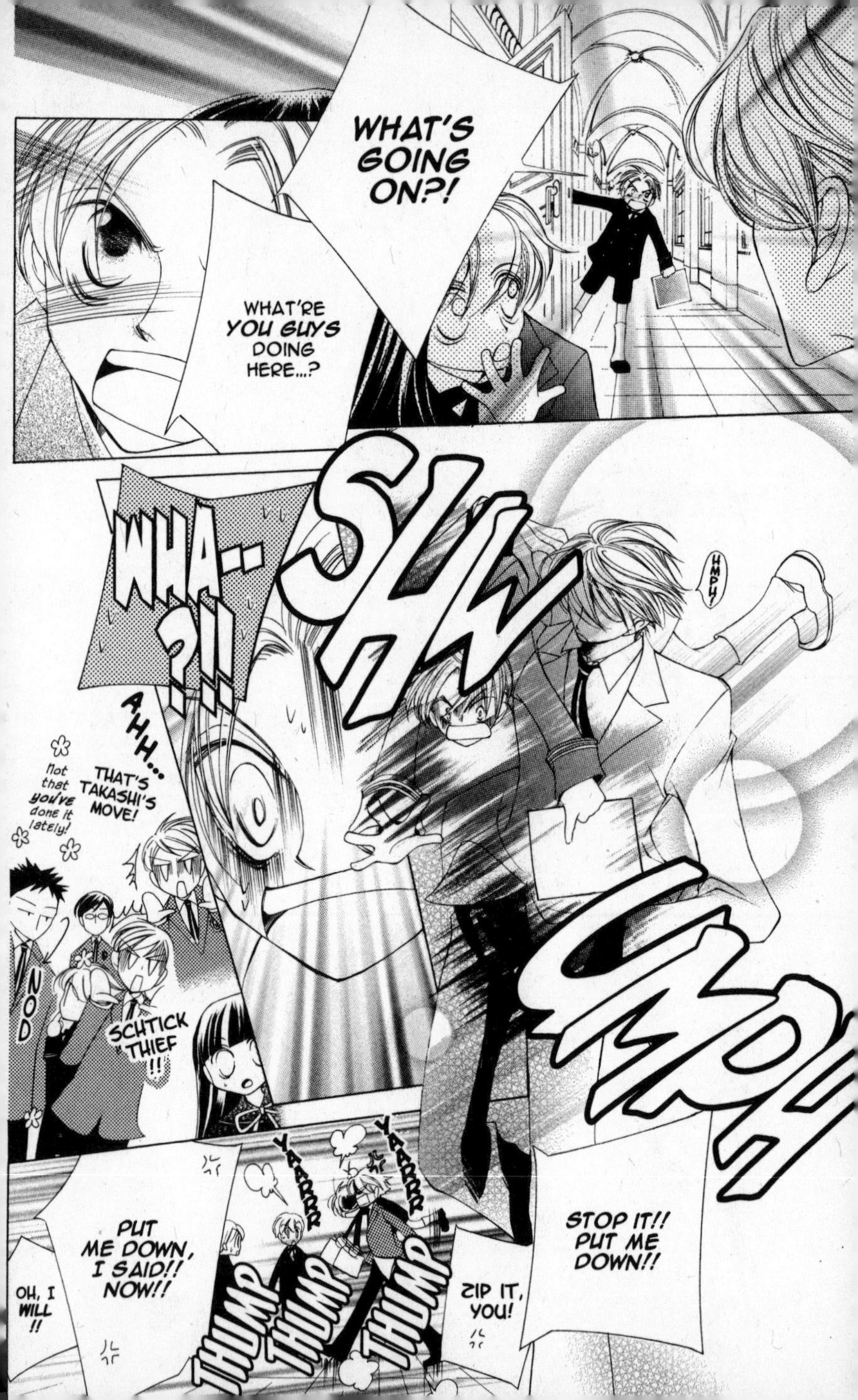
WHAT'S GOING ON?!
WHAT'RE YOU GUYS DOING HERE...?
SHW
HMPH!
UMPH
WHA...?!!
AHH... THAT'S TAKASHI'S MOVE!
Not that you've done it lately!
SCHTICK THIEF!!
NOD
STOP IT!! PUT ME DOWN!!
ZIP IT, YOU!
YAARRRR
YAARRRR
THUMP
THUMP
THUMP
PUT ME DOWN, I SAID!! NOW!!
OH, I WILL!!

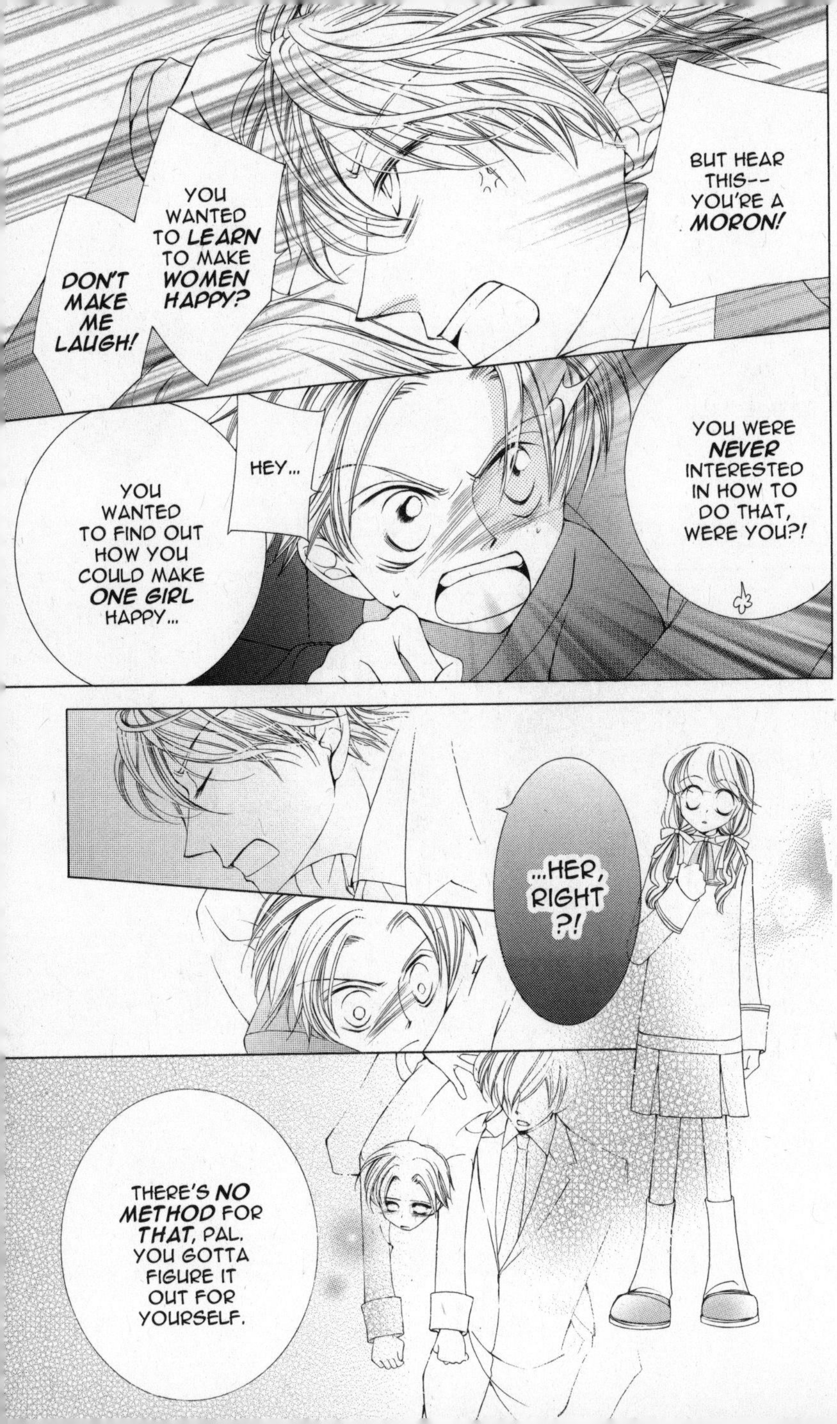
BUT HEAR THIS-- YOU'RE A **MORON!**
YOU WANTED TO **LEARN** TO MAKE **WOMEN HAPPY?**
DON'T MAKE ME LAUGH!
YOU WERE **NEVER** INTERESTED IN HOW TO DO THAT, WERE YOU?!
HEY...
YOU WANTED TO FIND OUT HOW YOU COULD MAKE **ONE GIRL** HAPPY...
...HER, RIGHT?!
THERE'S **NO METHOD** FOR **THAT,** PAL. YOU GOTTA FIGURE IT OUT FOR YOURSELF.

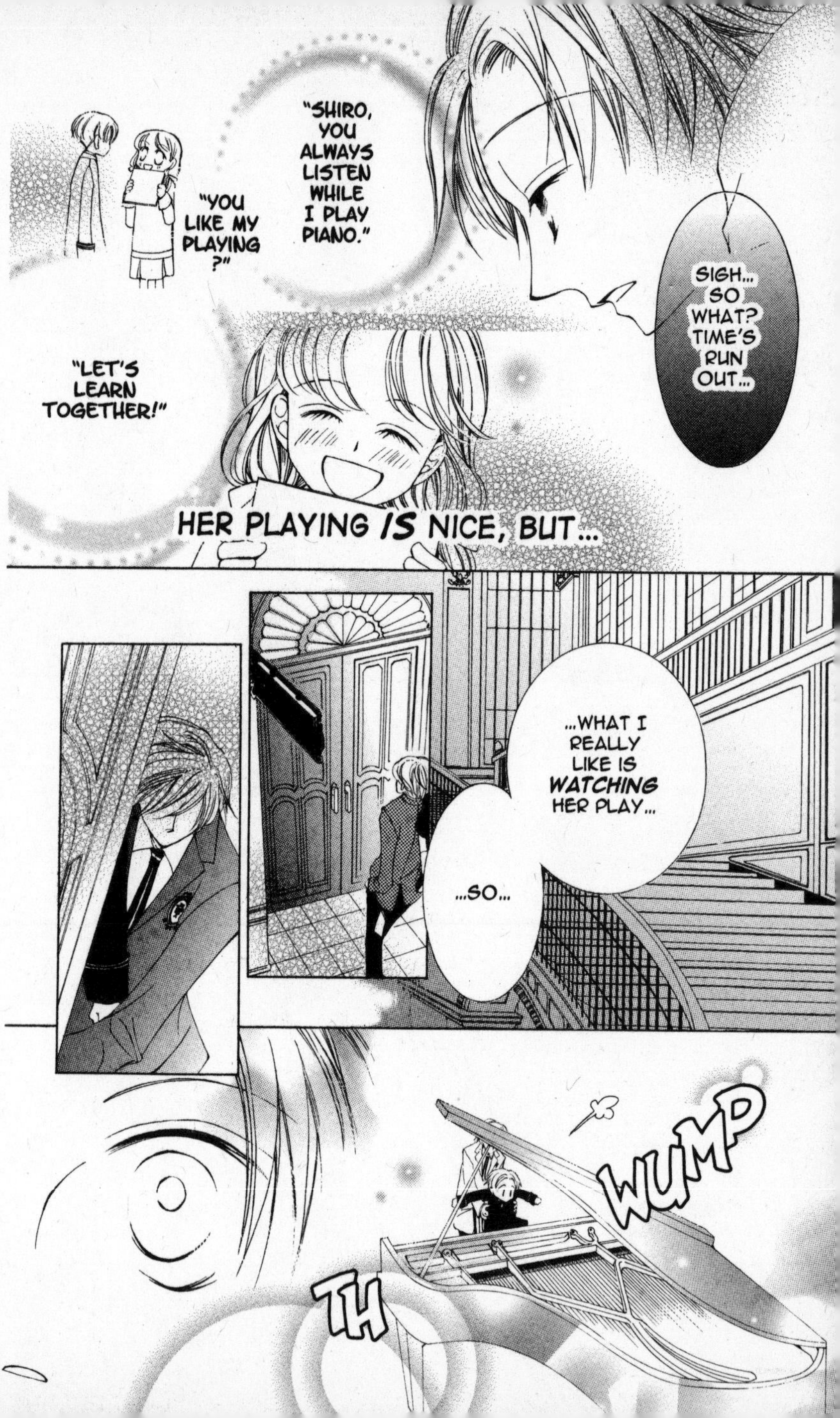
SIGH... SO WHAT? TIME'S RUN OUT...
"SHIRO, YOU ALWAYS LISTEN WHILE I PLAY PIANO."
"YOU LIKE MY PLAYING?"
"LET'S LEARN TOGETHER!"
HER PLAYING *IS* NICE, BUT...
...WHAT I REALLY LIKE IS *WATCHING* HER PLAY...
...SO...
WUMP
TH

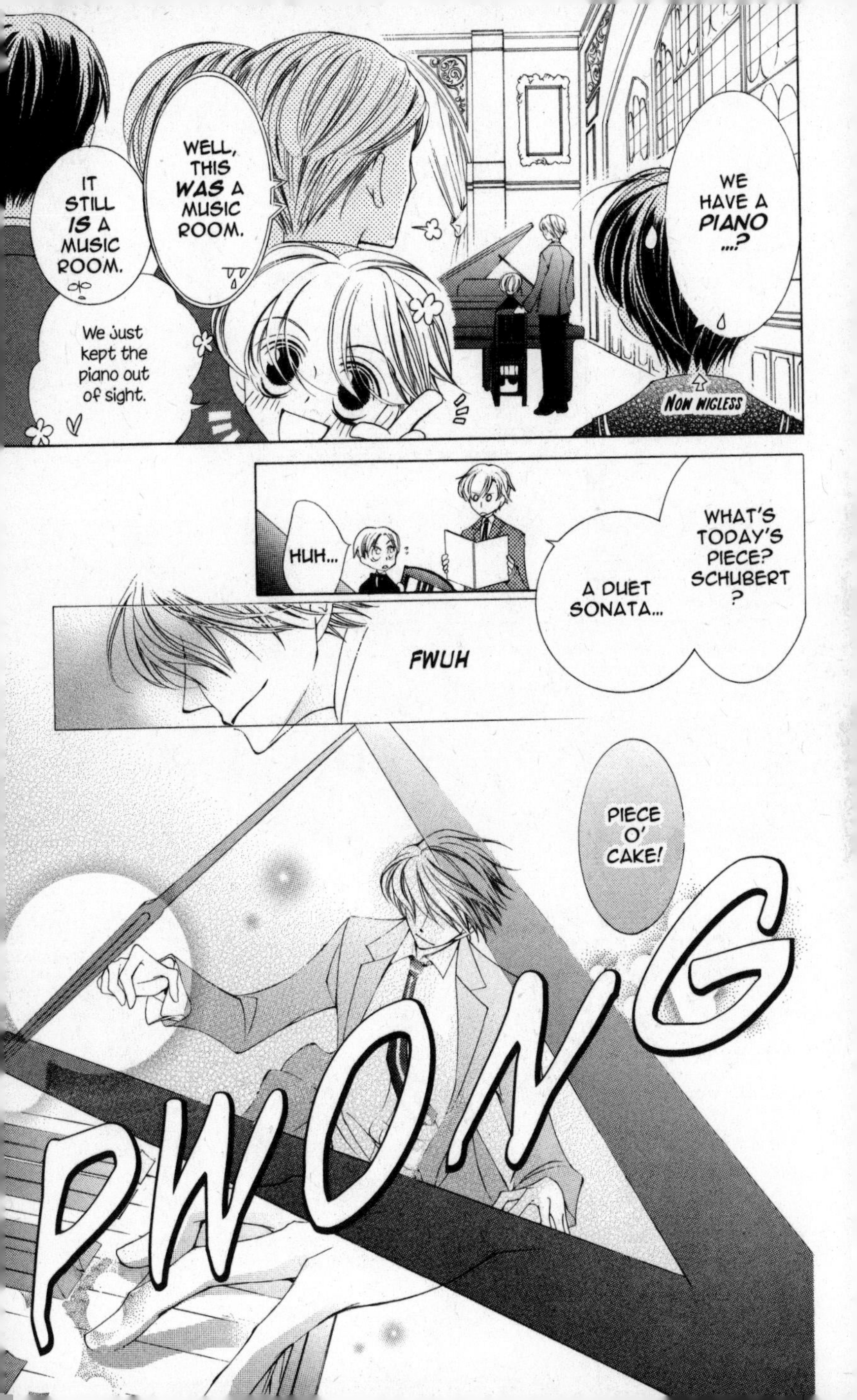
WE HAVE A PIANO ...?
NOW WIGLESS
WELL, THIS WAS A MUSIC ROOM.
IT STILL IS A MUSIC ROOM.
We just kept the piano out of sight.
WHAT'S TODAY'S PIECE? SCHUBERT ?
A DUET SONATA...
HUH...
FWUH
PIECE O' CAKE!
PWONG

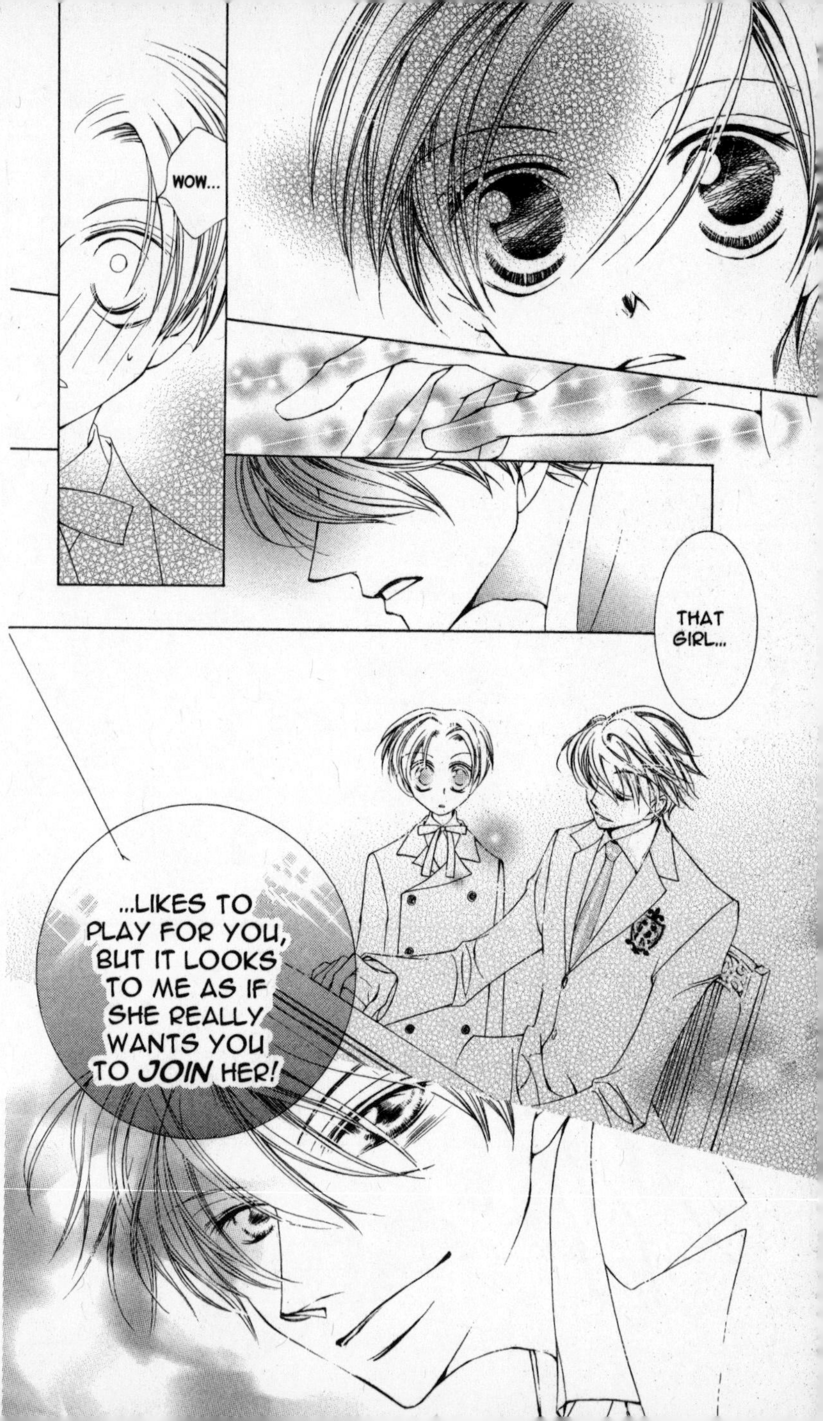
WOW...
THAT GIRL...
...LIKES TO PLAY FOR YOU, BUT IT LOOKS TO ME AS IF SHE REALLY WANTS YOU TO JOIN HER!

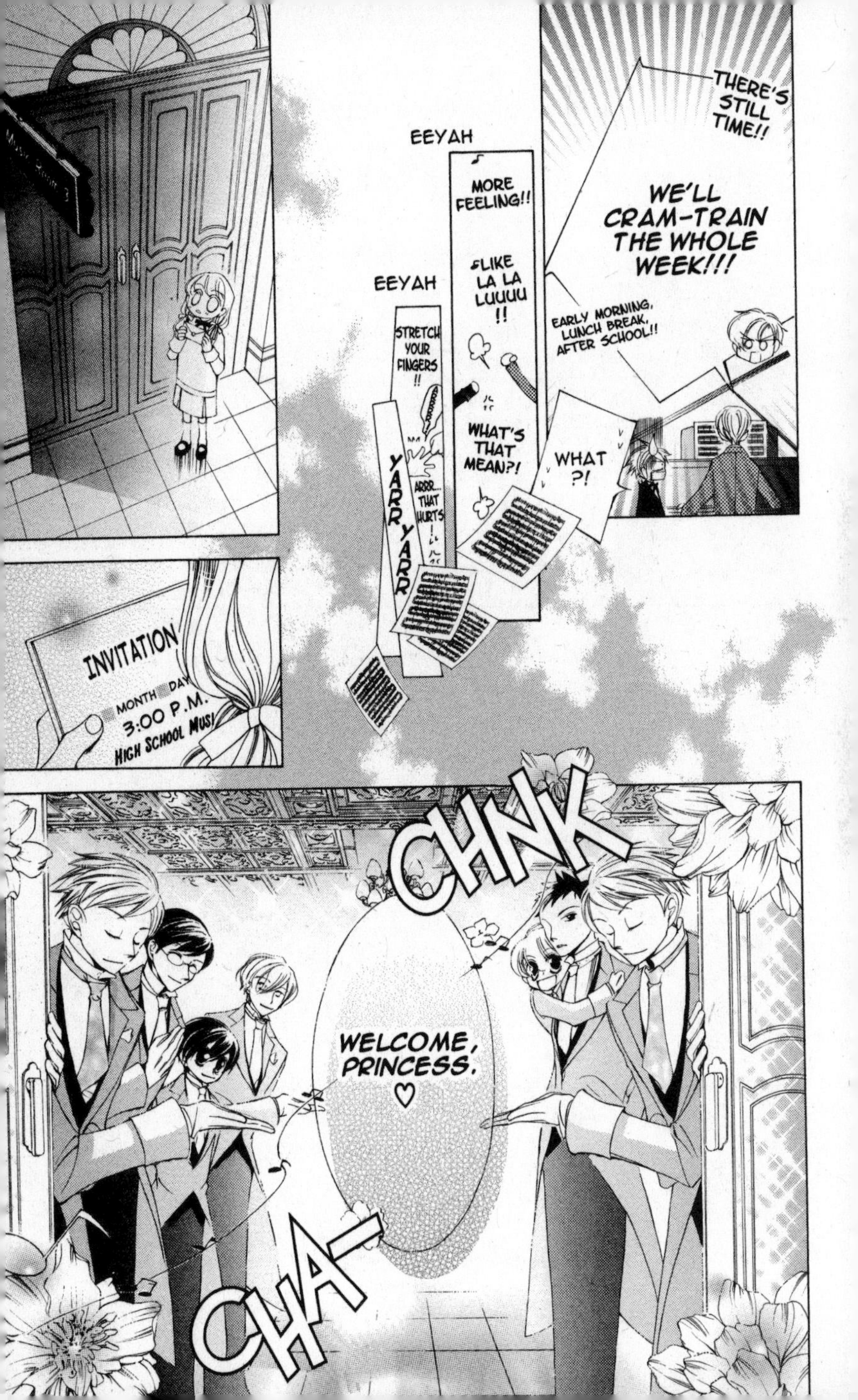
THERE'S STILL TIME!!
WE'LL CRAM-TRAIN THE WHOLE WEEK!!!
EARLY MORNING, LUNCH BREAK, AFTER SCHOOL!!
WHAT ?!
EEYAH
MORE FEELING!!
LIKE LA LA LUUUU !!
WHAT'S THAT MEAN?!
EEYAH
STRETCH YOUR FINGERS !!
YARR YARR
ARRR... THAT HURTS
INVITATION
MONTH DAY
3:00 P.M.
HIGH SCHOOL MUSI
CHA-
CHNK
WELCOME, PRINCESS. ♡

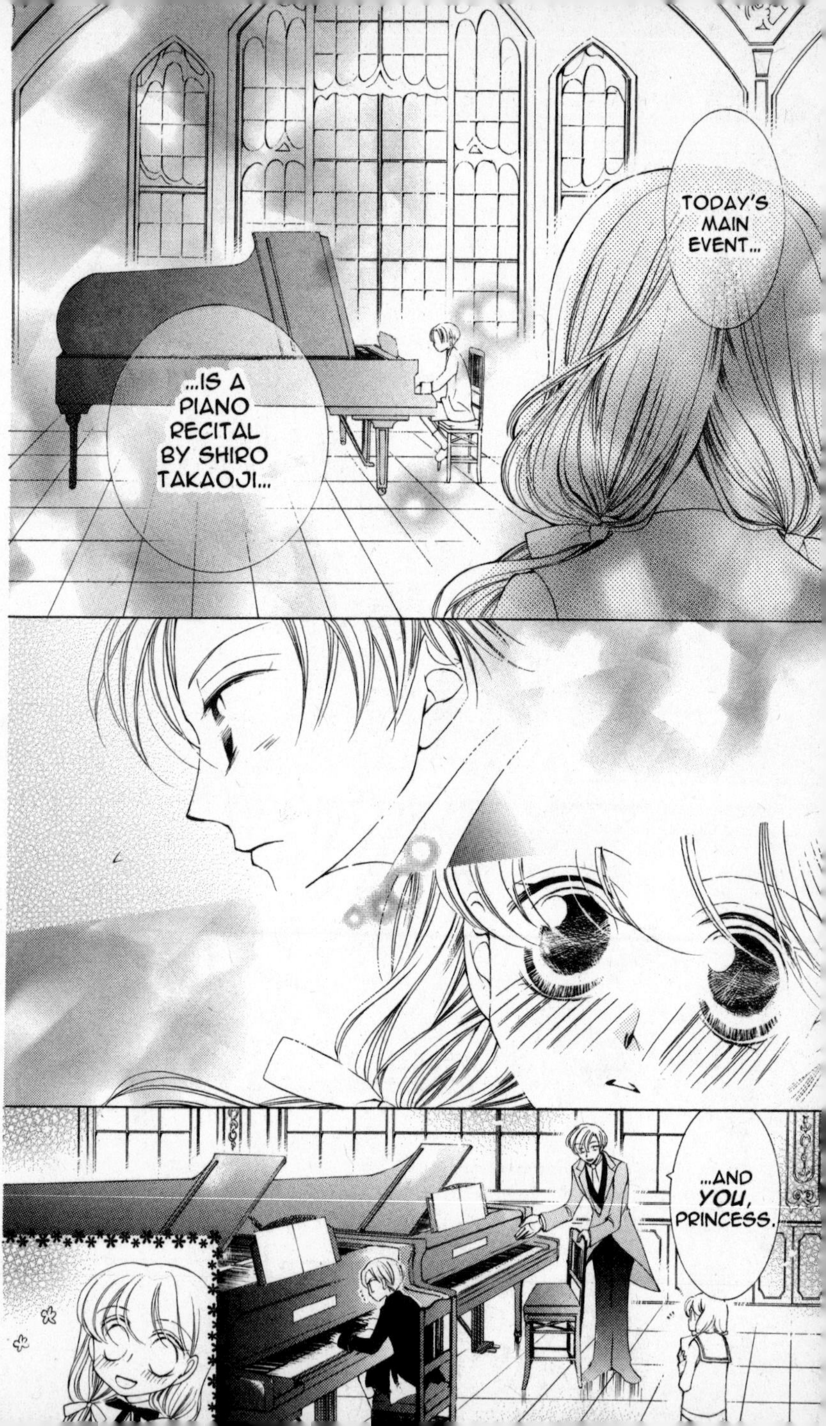
TODAY'S MAIN EVENT...
...IS A PIANO RECITAL BY SHIRO TAKAOJI...
...AND YOU, PRINCESS.

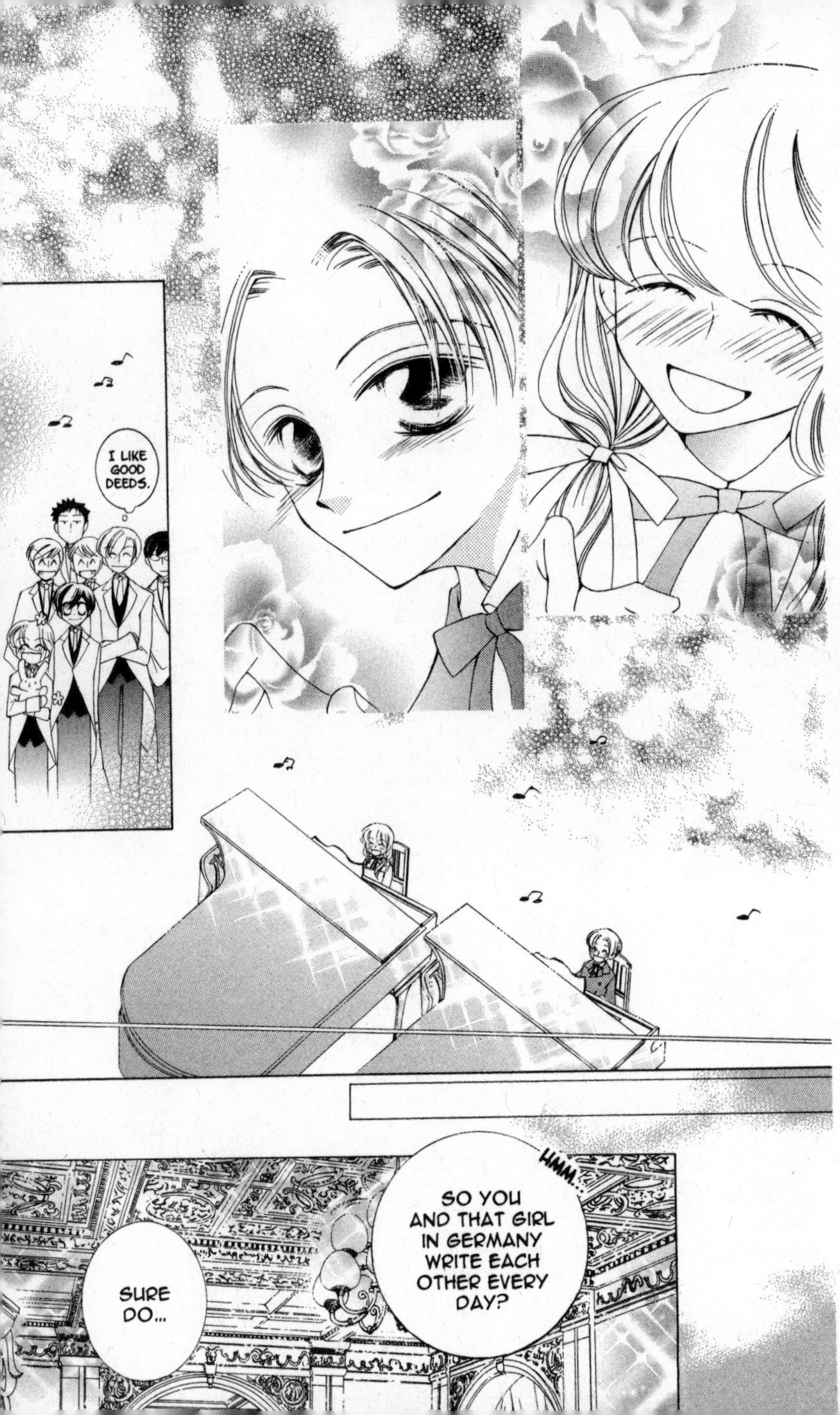
I LIKE GOOD DEEDS.
HMM...
SO YOU AND THAT GIRL IN GERMANY WRITE EACH OTHER EVERY DAY?
SURE DO...

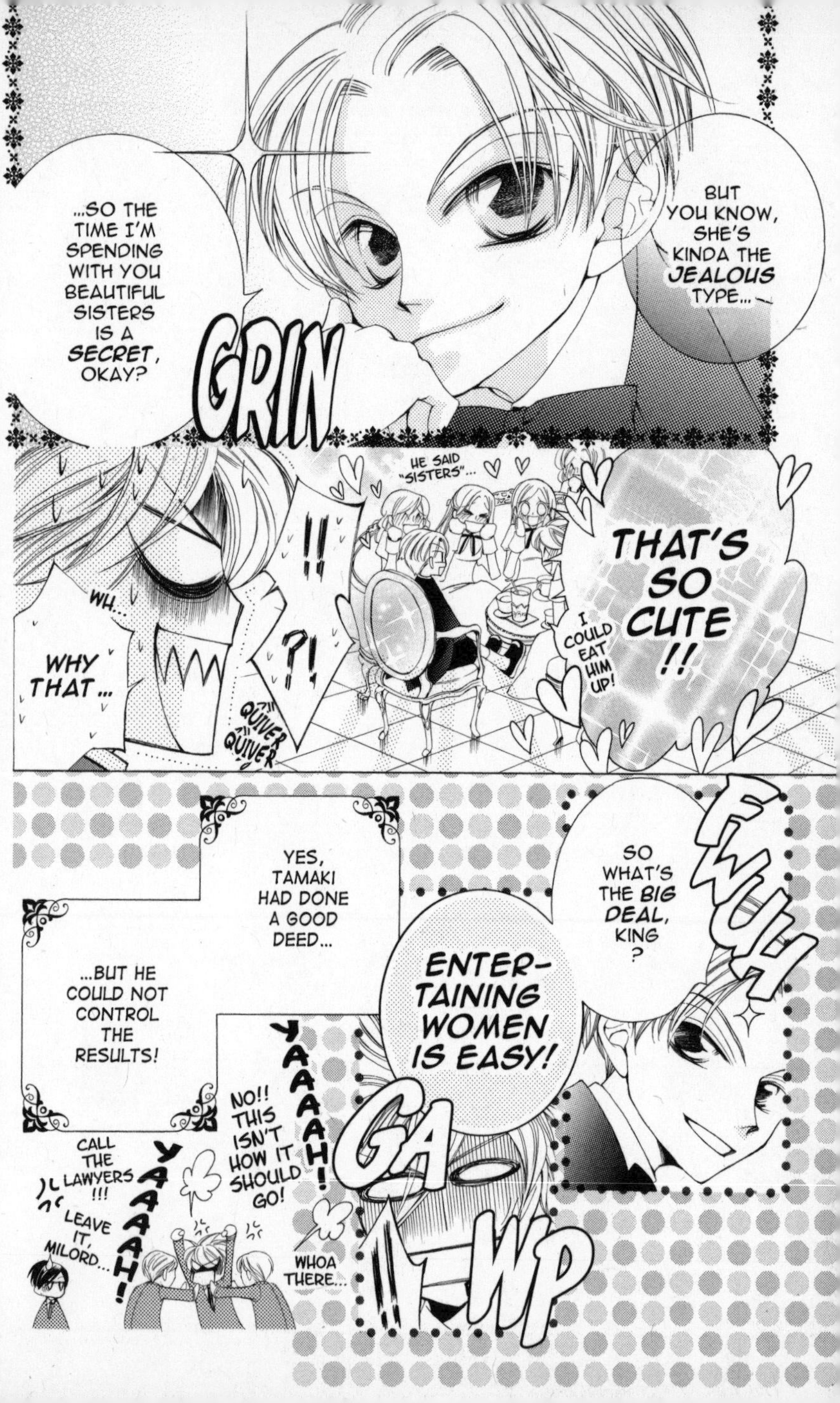
BUT YOU KNOW, SHE'S KINDA THE JEALOUS TYPE...
...SO THE TIME I'M SPENDING WITH YOU BEAUTIFUL SISTERS IS A SECRET, OKAY?
GRIN
THAT'S SO CUTE!!
I COULD EAT HIM UP!
HE SAID "SISTERS"...
!!
?!
QUIVER QUIVER
WH...
WHY THAT...
FWUH
SO WHAT'S THE BIG DEAL, KING?
ENTER-TAINING WOMEN IS EASY!
GA
WP
YES, TAMAKI HAD DONE A GOOD DEED...
...BUT HE COULD NOT CONTROL THE RESULTS!
YAAAAAH!
NO!! THIS ISN'T HOW IT SHOULD GO!
WHOA THERE...
YAAAAAH!
CALL THE LAWYERS!!!
LEAVE IT, MILORD...

BREAK TIME THEATER THE OURAN BATTLEGROUND

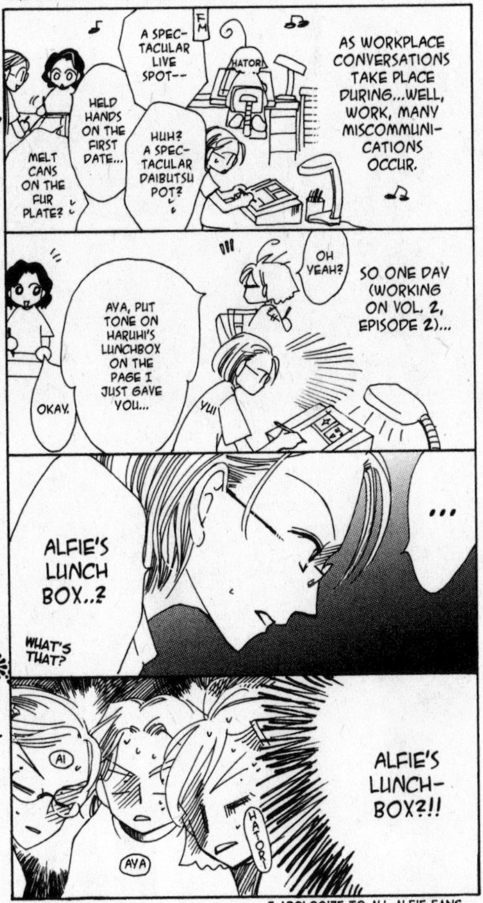
AS WORKPLACE CONVERSATIONS TAKE PLACE DURING...WELL, WORK, MANY MISCOMMUNICATIONS OCCUR.
A SPECTACULAR LIVE SPOT--
FM
HATORI
HUH? A SPECTACULAR DAIBUTSU POT?
HELD HANDS ON THE FIRST DATE...
AI→
MELT CANS ON THE FUR PLATE?
SO ONE DAY (WORKING ON VOL. 2, EPISODE 2)...
OH YEAH?
AYA, PUT TONE ON HARUHI'S LUNCHBOX ON THE PAGE I JUST GAVE YOU...
YUI
AYA→
OKAY.
...
ALFIE'S LUNCH BOX..?
WHAT'S THAT?
ALFIE'S LUNCH-BOX?!!
HATORI
AI
AYA

I APOLOGIZE TO ALL ALFIE FANS...

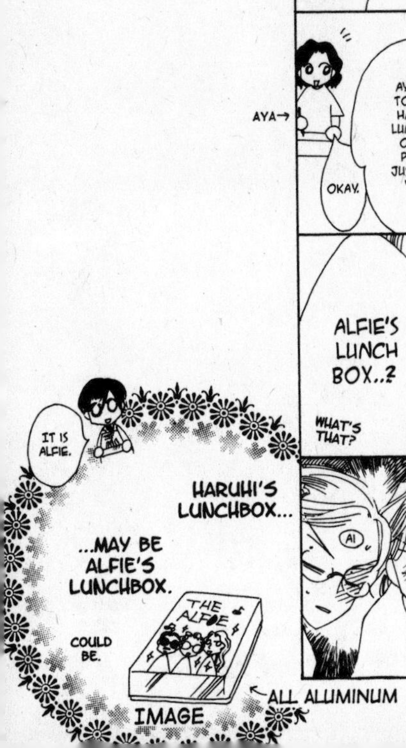
IT IS ALFIE.
HARUHI'S LUNCHBOX...
...MAY BE ALFIE'S LUNCHBOX.
THE ALFIE
COULD BE.
←ALL ALUMINUM
IMAGE

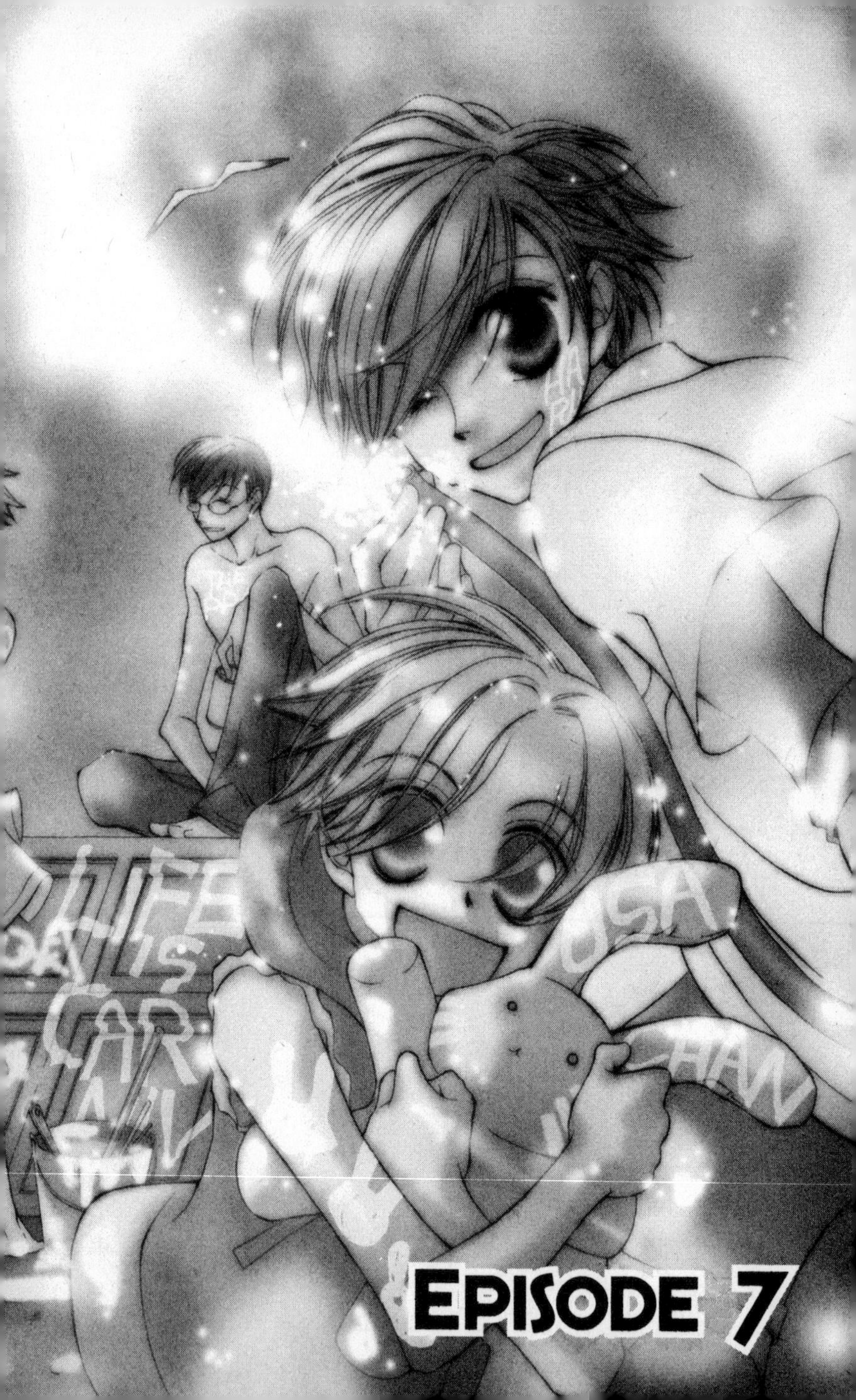
EPISODE 7

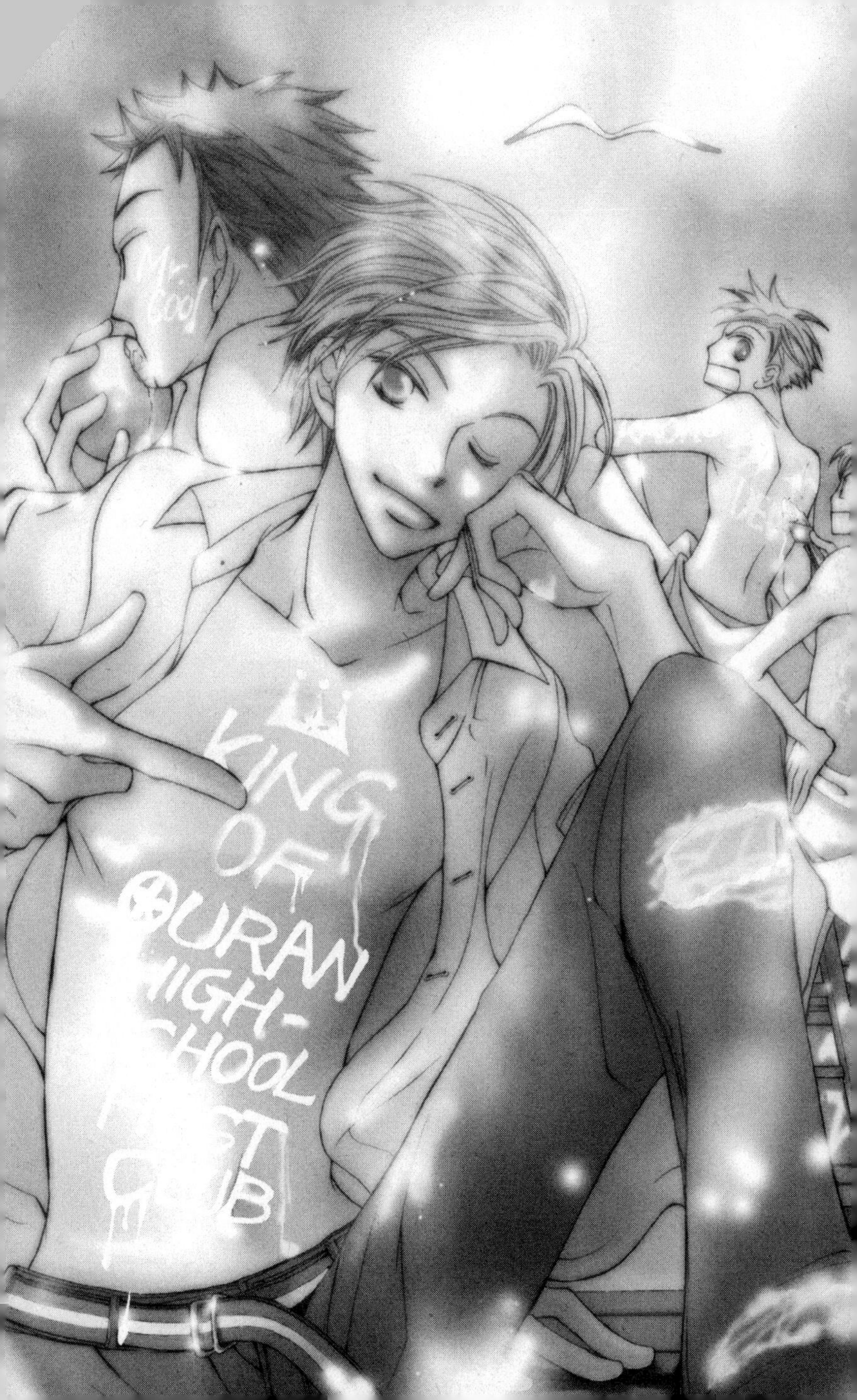
Mr. Cool
KING OF

OURAN THEATER OF LOVE ~ THE SUOH FAMILY STORY ~ (3)

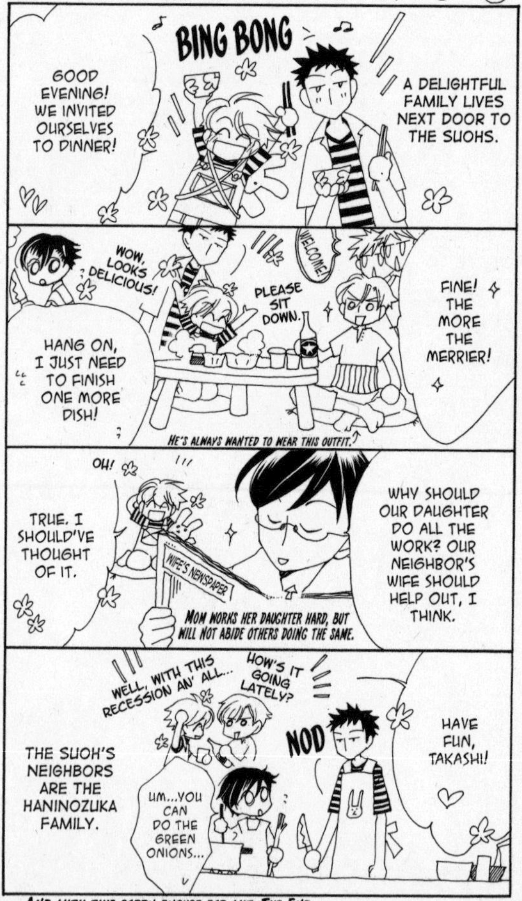
A DELIGHTFUL FAMILY LIVES NEXT DOOR TO THE SUOHS.
BING BONG
GOOD EVENING! WE INVITED OURSELVES TO DINNER!
FINE! THE MORE THE MERRIER!
WELCOME!
PLEASE SIT DOWN.
WOW, LOOKS DELICIOUS!
HANG ON, I JUST NEED TO FINISH ONE MORE DISH!
HE'S ALWAYS WANTED TO WEAR THIS OUTFIT.
WHY SHOULD OUR DAUGHTER DO ALL THE WORK? OUR NEIGHBOR'S WIFE SHOULD HELP OUT, I THINK.
OH!
WIFE'S NEWSPAPER
TRUE. I SHOULD'VE THOUGHT OF IT.
MOM WORKS HER DAUGHTER HARD, BUT WILL NOT ABIDE OTHERS DOING THE SAME.
HAVE FUN, TAKASHI!
HOW'S IT GOING LATELY?
WELL, WITH THIS RECESSION AN' ALL...
NOD
THE SUOH'S NEIGHBORS ARE THE HANINOZUKA FAMILY.
UM...YOU CAN DO THE GREEN ONIONS...

AND WITH THIS SORRY EXCUSE FOR WIT–THE END.

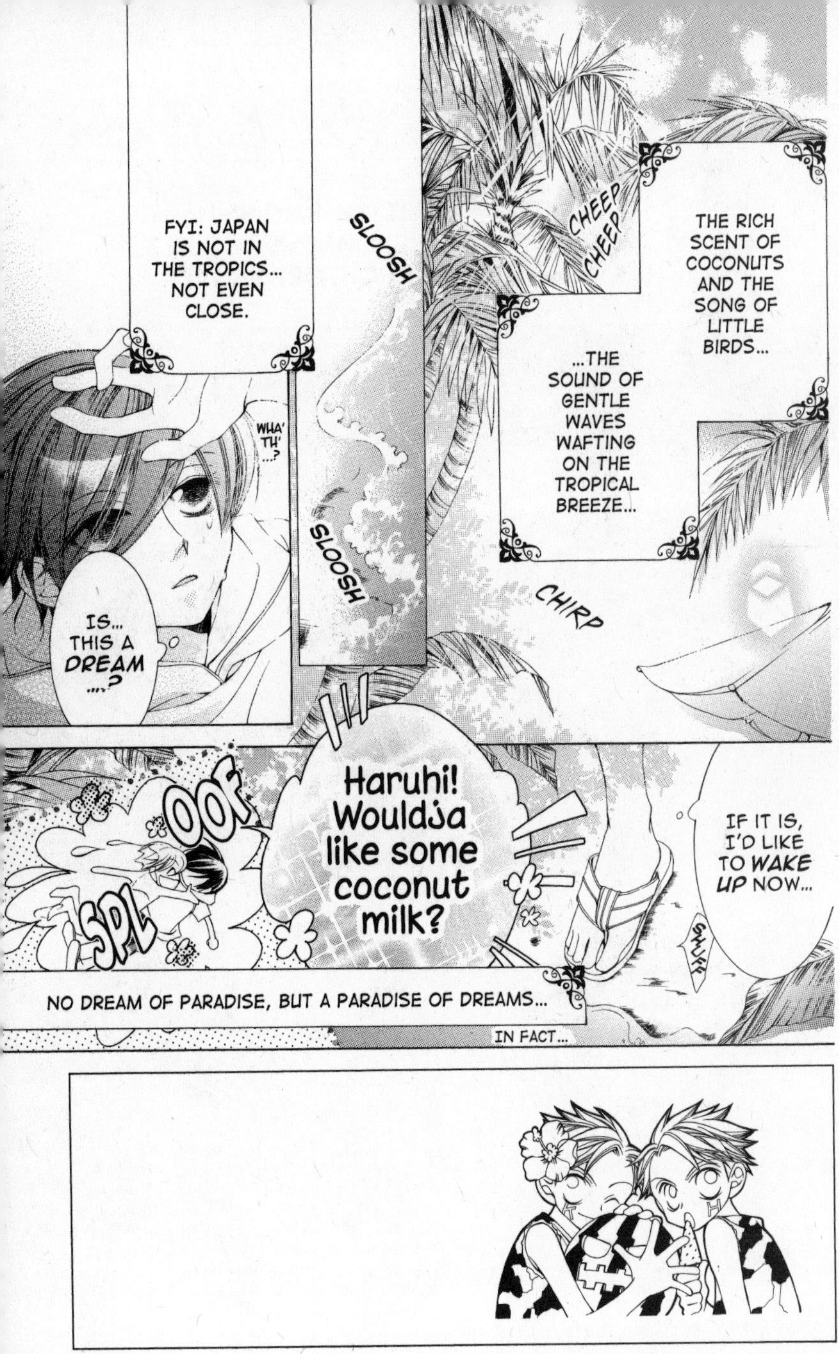

THE RICH SCENT OF COCONUTS AND THE SONG OF LITTLE BIRDS...
CHEEP CHEEP
...THE SOUND OF GENTLE WAVES WAFTING ON THE TROPICAL BREEZE...
CHIRP
SLOOSH
SLOOSH
FYI: JAPAN IS NOT IN THE TROPICS... NOT EVEN CLOSE.
WHA' TH' ...?
IS... THIS A *DREAM* ...?
IF IT IS, I'D LIKE TO ***WAKE UP*** NOW...
SHUFF
Haruhi! Wouldja like some coconut milk?
OOF
SPL
NO DREAM OF PARADISE, BUT A PARADISE OF DREAMS...
IN FACT...

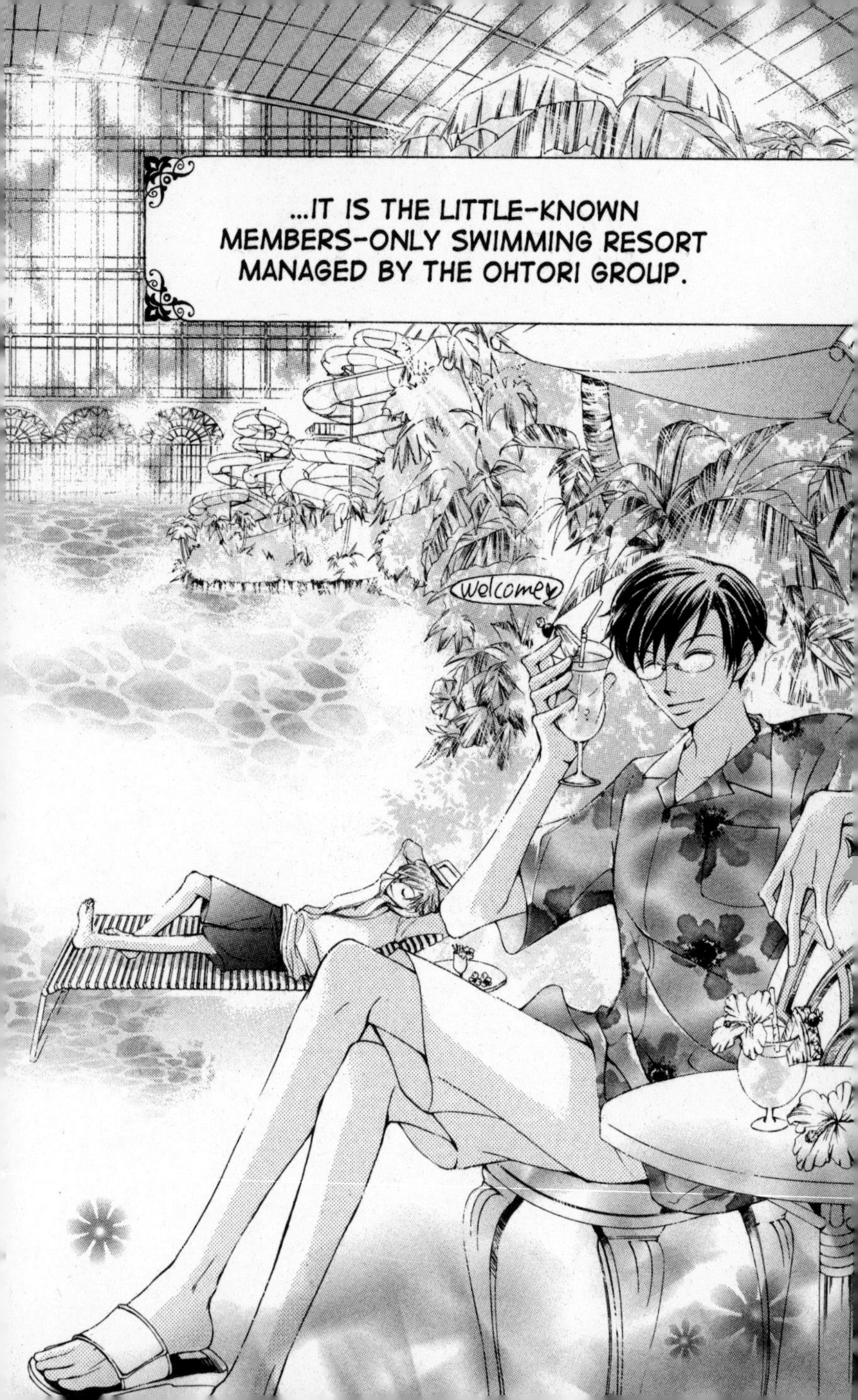
...IT IS THE LITTLE-KNOWN MEMBERS-ONLY SWIMMING RESORT MANAGED BY THE OHTORI GROUP.
Welcome

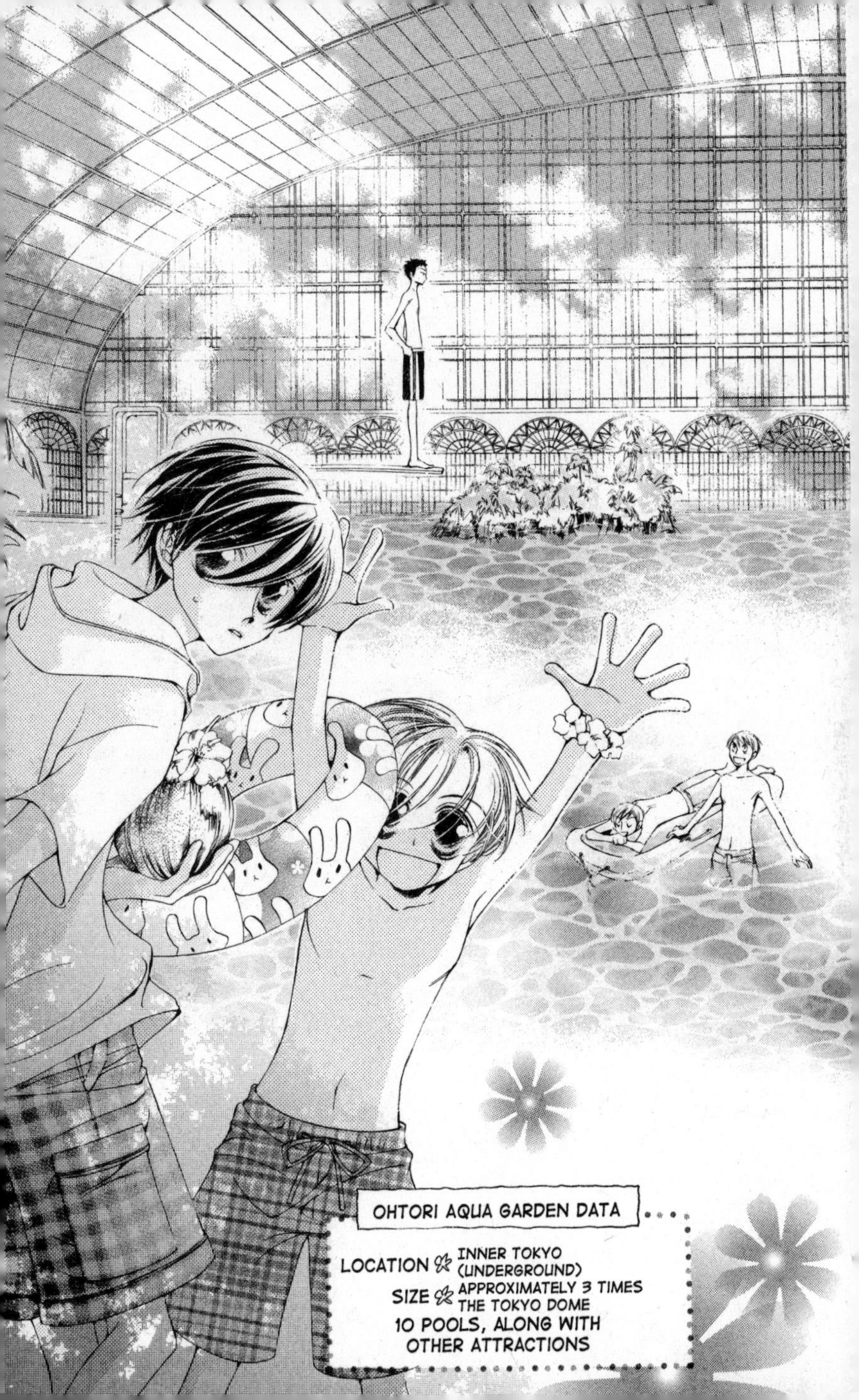
OHTORI AQUA GARDEN DATA
LOCATION ✿ INNER TOKYO (UNDERGROUND)
SIZE ✿ APPROXIMATELY 3 TIMES THE TOKYO DOME
10 POOLS, ALONG WITH OTHER ATTRACTIONS

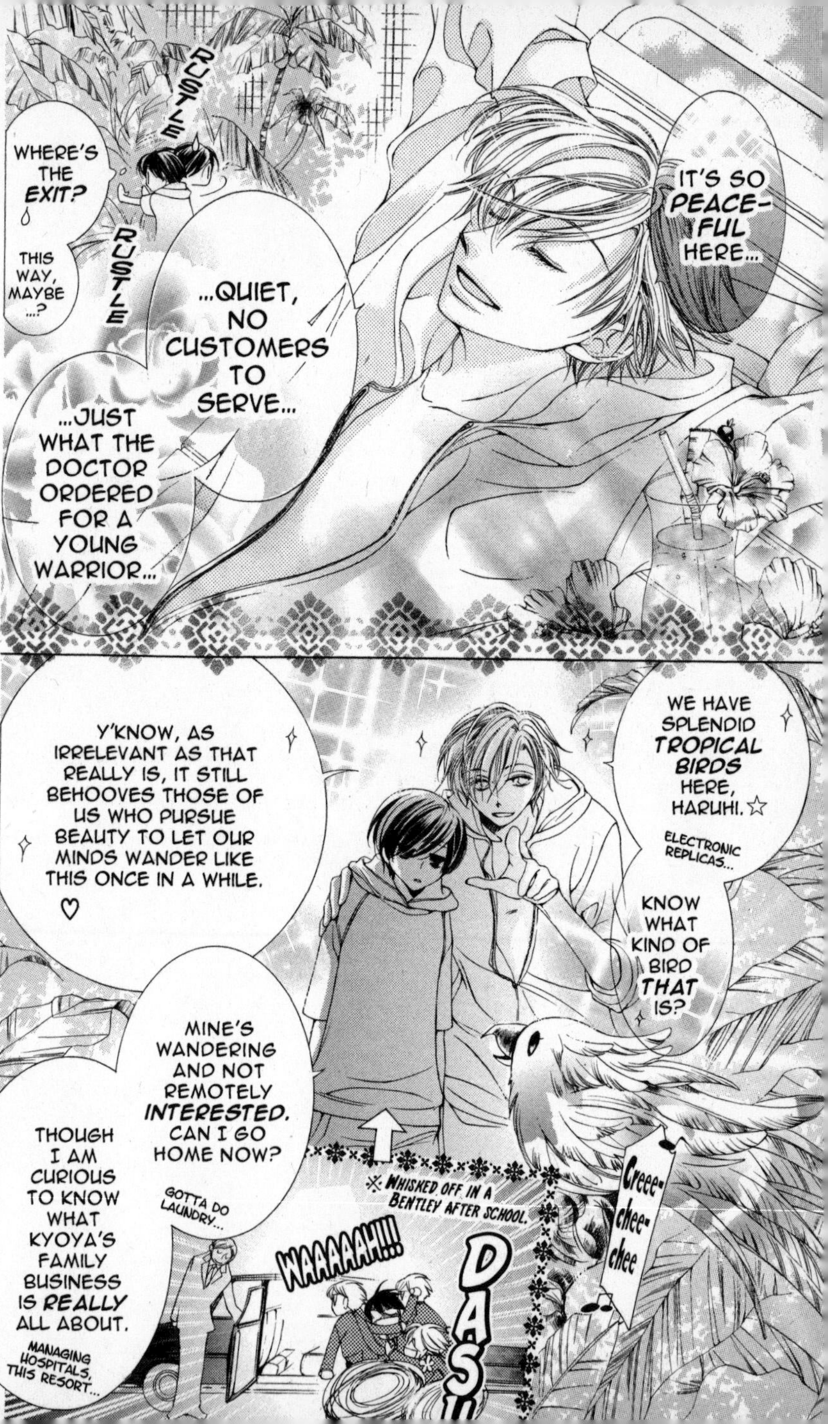

IT'S SO PEACE-FUL HERE...
...QUIET, NO CUSTOMERS TO SERVE...
...JUST WHAT THE DOCTOR ORDERED FOR A YOUNG WARRIOR...
RUSTLE
RUSTLE
WHERE'S THE EXIT?
THIS WAY, MAYBE ...?
WE HAVE SPLENDID TROPICAL BIRDS HERE, HARUHI. ☆
ELECTRONIC REPLICAS...
Y'KNOW, AS IRRELEVANT AS THAT REALLY IS, IT STILL BEHOOVES THOSE OF US WHO PURSUE BEAUTY TO LET OUR MINDS WANDER LIKE THIS ONCE IN A WHILE. ♡
KNOW WHAT KIND OF BIRD THAT IS?
Creee-chee-chee
MINE'S WANDERING AND NOT REMOTELY INTERESTED. CAN I GO HOME NOW?
GOTTA DO LAUNDRY...
THOUGH I AM CURIOUS TO KNOW WHAT KYOYA'S FAMILY BUSINESS IS REALLY ALL ABOUT.
MANAGING HOSPITALS, THIS RESORT...
※ WHISKED OFF IN A BENTLEY AFTER SCHOOL.
DASH
WAAAAAH!!!

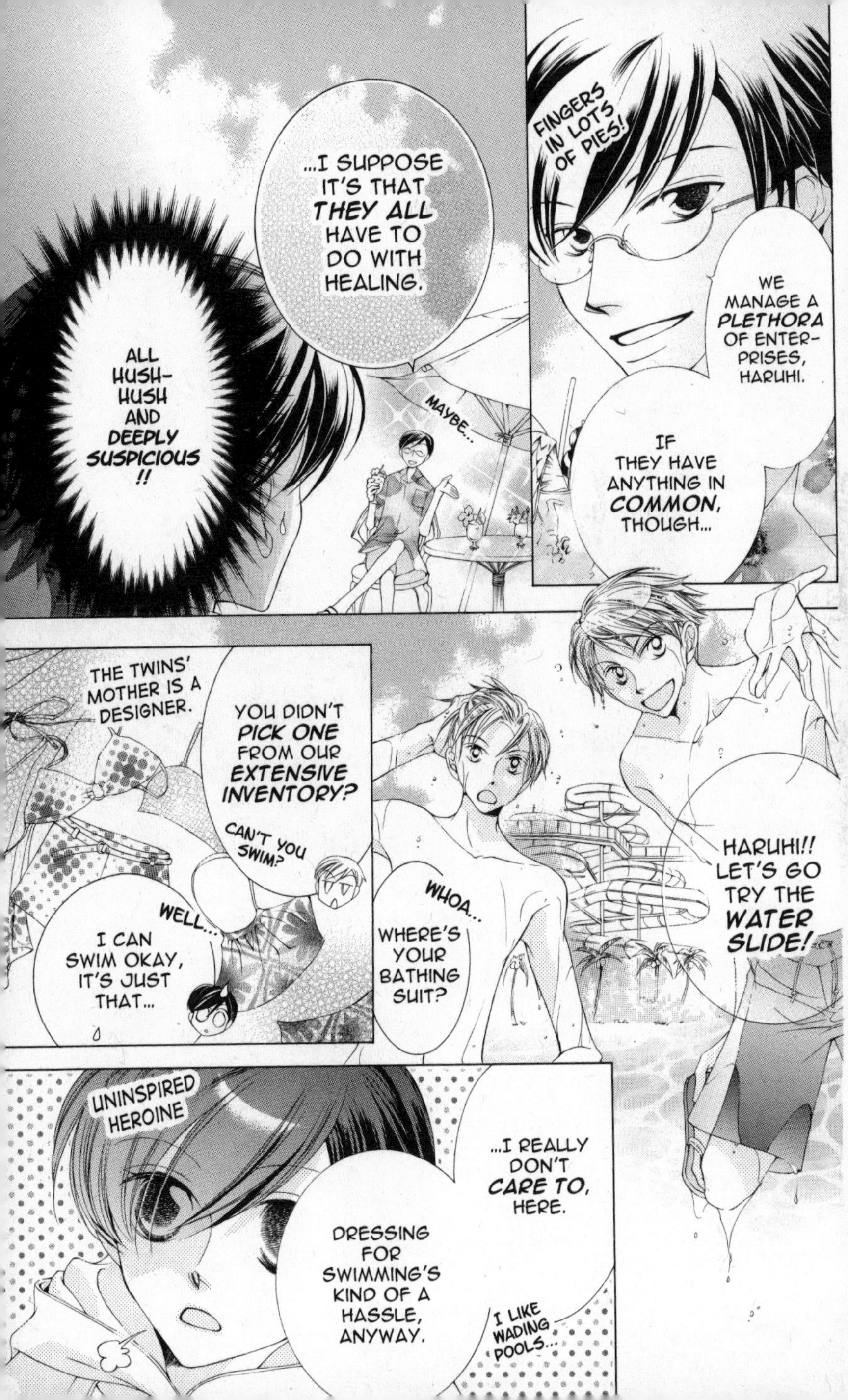
FINGERS IN LOTS OF PIES!
WE MANAGE A PLETHORA OF ENTER-PRISES, HARUHI.
IF THEY HAVE ANYTHING IN COMMON, THOUGH...
...I SUPPOSE IT'S THAT THEY ALL HAVE TO DO WITH HEALING.
MAYBE...
ALL HUSH-HUSH AND DEEPLY SUSPICIOUS!!
HARUHI!! LET'S GO TRY THE WATER SLIDE!
WHOA...
WHERE'S YOUR BATHING SUIT?
YOU DIDN'T PICK ONE FROM OUR EXTENSIVE INVENTORY?
THE TWINS' MOTHER IS A DESIGNER.
CAN'T YOU SWIM?
WELL...
I CAN SWIM OKAY, IT'S JUST THAT...
...I REALLY DON'T CARE TO, HERE.
UNINSPIRED HEROINE
DRESSING FOR SWIMMING'S KIND OF A HASSLE, ANYWAY.
I LIKE WADING POOLS...

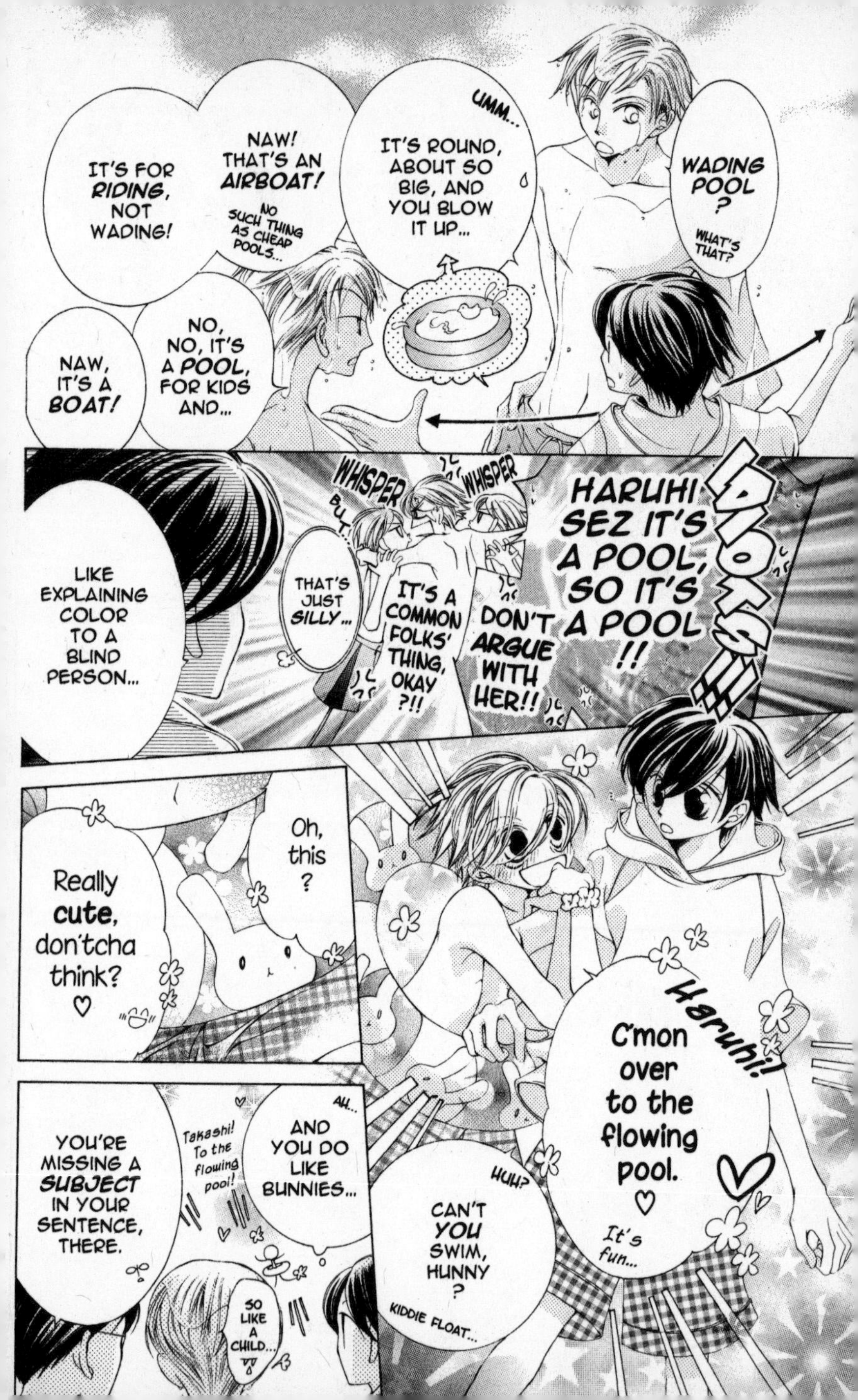
WADING POOL?
WHAT'S THAT?
UMM...
IT'S ROUND, ABOUT SO BIG, AND YOU BLOW IT UP...
NAW! THAT'S AN AIRBOAT!
NO SUCH THING AS CHEAP POOLS...
IT'S FOR RIDING, NOT WADING!
NO, NO, IT'S A POOL, FOR KIDS AND...
NAW, IT'S A BOAT!
IDIOTS!!
HARUHI SEZ IT'S A POOL, SO IT'S A POOL!!
DON'T ARGUE WITH HER!!
IT'S A COMMON FOLKS' THING, OKAY?!!
WHISPER
WHISPER
BUT...
THAT'S JUST SILLY...
LIKE EXPLAINING COLOR TO A BLIND PERSON...
Haruhi!
C'mon over to the flowing pool. ♡
It's fun...
HUH?
CAN'T YOU SWIM, HUNNY?
KIDDIE FLOAT...
Oh, this?
Really cute, don'tcha think? ♡
AH...
AND YOU DO LIKE BUNNIES...
Takashi! To the flowing pool!
YOU'RE MISSING A SUBJECT IN YOUR SENTENCE, THERE.
SO LIKE A CHILD...

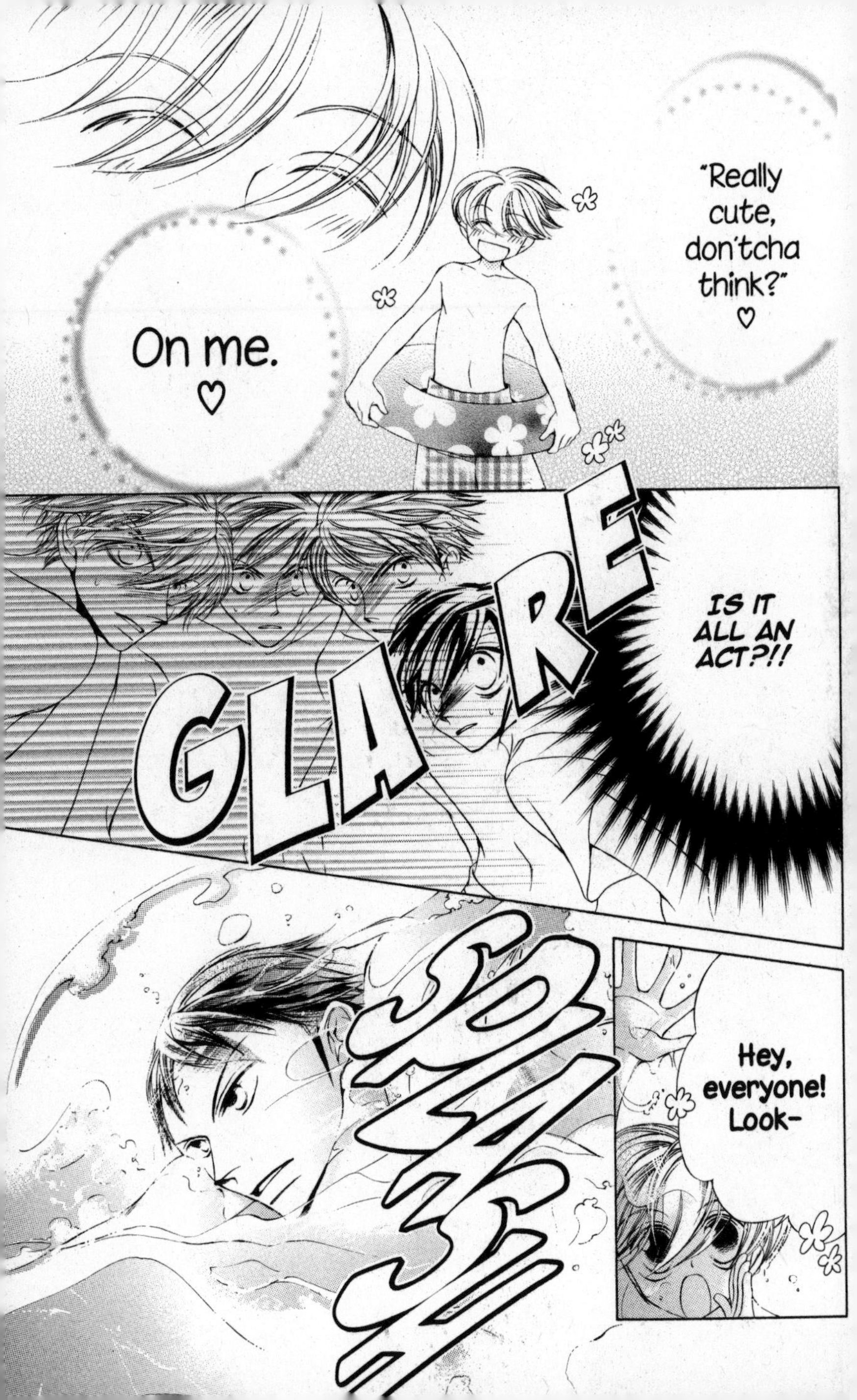
"Really cute, don'tcha think?" ♡
On me. ♡
IS IT ALL AN ACT?!!
GLARE
Hey, everyone! Look-
SPLASH!!

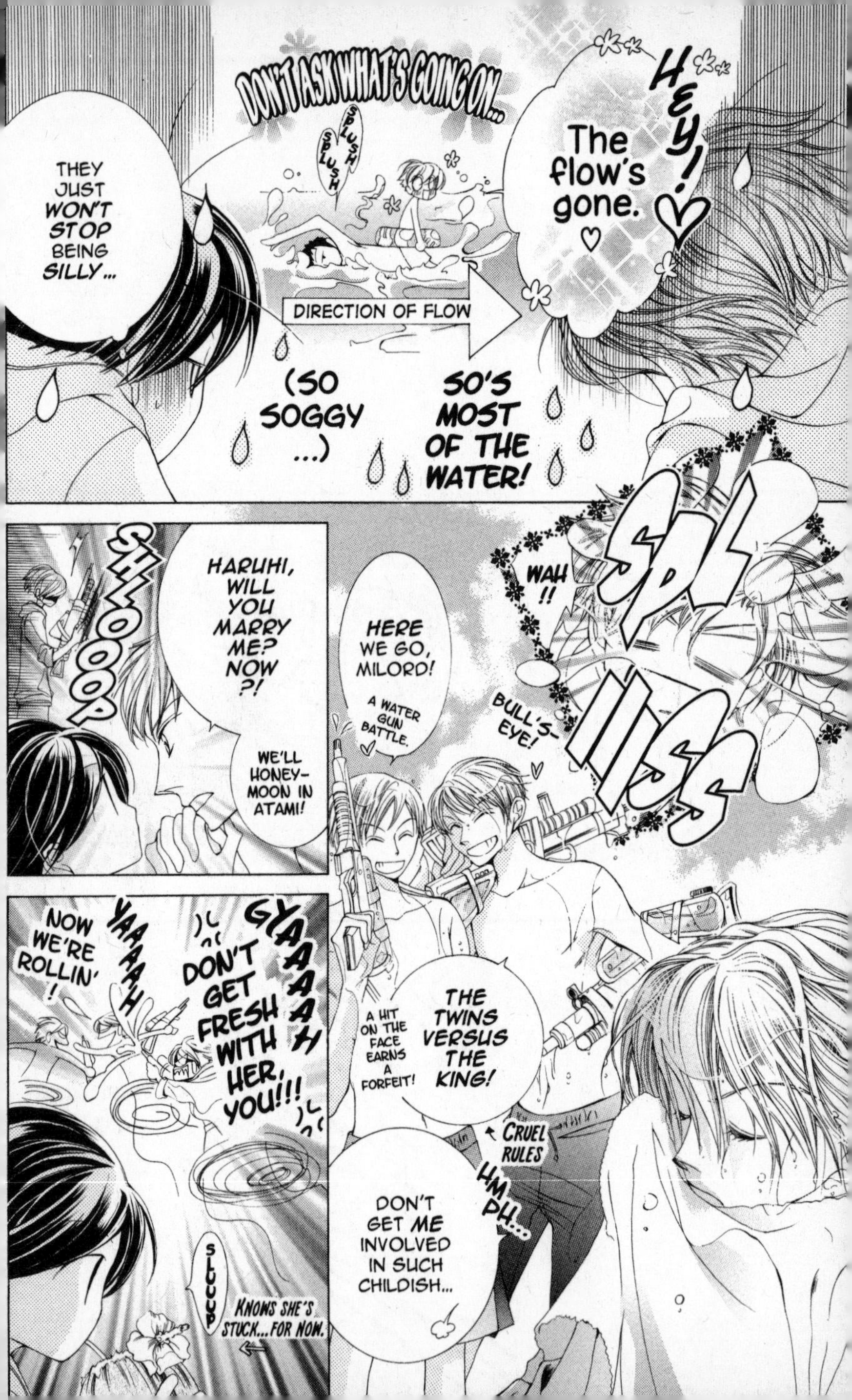
HEY! ♡
The flow's gone. ♡
DON'T ASK WHAT'S GOING ON...
SPLUSH SPLUSH
DIRECTION OF FLOW
SO'S MOST OF THE WATER!
(SO SOGGY ...)
THEY JUST WON'T STOP BEING SILLY...
SPLISS
WAH!!
BULL'S-EYE!
HERE WE GO, MILORD!
A WATER GUN BATTLE. ♡
THE TWINS VERSUS THE KING!
A HIT ON THE FACE EARNS A FORFEIT!
CRUEL RULES
HMPH...
DON'T GET ME INVOLVED IN SUCH CHILDISH...
SHLOOOP
HARUHI, WILL YOU MARRY ME? NOW?!
WE'LL HONEY-MOON IN ATAMI!
GYAAAAAH
DON'T GET FRESH WITH HER, YOU!!!
YAAAAH
NOW WE'RE ROLLIN'!
SLUUUP
KNOWS SHE'S STUCK...FOR NOW.

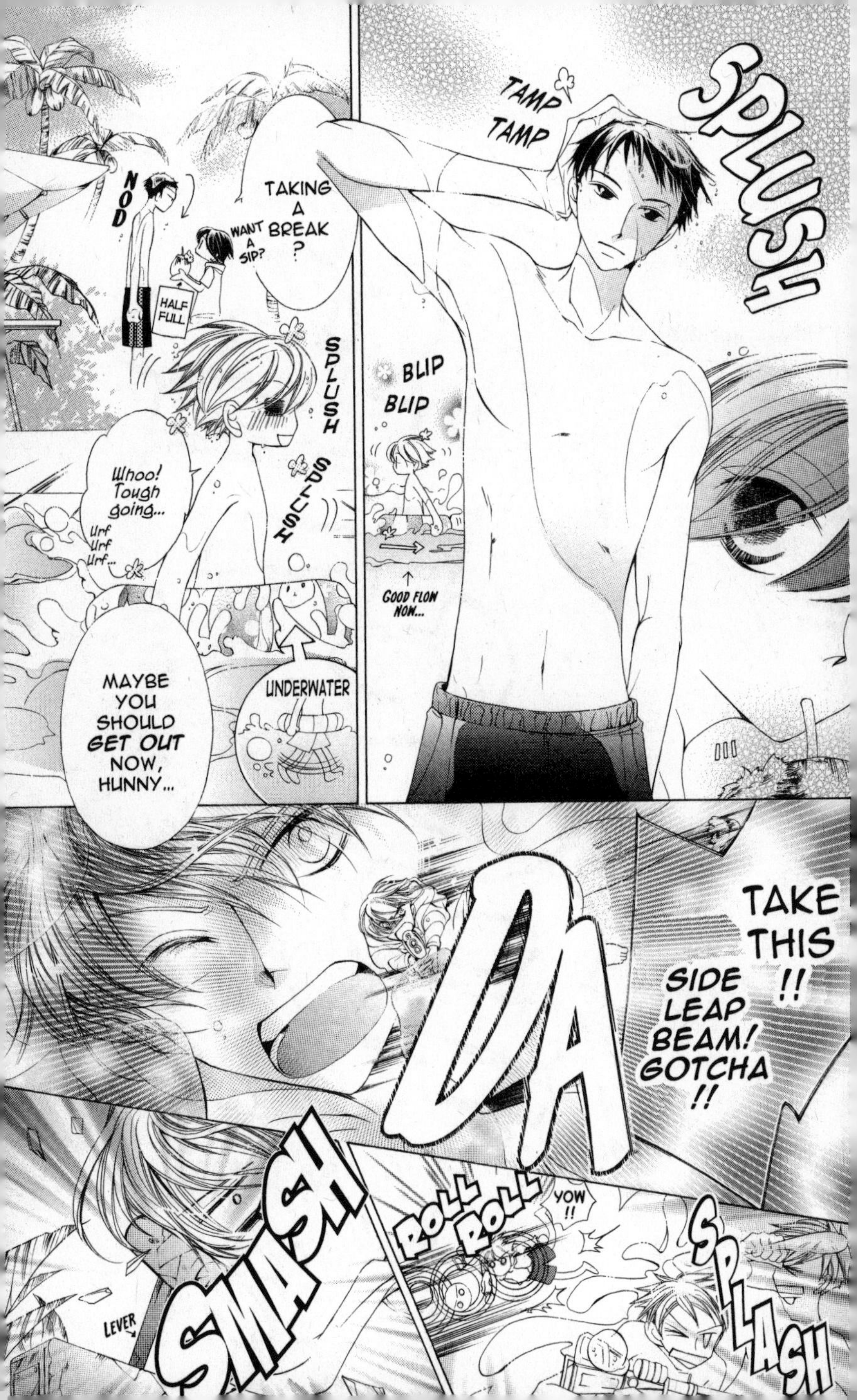
SPLUSH
TAMP TAMP
BLIP BLIP
GOOD FLOW NOW...
TAKING A BREAK?
NOD
WANT A SIP?
HALF FULL
SPLUSH
SPLUSH
Whoo! Tough going...
Urf Urf Urf...
UNDERWATER
MAYBE YOU SHOULD GET OUT NOW, HUNNY...
TAKE THIS!!
SIDE LEAP BEAM! GOTCHA!!
DA
SPLASH
YOW!!
ROLL ROLL
SMASH
LEVER

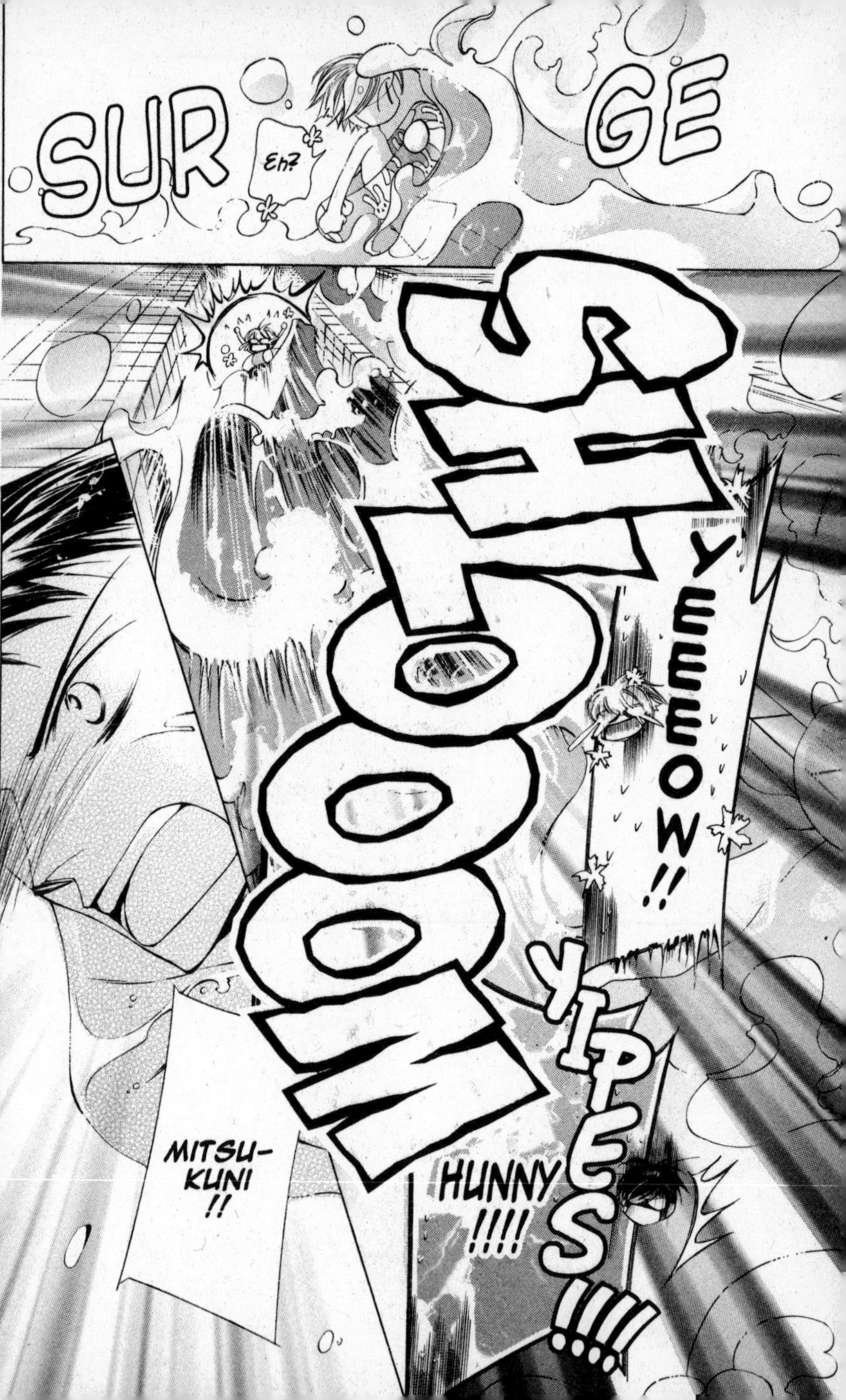
SURGE
Eh?
SHOOOM
YEEEOW!!
YIPES!!!!
HUNNY!!!!
MITSU-KUNI!!

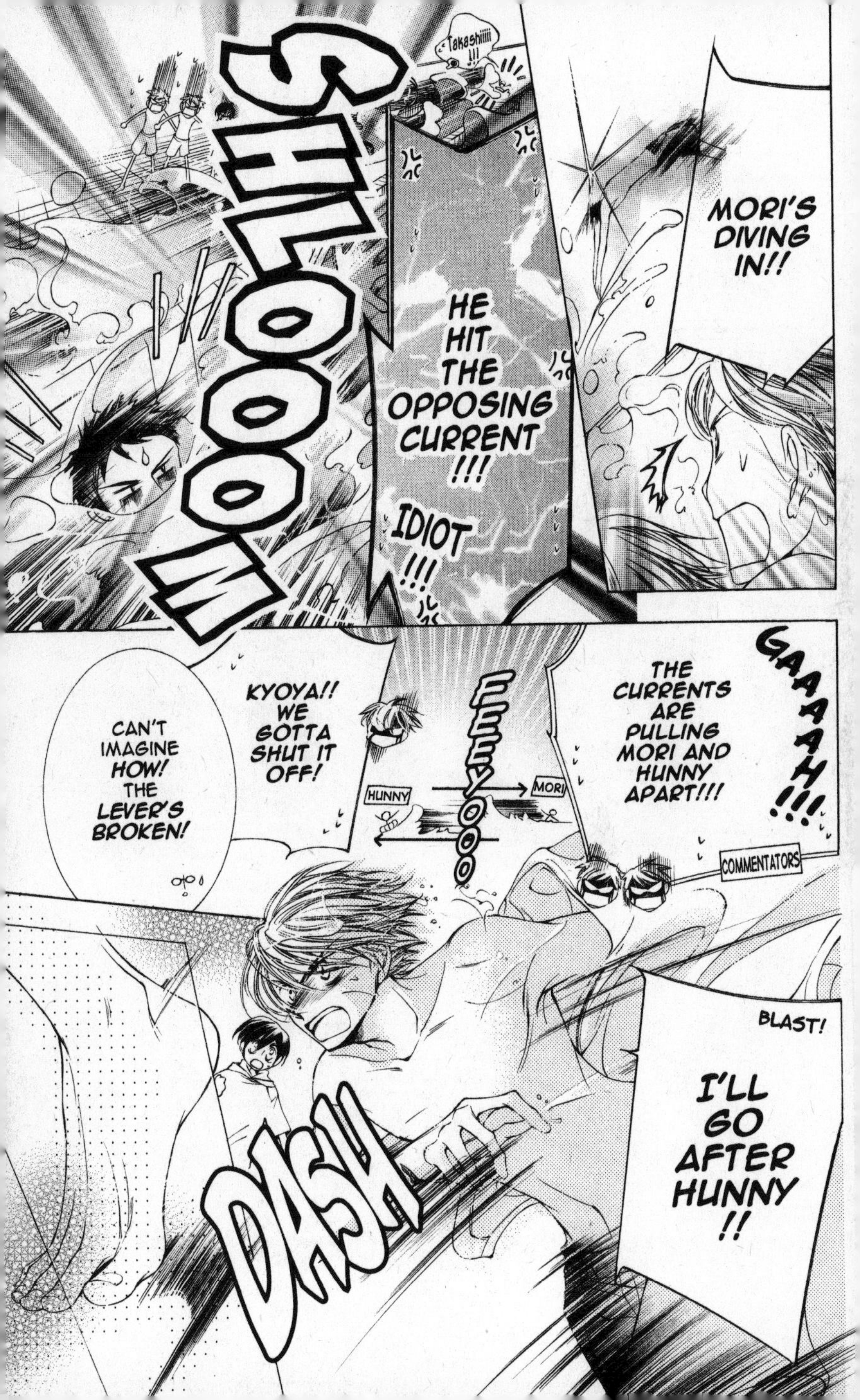
MORI'S DIVING IN!!
HE HIT THE OPPOSING CURRENT!!!
IDIOT!!!
Takashiiii!!!
SHLOOOOM!!
GAAAAAH!!!
THE CURRENTS ARE PULLING MORI AND HUNNY APART!!!
COMMENTATORS
FEEEYOOOO
MORI
HUNNY
KYOYA!! WE GOTTA SHUT IT OFF!
CAN'T IMAGINE HOW! THE LEVER'S BROKEN!
BLAST!
I'LL GO AFTER HUNNY!!
DASH

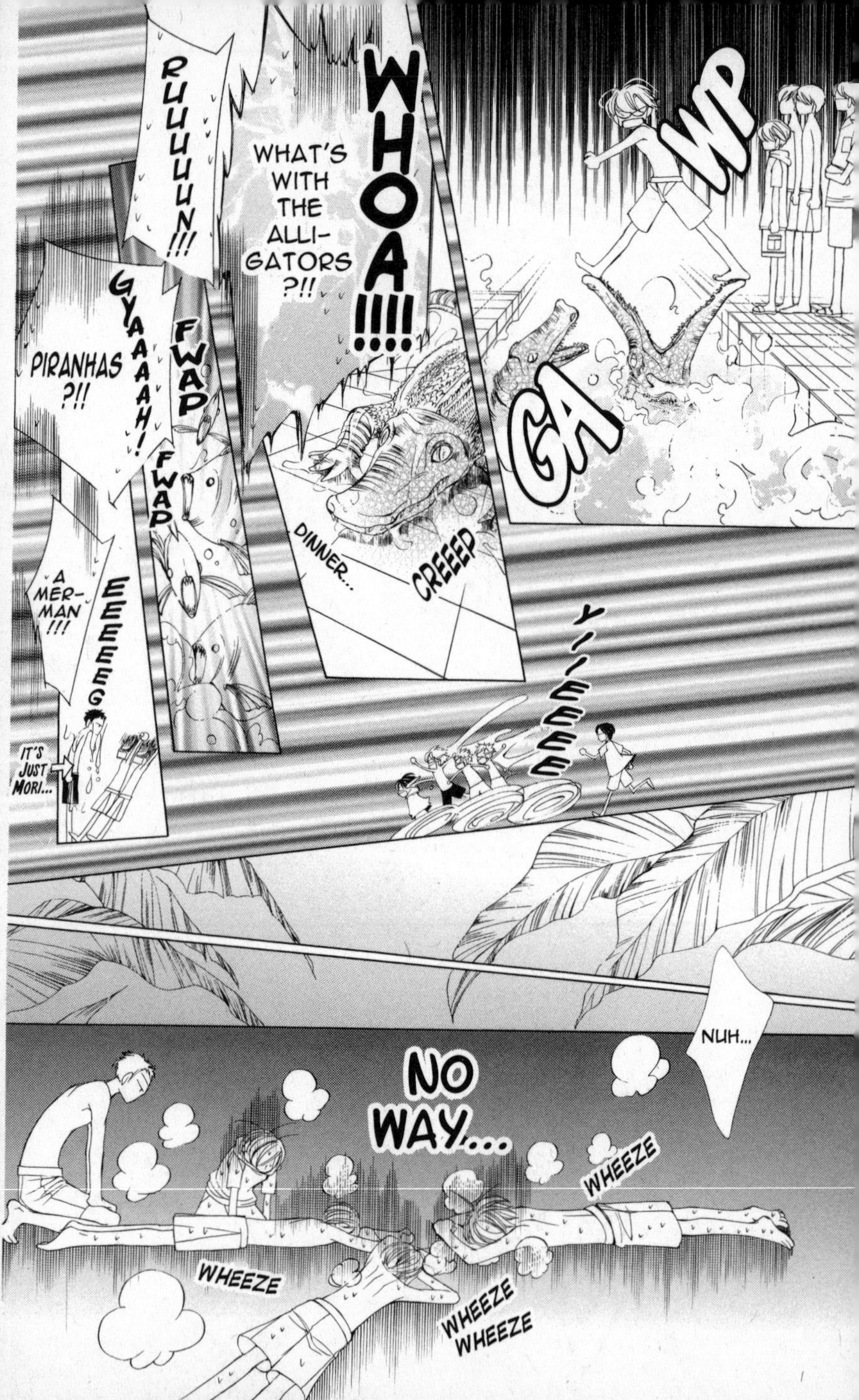
GAWP
WHOA!!!!
WHAT'S WITH THE ALLIGATORS?!!
CREEEP
DINNER...
RUUUUUUN!!!
GYAAAAAH!
FWAP
FWAP
PIRANHAS?!!
EEEEEEG
A MERMAN!!!
IT'S JUST MORI...
Y-I-IEEEEE
NUH...
NO WAY...
WHEEZE
WHEEZE
WHEEZE
WHEEZE

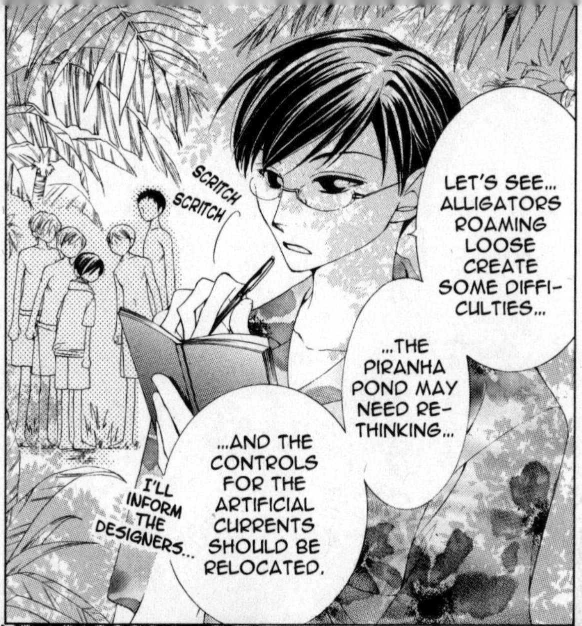
LET'S SEE... ALLIGATORS ROAMING LOOSE CREATE SOME DIFFI-CULTIES...
SCRITCH SCRITCH
...THE PIRANHA POND MAY NEED RE-THINKING...
...AND THE CONTROLS FOR THE ARTIFICIAL CURRENTS SHOULD BE RELOCATED.
I'LL INFORM THE DESIGNERS...

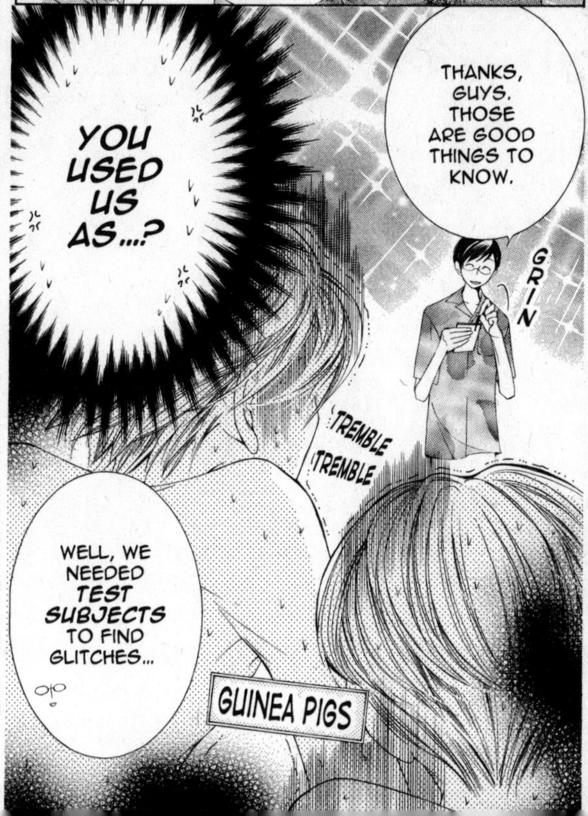
THANKS, GUYS. THOSE ARE GOOD THINGS TO KNOW.
GRIN
YOU USED US AS...?
TREMBLE TREMBLE
WELL, WE NEEDED TEST SUBJECTS TO FIND GLITCHES...
GUINEA PIGS

4

✿ FOR THE DRAMA CD, I HAVE RECKLESSLY WRITTEN AN EXTRA SHORT STORY, PLUS A HOLIDAY MESSAGE. I HAD A PROFESSIONAL WRITER EDIT IT, SO IT SHOULD BE MORE READABLE THAN MY PAST EFFORTS. SCENARIOS ARE SO DIFFICULT... MY LACK OF VOCABULARY IS PAINFULLY EVIDENT. ANYHOW, I HOPE YOU'LL ALL ENJOY IT.

✿ A CHANGE IN TOPIC. STARTING WITH THIS POOL EPISODE, THERE ARE NOW THREE EPISODES LABELED THE "BARE SKIN FESTIVAL" (LAUGH). SEEING AS IT IS THE SUMMER VOLUME...

PERSONALLY, I LIKE BOYS DRESSED UP BETTER THAN BARE, BUT SINCE WE ARE UNDERWAY WITH THIS, I HAD THEM "UNNECESSARILY" OUT OF THEIR CLOTHES, HOST CLUB STYLE (LAUGH). THEREFORE, THE NEXT VOLUME WILL START OFF THE SAME WAY. PLEASE, WATCH THE BOYS WITH YOUR TEPID EYES (LAUGH).

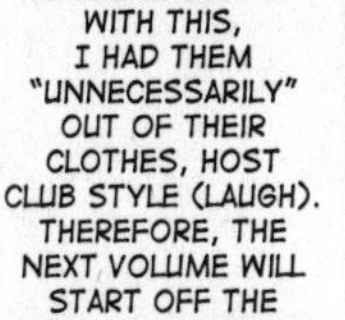
HAR!
I THINK TAMAKI IS REALLY THE SPEEDO TYPE... BUT I RESISTED THE URGE (LAUGH).
GOOD IDEA...

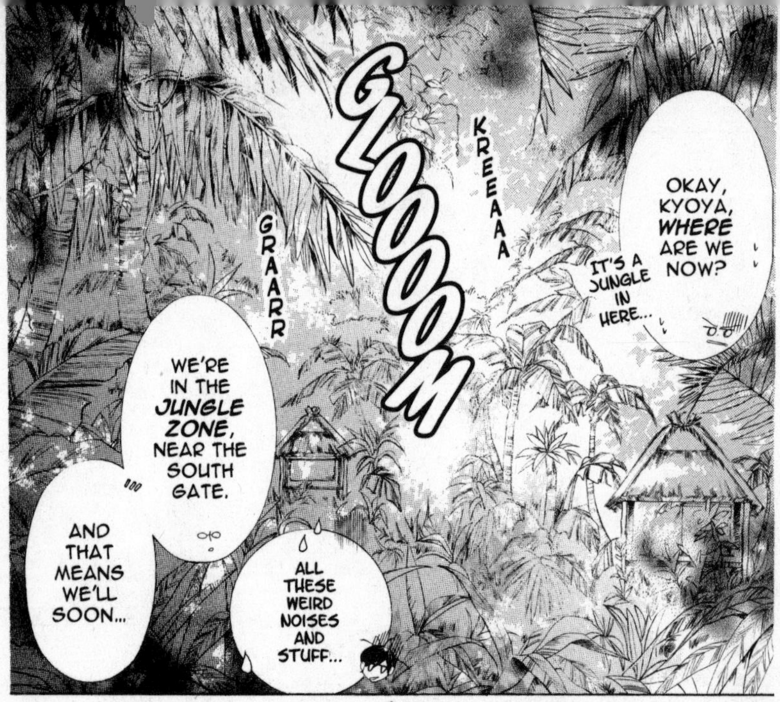
OKAY, KYOYA, WHERE ARE WE NOW?
IT'S A JUNGLE IN HERE...
KREEAAA
GLOOOOOM
GRAARR
WE'RE IN THE JUNGLE ZONE, NEAR THE SOUTH GATE.
ALL THESE WEIRD NOISES AND STUFF...
AND THAT MEANS WE'LL SOON...
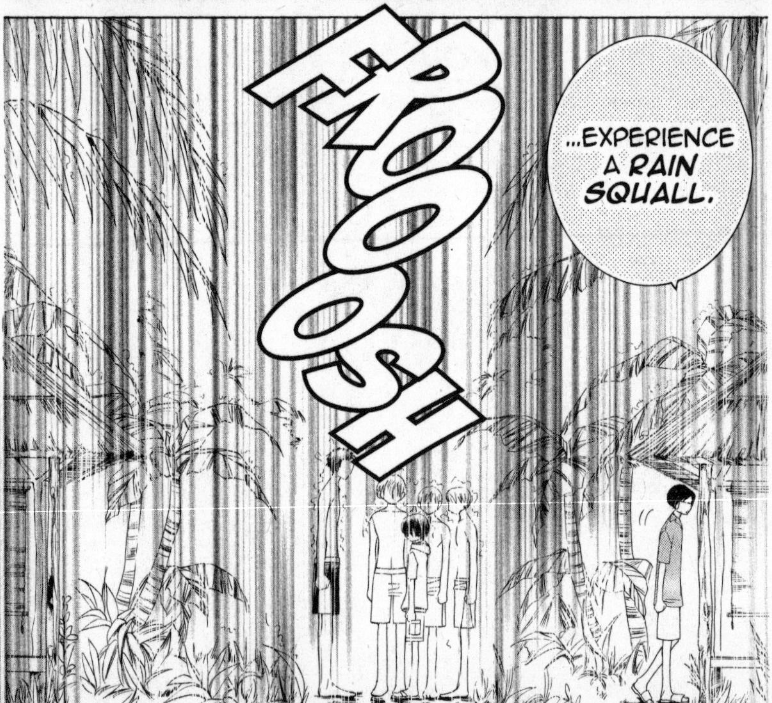
...EXPERIENCE A RAIN SQUALL.
FROOOSH

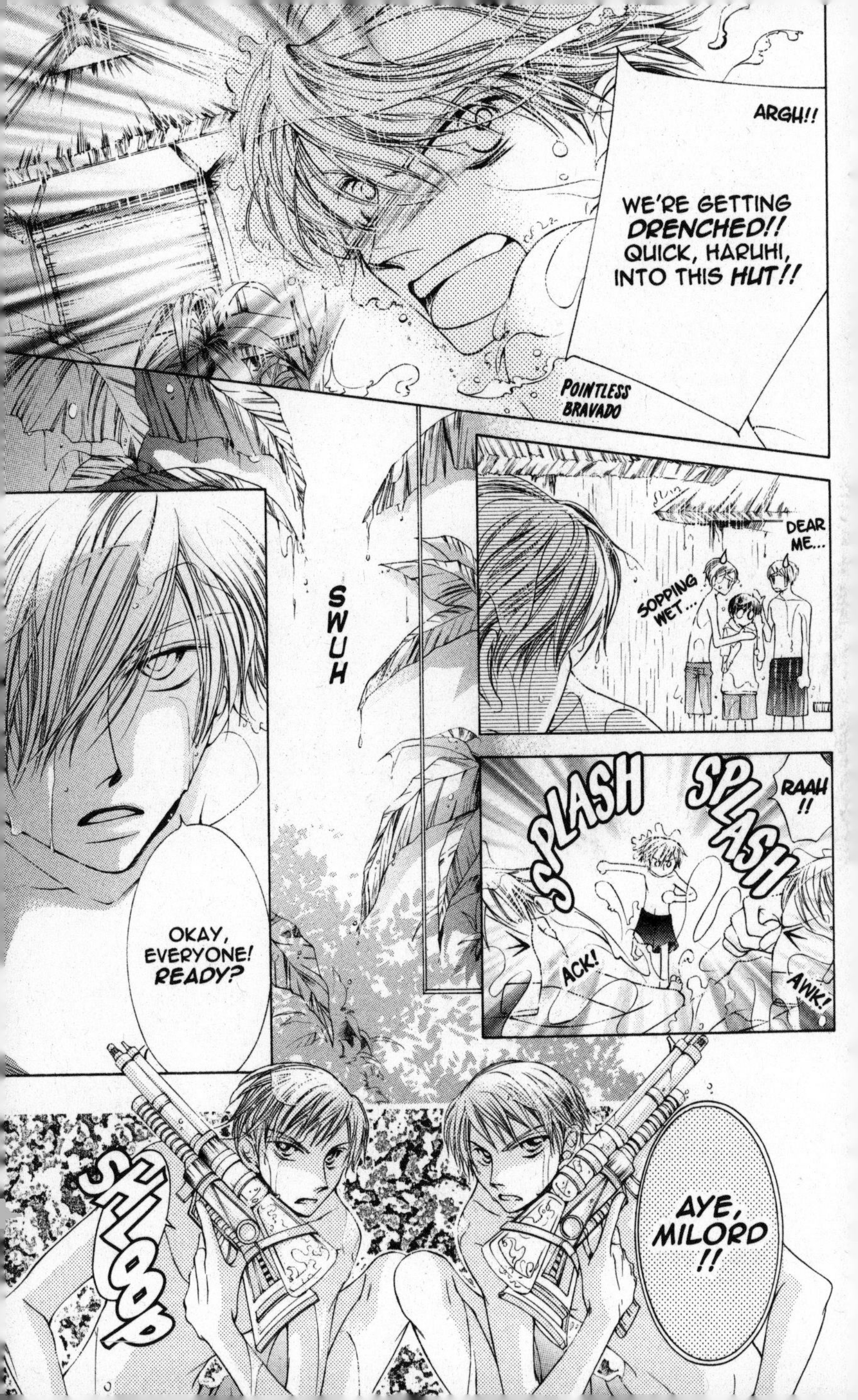
ARGH!!
WE'RE GETTING DRENCHED!! QUICK, HARUHI, INTO THIS HUT!!
POINTLESS BRAVADO
DEAR ME...
SOPPING WET...
RAAH!!
SPLASH
SPLASH
AWK!
ACK!
SWUH
OKAY, EVERYONE! READY?
AYE, MILORD!!
SHLOOP

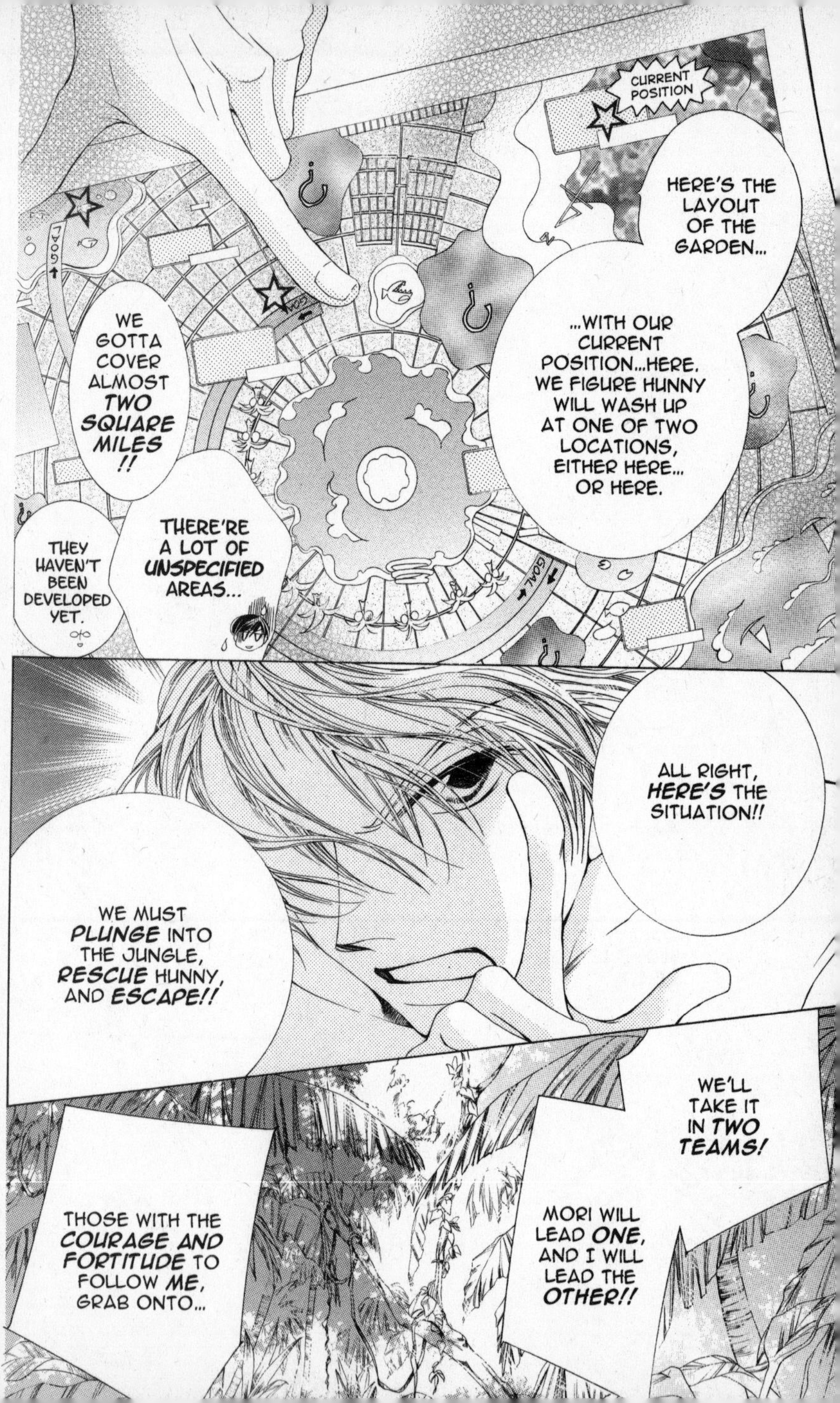
CURRENT POSITION
HERE'S THE LAYOUT OF THE GARDEN...
...WITH OUR CURRENT POSITION...HERE. WE FIGURE HUNNY WILL WASH UP AT ONE OF TWO LOCATIONS, EITHER HERE... OR HERE.
GOAL
WE GOTTA COVER ALMOST TWO SQUARE MILES!!
THERE'RE A LOT OF UNSPECIFIED AREAS...
THEY HAVEN'T BEEN DEVELOPED YET.
ALL RIGHT, HERE'S THE SITUATION!!
WE MUST PLUNGE INTO THE JUNGLE, RESCUE HUNNY, AND ESCAPE!!
WE'LL TAKE IT IN TWO TEAMS!
MORI WILL LEAD ONE, AND I WILL LEAD THE OTHER!!
THOSE WITH THE COURAGE AND FORTITUDE TO FOLLOW ME, GRAB ONTO...

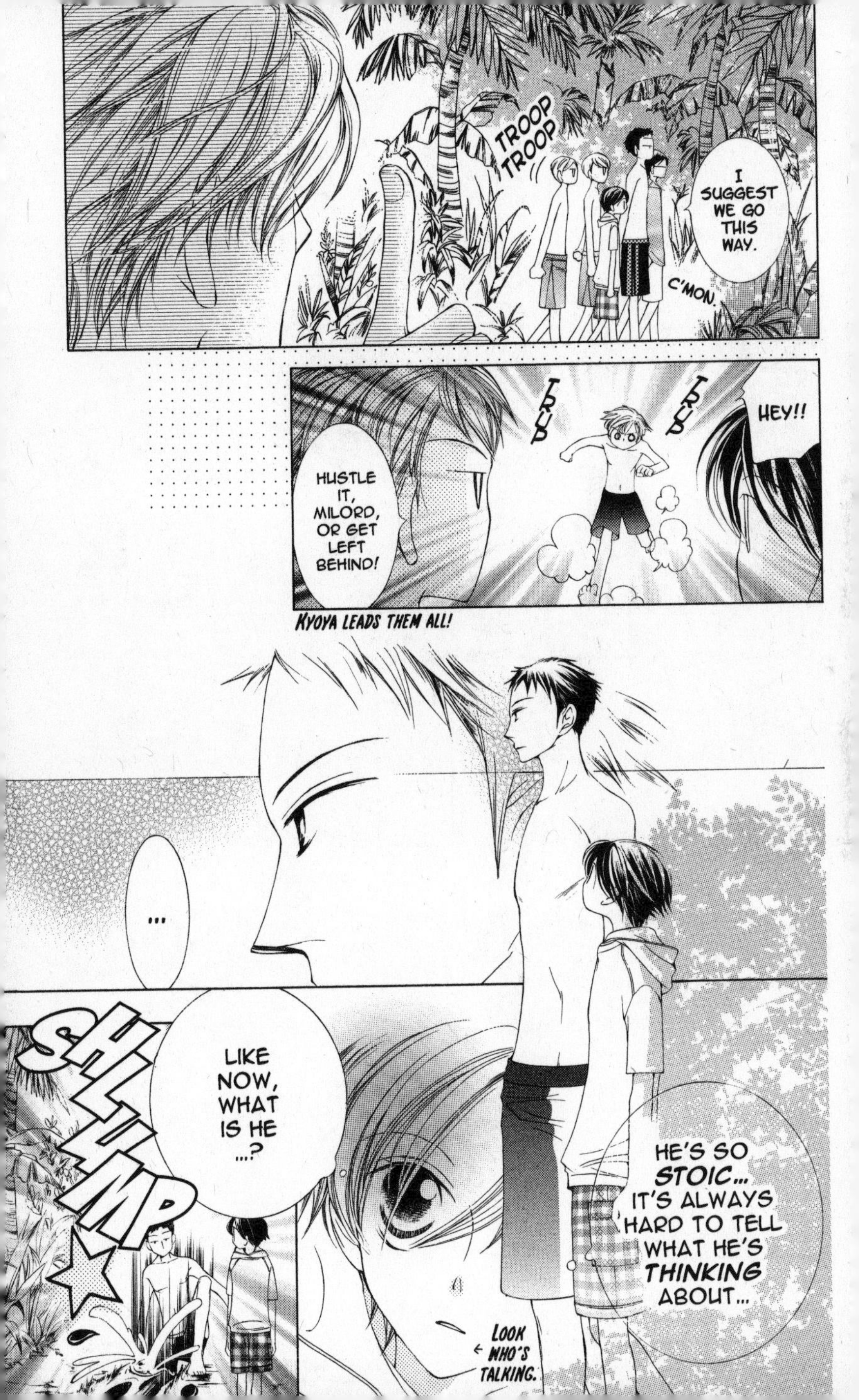
I SUGGEST WE GO THIS WAY.
C'MON.
TROOP TROOP
HEY!!
TRUP TRUP
HUSTLE IT, MILORD, OR GET LEFT BEHIND!
KYOYA LEADS THEM ALL!
...
HE'S SO STOIC... IT'S ALWAYS HARD TO TELL WHAT HE'S THINKING ABOUT...
LOOK ← WHO'S TALKING.
LIKE NOW, WHAT IS HE ...?
SHLUMP

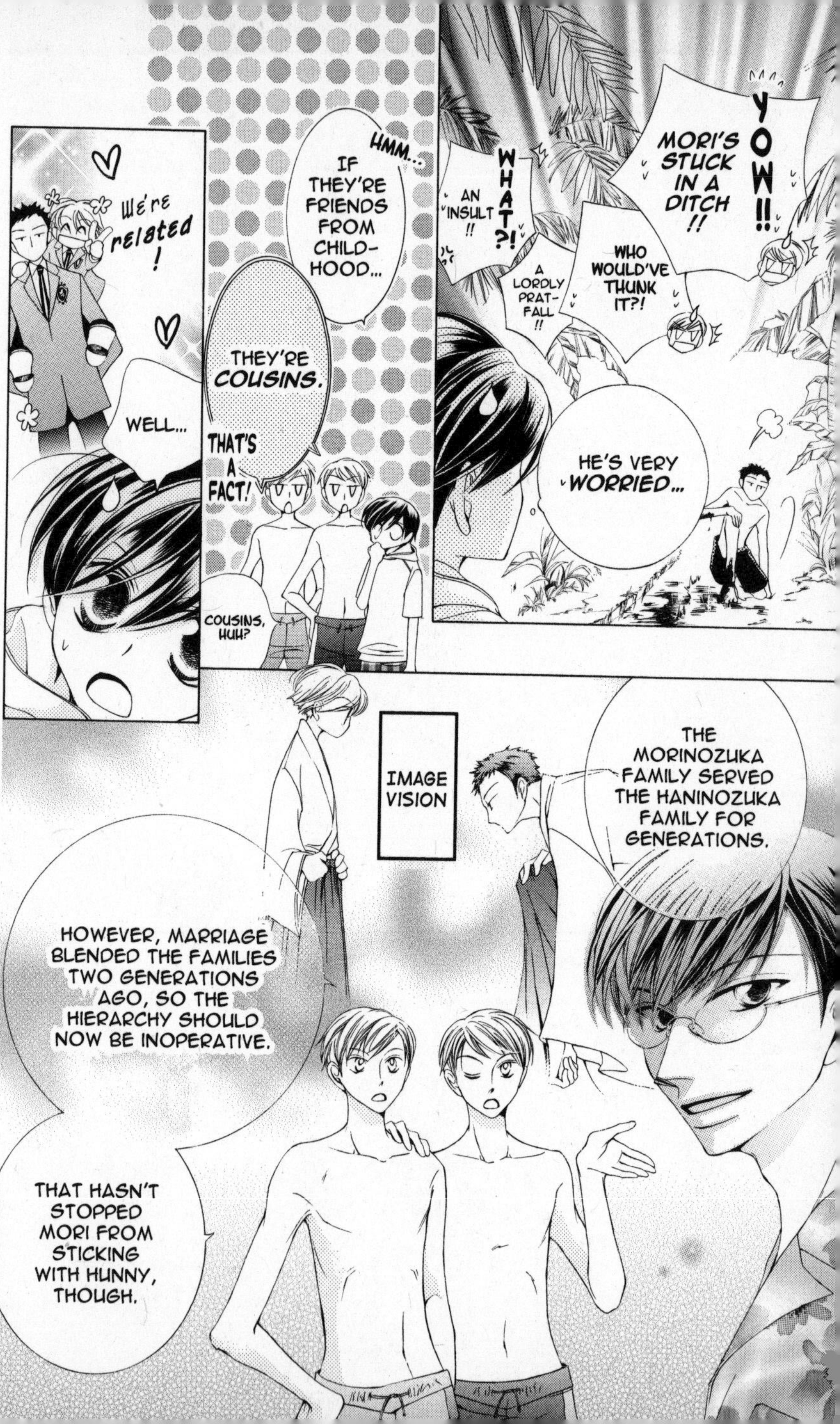
YOW!!
MORI'S STUCK IN A DITCH!!
WHAT?!
AN INSULT!!
WHO WOULD'VE THUNK IT?!
A LORDLY PRAT-FALL!!
HE'S VERY WORRIED...
HMM...
IF THEY'RE FRIENDS FROM CHILD-HOOD...
THEY'RE COUSINS.
THAT'S A FACT!
COUSINS, HUH?
We're related!
WELL...
THE MORINOZUKA FAMILY SERVED THE HANINOZUKA FAMILY FOR GENERATIONS.
IMAGE VISION
HOWEVER, MARRIAGE BLENDED THE FAMILIES TWO GENERATIONS AGO, SO THE HIERARCHY SHOULD NOW BE INOPERATIVE.
THAT HASN'T STOPPED MORI FROM STICKING WITH HUNNY, THOUGH.

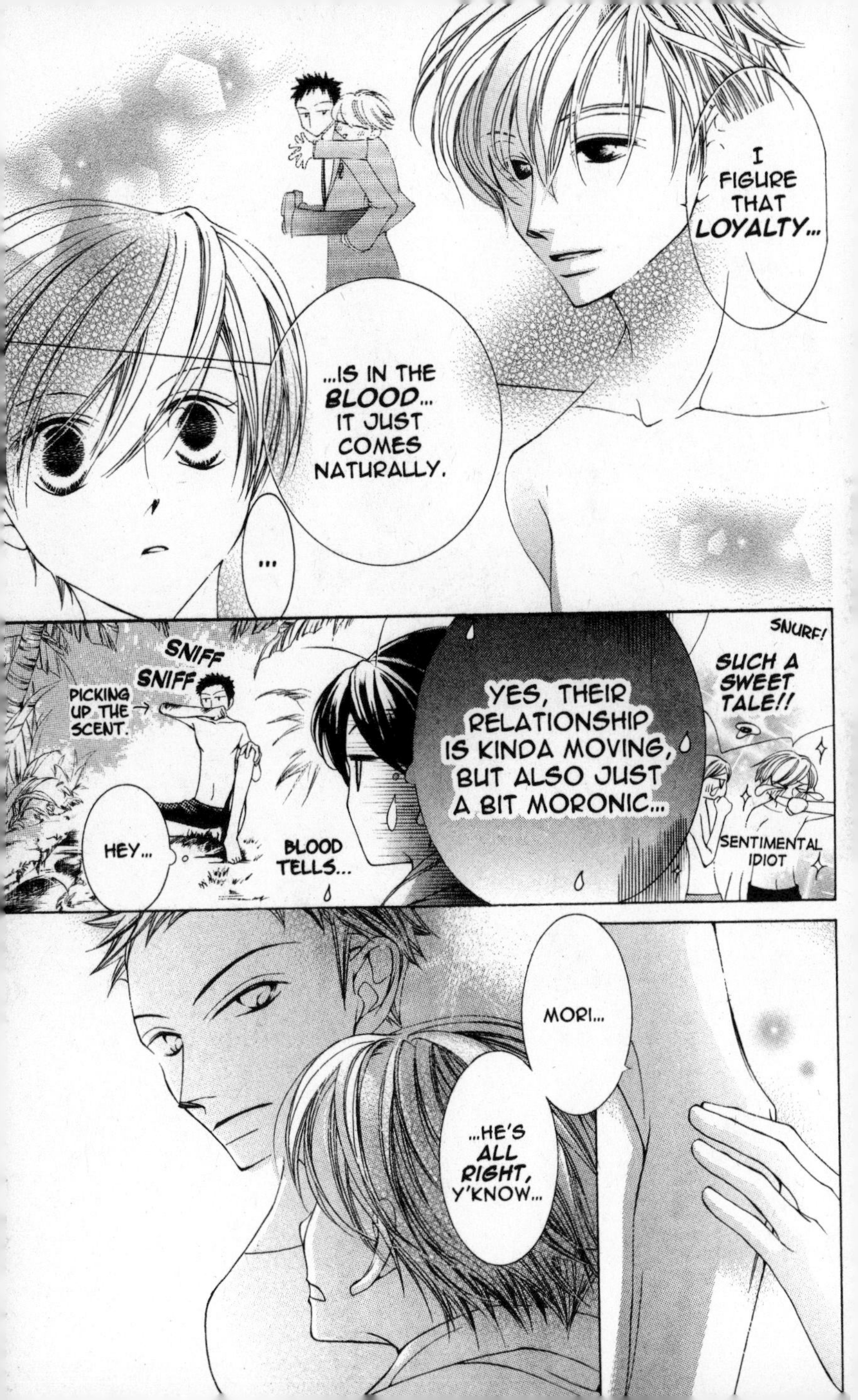
I FIGURE THAT LOYALTY...
...IS IN THE BLOOD... IT JUST COMES NATURALLY.
...
SNURF!
SUCH A SWEET TALE!!
SENTIMENTAL IDIOT
YES, THEIR RELATIONSHIP IS KINDA MOVING, BUT ALSO JUST A BIT MORONIC...
BLOOD TELLS...
SNIFF SNIFF
PICKING UP THE SCENT.
HEY...
MORI...
...HE'S ALL RIGHT, Y'KNOW...

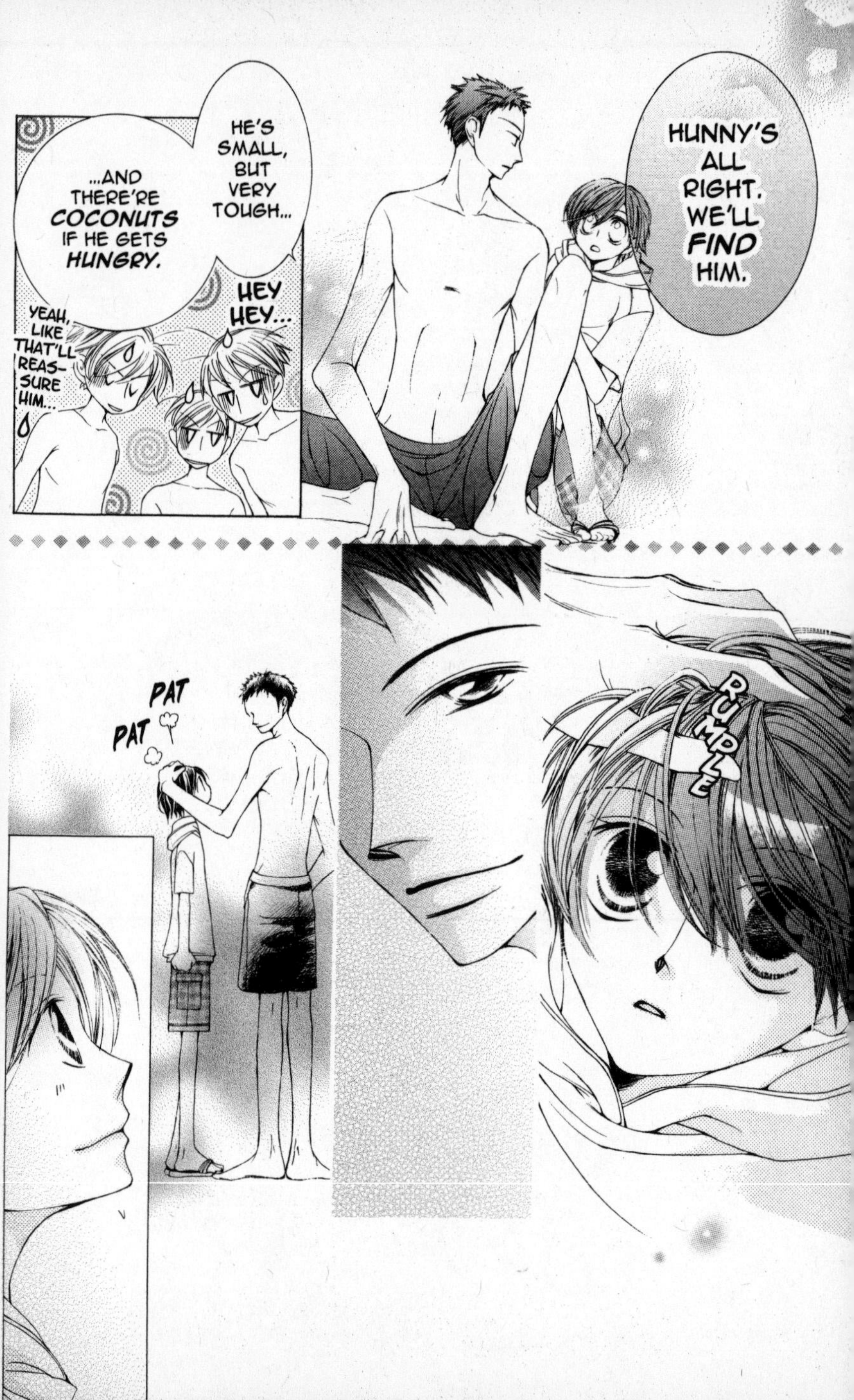
HUNNY'S ALL RIGHT. WE'LL FIND HIM.
HE'S SMALL, BUT VERY TOUGH...
...AND THERE'RE COCONUTS IF HE GETS HUNGRY.
HEY HEY...
YEAH, LIKE THAT'LL REAS-SURE HIM...
RUMPLE
PAT
PAT

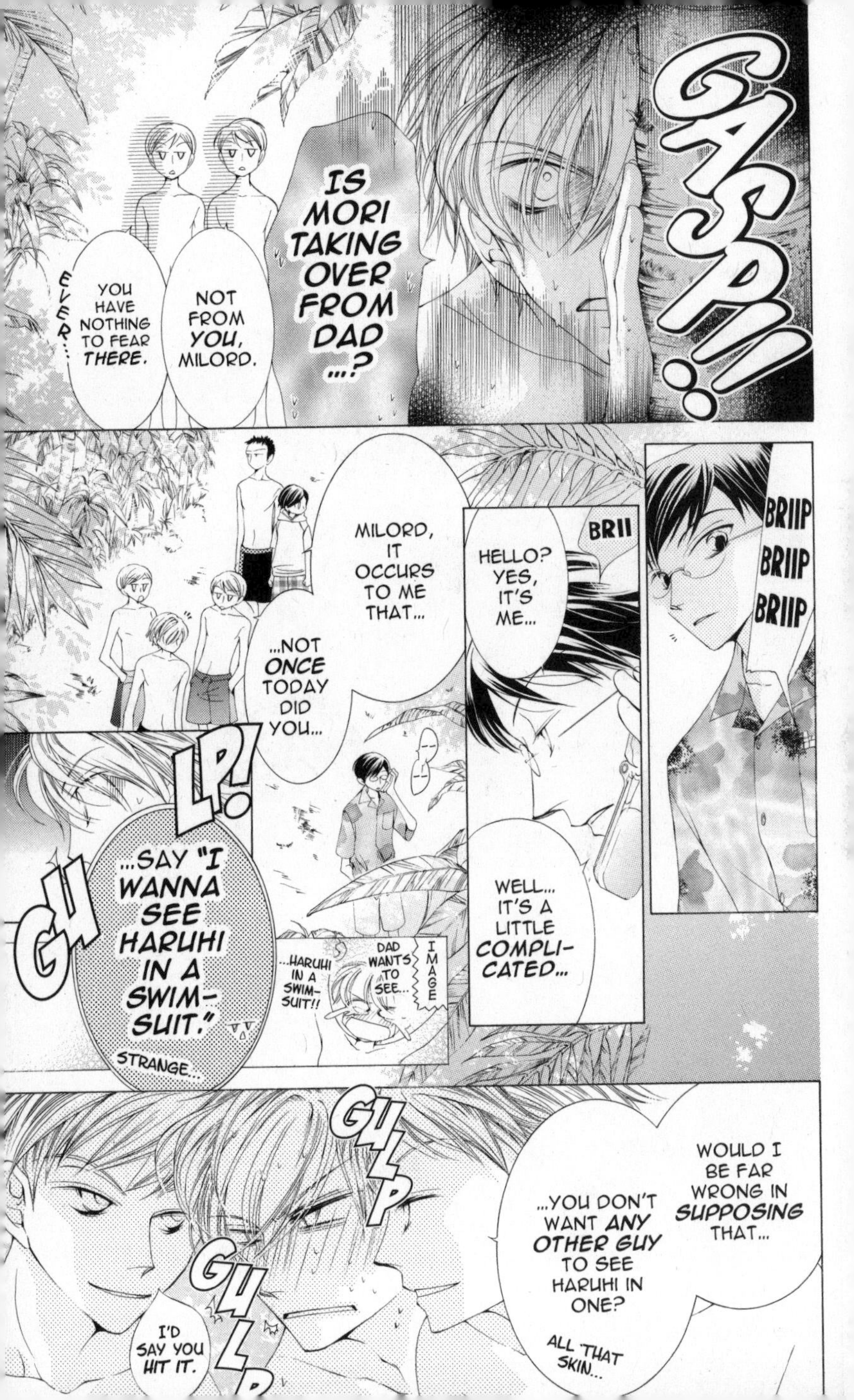
GASP!!..
IS MORI TAKING OVER FROM DAD ...?
NOT FROM YOU, MILORD.
YOU HAVE NOTHING TO FEAR THERE.
EVER...
BRIIP BRIIP BRIIP
BRII
HELLO? YES, IT'S ME...
WELL... IT'S A LITTLE COMPLICATED...
MILORD, IT OCCURS TO ME THAT...
...NOT ONCE TODAY DID YOU...
...SAY "I WANNA SEE HARUHI IN A SWIM-SUIT."
GULP!
STRANGE...
IMAGE
DAD WANTS TO SEE...
...HARUHI IN A SWIM-SUIT!!
WOULD I BE FAR WRONG IN SUPPOSING THAT...
...YOU DON'T WANT ANY OTHER GUY TO SEE HARUHI IN ONE?
ALL THAT SKIN...
GULP
GULP
I'D SAY YOU HIT IT.

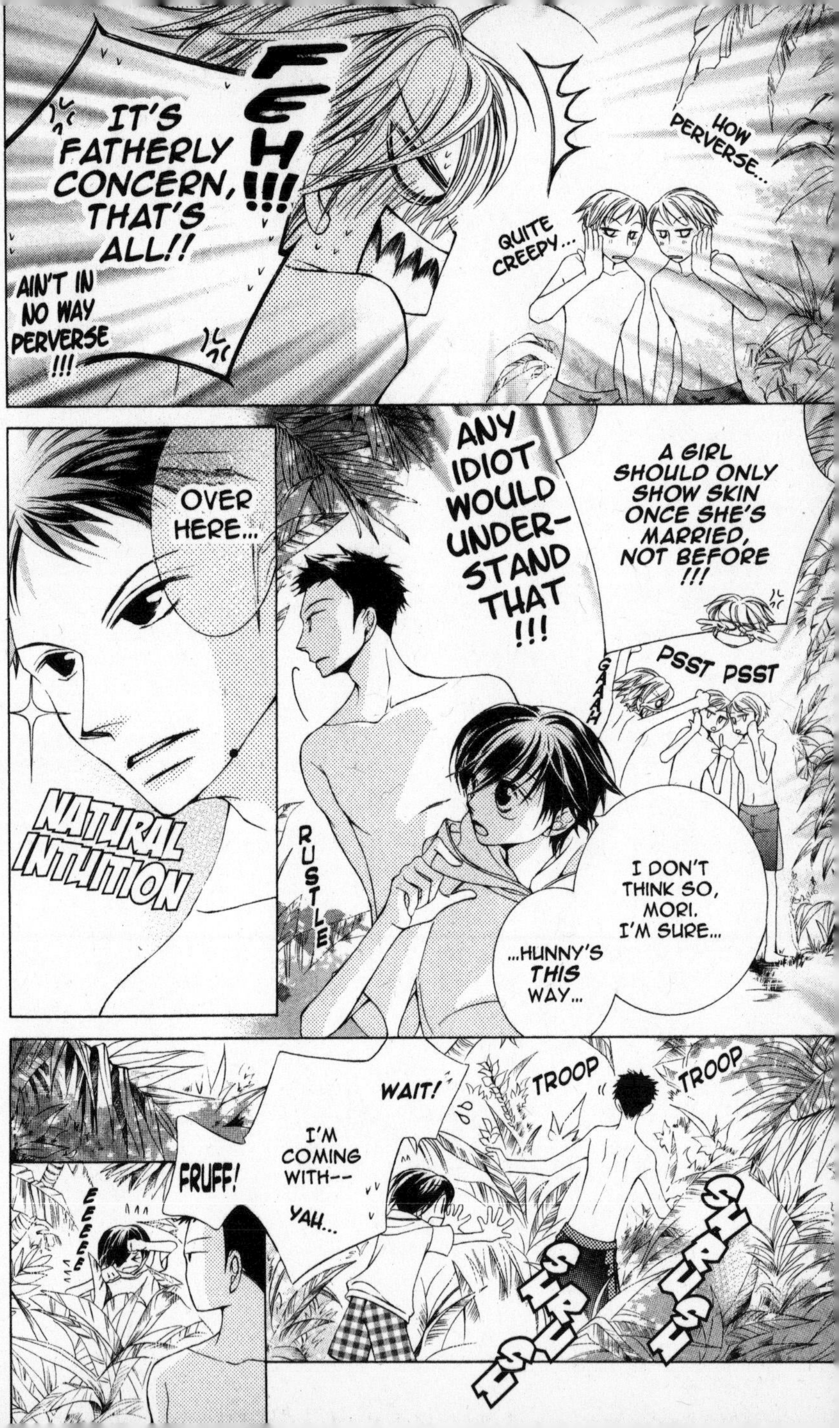
HOW PERVERSE...
QUITE CREEPY...
FEH!!!
IT'S FATHERLY CONCERN, THAT'S ALL!!
AIN'T IN NO WAY PERVERSE!!!
A GIRL SHOULD ONLY SHOW SKIN ONCE SHE'S MARRIED, NOT BEFORE!!!
ANY IDIOT WOULD UNDERSTAND THAT!!!
GAAAH
PSST PSST
I DON'T THINK SO, MORI. I'M SURE...
...HUNNY'S THIS WAY...
RUSTLE
OVER HERE...
NATURAL INTUITION
TROOP
TROOP
SHRUSH
WAIT!
I'M COMING WITH--
SHRUSH
YAH...
FRUFF!
EEEEE

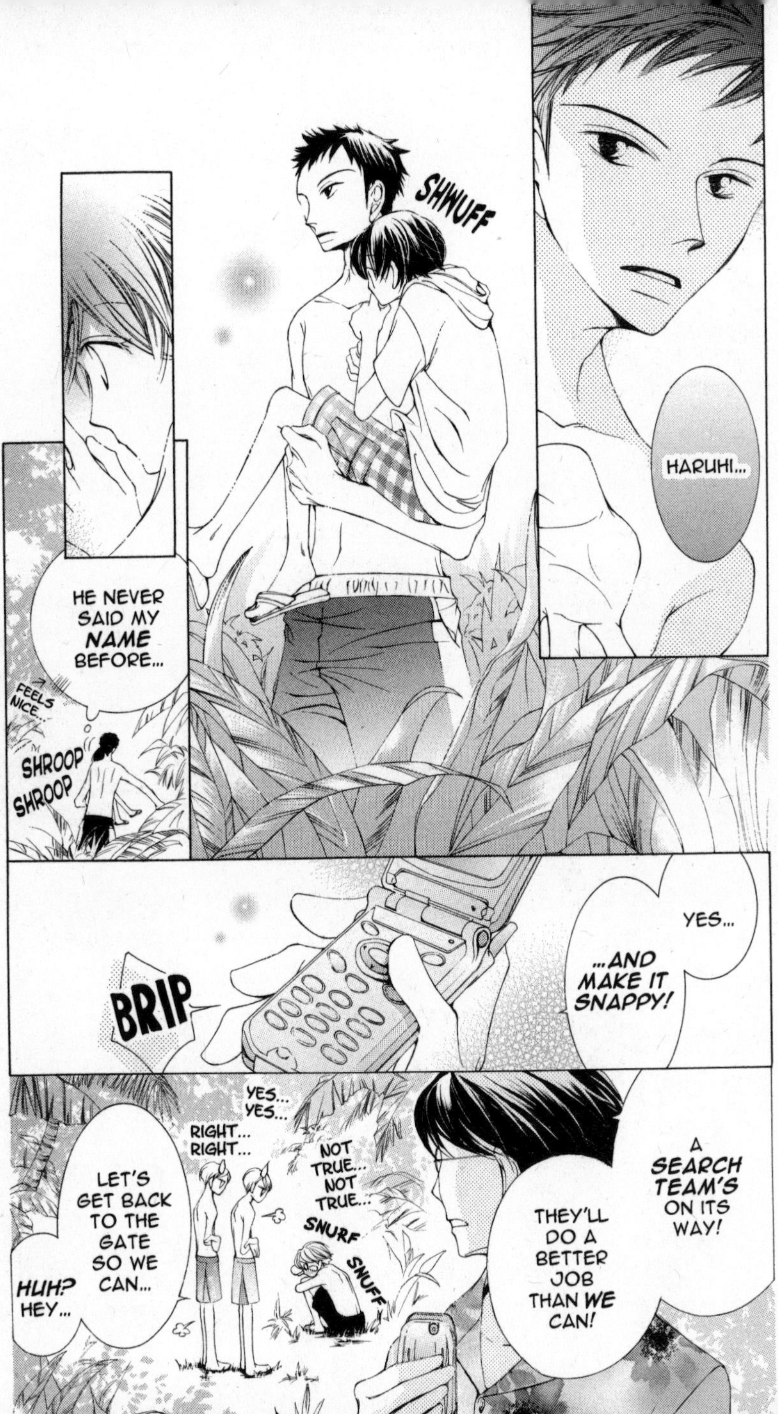
HARUHI...
SHWUFF
HE NEVER SAID MY NAME BEFORE...
FEELS NICE...
SHROOP SHROOP
YES...
...AND MAKE IT SNAPPY!
BRIP
A SEARCH TEAM'S ON ITS WAY!
THEY'LL DO A BETTER JOB THAN WE CAN!
YES... YES...
NOT TRUE... NOT TRUE...
SNURF
SNUFF
RIGHT... RIGHT...
LET'S GET BACK TO THE GATE SO WE CAN...
HUH? HEY...

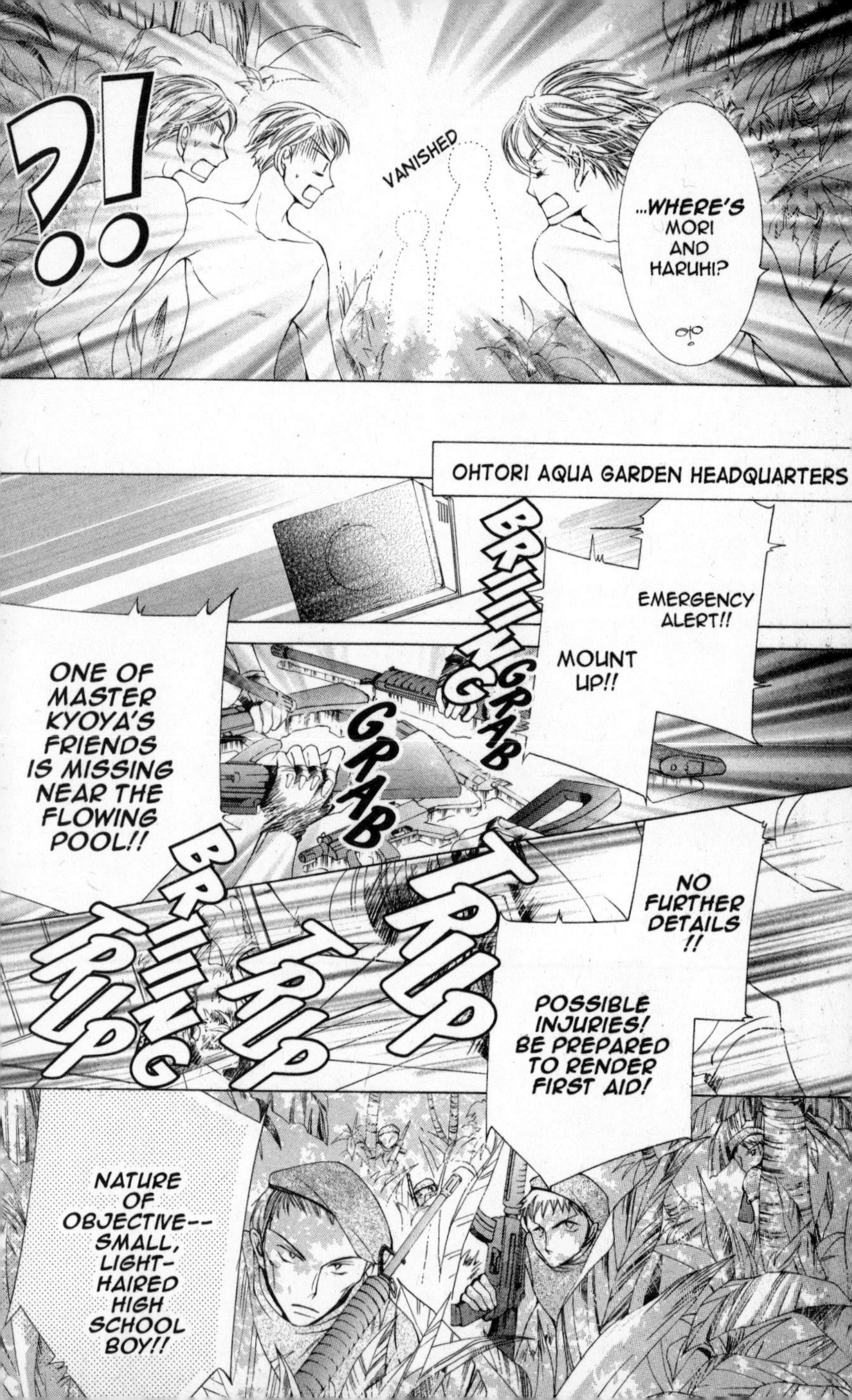
...WHERE'S MORI AND HARUHI?
VANISHED
?!
OHTORI AQUA GARDEN HEADQUARTERS
BRIIING
EMERGENCY ALERT!!
MOUNT UP!!
GRAB
GRAB
ONE OF MASTER KYOYA'S FRIENDS IS MISSING NEAR THE FLOWING POOL!!
NO FURTHER DETAILS!!
TRIP
TRIP
BRIIING
TRIP
POSSIBLE INJURIES! BE PREPARED TO RENDER FIRST AID!
NATURE OF OBJECTIVE-- SMALL, LIGHT-HAIRED HIGH SCHOOL BOY!!

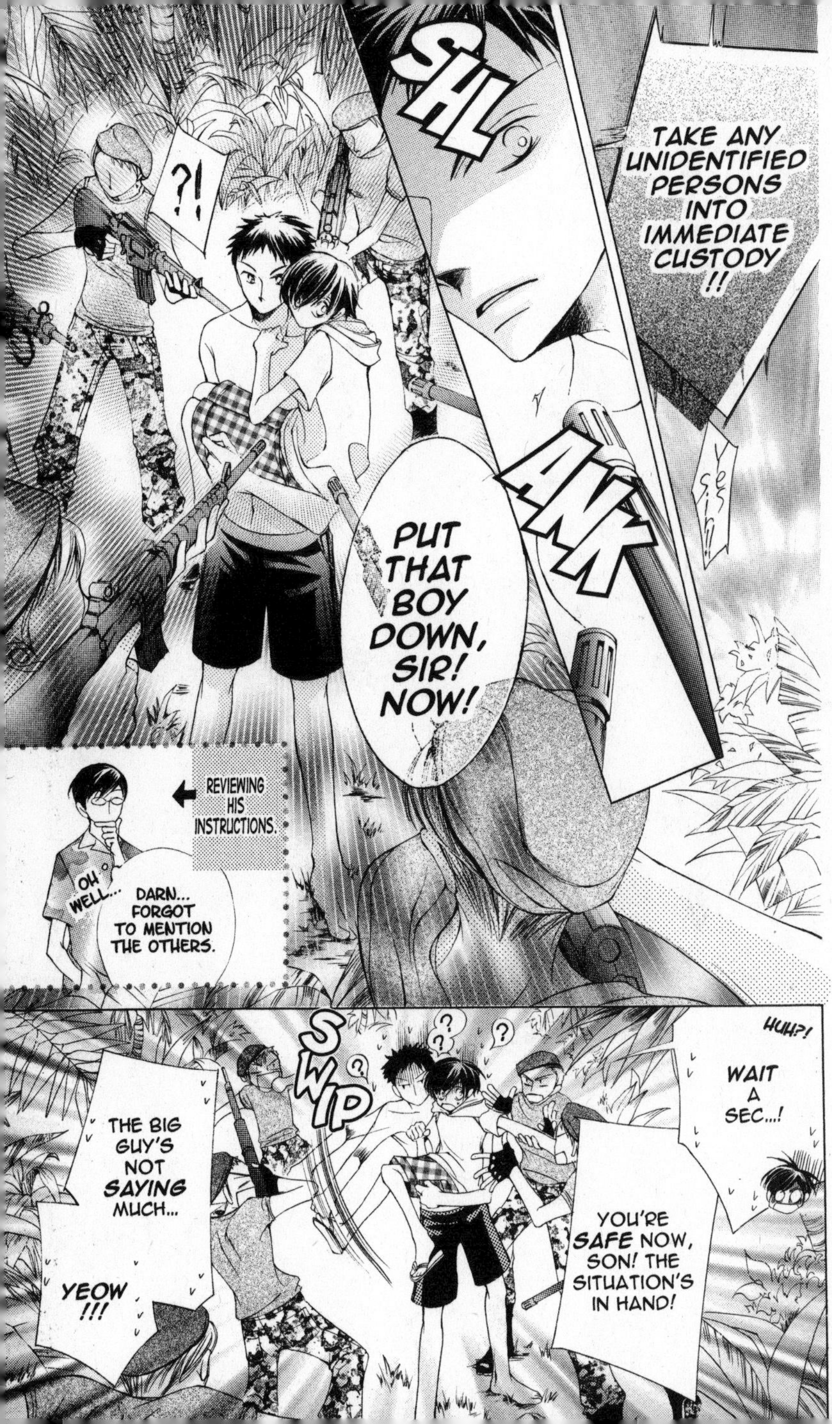
SHL
TAKE ANY UNIDENTIFIED PERSONS INTO IMMEDIATE CUSTODY!!
Yes sir!
ANK
PUT THAT BOY DOWN, SIR! NOW!
?!
REVIEWING HIS INSTRUCTIONS.
DARN... FORGOT TO MENTION THE OTHERS.
OH WELL...
HUH?!
WAIT A SEC...!
YOU'RE SAFE NOW, SON! THE SITUATION'S IN HAND!
SWIP
THE BIG GUY'S NOT SAYING MUCH...
YEOW!!!

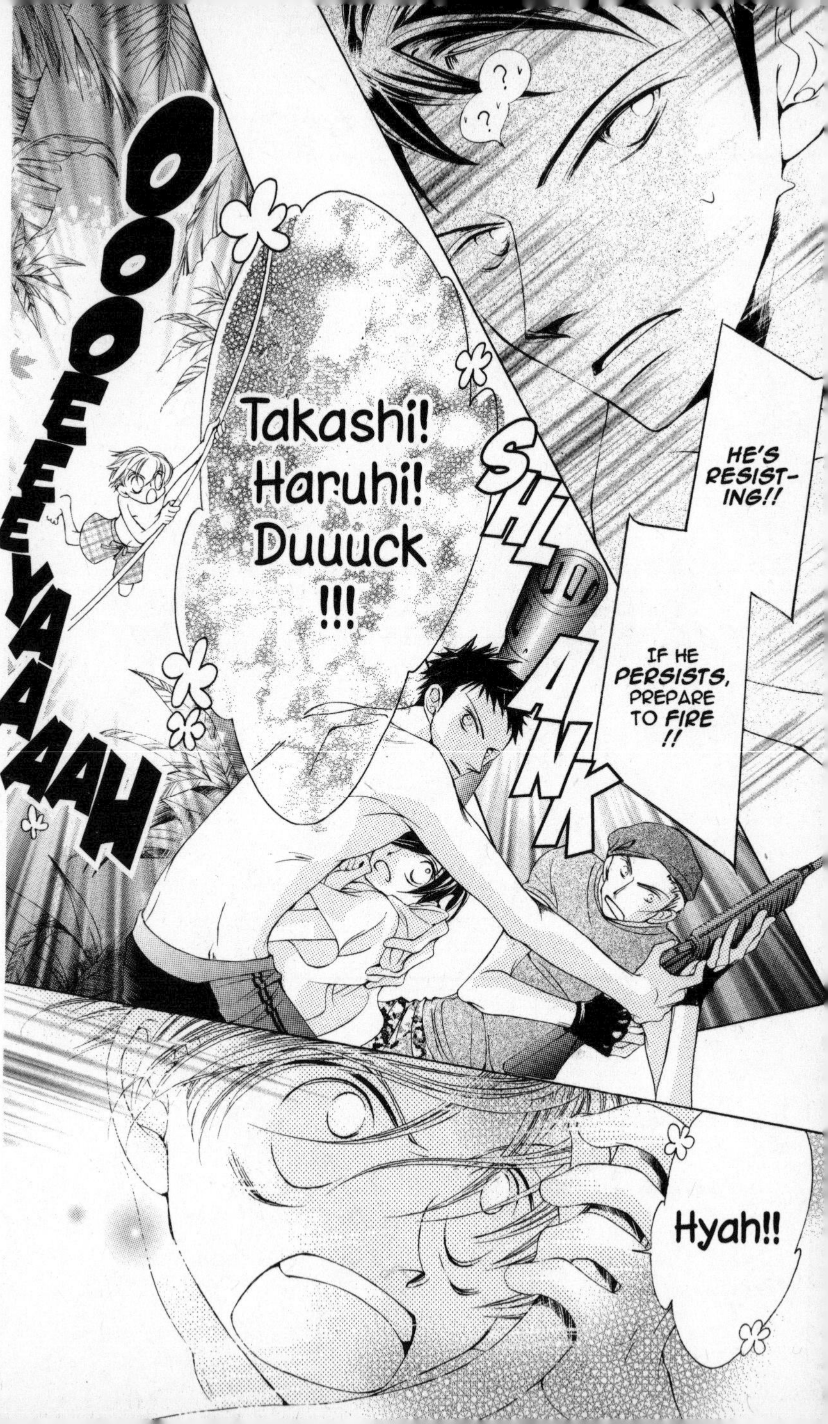

HE'S RESISTING!!
IF HE PERSISTS, PREPARE TO FIRE!!
SHLANK
Takashi! Haruhi! Duuuck!!!
OOOOEEEEYAAAAAH
Hyah!!

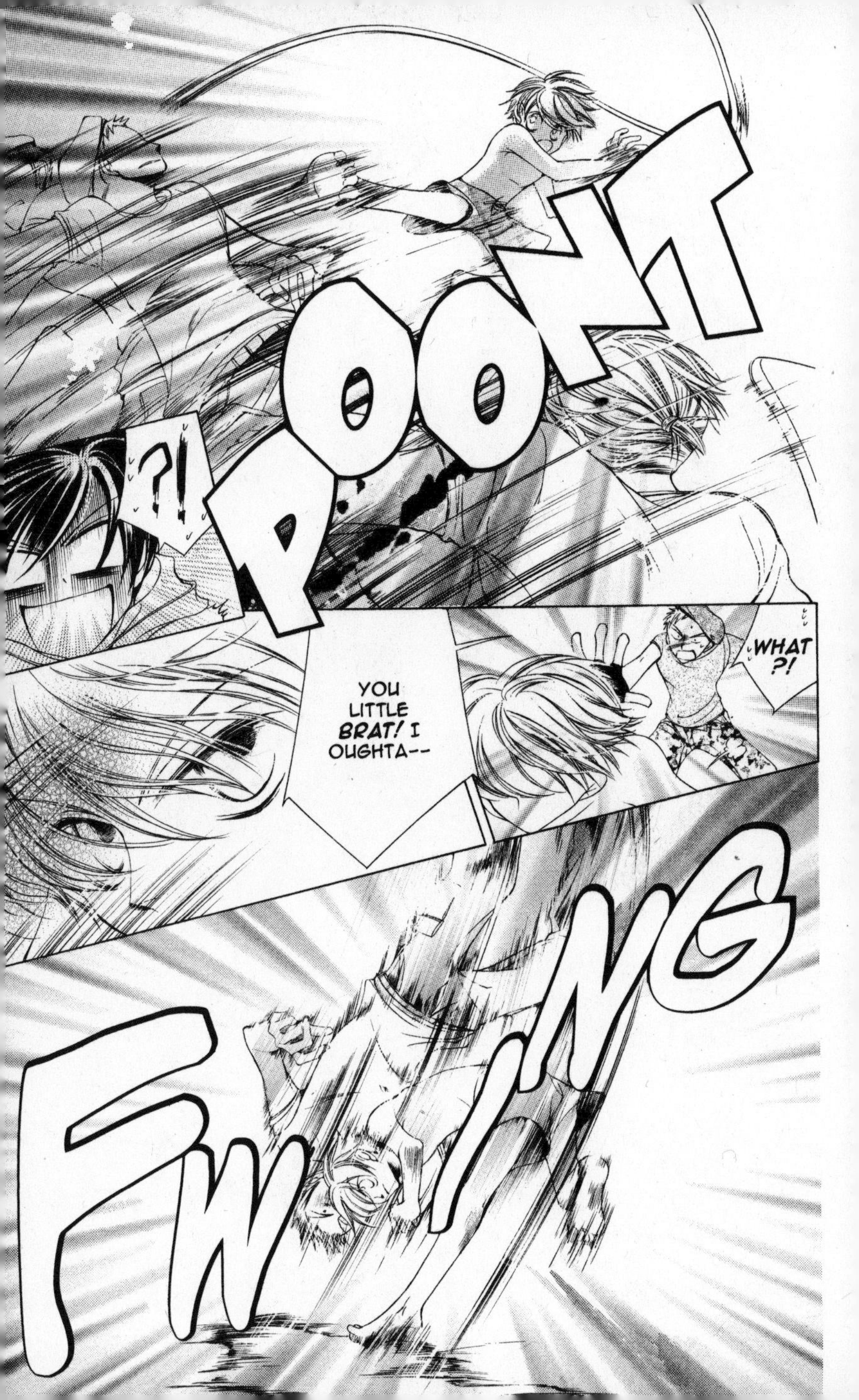
POONT
?!
WHAT?!
YOU LITTLE BRAT! I OUGHTA--

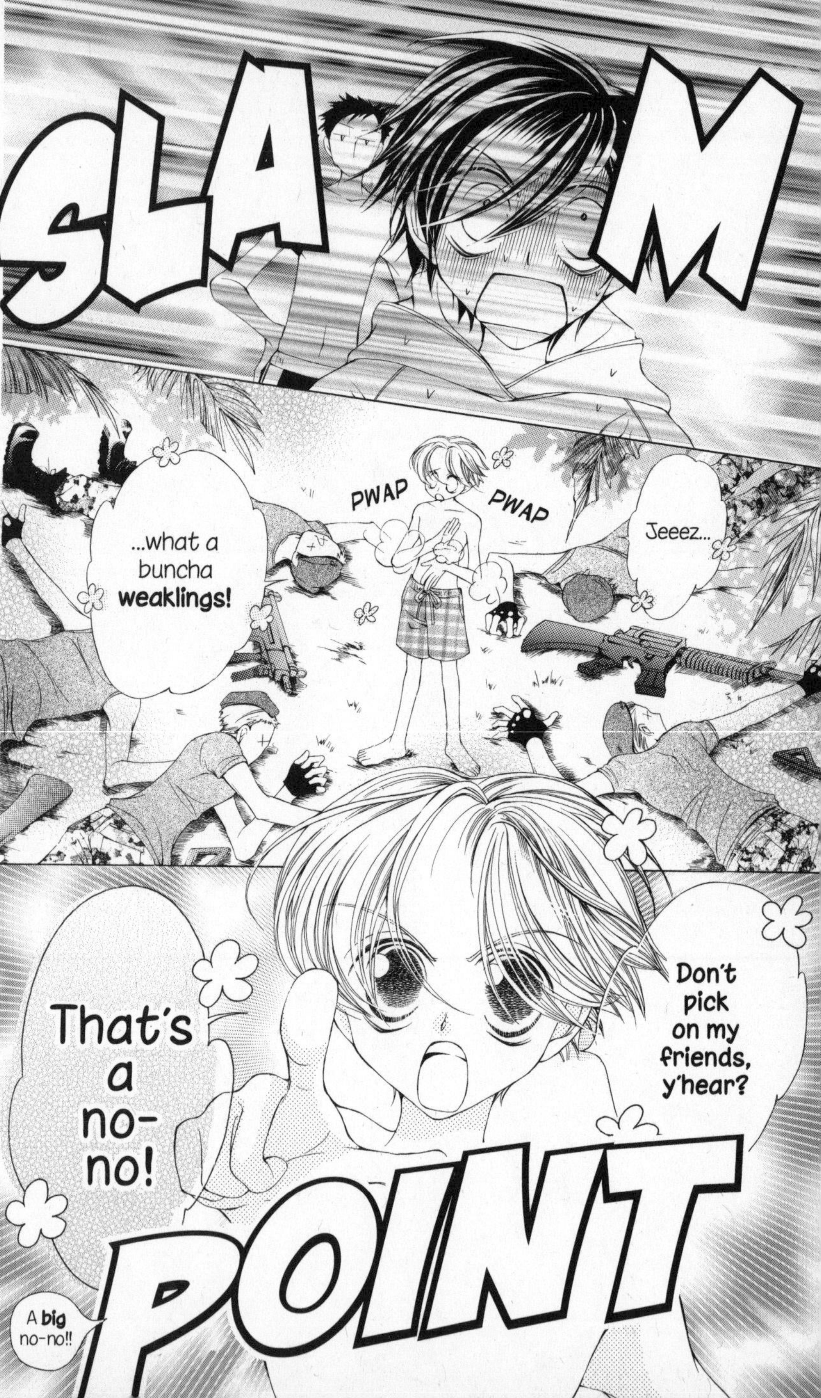
SLAM
Jeeez...
PWAP
PWAP
...what a buncha weaklings!
Don't pick on my friends, y'hear?
That's a no-no!
POINT
A big no-no!!

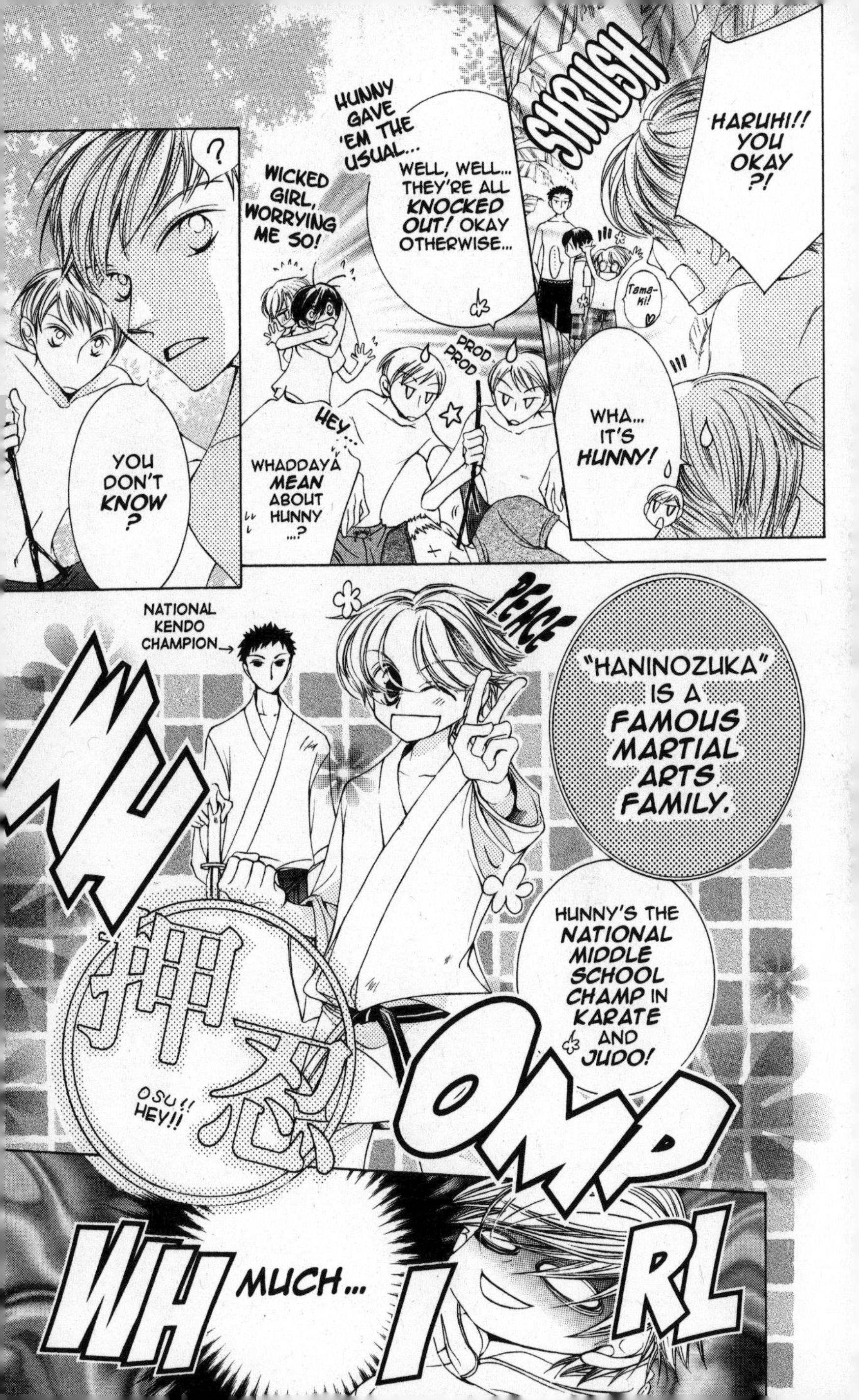
SHRUSH
HARUHI!! YOU OKAY ?!
Tama-ki!
WHA... IT'S HUNNY!
HUNNY GAVE 'EM THE USUAL...
WELL, WELL... THEY'RE ALL KNOCKED OUT! OKAY OTHERWISE...
WICKED GIRL, WORRYING ME SO!
PROD PROD
HEY...
WHADDAYA MEAN ABOUT HUNNY ...?
?
YOU DON'T KNOW ?
PEACE
"HANINOZUKA" IS A FAMOUS MARTIAL ARTS FAMILY.
NATIONAL KENDO CHAMPION
HUNNY'S THE NATIONAL MIDDLE SCHOOL CHAMP IN KARATE AND JUDO!
WH OMP
OSU!! HEY!!
WH I RL
MUCH...

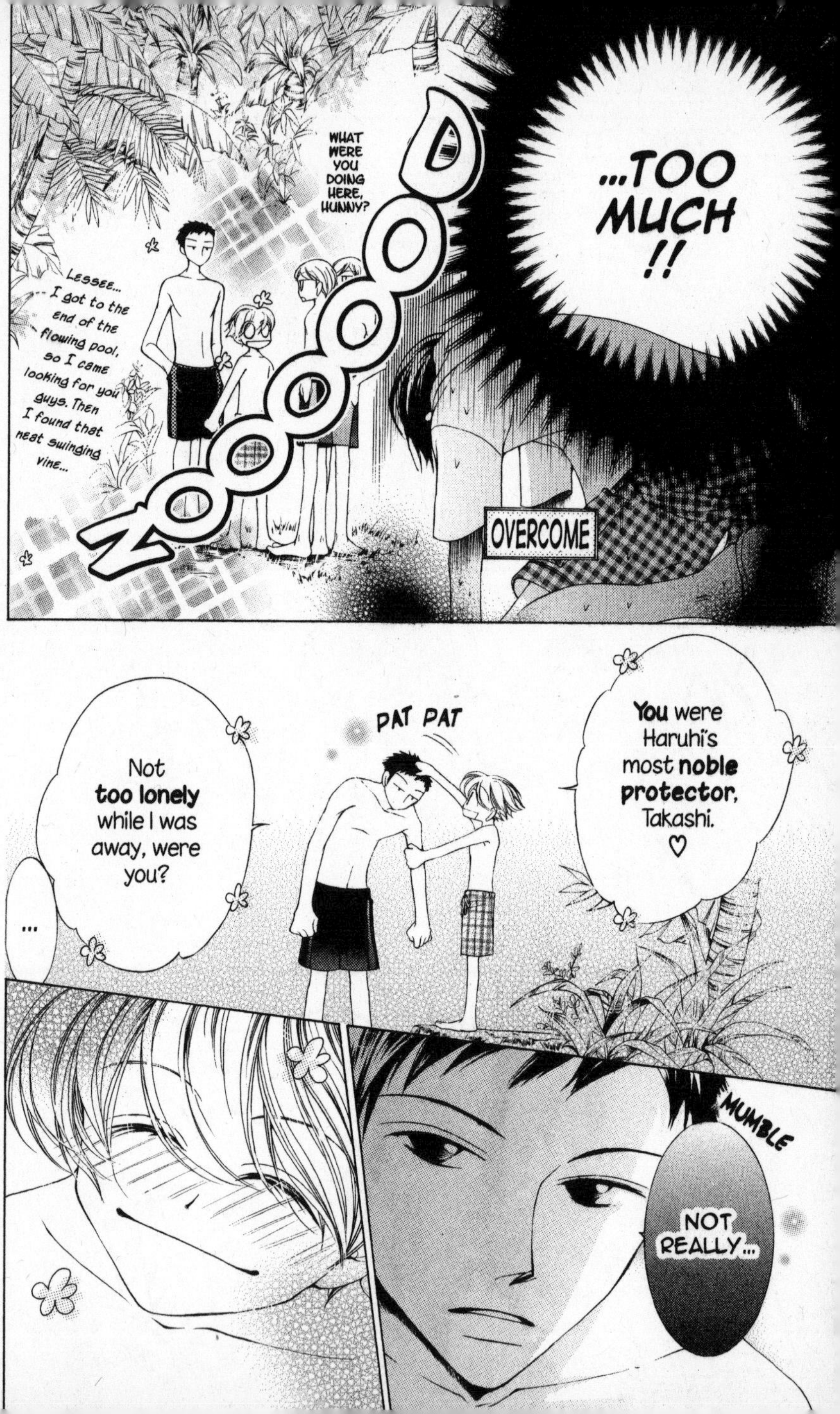
...TOO MUCH!!
DOOOOON
OVERCOME
WHAT WERE YOU DOING HERE, HUNNY?
Lessee... I got to the end of the flowing pool, so I came looking for you guys. Then I found that neat swinging vine...
You were Haruhi's most noble protector, Takashi. ♡
PAT PAT
Not too lonely while I was away, were you?
...
MUMBLE
NOT REALLY...

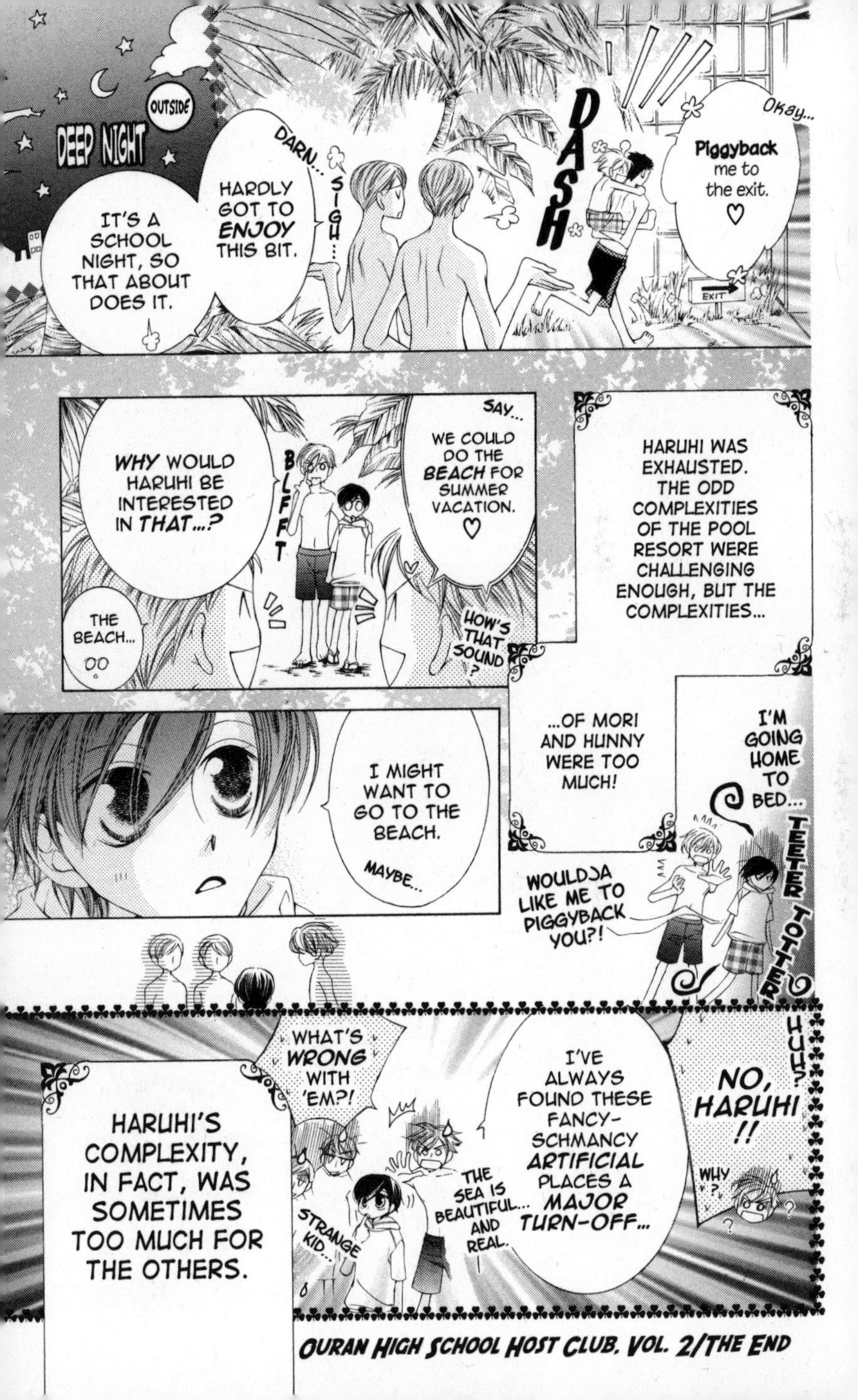

Okay...
Piggyback me to the exit. ♡
DASH
DARN... SIGH...
HARDLY GOT TO ENJOY THIS BIT.
IT'S A SCHOOL NIGHT, SO THAT ABOUT DOES IT.
OUTSIDE
DEEP NIGHT
EXIT
HARUHI WAS EXHAUSTED. THE ODD COMPLEXITIES OF THE POOL RESORT WERE CHALLENGING ENOUGH, BUT THE COMPLEXITIES...
SAY...
WE COULD DO THE BEACH FOR SUMMER VACATION. ♡
HOW'S THAT SOUND?
BLFFT
WHY WOULD HARUHI BE INTERESTED IN THAT...?
THE BEACH...
I'M GOING HOME TO BED...
TEETER TOTTER
WOULDJA LIKE ME TO PIGGYBACK YOU?!
...OF MORI AND HUNNY WERE TOO MUCH!
I MIGHT WANT TO GO TO THE BEACH.
MAYBE...
HUH?
NO, HARUHI!!
WHY?
I'VE ALWAYS FOUND THESE FANCY-SCHMANCY ARTIFICIAL PLACES A MAJOR TURN-OFF...
THE SEA IS BEAUTIFUL... AND REAL.
WHAT'S WRONG WITH 'EM?!
STRANGE KID...
HARUHI'S COMPLEXITY, IN FACT, WAS SOMETIMES TOO MUCH FOR THE OTHERS.
OURAN HIGH SCHOOL HOST CLUB. VOL. 2/THE END

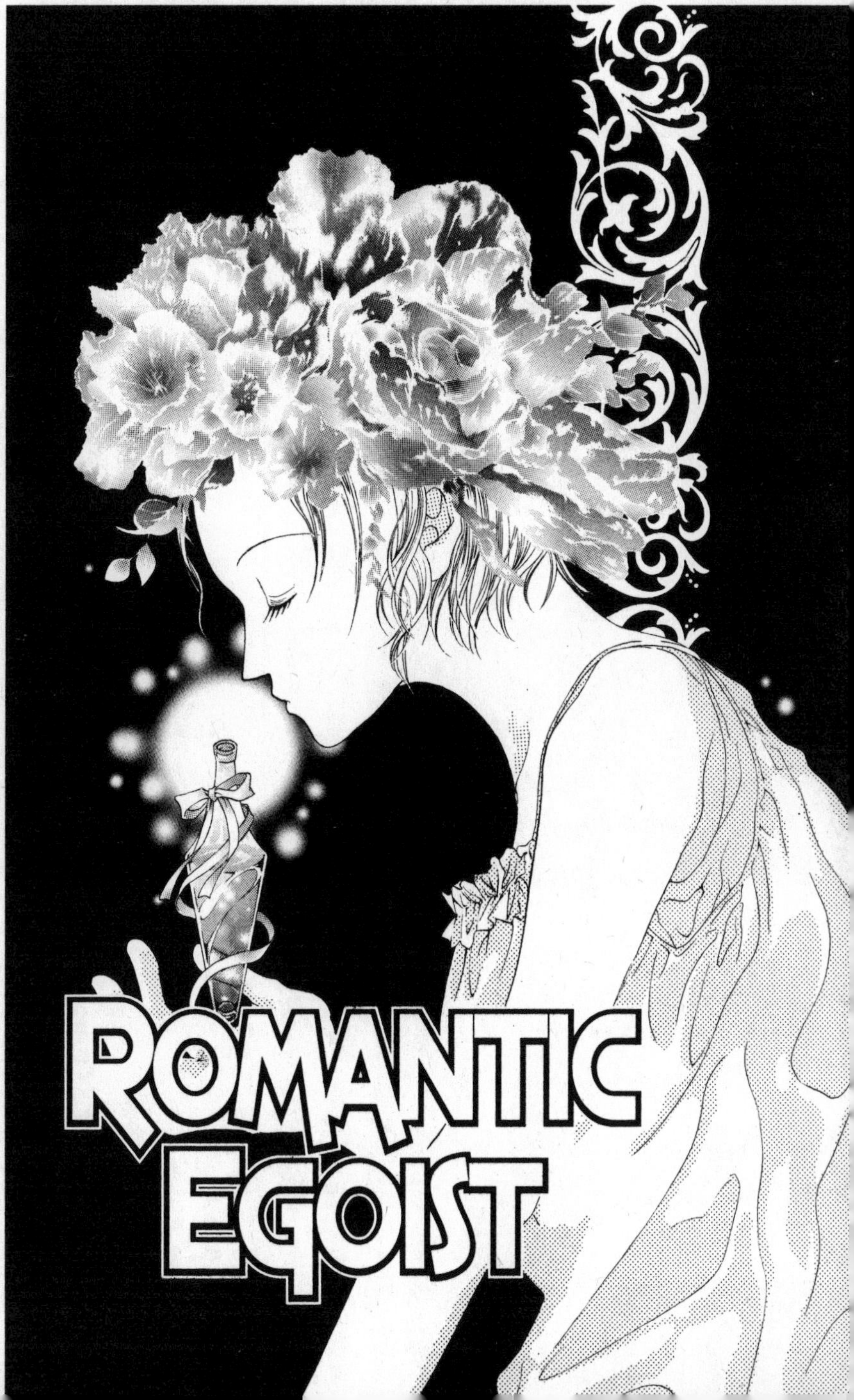
ROMANTIC
EGOIST

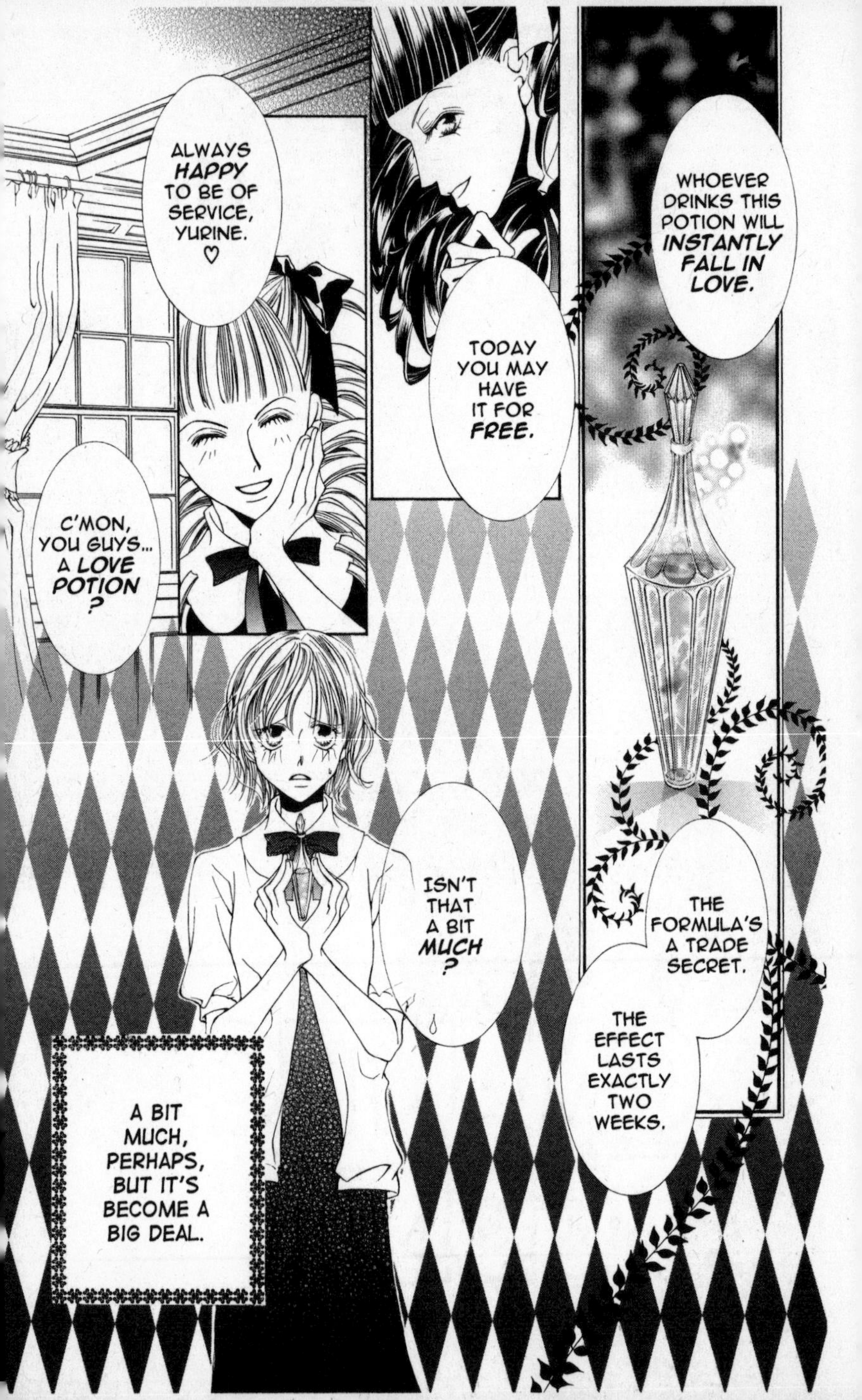
WHOEVER DRINKS THIS POTION WILL INSTANTLY FALL IN LOVE.
THE FORMULA'S A TRADE SECRET.
THE EFFECT LASTS EXACTLY TWO WEEKS.
TODAY YOU MAY HAVE IT FOR FREE.
ALWAYS HAPPY TO BE OF SERVICE, YURINE. ♡
C'MON, YOU GUYS... A LOVE POTION?
ISN'T THAT A BIT MUCH?
A BIT MUCH, PERHAPS, BUT IT'S BECOME A BIG DEAL.

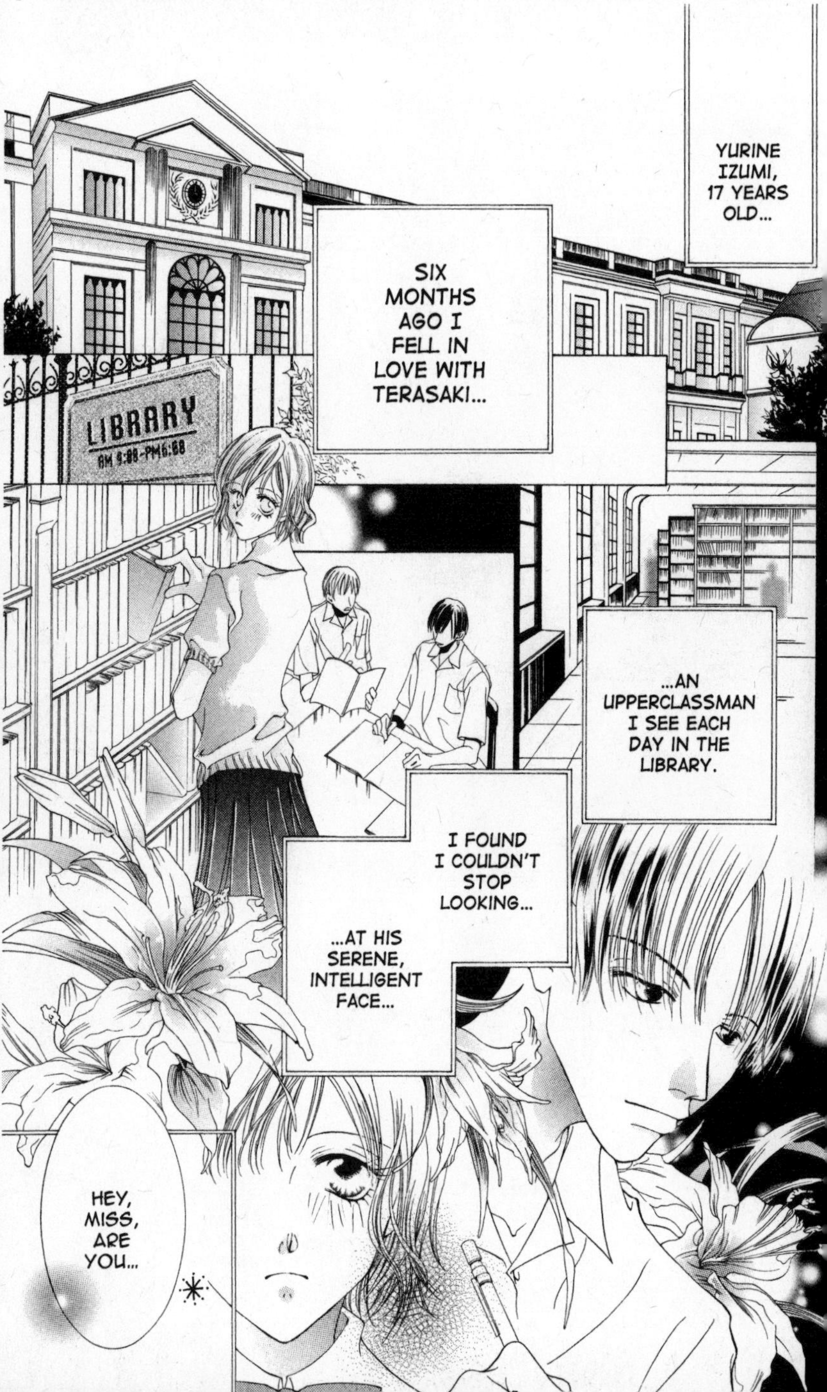
YURINE IZUMI, 17 YEARS OLD...
SIX MONTHS AGO I FELL IN LOVE WITH TERASAKI...
LIBRARY
AM 9:00-PM6:00
...AN UPPERCLASSMAN I SEE EACH DAY IN THE LIBRARY.
I FOUND I COULDN'T STOP LOOKING...
...AT HIS SERENE, INTELLIGENT FACE...
HEY, MISS, ARE YOU...

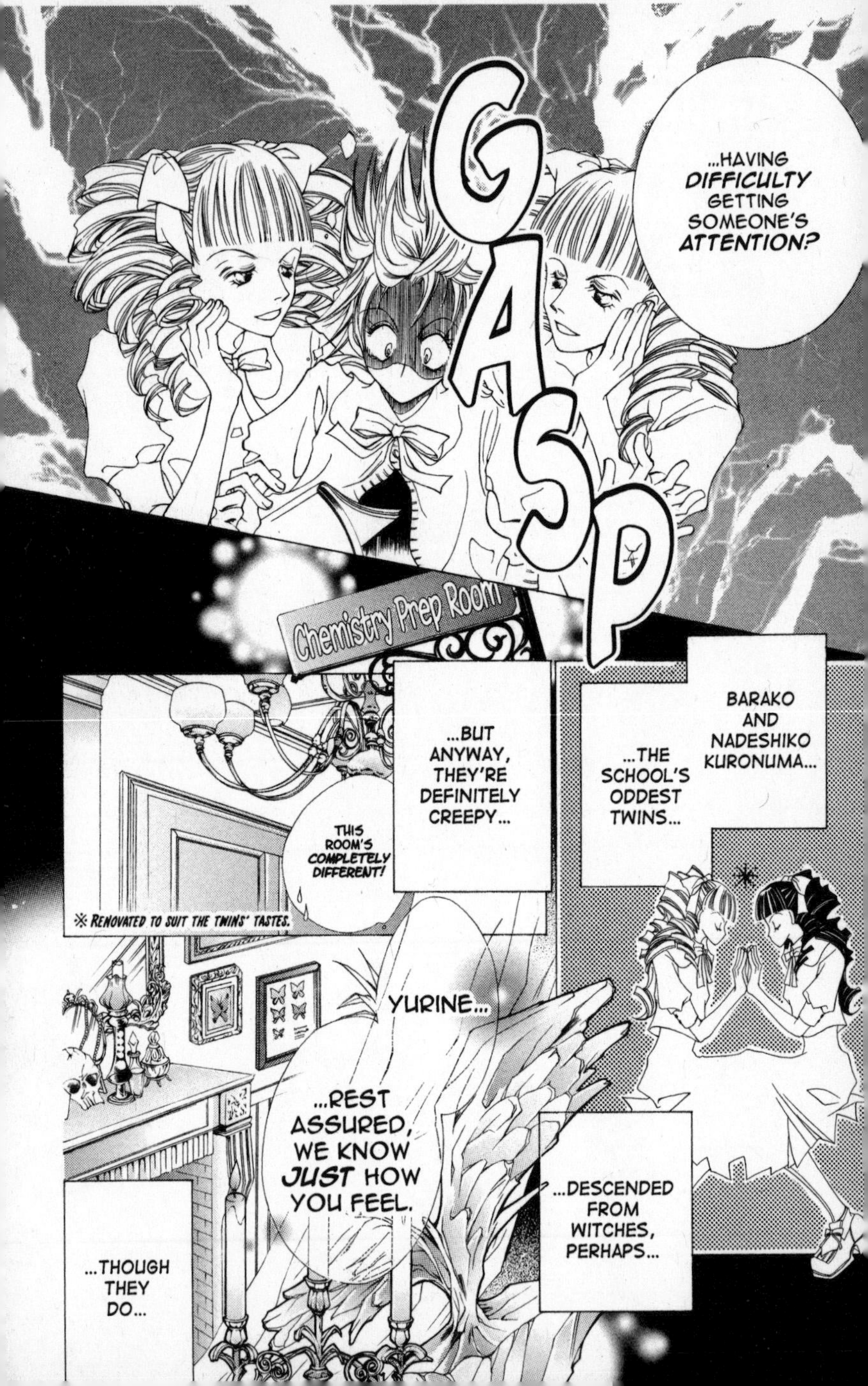
...HAVING DIFFICULTY GETTING SOMEONE'S ATTENTION?
GASP
Chemistry Prep Room
BARAKO AND NADESHIKO KURONUMA...
...THE SCHOOL'S ODDEST TWINS...
...BUT ANYWAY, THEY'RE DEFINITELY CREEPY...
THIS ROOM'S COMPLETELY DIFFERENT!
※ RENOVATED TO SUIT THE TWINS' TASTES.
...DESCENDED FROM WITCHES, PERHAPS...
YURINE...
...REST ASSURED, WE KNOW JUST HOW YOU FEEL.
...THOUGH THEY DO...

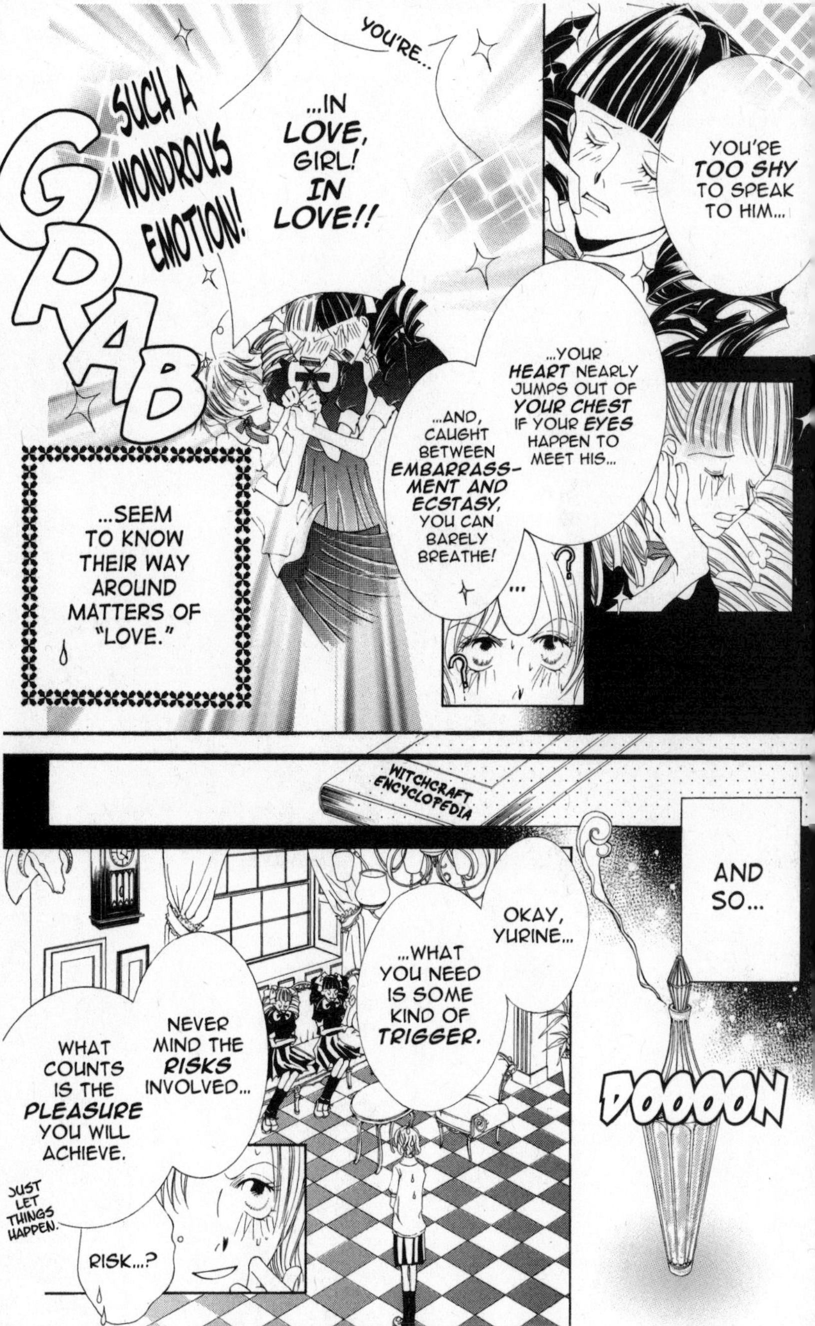
YOU'RE TOO SHY TO SPEAK TO HIM...
...YOUR HEART NEARLY JUMPS OUT OF YOUR CHEST IF YOUR EYES HAPPEN TO MEET HIS...
...AND, CAUGHT BETWEEN EMBARRASSMENT AND ECSTASY, YOU CAN BARELY BREATHE!
...
YOU'RE...
...IN LOVE, GIRL! IN LOVE!!
SUCH A WONDROUS EMOTION!
GRAB
...SEEM TO KNOW THEIR WAY AROUND MATTERS OF "LOVE."
WITCHCRAFT ENCYCLOPEDIA
AND SO...
DOOOON
OKAY, YURINE...
...WHAT YOU NEED IS SOME KIND OF TRIGGER.
NEVER MIND THE RISKS INVOLVED...
WHAT COUNTS IS THE PLEASURE YOU WILL ACHIEVE.
JUST LET THINGS HAPPEN.
RISK...?

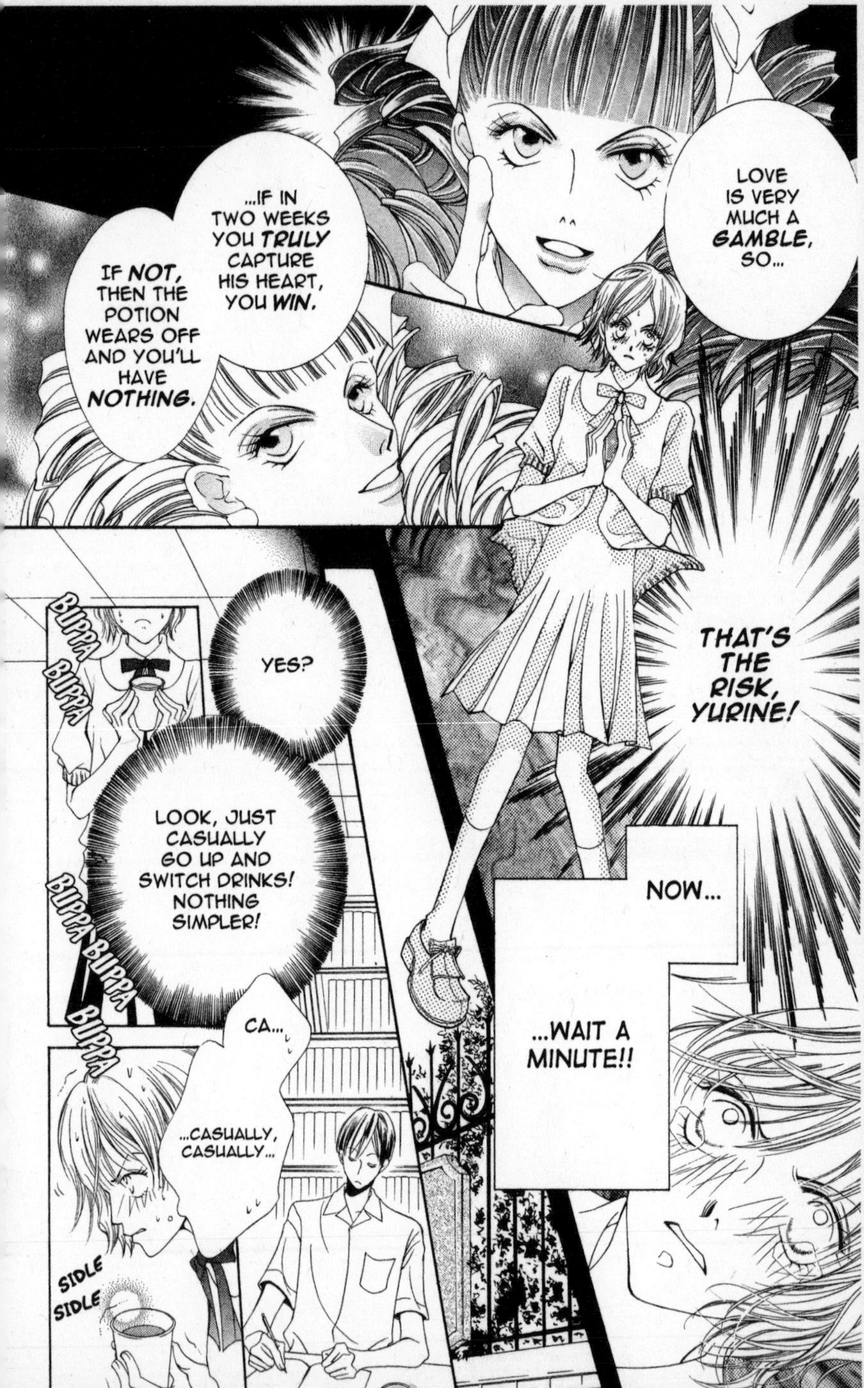
LOVE IS VERY MUCH A GAMBLE, SO...
...IF IN TWO WEEKS YOU TRULY CAPTURE HIS HEART, YOU WIN.
IF NOT, THEN THE POTION WEARS OFF AND YOU'LL HAVE NOTHING.
THAT'S THE RISK, YURINE!
NOW...
...WAIT A MINUTE!!
YES?
BUPPA BUPPA BUPPA
LOOK, JUST CASUALLY GO UP AND SWITCH DRINKS! NOTHING SIMPLER!
BUPPA BUPPA BUPPA BUPPA
CA...
...CASUALLY, CASUALLY...
SIDLE SIDLE

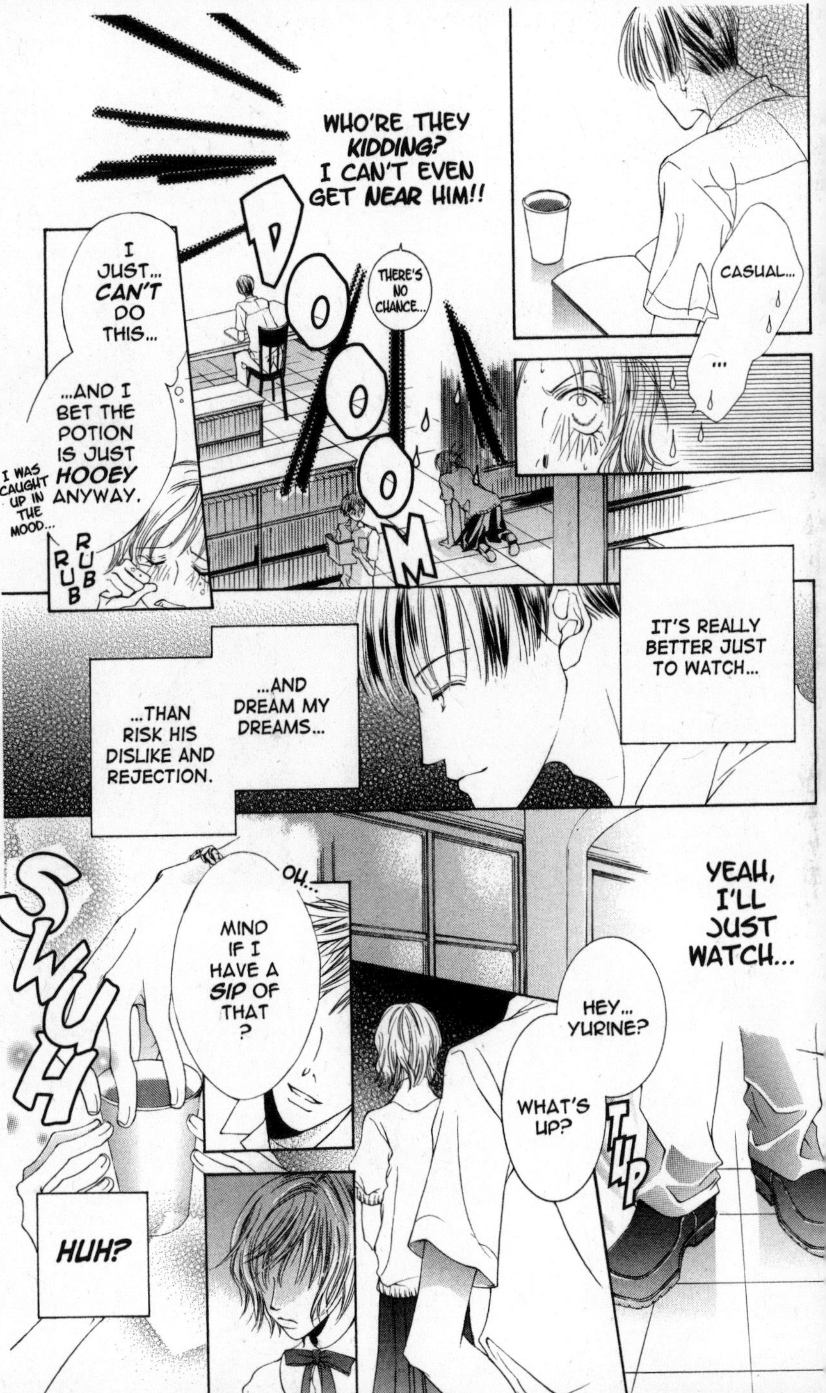
CASUAL...
...
WHO'RE THEY KIDDING? I CAN'T EVEN GET NEAR HIM!!
DOOOOM
THERE'S NO CHANCE...
I JUST... CAN'T DO THIS...
...AND I BET THE POTION IS JUST HOOEY ANYWAY.
I WAS CAUGHT UP IN THE MOOD...
RUB RUB
IT'S REALLY BETTER JUST TO WATCH...
...AND DREAM MY DREAMS...
...THAN RISK HIS DISLIKE AND REJECTION.
YEAH, I'LL JUST WATCH...
HEY... YURINE?
WHAT'S UP?
TUP
OH...
MIND IF I HAVE A SIP OF THAT?
SWUH
HUH?

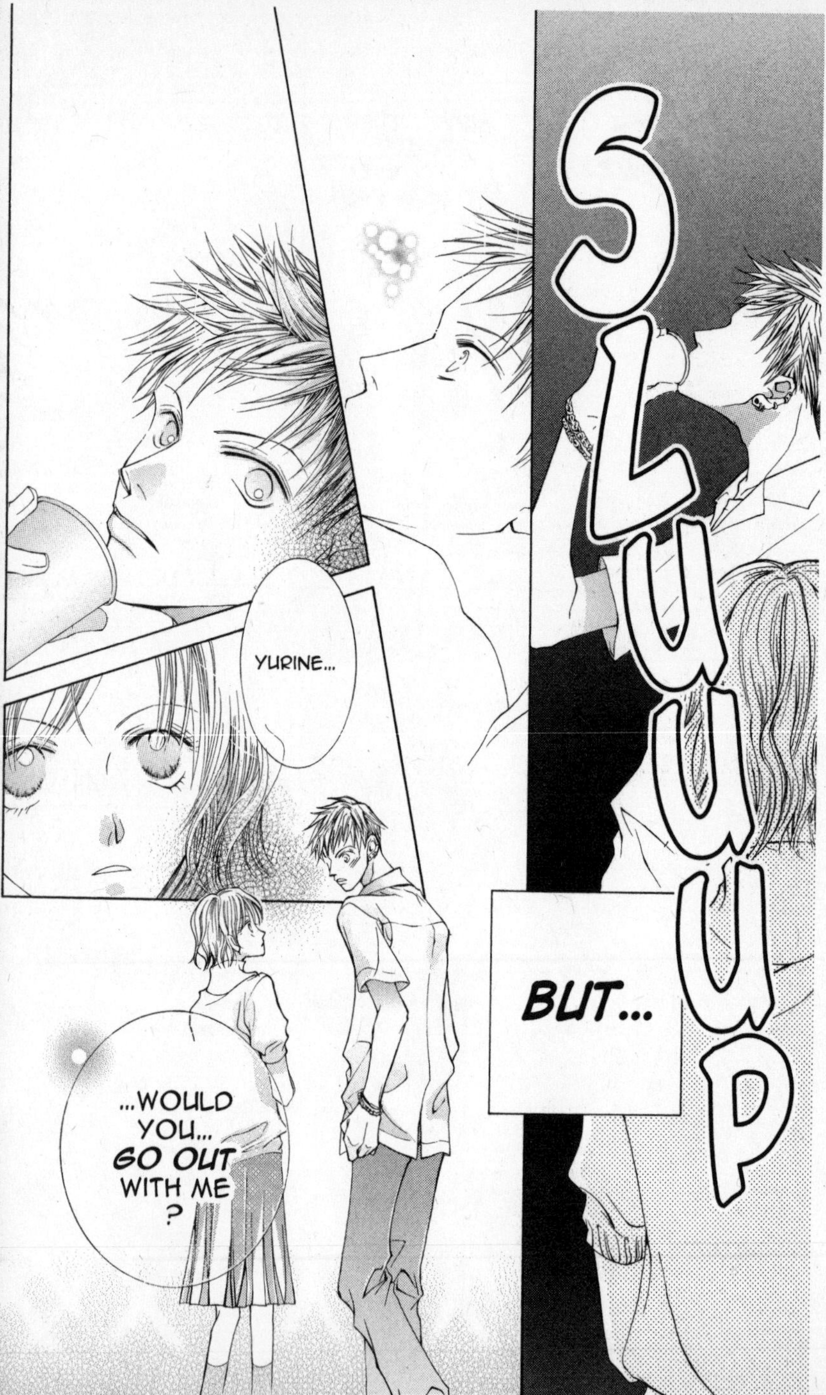
SLUUUP
BUT...
YURINE...
...WOULD YOU... GO OUT WITH ME?

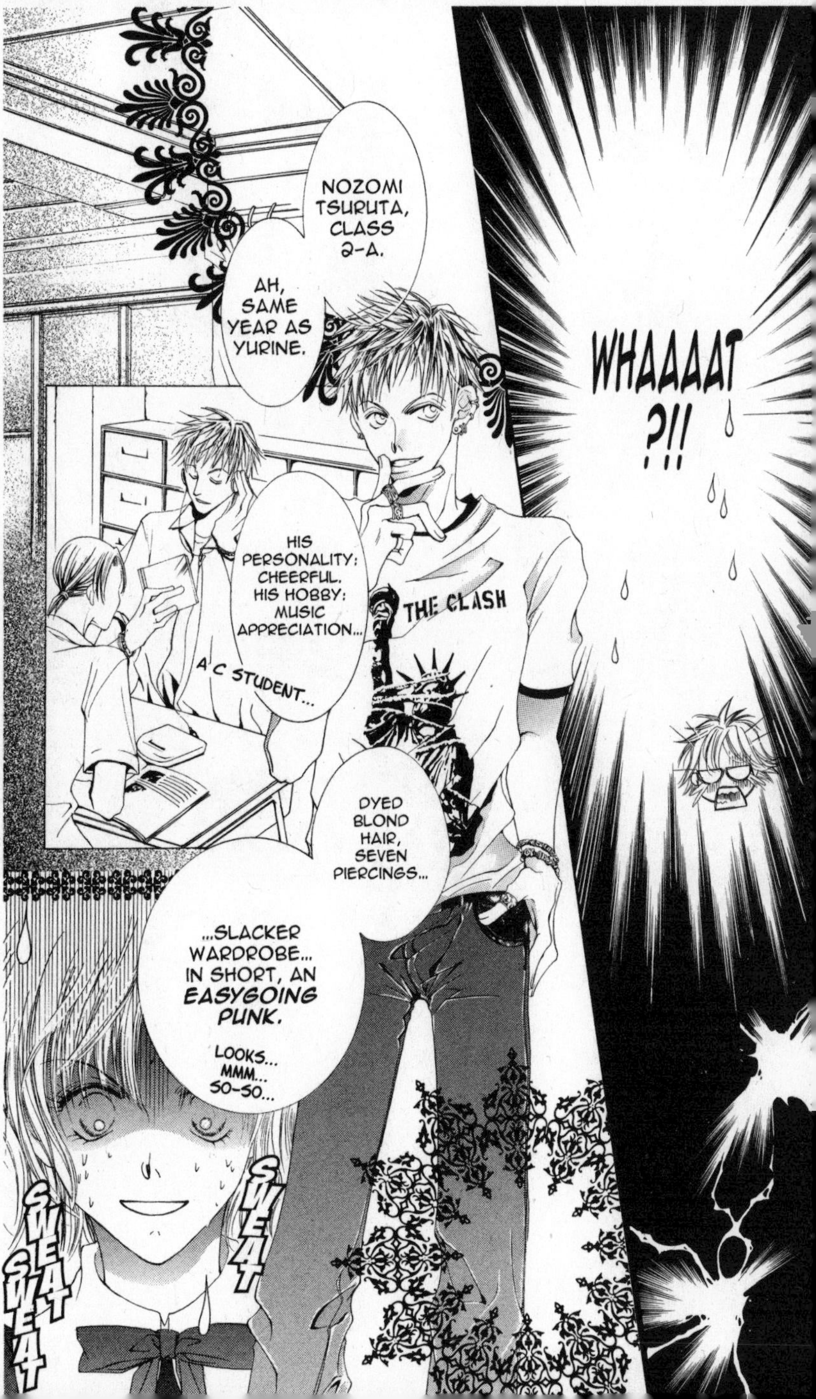
WHAAAAT?!!
NOZOMI TSURUTA, CLASS 2-A.
AH, SAME YEAR AS YURINE.
HIS PERSONALITY: CHEERFUL. HIS HOBBY: MUSIC APPRECIATION...
A C STUDENT...
THE CLASH
DYED BLOND HAIR, SEVEN PIERCINGS...
...SLACKER WARDROBE... IN SHORT, AN **EASYGOING PUNK.**
LOOKS... MMM... SO-SO...
SWEAT
SWEAT
SWEAT

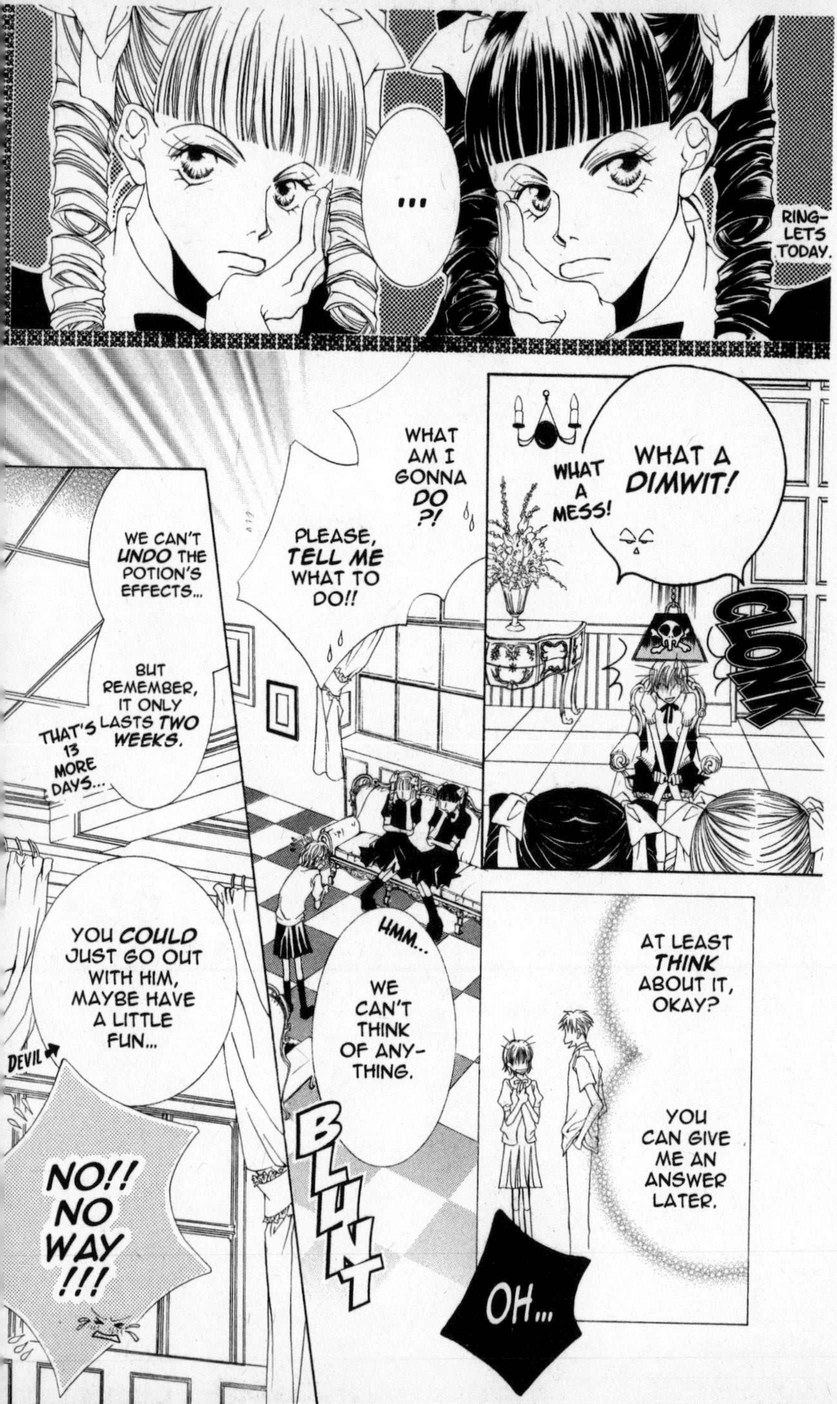
RING-LETS TODAY.
...
WHAT A DIMWIT!
WHAT A MESS!
CLONK
AT LEAST THINK ABOUT IT, OKAY?
YOU CAN GIVE ME AN ANSWER LATER.
OH...
WHAT AM I GONNA DO ?!
PLEASE, TELL ME WHAT TO DO!!
WE CAN'T UNDO THE POTION'S EFFECTS...
BUT REMEMBER, IT ONLY LASTS TWO WEEKS.
THAT'S 13 MORE DAYS...
HMM...
WE CAN'T THINK OF ANY-THING.
BLUNT
YOU COULD JUST GO OUT WITH HIM, MAYBE HAVE A LITTLE FUN...
DEVIL
NO!! NO WAY!!!

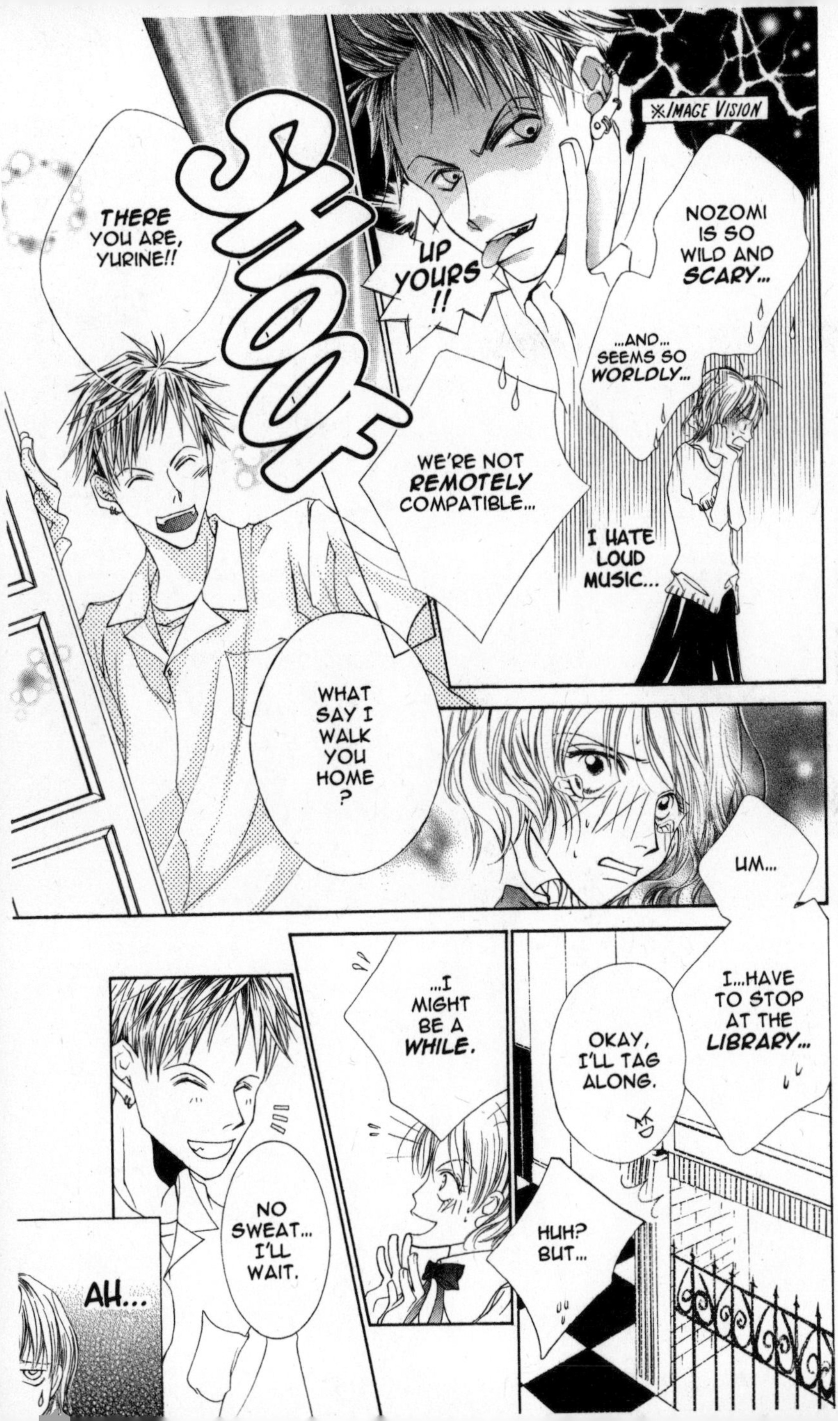
※IMAGE VISION
UP YOURS !!
NOZOMI IS SO WILD AND SCARY...
...AND... SEEMS SO WORLDLY...
WE'RE NOT REMOTELY COMPATIBLE...
I HATE LOUD MUSIC...
UM...
THERE YOU ARE, YURINE!!
SHOOT
WHAT SAY I WALK YOU HOME ?
I...HAVE TO STOP AT THE LIBRARY...
OKAY, I'LL TAG ALONG.
...I MIGHT BE A WHILE.
HUH? BUT...
NO SWEAT... I'LL WAIT.
AH...

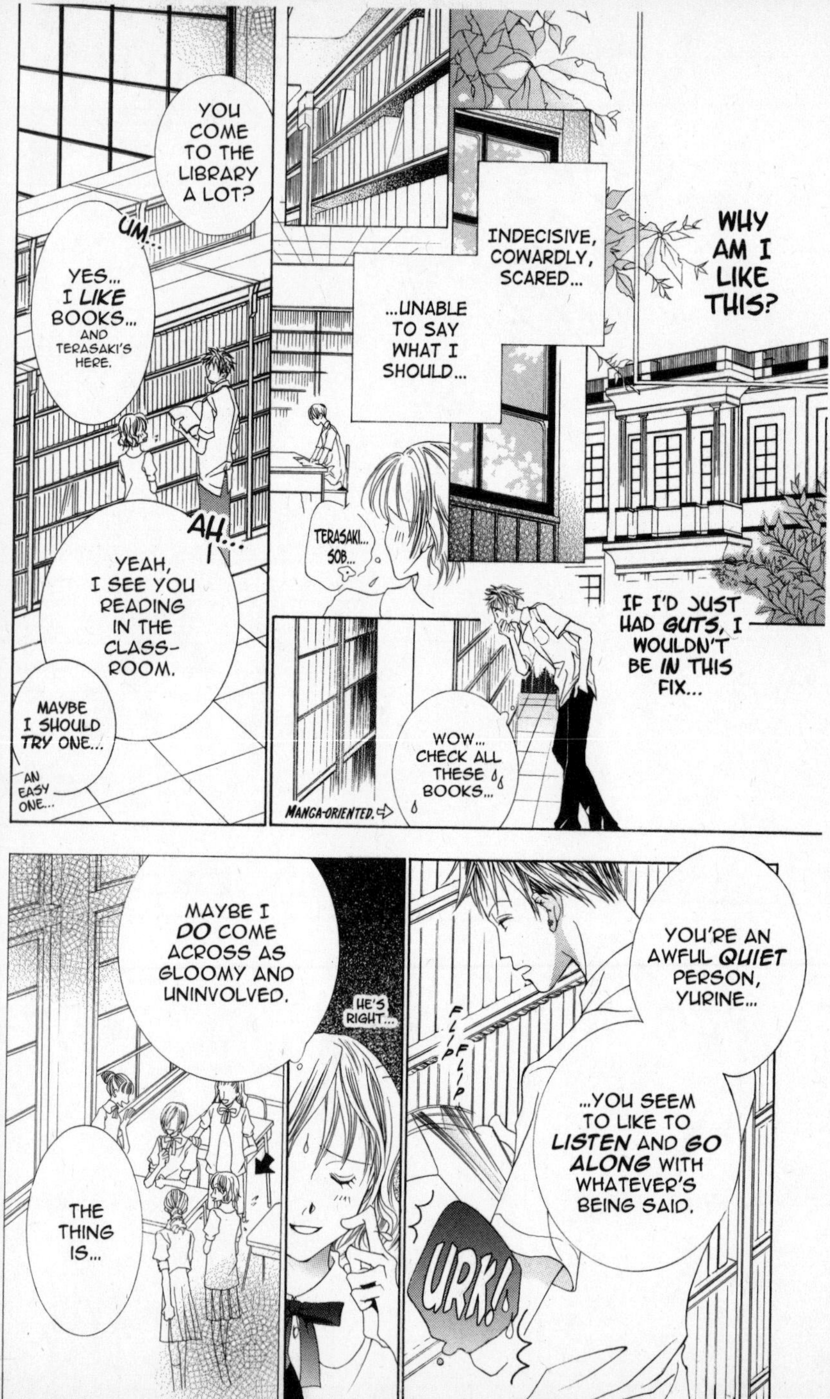
WHY AM I LIKE THIS?
INDECISIVE, COWARDLY, SCARED...
...UNABLE TO SAY WHAT I SHOULD...
TERASAKI... SOB...
IF I'D JUST HAD GUTS, I WOULDN'T BE IN THIS FIX...
WOW... CHECK ALL THESE BOOKS...
MANGA-ORIENTED.
YOU COME TO THE LIBRARY A LOT?
UM...
YES... I LIKE BOOKS... AND TERASAKI'S HERE.
AH...
YEAH, I SEE YOU READING IN THE CLASSROOM.
MAYBE I SHOULD TRY ONE...
AN EASY ONE...
YOU'RE AN AWFUL QUIET PERSON, YURINE...
FLIP FLIP
...YOU SEEM TO LIKE TO LISTEN AND GO ALONG WITH WHATEVER'S BEING SAID.
URK!
HE'S RIGHT...
MAYBE I DO COME ACROSS AS GLOOMY AND UNINVOLVED.
THE THING IS...

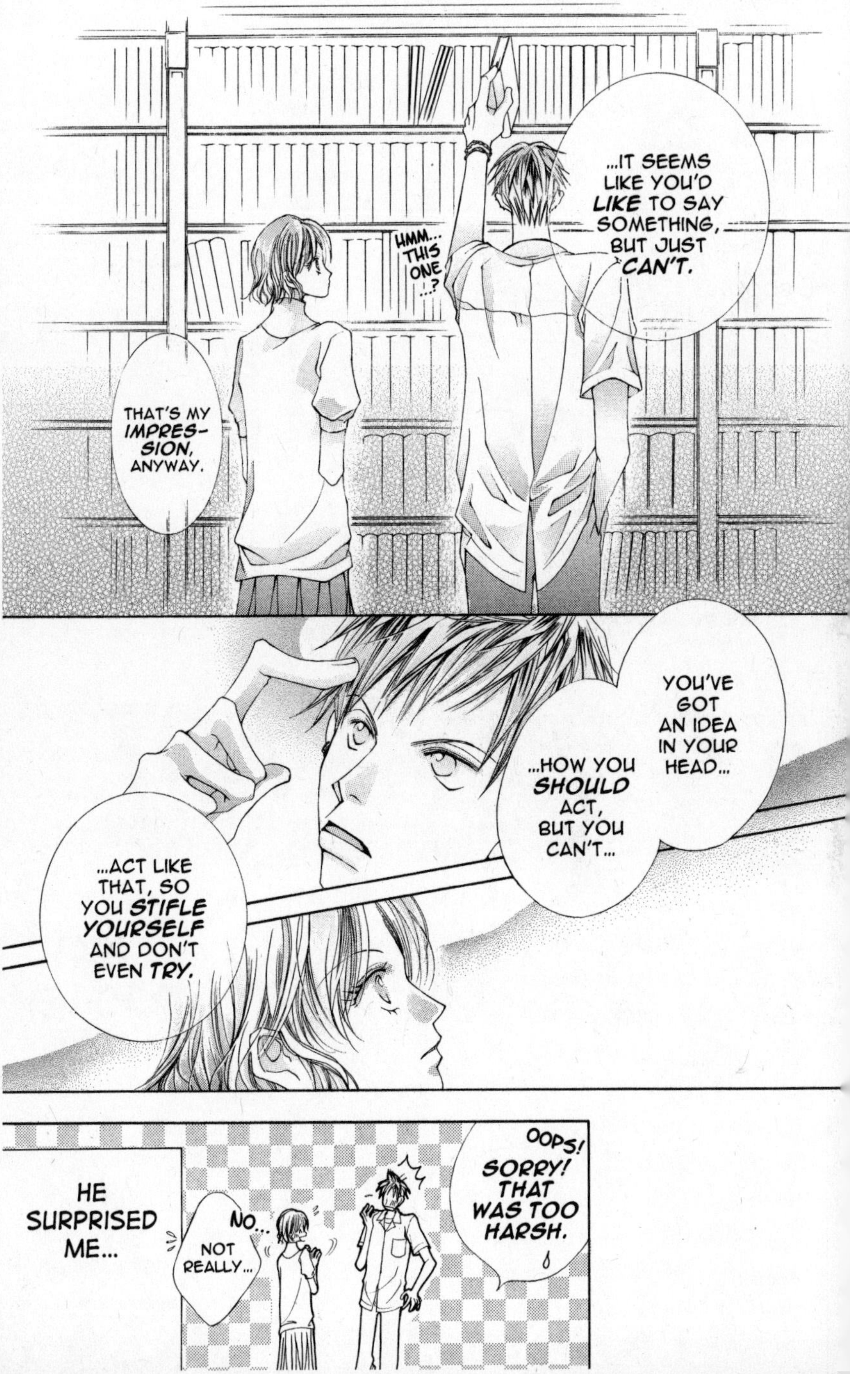
...IT SEEMS LIKE YOU'D LIKE TO SAY SOMETHING, BUT JUST CAN'T.
HMM... THIS ONE ...?
THAT'S MY IMPRESSION, ANYWAY.
YOU'VE GOT AN IDEA IN YOUR HEAD...
...HOW YOU SHOULD ACT, BUT YOU CAN'T...
...ACT LIKE THAT, SO YOU STIFLE YOURSELF AND DON'T EVEN TRY.
OOPS! SORRY! THAT WAS TOO HARSH.
NO... NOT REALLY...
HE SURPRISED ME...

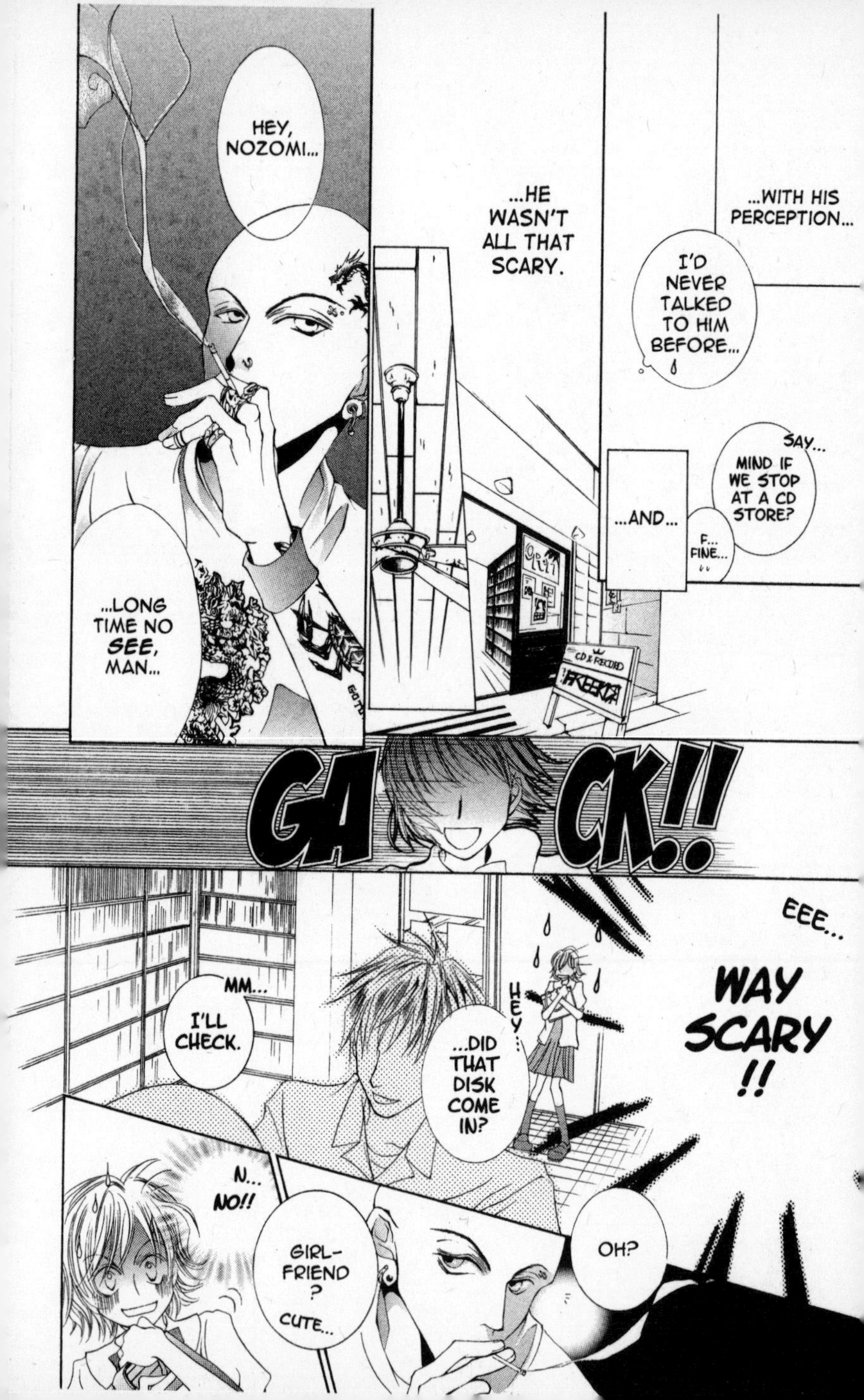
...WITH HIS PERCEPTION...
I'D NEVER TALKED TO HIM BEFORE...
SAY... MIND IF WE STOP AT A CD STORE?
F... FINE...
...AND...
...HE WASN'T ALL THAT SCARY.
CD & RECORD
HEY, NOZOMI...
...LONG TIME NO SEE, MAN...
GA CK!!
EEE...
WAY SCARY!!
HEY...
...DID THAT DISK COME IN?
MM... I'LL CHECK.
OH?
GIRL-FRIEND? CUTE...
N... NO!!

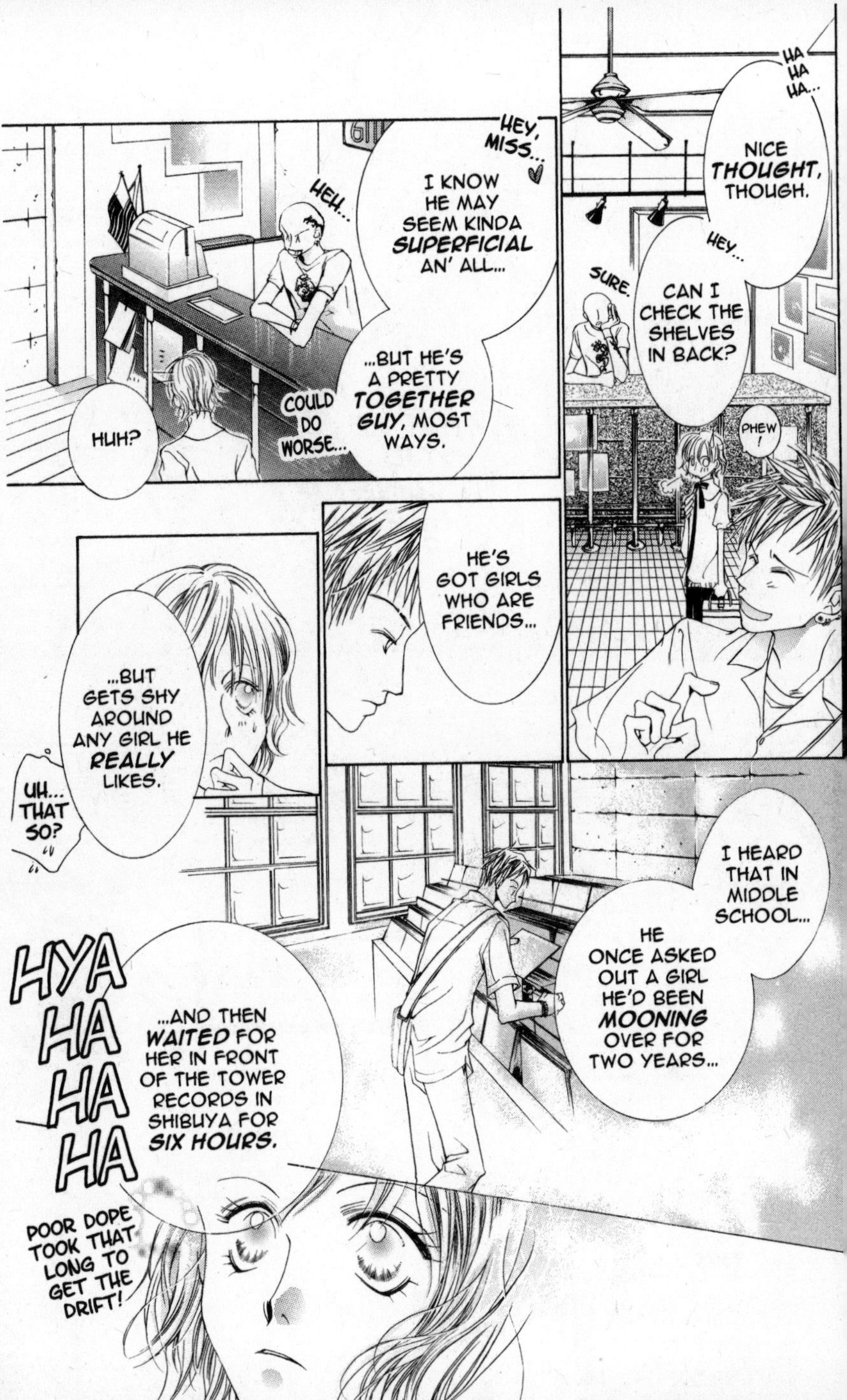
HA HA HA...
NICE THOUGHT, THOUGH.
HEY...
CAN I CHECK THE SHELVES IN BACK?
SURE.
PHEW!
HEY, MISS...
I KNOW HE MAY SEEM KINDA SUPERFICIAL AN' ALL...
HEH...
...BUT HE'S A PRETTY TOGETHER GUY, MOST WAYS.
COULD DO WORSE...
HUH?
HE'S GOT GIRLS WHO ARE FRIENDS...
...BUT GETS SHY AROUND ANY GIRL HE REALLY LIKES.
UH... THAT SO?
I HEARD THAT IN MIDDLE SCHOOL...
HE ONCE ASKED OUT A GIRL HE'D BEEN MOONING OVER FOR TWO YEARS...
...AND THEN WAITED FOR HER IN FRONT OF THE TOWER RECORDS IN SHIBUYA FOR SIX HOURS.
HYA HA HA HA
POOR DOPE TOOK THAT LONG TO GET THE DRIFT!

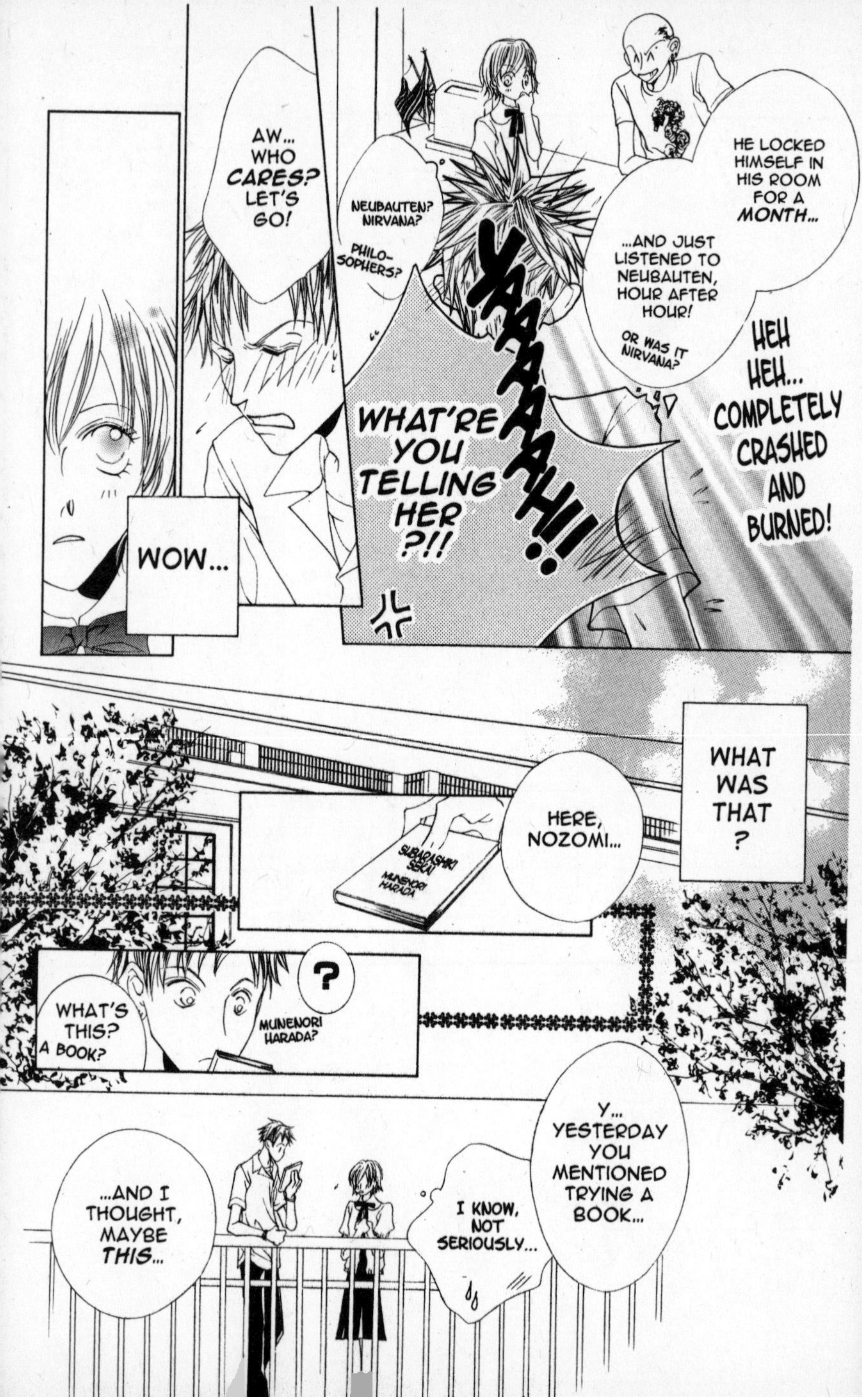
HE LOCKED HIMSELF IN HIS ROOM FOR A MONTH...
...AND JUST LISTENED TO NEUBAUTEN, HOUR AFTER HOUR!
OR WAS IT NIRVANA?
HEH HEH... COMPLETELY CRASHED AND BURNED!
YAAAAAAH!!!
WHAT'RE YOU TELLING HER?!!
NEUBAUTEN? NIRVANA?
PHILO-SOPHERS?
AW... WHO CARES? LET'S GO!
WOW...
WHAT WAS THAT?
HERE, NOZOMI...
SUBARASHIKI SEKAI
MUNENORI HARADA
?
MUNENORI HARADA?
WHAT'S THIS? A BOOK?
Y... YESTERDAY YOU MENTIONED TRYING A BOOK...
I KNOW, NOT SERIOUSLY...
...AND I THOUGHT, MAYBE THIS...

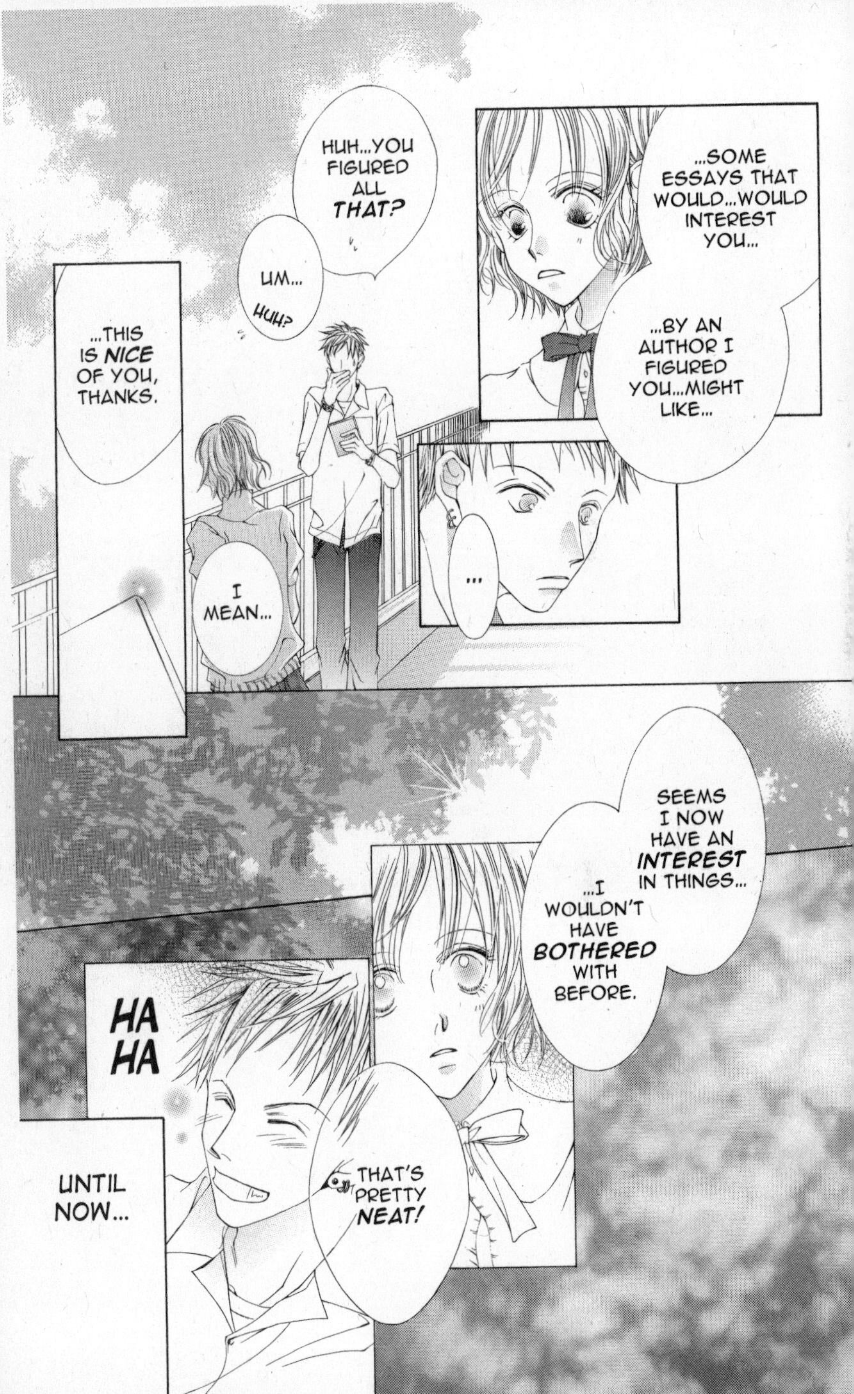
...SOME ESSAYS THAT WOULD...WOULD INTEREST YOU...
...BY AN AUTHOR I FIGURED YOU...MIGHT LIKE...
...
HUH...YOU FIGURED ALL THAT?
UM...
HUH?
I MEAN...
...THIS IS NICE OF YOU, THANKS.
SEEMS I NOW HAVE AN INTEREST IN THINGS...
...I WOULDN'T HAVE BOTHERED WITH BEFORE.
HA HA
THAT'S PRETTY NEAT!
UNTIL NOW...

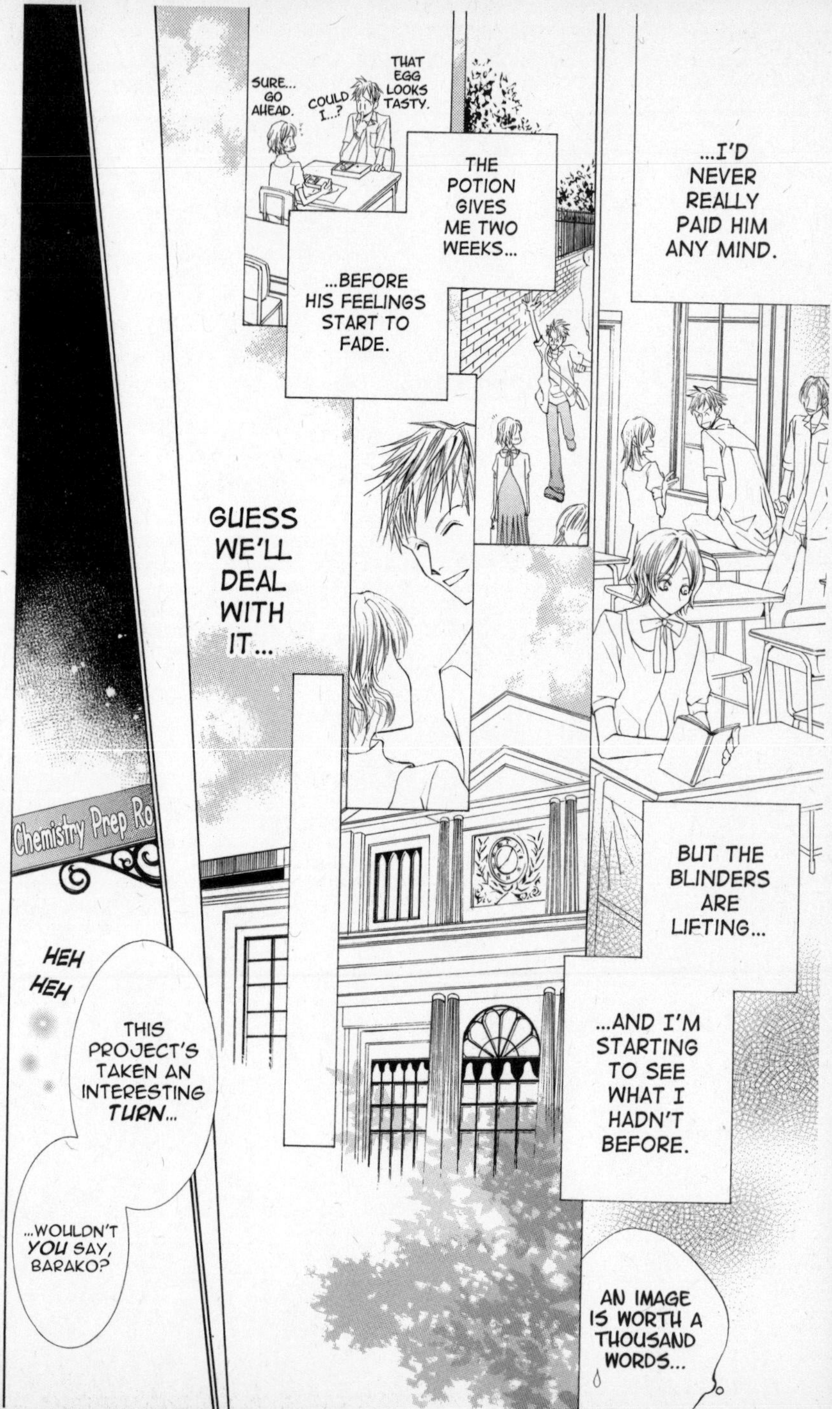

...I'D NEVER REALLY PAID HIM ANY MIND.
BUT THE BLINDERS ARE LIFTING...
...AND I'M STARTING TO SEE WHAT I HADN'T BEFORE.
AN IMAGE IS WORTH A THOUSAND WORDS...
THAT EGG LOOKS TASTY.
COULD I...?
SURE... GO AHEAD.
THE POTION GIVES ME TWO WEEKS...
...BEFORE HIS FEELINGS START TO FADE.
GUESS WE'LL DEAL WITH IT...
Chemistry Prep Ro
HEH HEH
THIS PROJECT'S TAKEN AN INTERESTING TURN...
...WOULDN'T YOU SAY, BARAKO?

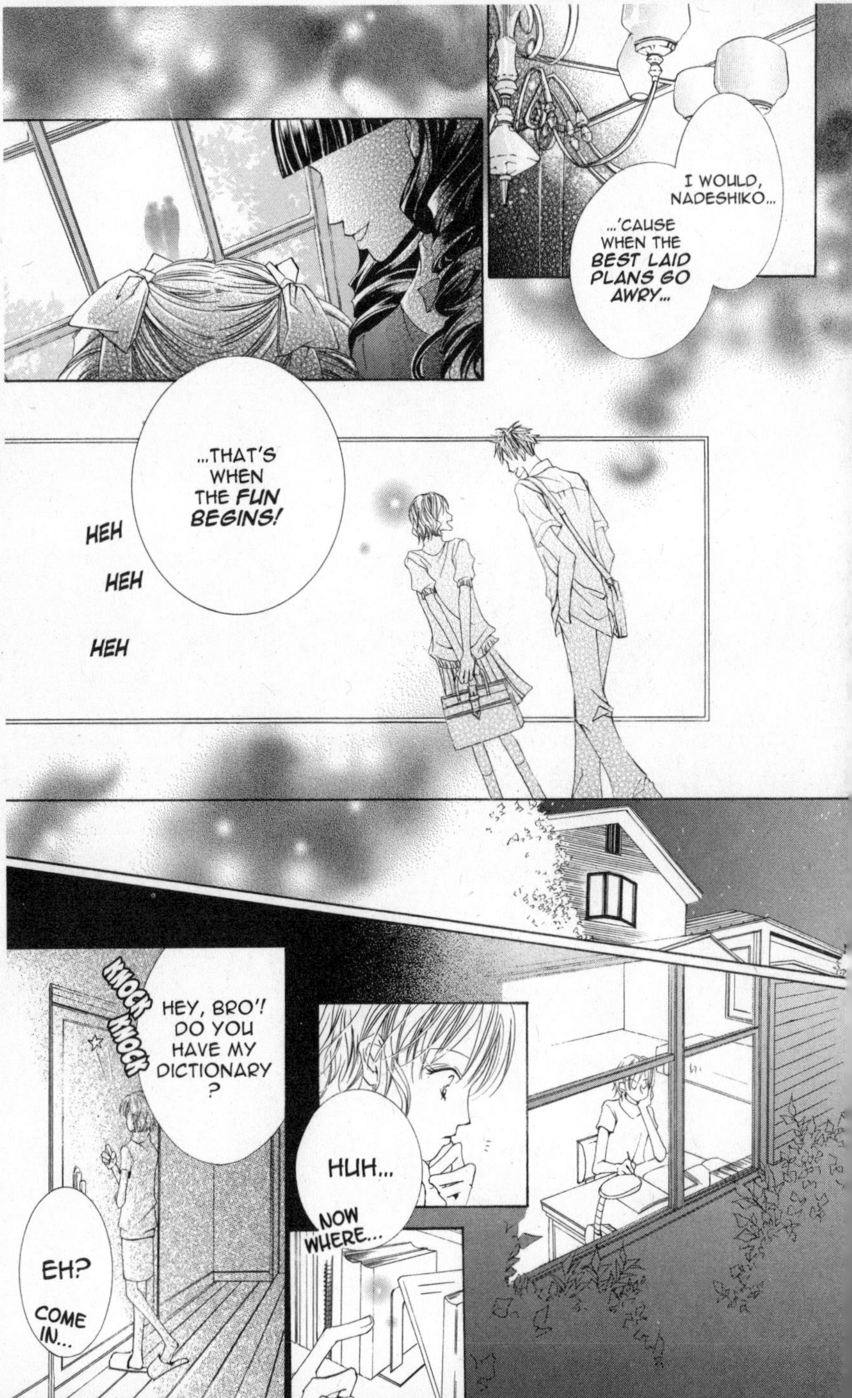
I WOULD, NADESHIKO...
...'CAUSE WHEN THE BEST LAID PLANS GO AWRY...
...THAT'S WHEN THE FUN BEGINS!
HEH
HEH
HEH
HUH...
NOW WHERE...
KNOCK KNOCK
HEY, BRO'! DO YOU HAVE MY DICTIONARY?
EH?
COME IN...

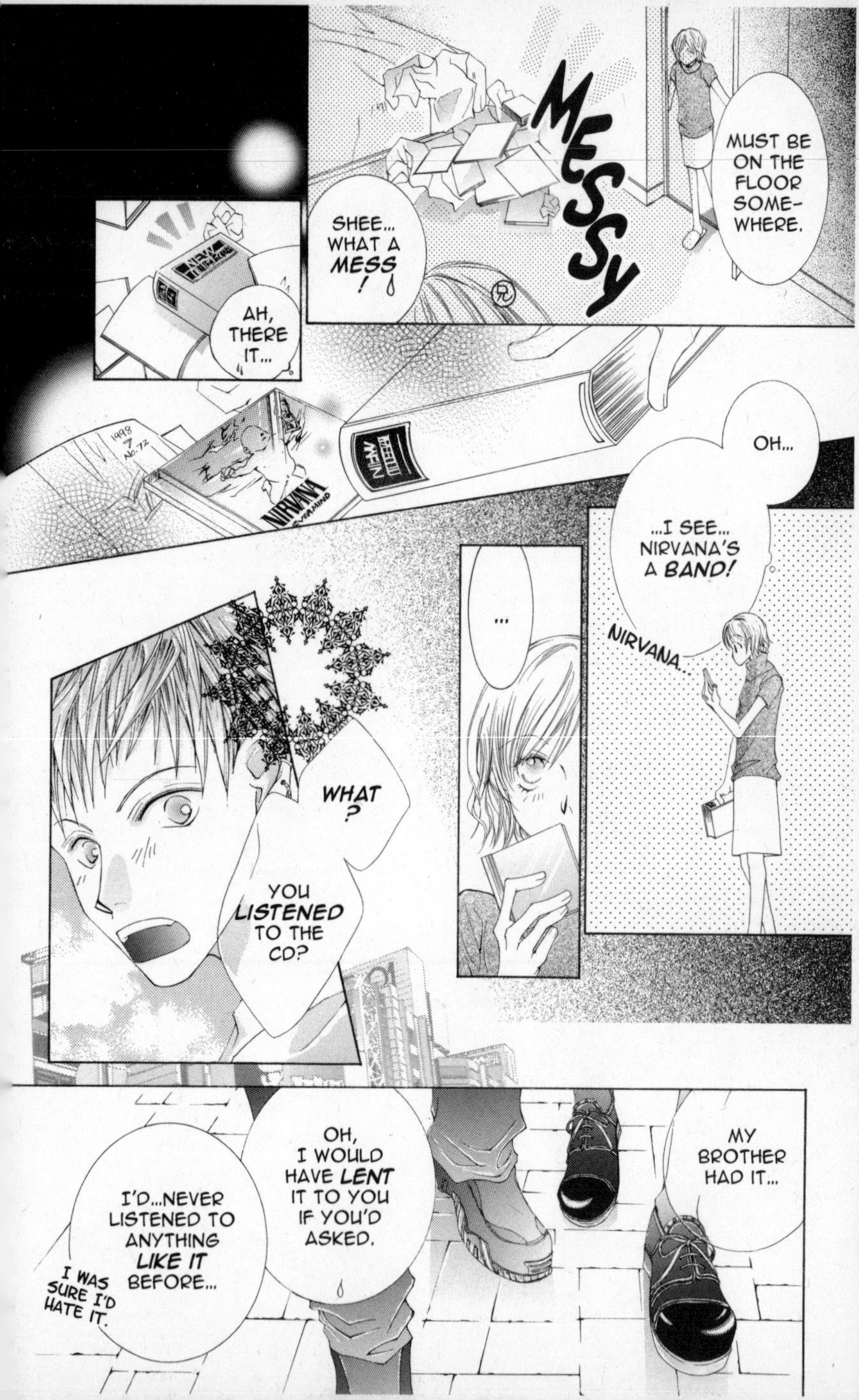
MUST BE ON THE FLOOR SOMEWHERE.
MESSY
SHEE... WHAT A *MESS*!
AH, THERE IT...
OH...
...I SEE... NIRVANA'S A *BAND!*
NIRVANA...
...
WHAT?
YOU *LISTENED* TO THE CD?
MY BROTHER HAD IT...
OH, I WOULD HAVE *LENT* IT TO YOU IF YOU'D ASKED.
I'D...NEVER LISTENED TO ANYTHING *LIKE IT* BEFORE...
I WAS SURE I'D HATE IT.

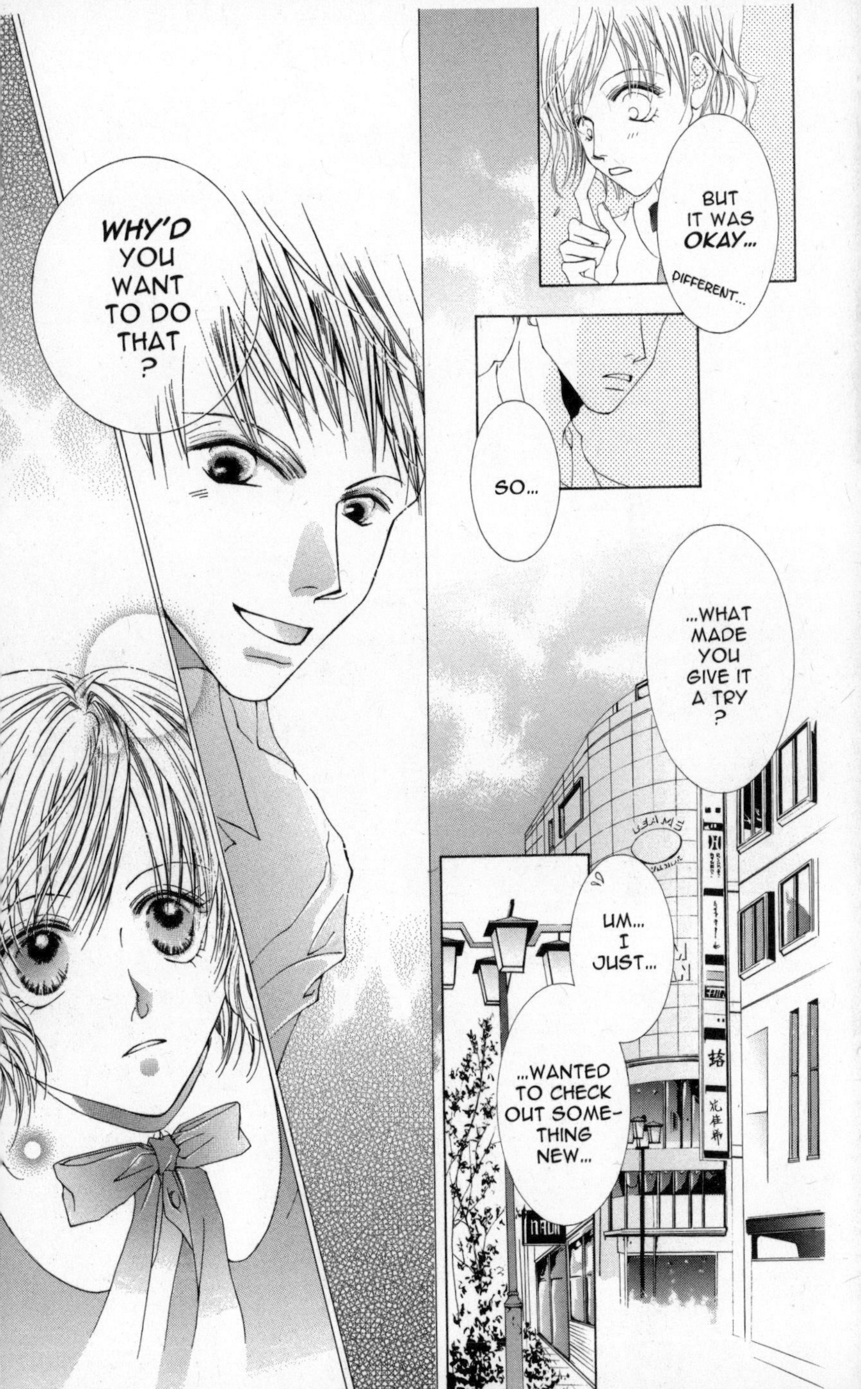

BUT IT WAS OKAY...
DIFFERENT...
SO...
...WHAT MADE YOU GIVE IT A TRY?
UM... I JUST...
...WANTED TO CHECK OUT SOME-THING NEW...
WHY'D YOU WANT TO DO THAT?

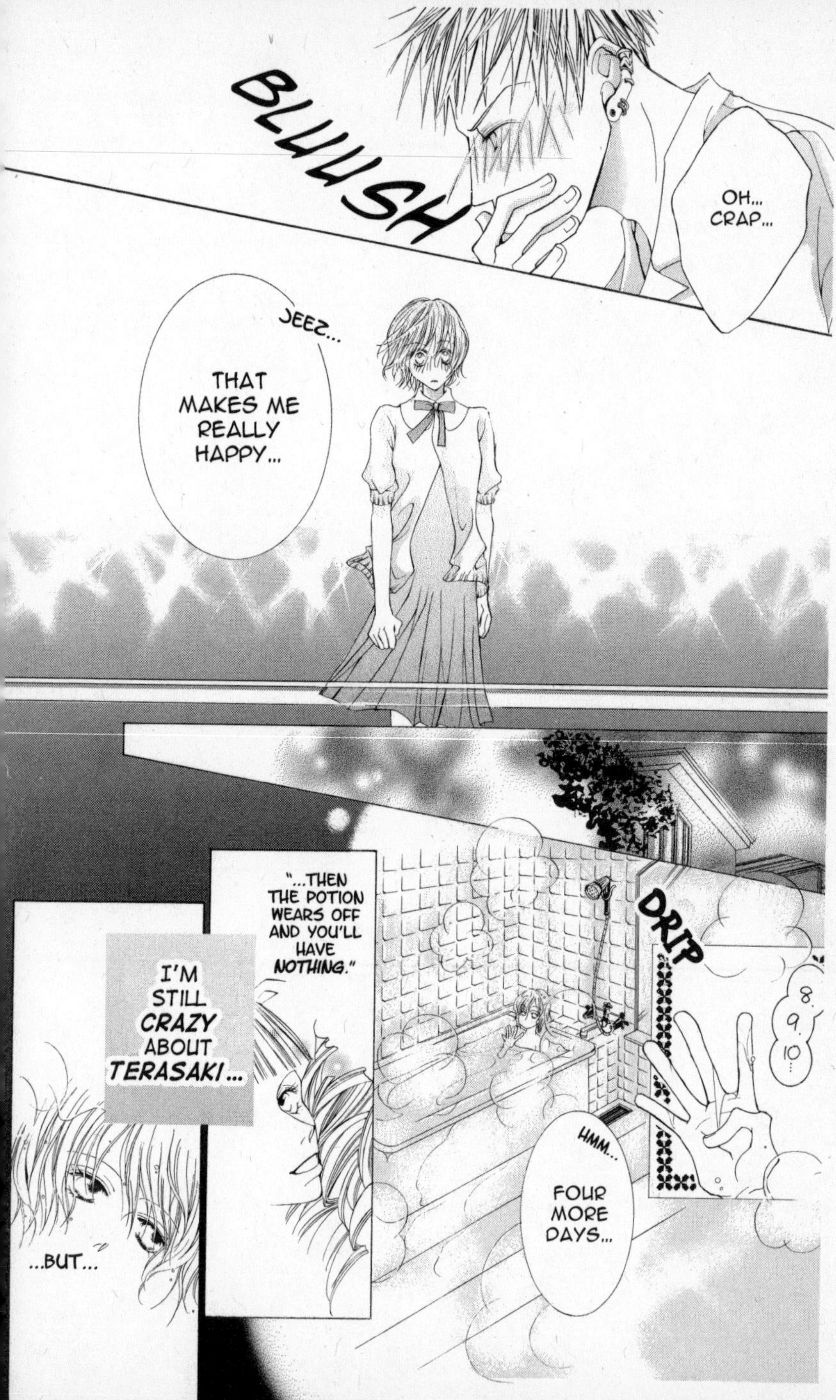
OH... CRAP...
BLUUSH
JEEZ...
THAT MAKES ME REALLY HAPPY...
8. 9. 10...
DRIP
HMM...
FOUR MORE DAYS...
"...THEN THE POTION WEARS OFF AND YOU'LL HAVE NOTHING."
I'M STILL CRAZY ABOUT TERASAKI...
...BUT...

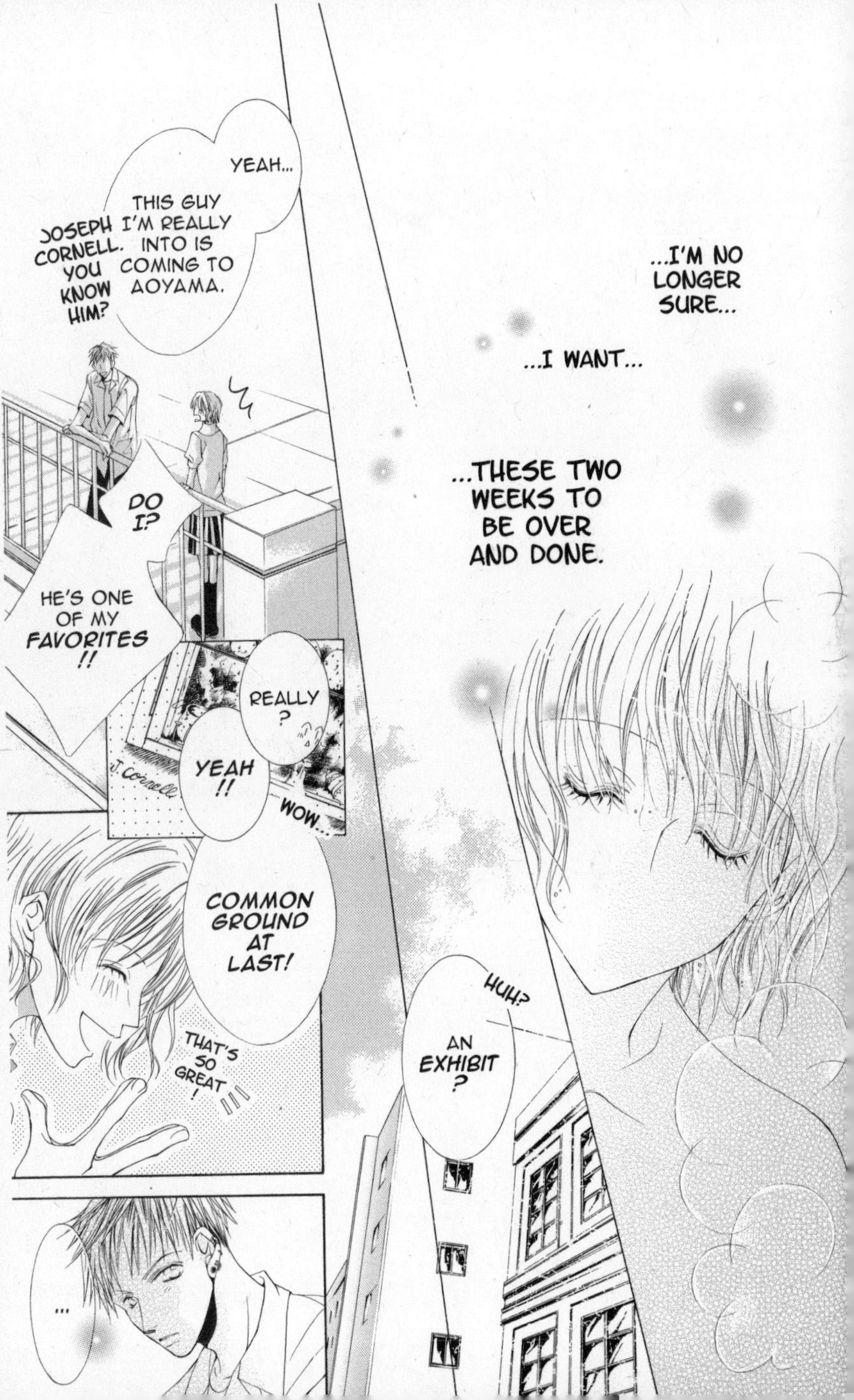
...I'M NO LONGER SURE...
...I WANT...
...THESE TWO WEEKS TO BE OVER AND DONE.
HUH?
AN EXHIBIT?
YEAH...
THIS GUY I'M REALLY INTO IS COMING TO AOYAMA.
JOSEPH CORNELL. YOU KNOW HIM?
DO I?
HE'S ONE OF MY FAVORITES!!
REALLY?
YEAH!!
J. Cornell
WOW...
COMMON GROUND AT LAST!
THAT'S SO GREAT!
...

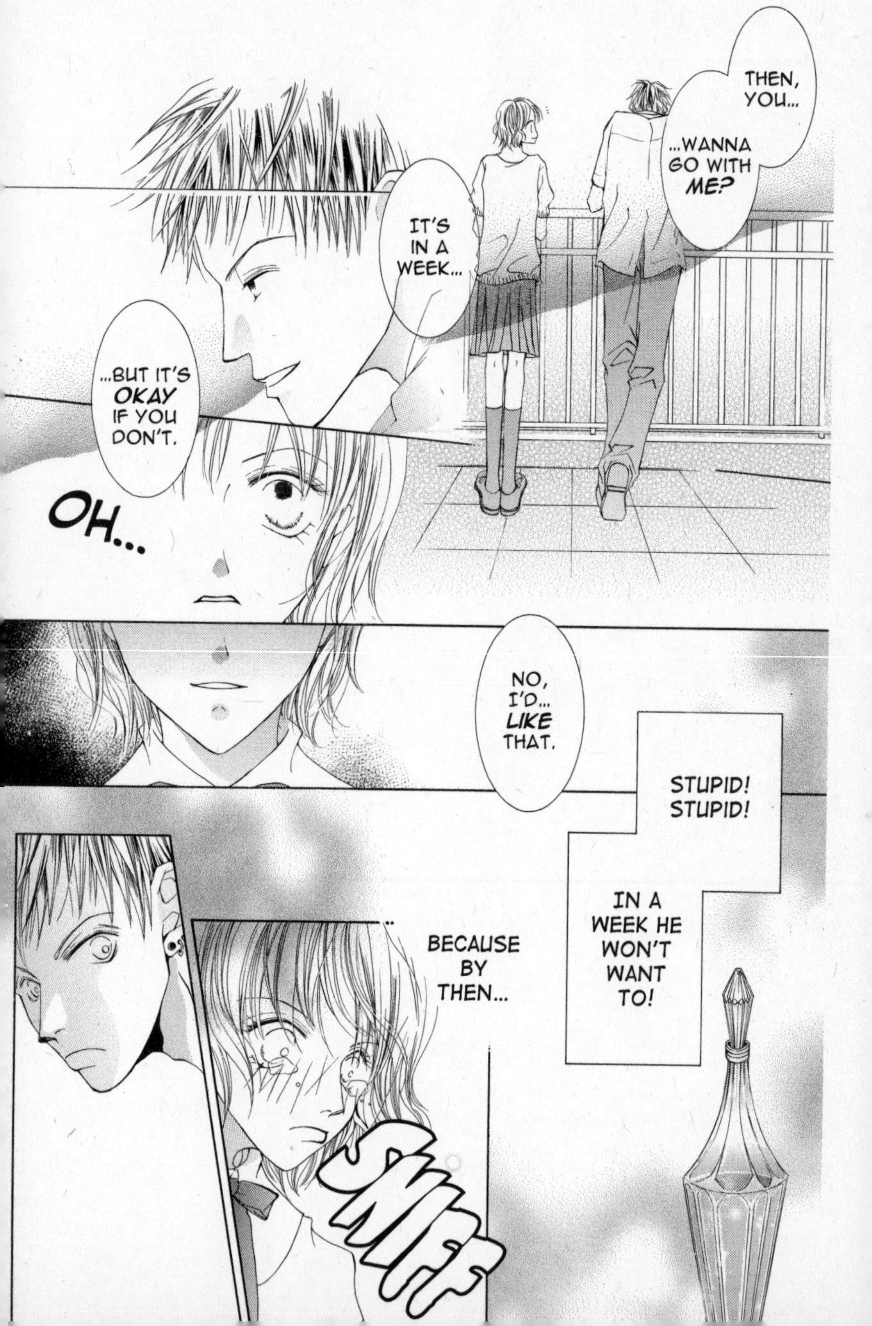
THEN, YOU...
...WANNA GO WITH ME?
IT'S IN A WEEK...
...BUT IT'S OKAY IF YOU DON'T.
OH...
NO, I'D... LIKE THAT.
STUPID! STUPID!
IN A WEEK HE WON'T WANT TO!
BECAUSE BY THEN...
SNIFF

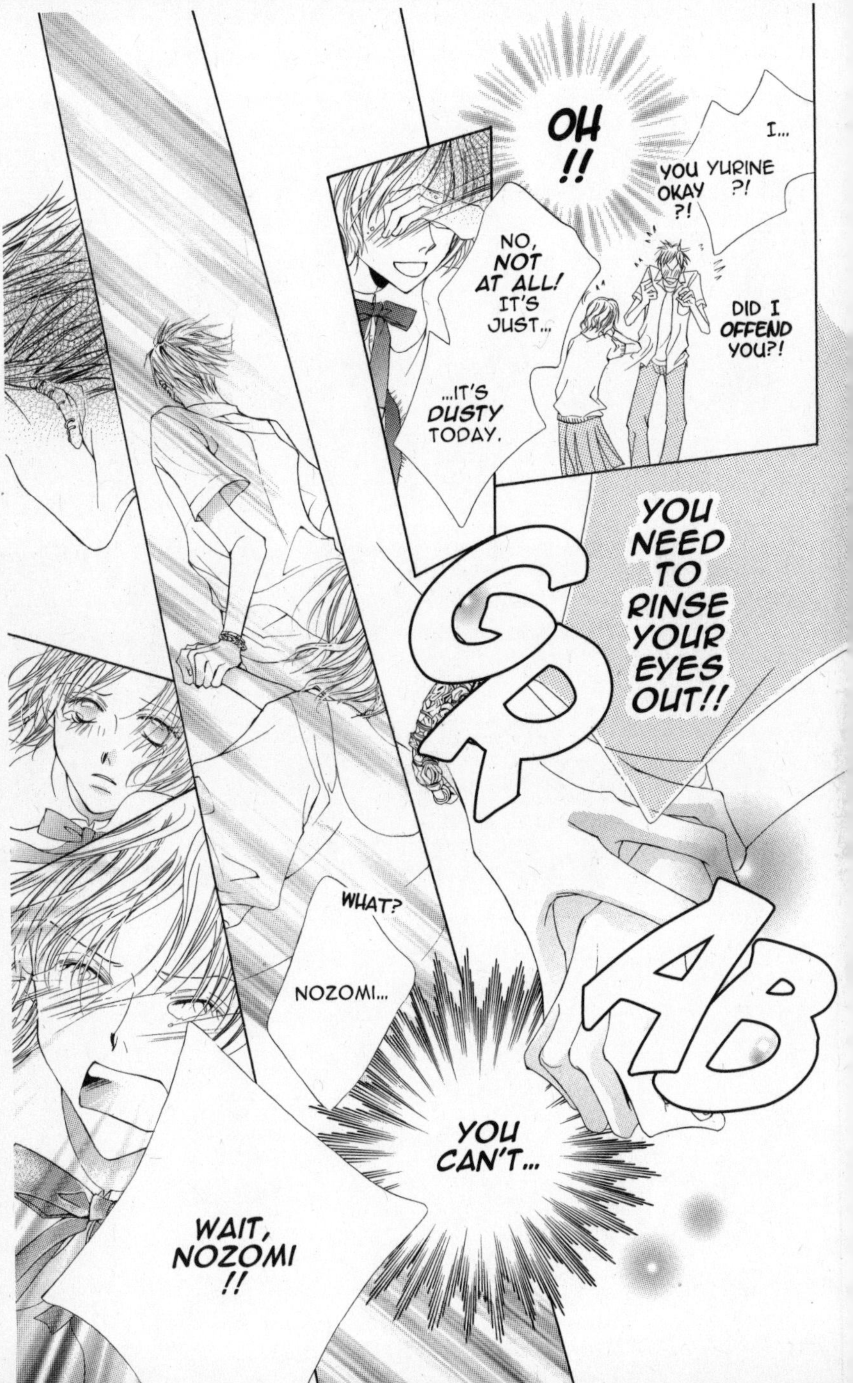
I...
YURINE ?!
YOU OKAY ?!
DID I OFFEND YOU?!
OH !!
NO, NOT AT ALL! IT'S JUST...
...IT'S DUSTY TODAY.
YOU NEED TO RINSE YOUR EYES OUT!!
GR
AB
WHAT?
NOZOMI...
YOU CAN'T...
WAIT, NOZOMI !!

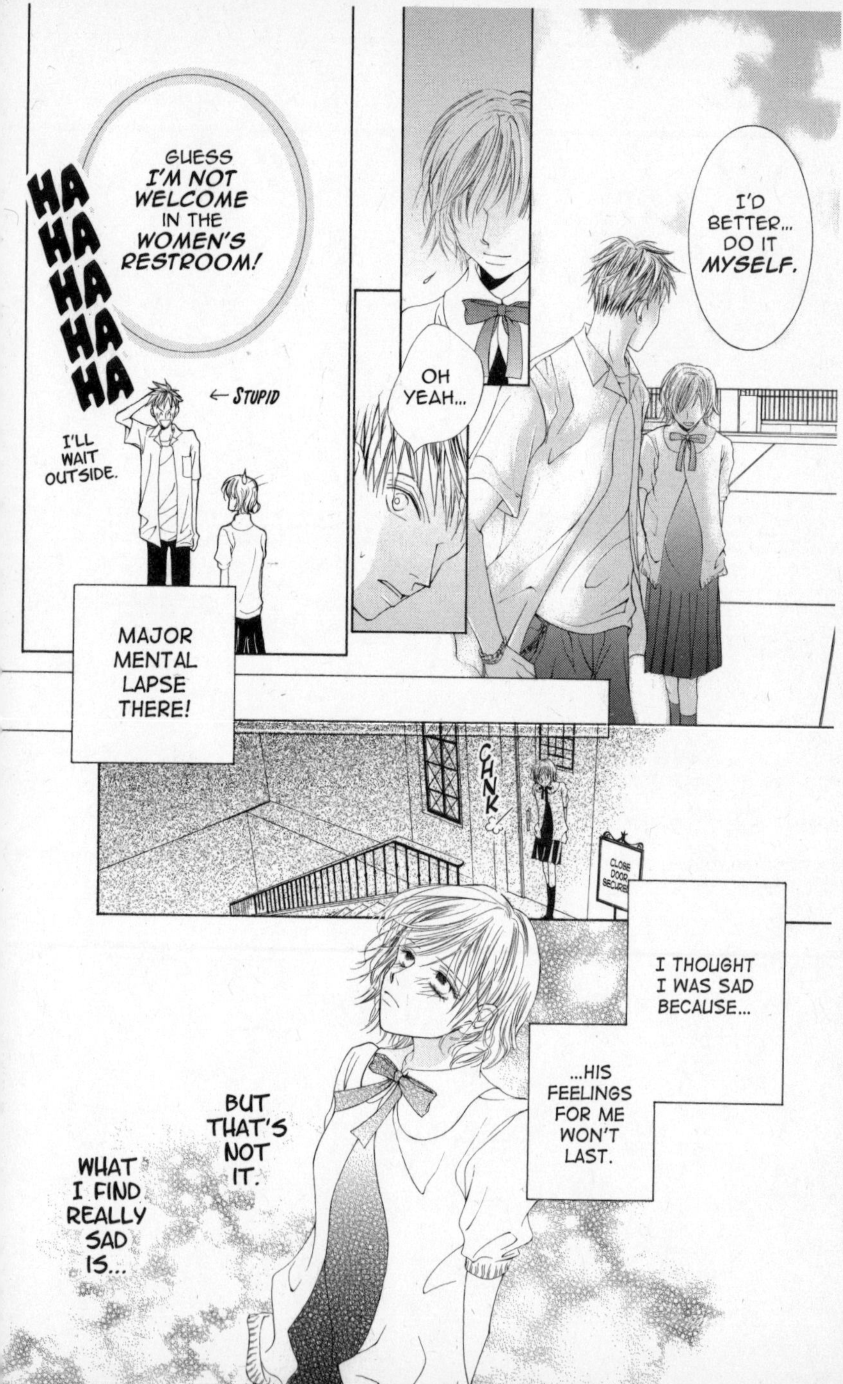
I'D BETTER... DO IT MYSELF.
OH YEAH...
GUESS I'M NOT WELCOME IN THE WOMEN'S RESTROOM!
HAHAHAHAHA
← STUPID
I'LL WAIT OUTSIDE.
MAJOR MENTAL LAPSE THERE!
CHNK
I THOUGHT I WAS SAD BECAUSE...
...HIS FEELINGS FOR ME WON'T LAST.
BUT THAT'S NOT IT.
WHAT I FIND REALLY SAD IS...

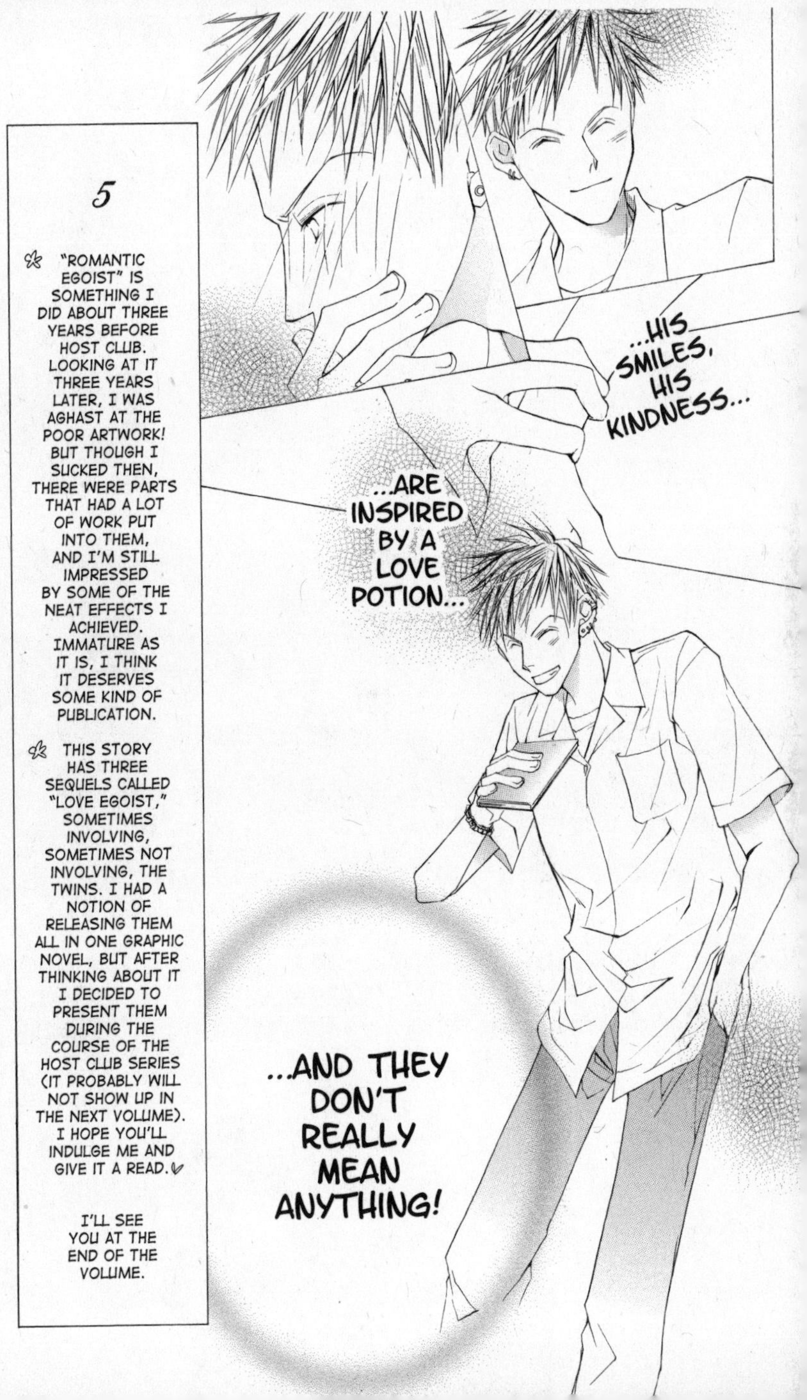
...HIS SMILES, HIS KINDNESS...
...ARE INSPIRED BY A LOVE POTION...
...AND THEY DON'T REALLY MEAN ANYTHING!

5

✿ "ROMANTIC EGOIST" IS SOMETHING I DID ABOUT THREE YEARS BEFORE HOST CLUB. LOOKING AT IT THREE YEARS LATER, I WAS AGHAST AT THE POOR ARTWORK! BUT THOUGH I SUCKED THEN, THERE WERE PARTS THAT HAD A LOT OF WORK PUT INTO THEM, AND I'M STILL IMPRESSED BY SOME OF THE NEAT EFFECTS I ACHIEVED. IMMATURE AS IT IS, I THINK IT DESERVES SOME KIND OF PUBLICATION.

✿ THIS STORY HAS THREE SEQUELS CALLED "LOVE EGOIST," SOMETIMES INVOLVING, SOMETIMES NOT INVOLVING, THE TWINS. I HAD A NOTION OF RELEASING THEM ALL IN ONE GRAPHIC NOVEL, BUT AFTER THINKING ABOUT IT I DECIDED TO PRESENT THEM DURING THE COURSE OF THE HOST CLUB SERIES (IT PROBABLY WILL NOT SHOW UP IN THE NEXT VOLUME). I HOPE YOU'LL INDULGE ME AND GIVE IT A READ. ♥

I'LL SEE YOU AT THE END OF THE VOLUME.

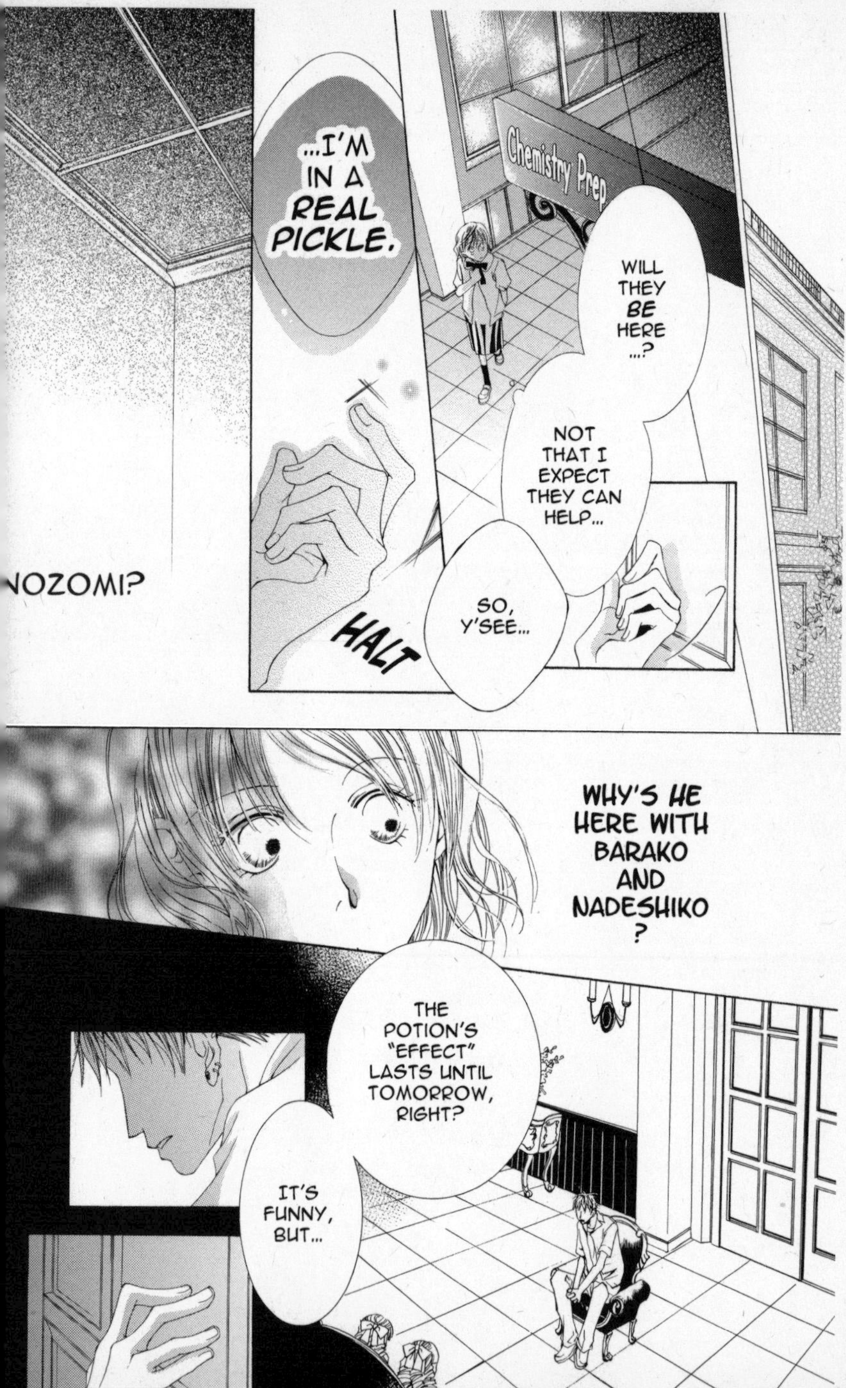

Chemistry Prep
WILL THEY BE HERE ...?
NOT THAT I EXPECT THEY CAN HELP...
SO, Y'SEE...
...I'M IN A REAL PICKLE.
HALT
NOZOMI?
WHY'S HE HERE WITH BARAKO AND NADESHIKO ?
THE POTION'S "EFFECT" LASTS UNTIL TOMORROW, RIGHT?
IT'S FUNNY, BUT...

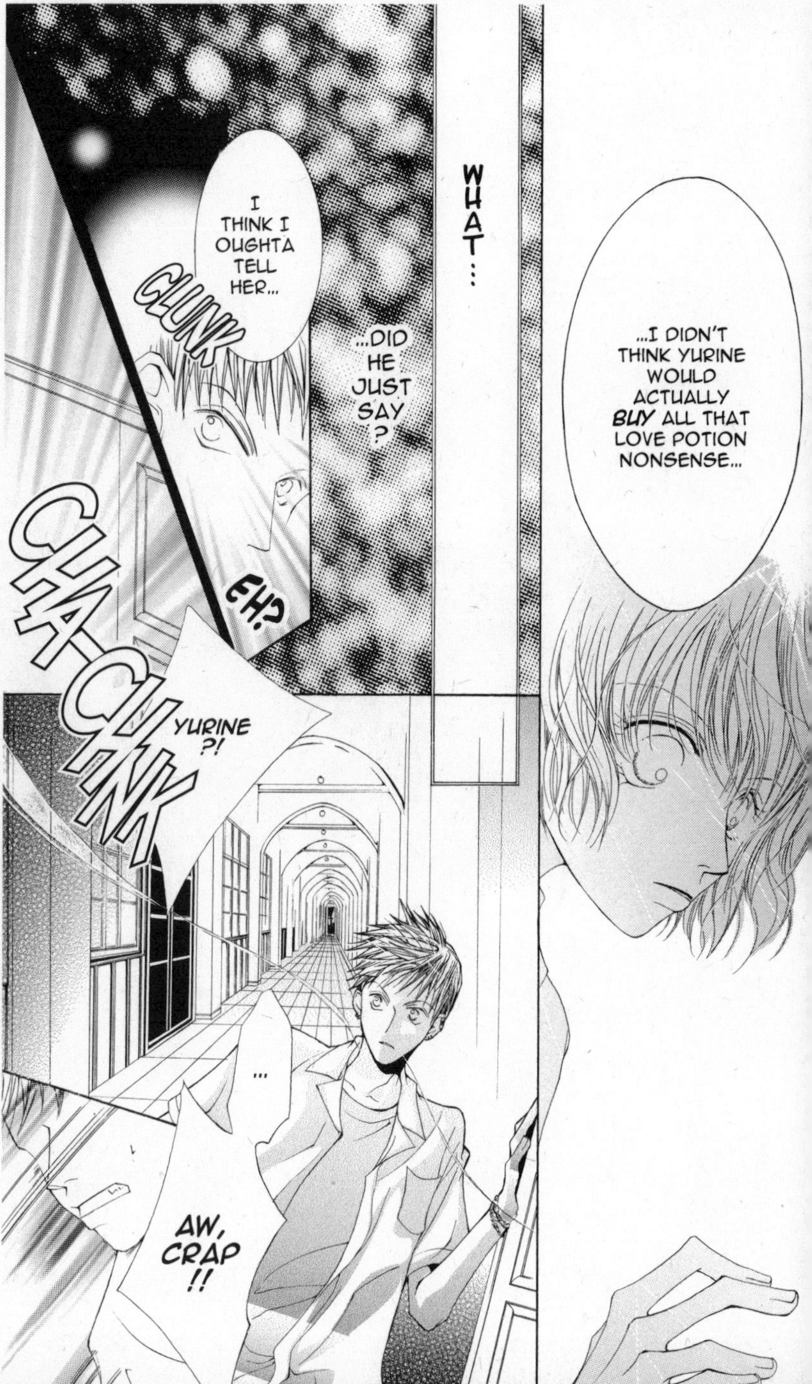

...I DIDN'T THINK YURINE WOULD ACTUALLY BUY ALL THAT LOVE POTION NONSENSE...
WHAT...
I THINK I OUGHTA TELL HER...
...DID HE JUST SAY ?
CLUNK
EH?
CHA-CHINK
YURINE ?!
...
AW, CRAP !!

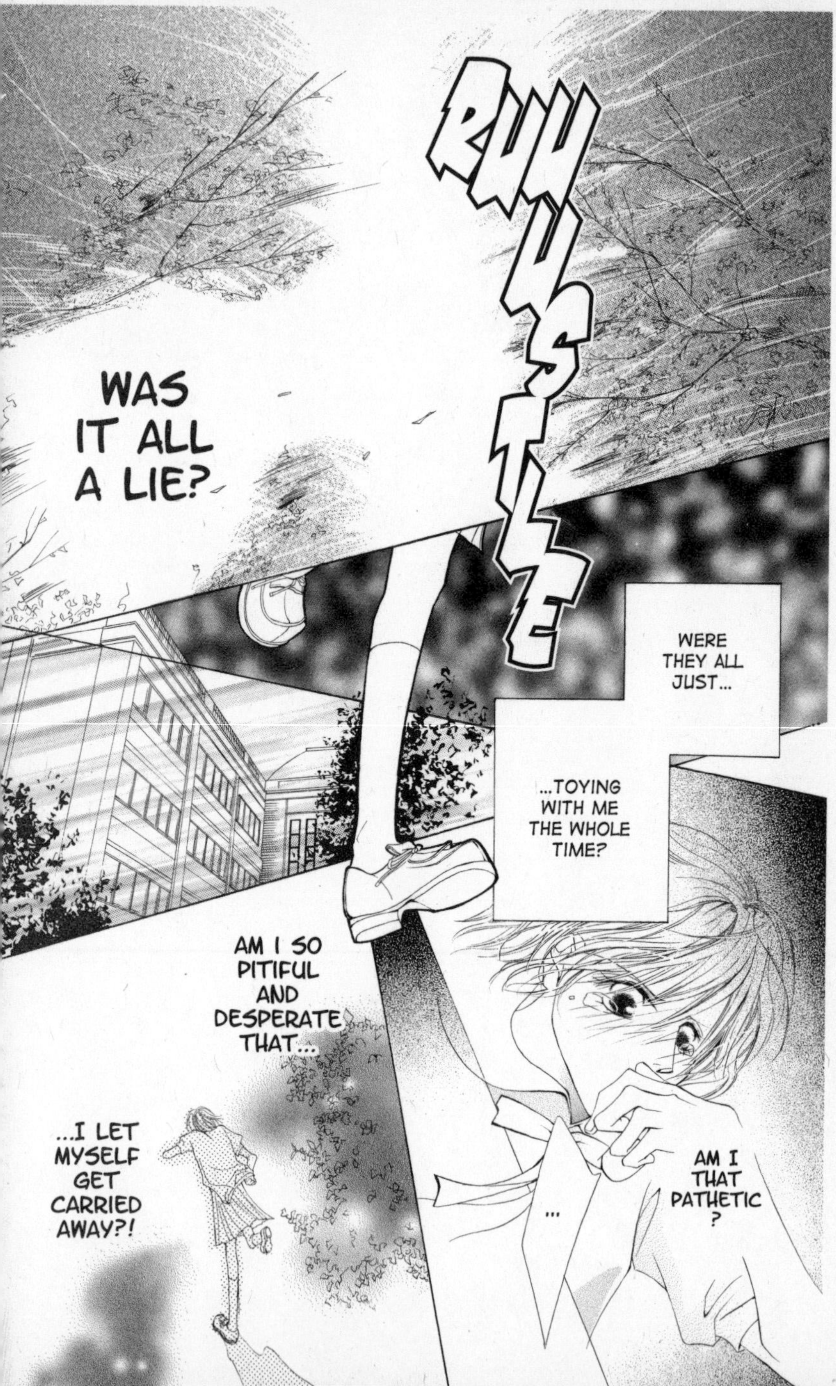
RUUUSTLE
WAS IT ALL A LIE?
WERE THEY ALL JUST...
...TOYING WITH ME THE WHOLE TIME?
AM I THAT PATHETIC?
...
AM I SO PITIFUL AND DESPERATE THAT...
...I LET MYSELF GET CARRIED AWAY?!

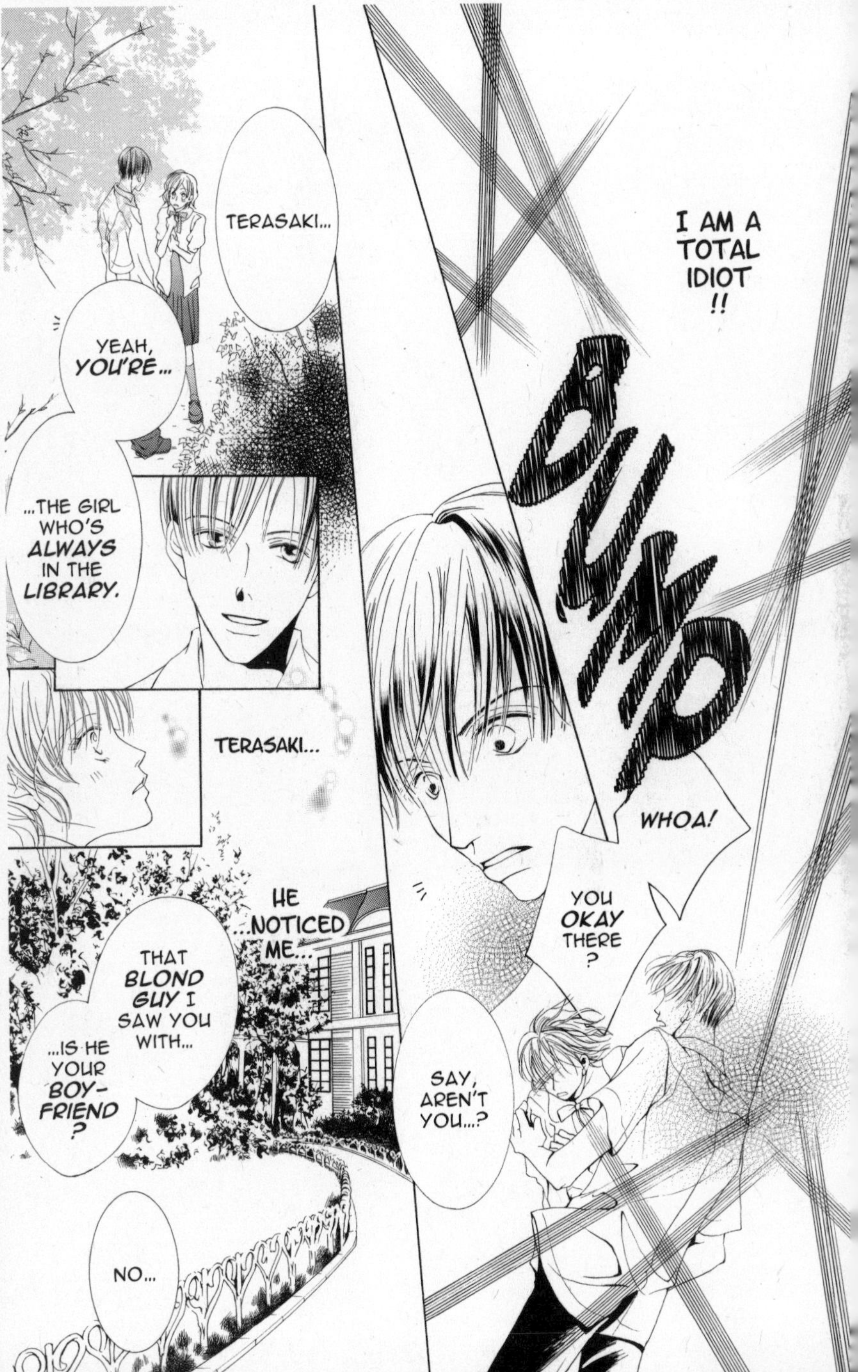
I AM A TOTAL IDIOT!!
BUMP
WHOA!
YOU OKAY THERE?
SAY, AREN'T YOU...?
TERASAKI...
YEAH, YOU'RE...
...THE GIRL WHO'S ALWAYS IN THE LIBRARY.
TERASAKI...
HE ...NOTICED ME...
THAT BLOND GUY I SAW YOU WITH...
...IS HE YOUR BOY-FRIEND?
NO...

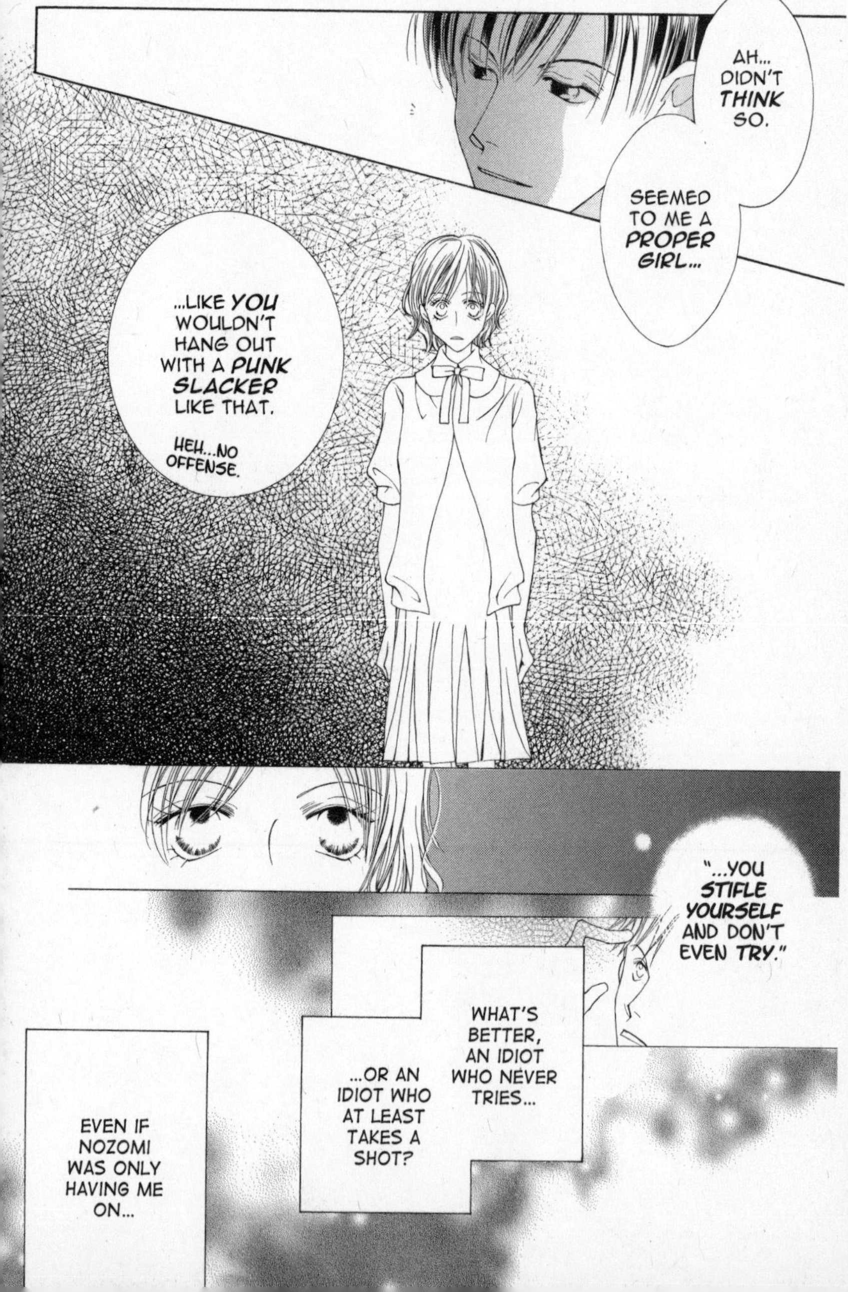
AH... DIDN'T THINK SO.
SEEMED TO ME A PROPER GIRL...
...LIKE YOU WOULDN'T HANG OUT WITH A PUNK SLACKER LIKE THAT.
HEH...NO OFFENSE.
"...YOU STIFLE YOURSELF AND DON'T EVEN TRY."
WHAT'S BETTER, AN IDIOT WHO NEVER TRIES...
...OR AN IDIOT WHO AT LEAST TAKES A SHOT?
EVEN IF NOZOMI WAS ONLY HAVING ME ON...

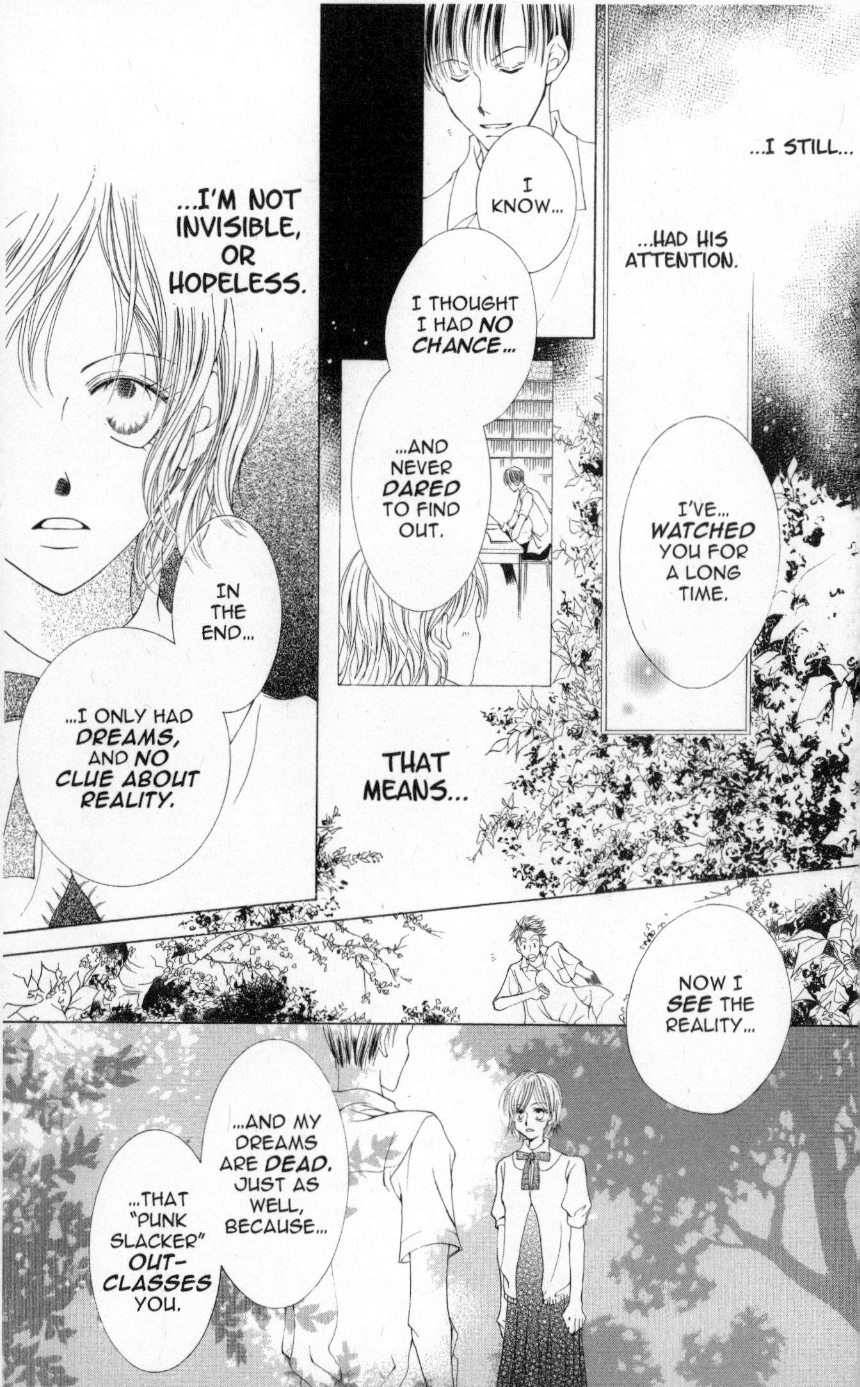
...I STILL...
...HAD HIS ATTENTION.
I'VE... WATCHED YOU FOR A LONG TIME.
I KNOW...
I THOUGHT I HAD NO CHANCE...
...AND NEVER DARED TO FIND OUT.
THAT MEANS...
...I'M NOT INVISIBLE, OR HOPELESS.
IN THE END...
...I ONLY HAD DREAMS, AND NO CLUE ABOUT REALITY.
NOW I SEE THE REALITY...
...AND MY DREAMS ARE DEAD. JUST AS WELL, BECAUSE...
...THAT "PUNK SLACKER" OUT-CLASSES YOU.

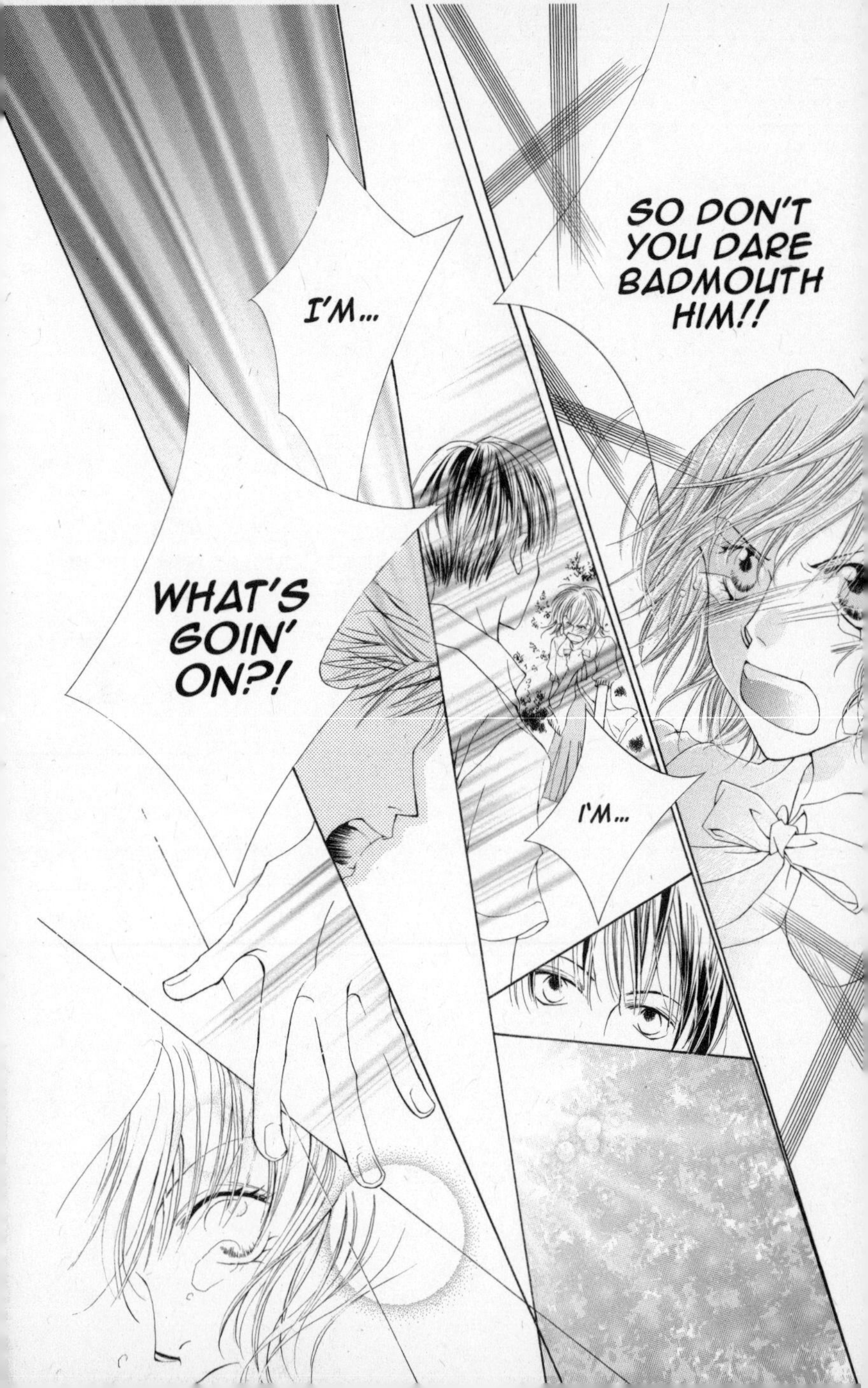
SO DON'T YOU DARE BADMOUTH HIM!!
I'M...
WHAT'S GOIN' ON?!
I'M...

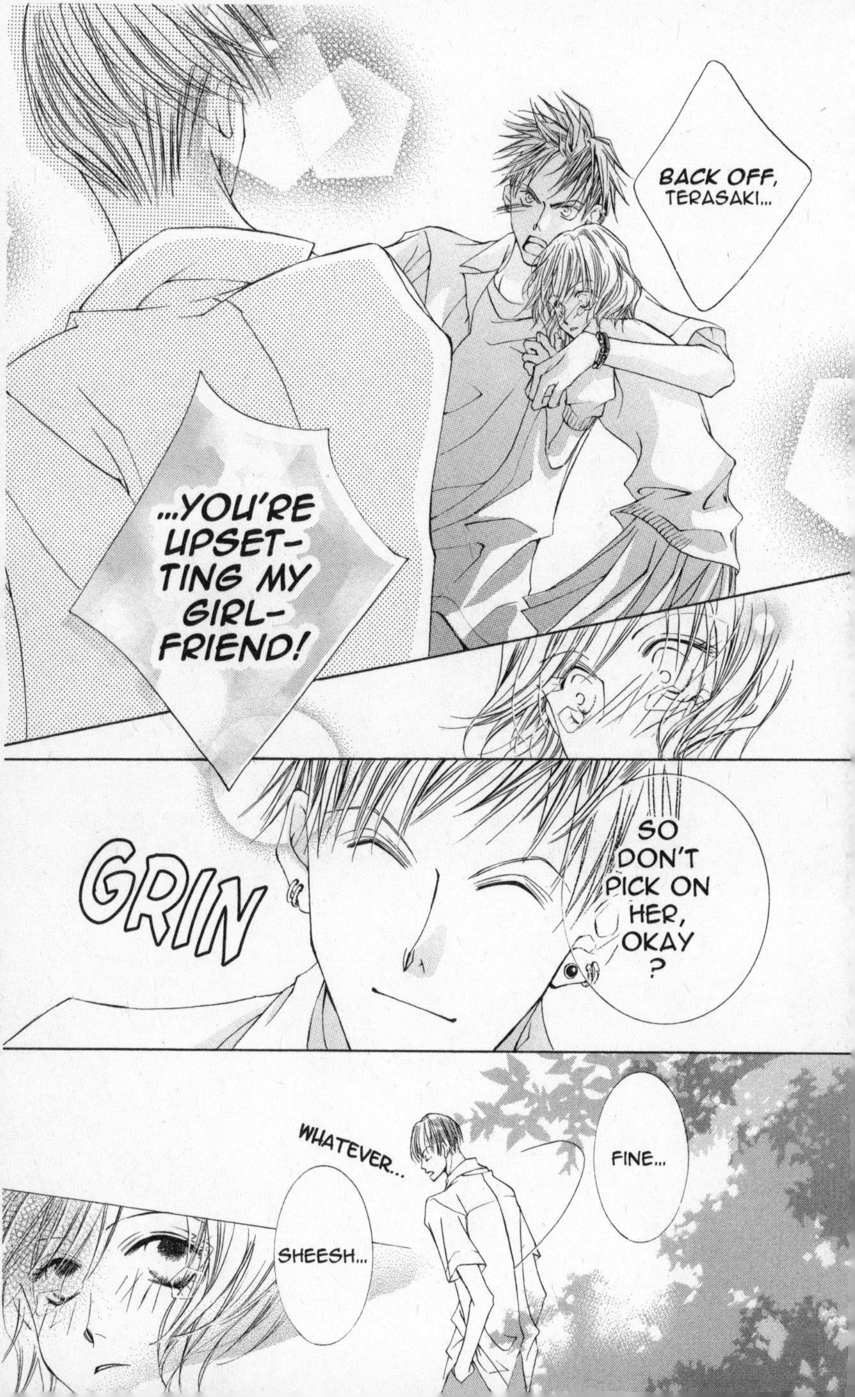
BACK OFF, TERASAKI...
...YOU'RE UPSET-TING MY GIRL-FRIEND!
SO DON'T PICK ON HER, OKAY?
GRIN
FINE...
WHATEVER...
SHEESH...

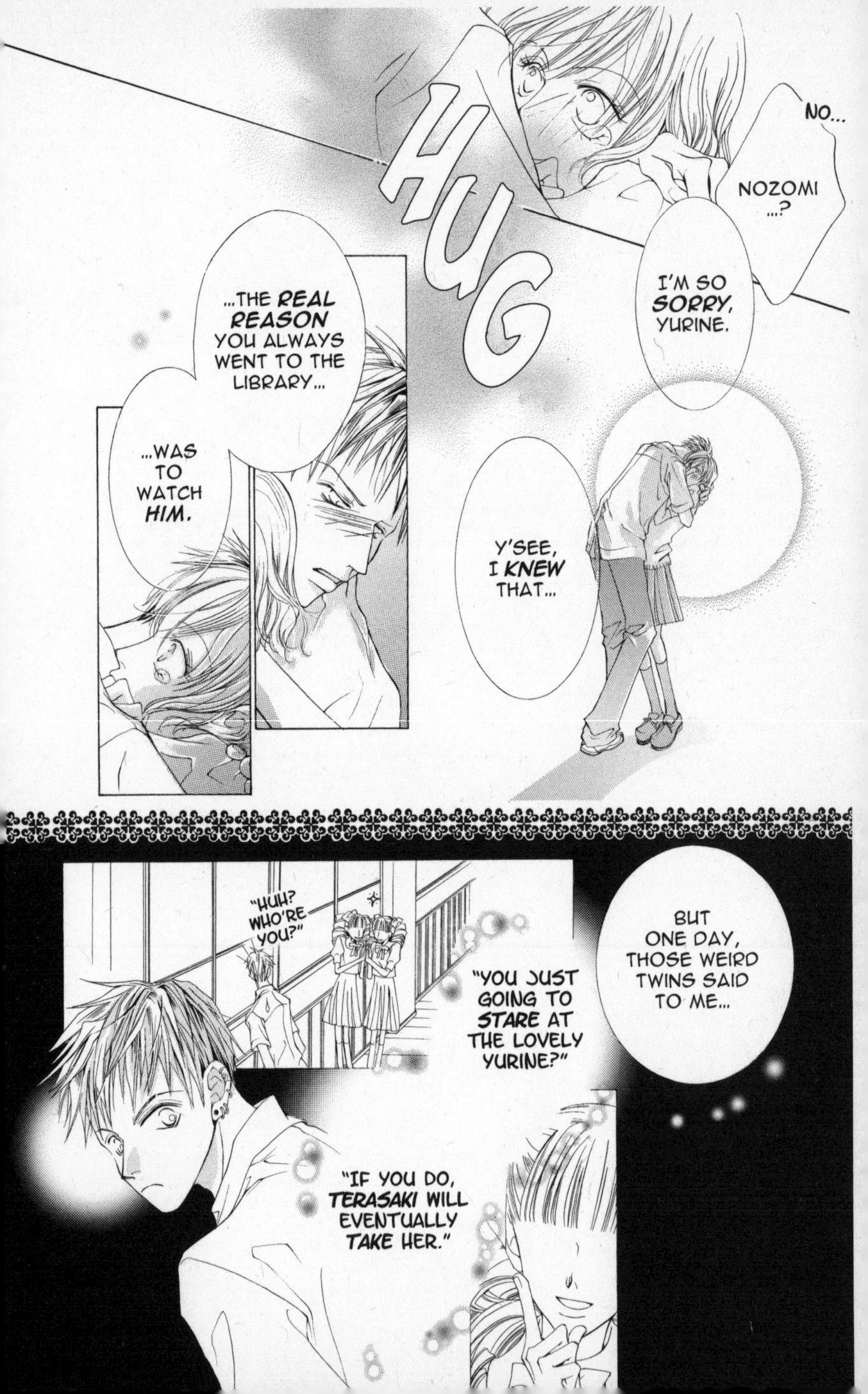
NO...
NOZOMI ...?
HUG
I'M SO SORRY, YURINE.
Y'SEE, I KNEW THAT...
...THE REAL REASON YOU ALWAYS WENT TO THE LIBRARY...
...WAS TO WATCH HIM.
BUT ONE DAY, THOSE WEIRD TWINS SAID TO ME...
"HUH? WHO'RE YOU?"
"YOU JUST GOING TO STARE AT THE LOVELY YURINE?"
"IF YOU DO, TERASAKI WILL EVENTUALLY TAKE HER."

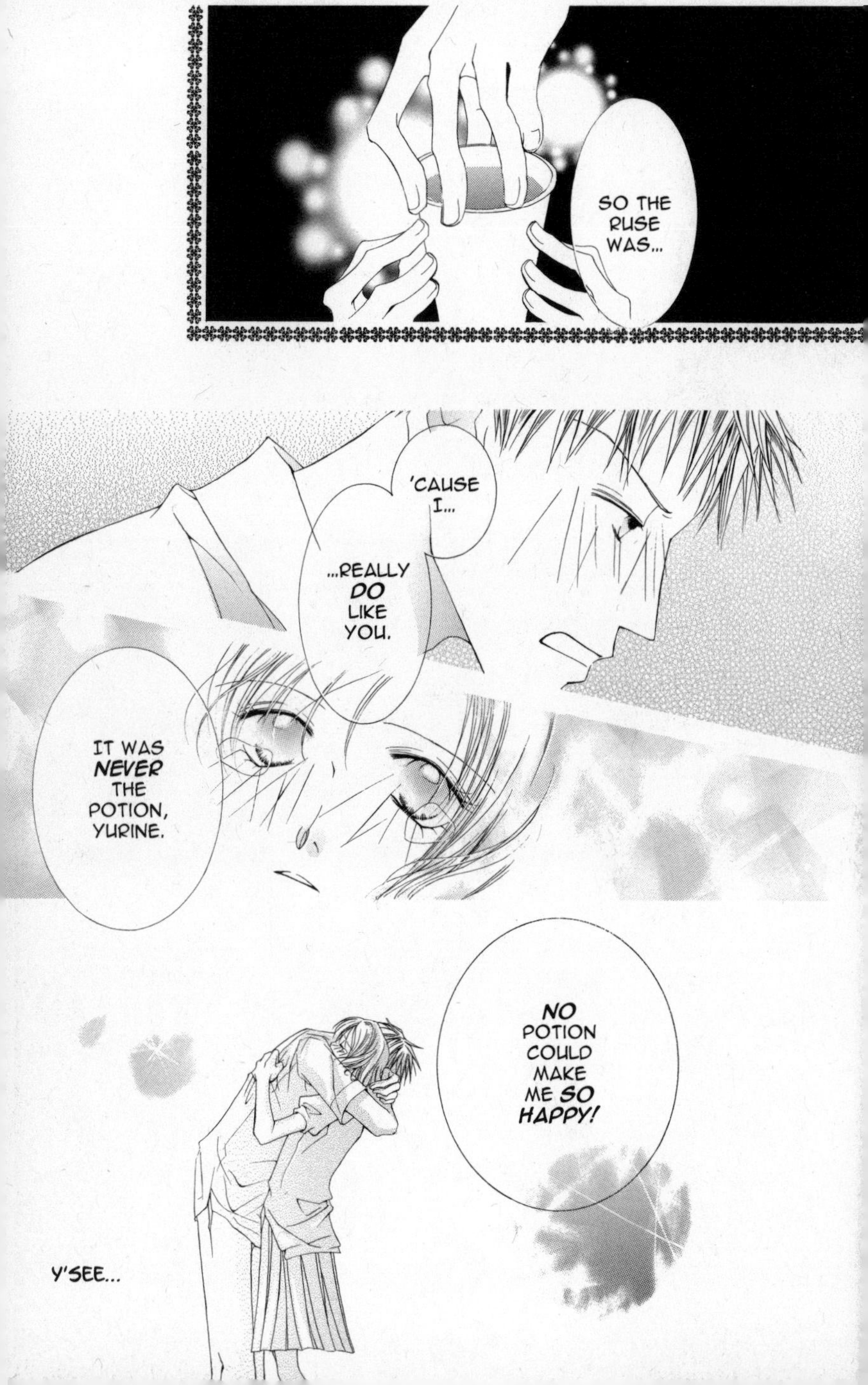
SO THE RUSE WAS...
'CAUSE I...
...REALLY DO LIKE YOU.
IT WAS NEVER THE POTION, YURINE.
NO POTION COULD MAKE ME SO HAPPY!
Y'SEE...

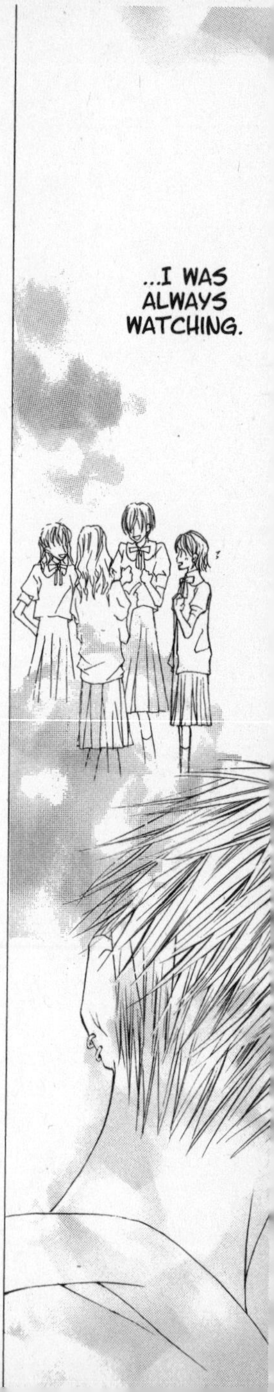
...I WAS ALWAYS WATCHING.

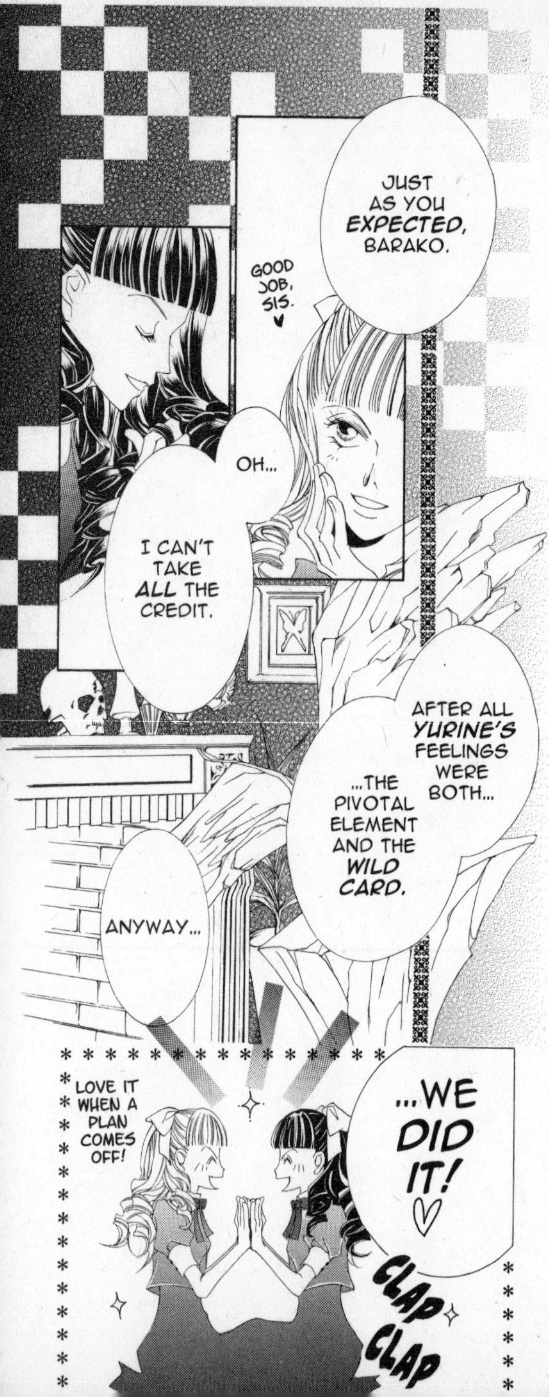
JUST AS YOU EXPECTED, BARAKO.
GOOD JOB, SIS. ♥
OH...
I CAN'T TAKE ALL THE CREDIT.
AFTER ALL YURINE'S FEELINGS WERE BOTH...
...THE PIVOTAL ELEMENT AND THE WILD CARD.
ANYWAY...
...WE DID IT! ♥
LOVE IT WHEN A PLAN COMES OFF!
CLAP CLAP

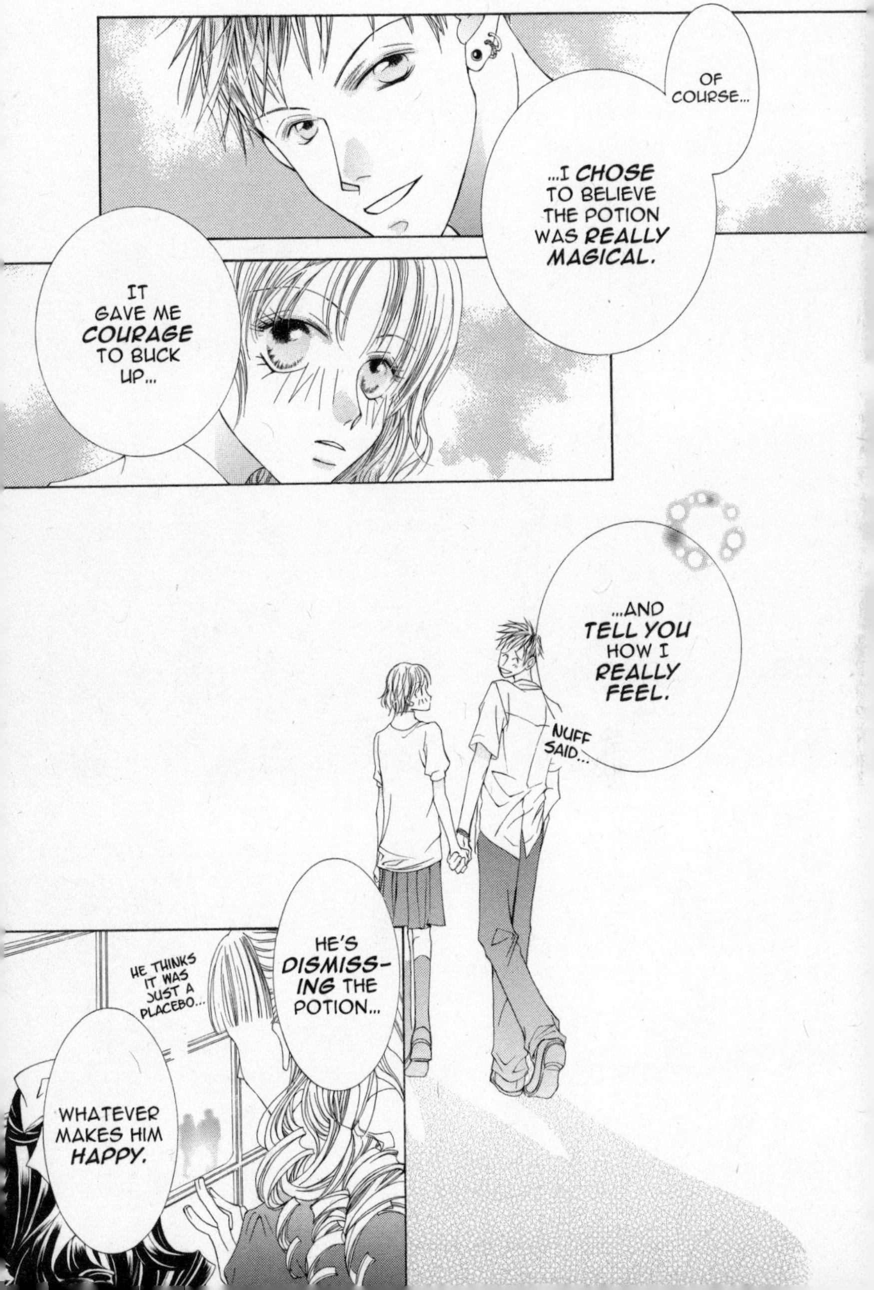
OF COURSE...
...I CHOSE TO BELIEVE THE POTION WAS REALLY MAGICAL.
IT GAVE ME COURAGE TO BUCK UP...
...AND TELL YOU HOW I REALLY FEEL.
NUFF SAID...
HE'S DISMISSING THE POTION...
HE THINKS IT WAS JUST A PLACEBO...
WHATEVER MAKES HIM HAPPY.

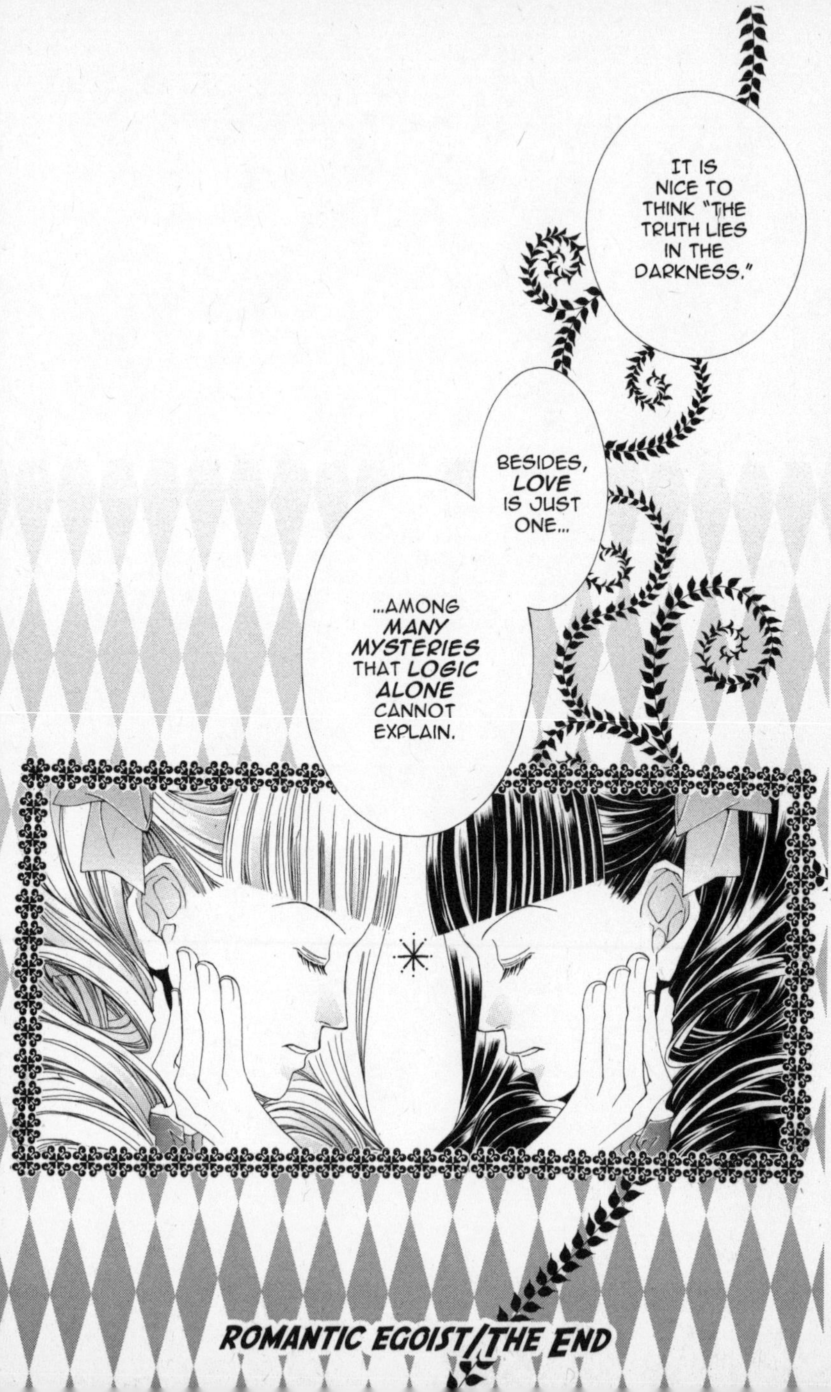
IT IS NICE TO THINK "THE TRUTH LIES IN THE DARKNESS."
BESIDES, LOVE IS JUST ONE...
...AMONG MANY MYSTERIES THAT LOGIC ALONE CANNOT EXPLAIN.
ROMANTIC EGOIST/THE END

EGOISTIC CLUB

HELLO EVERYONE!! THANK YOU FOR STICKING AROUND FOR *HOST CLUB*, VOLUME 2.

TAMAKI'S "IT'S ALL ACCORDING TO PLAN!!" POSE, DRAWN AS HATORI STRIKES SAID POSE IN A MIRROR. (ART'S A LONELY BUSINESS! HAH!)

HURF... URF... CRAMPING UP

I AM THE HOST CLUB'S MOTHER, BISCOTTI HATORINE.

WELCOME... Y'ALL!

WE WILL BEGIN WITH THE CHARACTER RANKINGS FROM THE FIRST EPISODE (FOUR EPISODES TOTAL). THANK YOU ALL FOR YOUR LETTERS!!

1ST (PREVIOUSLY 1ST) HUH?

2ND (PREVIOUSLY 3RD) NICE!! WELL DONE!!

3RD (PREVIOUSLY 6TH) SWEET!! CLENCH

INDIVIDUALLY, HIKARU > KAORU

4TH (PREVIOUSLY 2ND) ...

5TH (PREVIOUSLY 4TH)

6TH (PREVIOUSLY 5TH) BWAAAH

THERE, THERE, MITSUKUNI...

THE DIFFERENCE BETWEEN HARUHI AND TAMAKI WAS 80 VOTES...TAMAKI AND THE TWINS, 75. THE SPREADS OPENED UP A LOT AFTER THAT.

APOLOGIES

IN "THE TWINS FIGHT" EPISODE THAT WAS PUBLISHED IN THE MAGAZINE, THE MATTER OF HAIR PARTINGS SEEMS TO HAVE BEEN INCORRECT.. SORRY!!

IT WAS FIXED WHEN THE GRAPHIC NOVEL WAS PUBLISHED.

HIKARU — ✕ LEFT PART ○ RIGHT PART

KAORU — ✕ RIGHT PART ○ LEFT PART

✕ PARTING TO THE LEFT IS A LEFT PART

○ HAVING THE PART ON THE LEFT IS A LEFT PART

COULD I HAVE MISUNDERSTOOD THIS ALL MY LIFE?

IN VOL. 1 I ALSO STATED "THE FINDER GETS 30%," BUT 5-20% IS THE TRUTH.

I AM SO SORRY!!!

MISLETTERING, CARELESS MISTAKES, IGNORANCE, AND LACK OF RESEARCH ARE ALL THINGS I REFLECT UPON DAILY. I AM ASHAMED BY MY SHORTCOMINGS, BUT I WILL TRY HARDER.

DEEPLY, DEEPLY SORRY!!

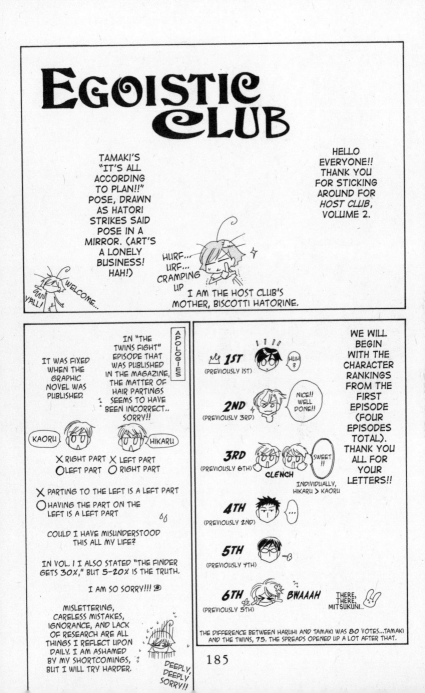

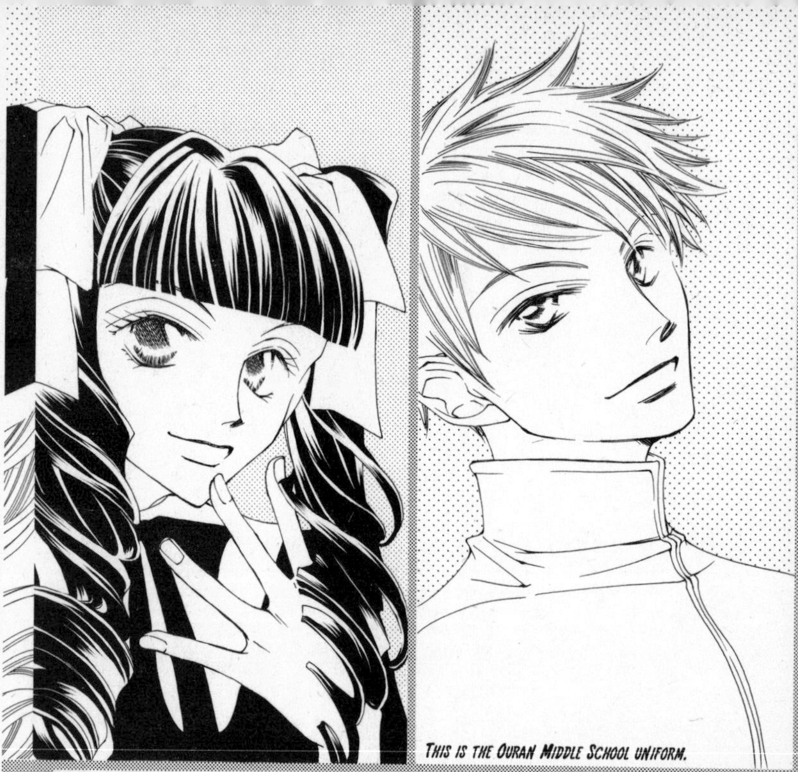
THIS IS THE OURAN MIDDLE SCHOOL UNIFORM.

WITH THEIR MISCHIEVOUS PERSONALITIES, IT WOULD BE NO SURPRISE IF THESE FOUR ARE ALL RELATED.

✿ I LIKE TWINS. I LIKE SYMMETRY, IMAGES WITH MANY IDENTICAL ITEMS, PRIVATE SCHOOLS, EUROPEAN BUILDINGS, AND CHANDELIERS. WITH THE PUBLICATION OF "ROMANTIC EGOIST" IN THIS BOOK, IT SHOULD BE PRETTY OBVIOUS, SO I'LL TELL ALL. PLEASE BEAR WITH ME.

✿ MY INTEREST IN TWINS STARTED WHEN I WAS IN ELEMENTARY SCHOOL, BUT THE REAL TRIGGER WAS PROBABLY A FOREIGN CHILDREN'S BOOK, *OCHAMENA FUTAGO* (THE TWINS) SERIES BY ENID BLYTON, AND KESTNER'S *FUTARI NO LOTTE* (THE TWO LOTTES). I'D ALREADY BEEN FASCINATED BY ENGLAND AND BOARDING SCHOOLS, AND THIS DEFINITELY FUELED MY "I WANT TO WRITE" FEVER, SO THAT THERE WERE TWINS (MALE) IN ONE WORK I SUBMITTED, AND A BOARDING SCHOOL IN ANOTHER. EVEN AFTER MY DEBUT, THERE WAS ONE REJECTED WORK INVOLVING MALE TWINS. THE KURONUMA SISTERS WERE TAKEN FROM A REJECTED WORK AND REUSED TO GIVE BIRTH TO "ROMANTIC EGOIST." THEY HAVE QUITE A STICKY HISTORY. I FINALLY WAS ABLE TO WRITE ABOUT MALE TWINS IN *HOST CLUB*, SO MAYBE NEXT I'LL TRY PATERNAL TWINS...(YOU'RE STILL PLANNING ON WRITING?) WHAT'S SAD WAS THAT NOBODY AROUND ME HAD THE SAME INTEREST IN TWINS, AND I WAS TOLD BY MY 25-YEAR-OLD FRIEND, "THIS IS THE FIRST TIME IN MY LIFE I'VE RUN INTO SOMEONE SO INTO TWINS LIKE THIS." BUT THAT'S FINE...THE WORLD HAS BEEN GIVEN MANY FINE WORKS INVOLVING TWINS (EVEN IF THEY'RE NOT THE MAIN CHARACTERS). AT TIMES, I GET LETTERS SAYING, "WE ARE TWINS.♡" AND "I LIKE TWINS, TOO♡," SO I'M CONTENT. HEH HEH. THE PROBLEM WITH THE KURONUMA SISTERS AND

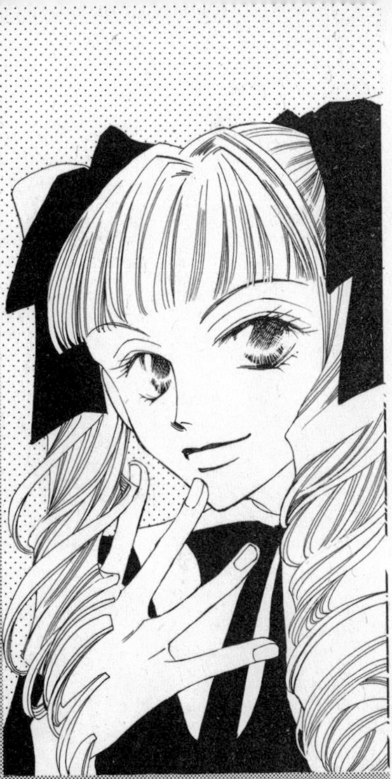

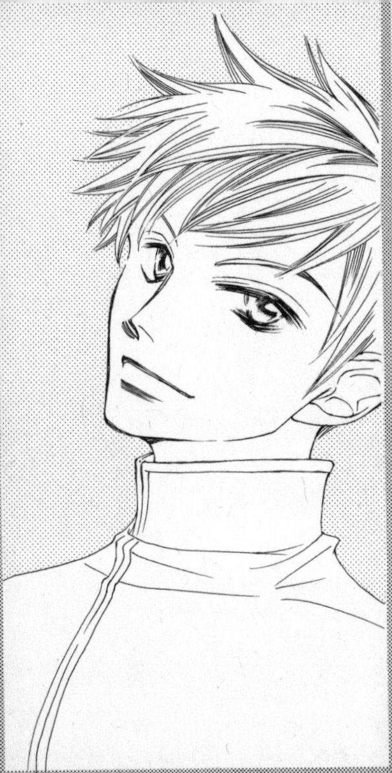

THE HITACHIIN BROTHERS IS THAT THEY LOOK SIMILAR TO A LOT OF OTHER CHARACTERS. (REGARDING THE KURONUMA SISTERS, I WAS TOLD THEY "LOOK LIKE THE TWINS IN ..." FROM ABOUT THREE OR SO DIFFERENT WORKS). I CONSTANTLY THINK I SHOULD TRY TO BE MORE ORIGINAL IN MY DRAFTSMANSHIP. I AM SORRY. OH!! BY THE WAY, THOUGH I'VE TALKED ON AND ON ABOUT THIS ALREADY, PLEASE DON'T THINK I'M BIASED TOWARDS HIKARU AND KAORU IN *HOST CLUB* (I THINK...!!) THE REASON THEY APPEAR SO OFTEN IS BECAUSE THEY ARE EASY TO DRAW, AND THEY ARE JUST "THAT TYPE OF CHARACTER" (I THINK...!!). THE REAL-LIVE HATORI IS ALWAYS COMING UP WITH TWISTED COMMENTS LIKE THE ONES UTTERED BY THOSE TWO AND KYOYA. ON TOP OF THAT, I'VE LATELY BEEN PRONE TO SAY, "I DON'T LIKE EVENTS THAT MUCH," AND IT'S BEEN POINTED OUT THAT THAT'S QUITE SIMILAR TO HARUHI, MAKING ME FEEL EVEN MORE BLUE (LAUGH). HATORI THINKS TAMAKI ACTUALLY HAS THE BEST PERSONALITY WITHIN THE HOST CLUB...IT'S JUST THAT THEY DON'T MESH WELL (A HUGE PROBLEM).

PLEASE SUPPORT THIS BENIGHTED MANGA, IN WHICH HAPPINESS PROVES ELUSIVE NO MATTER WHICH CHARACTERS YOU ROOT FOR!!! (I ACCEPT ALL BON MOTS AND BRICKBATS!)

I HOPE I WILL SEE YOU ALL IN VOLUME 3. ♡THANK YOU VERY MUCH FOR READING!!!

2003☆Nov. Bisco☆H©

PRESENTED PER NO ONE'S REQUEST: THE USUAL FLIRTATIOUS DRAWING TO END THE VOLUME.

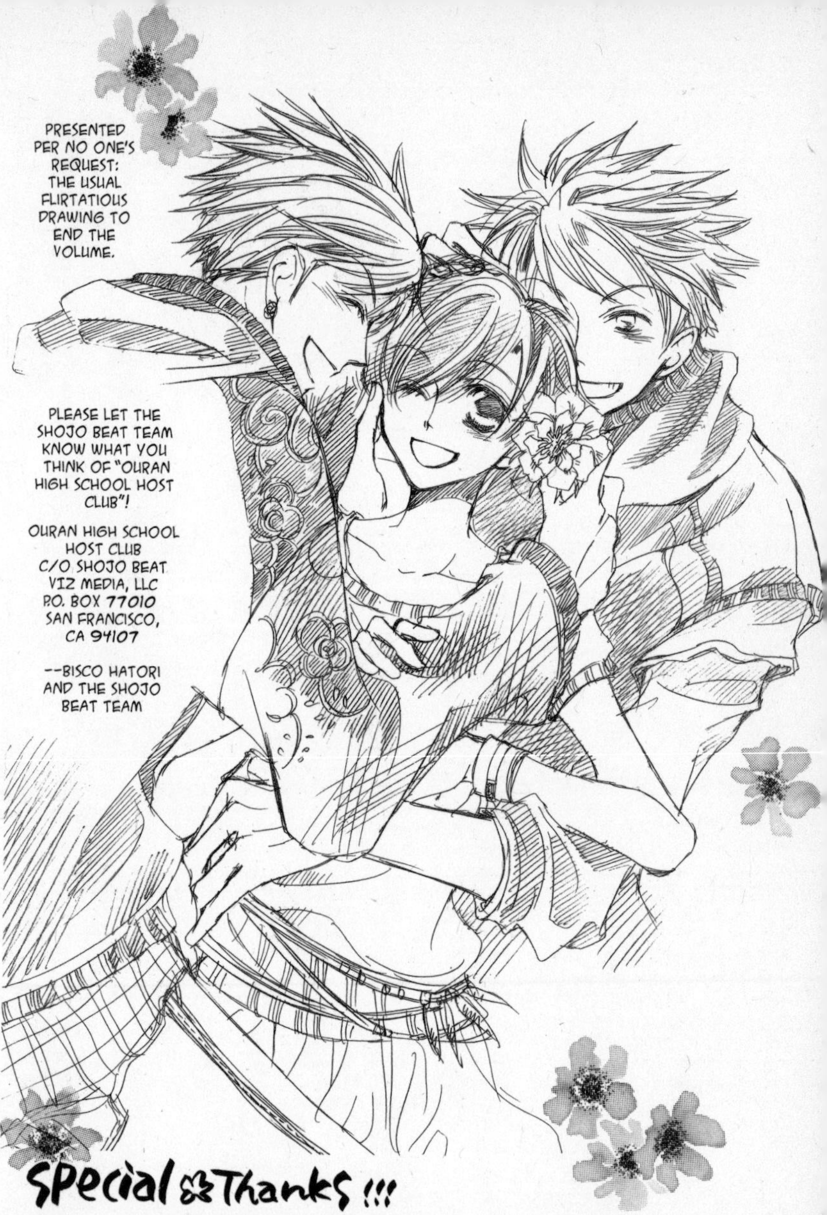

PLEASE LET THE SHOJO BEAT TEAM KNOW WHAT YOU THINK OF "OURAN HIGH SCHOOL HOST CLUB"!

OURAN HIGH SCHOOL HOST CLUB
C/O SHOJO BEAT
VIZ MEDIA, LLC
P.O. BOX 77010
SAN FRANCISCO, CA 94107

--BISCO HATORI AND THE SHOJO BEAT TEAM

Special ✿ Thanks !!!

MASTER YAMASHITA ✿ EVERYONE IN THE EDITING DEPARTMENT ✿ EVERYONE INVOLVED IN PUBLISHING THIS BOOK ✿ FAMILY, FRIENDS, KIMIKO HATANAKA
YUI NATSUKI ✿ AYA AOMURA ✿ AI SATAKE ✿ AKANE KORYO ✿
AND ESPECIALLY YOU, THE READER. ♡

EGOISTIC CLUB/THE END

Author Bio

Bisco Hatori made her manga debut with **Isshun kan no Romance (A Moment of Romance)** in **LaLa DX** magazine. The comedy **Ouran High School Host Club** is her breakout hit. When she's stuck thinking up characters' names, she gets inspired by loud, upbeat music (her radio is set to NACK5 FM). She enjoys reading all kinds of manga, but she's especially fond of the sci-fi drama **Please Save My Earth** and **Slam Dunk**, a basketball classic.

OURAN HIGH SCHOOL HOST CLUB
VOL. 2
Shojo Beat Edition

STORY AND ART BY BISCO HATORI

English Adaptation/Gary Leach
Translation/Kenichiro Yagi
Touch-up Art & Lettering/Curtis Yee
Graphic Design/Izumi Evers
Editor/Yuki Takagaki

Ouran Koko Host Club by Bisco Hatori © Bisco Hatori 2000. All rights reserved. First published in Japan in 2003 by HAKUSENSHA, Inc., Tokyo. English language translation rights arranged with HAKUSENSHA, Inc., Tokyo.

The rights of the author(s) of the work(s) in this publication to be so identified have been asserted in accordance with the Copyright, Designs and Patents Act 1988. A CIP catalogue record for this book is available from the British Library.

The stories, characters and incidents mentioned in this publication are entirely fictional.

No portion of this book may be reproduced or transmitted in any form or by any means without written permission from the copyright holders.

Printed in the U.S.A.

Published by VIZ Media, LLC
P.O. Box 77010
San Francisco, CA 94107

12
First printing, August 2005
Twelfth printing, January 2012

www.viz.com   www.shojobeat.com

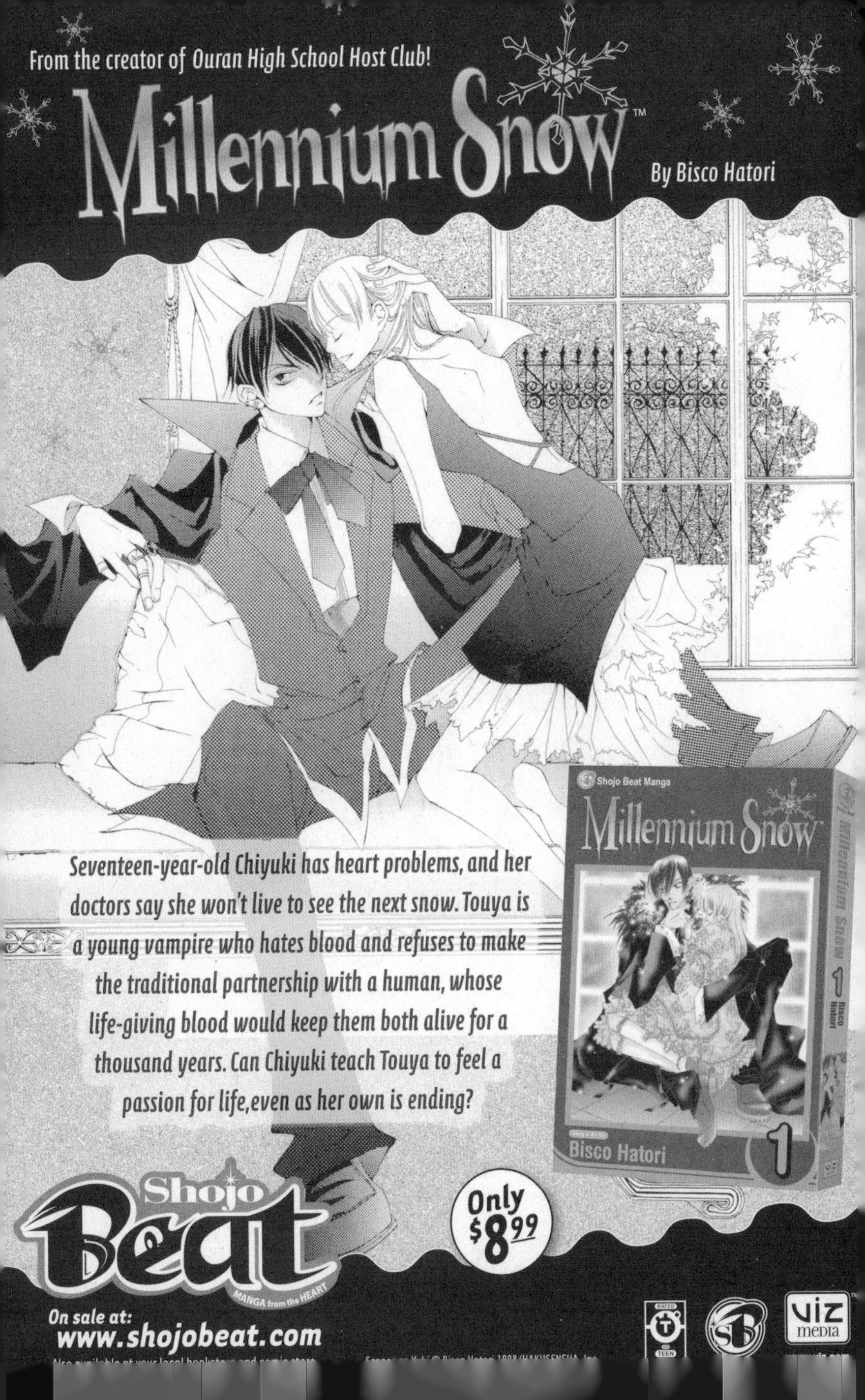
From the creator of Ouran High School Host Club!
Millennium Snow™
By Bisco Hatori
Seventeen-year-old Chiyuki has heart problems, and her doctors say she won't live to see the next snow. Touya is a young vampire who hates blood and refuses to make the traditional partnership with a human, whose life-giving blood would keep them both alive for a thousand years. Can Chiyuki teach Touya to feel a passion for life,even as her own is ending?
Shojo Beat Manga
Millennium Snow
Bisco Hatori
1
Only $8.99
Shojo Beat
MANGA from the HEART
On sale at:
www.shojobeat.com
RATED T TEEN
VIZ media

Kyoko Mogami followed her true love Sho to Tokyo to support him while he made it big as an idol. But he's casting her out now that he's famous enough! Kyoko won't suffer in silence— she's going to get her sweet revenge by beating Sho in show biz!

Vol. 1 ISBN: 978-1-4215-4226-3

Vol. 2 ISBN: 978-1-4215-4227-0

Vol. 3 ISBN: 978-1-4215-4228-7

Only $14.99 for each volume! ($16.99 in Canada)

Show biz is sweet...but revenge is sweeter!

Skip·Beat!

Story and Art by YOSHIKI NAKAMURA

In Stores Now!

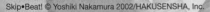

www.viz.com